THE CAMBRIDGE COMPANION TO

FREUD

The Cambridge Companion to

FREUD

Edited by Jerome Neu

CAMBRIDGE
UNIVERSITY PRESS

Published by the Press Syndicate of the University of Cambridge
The Pitt Building, Trumpington Street, Cambridge CB2 IRP
40 West 20th Street, New York, NY 10011-4211, USA
10 Stamford Road, Oakleigh, Victoria 3166, Australia

© Cambridge University Press 1991

First published 1992
Reprinted 1992

Printed in the United States of America

Library of Congress Cataloging-in-Publication Data
The Cambridge companion to Freud / edited by Jerome Neu.
p.   cm. – (Cambridge companions to philosophy)
Includes bibliographical references and index.
ISBN 0-521-37424-3. – ISBN 0-521-37779-X (pbk.)
1. Freud, Sigmund, 1856–1939.   I. Neu, Jerome.   II. Series.
BF109.F74C36   1991
150.19′52–DC20   91-21206
                                                         CIP

A catalog record for this book is available from the British Library.

ISBN 0-521-37424-3 hardback
ISBN 0-521-37779-X paperback

CONTENTS

v

vi   Contents

CONTRIBUTORS

RACHEL B. BLASS is a graduate student in clinical psychology at the Hebrew University of Jerusalem. She is working at the Sigmund Freud Center on a series of papers reexamining and reconceptualizing traditional psychoanalytic theories of development.

NANCY J. CHODOROW is Professor of Sociology at the University of California, Berkeley. She is an advanced candidate at the San Francisco Psychoanalytic Institute and author of *The Reproduction of Mothering: Psychoanalysis and the Sociology of Gender* and *Feminism and Psychoanalytic Theory*.

JENNIFER CHURCH teaches philosophy at Vassar College. She has written several articles on consciousness and irrationality.

JOHN DEIGH teaches moral and political philosophy at Northwestern University. He is an associate editor of *Ethics*.

SEBASTIAN GARDNER is Lecturer in Philosophy at Birkbeck College, University of London.

CLARK GLYMOUR is Alumni Professor of Philosophy at Carnegie Mellon University and Adjunct Professor of History and Philosophy of Science at the University of Pittsburgh. He is completing a book on Freud and the foundations of cognitive science.

JAMES HOPKINS is Lecturer in Philosophy at King's College, London, and assistant editor of *Mind*. He is coeditor with Richard Wollheim of *Philosophical Essays on Freud*, and with Anthony Savile of *Psychoanalysis, Mind, and Art: Essays for Richard Wollheim* (forthcoming).

vii

GERALD N. IZENBERG teaches modern European intellectual history at Washington University. He is also an advanced candidate and instructor at the St. Louis Psychoanalytic Institute.

JEROME NEU teaches philosophy at the University of California, Santa Cruz. He was for two years a Guest Student at the Boston Psychoanalytic Institute, and is the author of *Emotion, Thought, and Therapy.*

ROBERT A. PAUL is Candler Professor of Anthropology in the Institute of Liberal Arts at Emory University. He is an advanced candidate in the Emory University Psychoanalytic Institute. He is editor of *Ethos: Journal of the Society for Psychological Anthropology.*

DAVID SACHS has published essays on Plato, Aristotle, Wittgenstein, and Freud, and also on moral psychology. He is Professor of Philosophy at The Johns Hopkins University.

CARL E. SCHORSKE, a retired Professor of History, directed Princeton University's program in European Cultural Studies. He is the author of *Fin-de-siècle Vienna: Politics and Culture.*

BENNETT SIMON is training and supervising analyst at the Boston Psychoanalytic Society and Institute, and Clinical Associate Professor of Psychiatry, Harvard Medical School. In 1989–90, he was Sigmund Freud Professor of Psychoanalysis at the Hebrew University of Jerusalem. He has written on problems of the Oedipus complex and is author of *Mind and Madness in Ancient Greece* and *Tragic Drama and the Family: Psychoanalytic Studies from Aeschylus to Beckett.*

RICHARD WOLLHEIM teaches philosophy and the humanities at the University of California, Berkeley, and the University of California, Davis. As well as being the author of *Sigmund Freud*, he is the author of several psychoanalytically influenced books, such as *The Thread of Life* and *Painting as an Art*. He is Honourary Associate of the British Psycho-Analytic Society.

ACKNOWLEDGMENTS

Earlier versions of the following essays have appeared as indicated. The essays are published here with the permission of the copyright holders.

Jerome Neu, "Freud and Perversion," in *Sexuality and Medicine*, vol. 1, ed. E. E. Shelp (Dordrecht, The Netherlands: D. Reidel, 1987). Copyright Jerome Neu.

David Sachs, "In Fairness to Freud," *The Philosophical Review* 98 (1989). Copyright David Sachs.

Carl Schorske, "Freud: The Psycho-archeology of Civilizations," *The Proceedings of the Massachusetts Historical Society* 92 (1980). Copyright Massachusetts Historical Society.

Richard Wollheim, "Freud and the Understanding of Art," *British Journal of Aesthetics* 10 (1970) and in Wollheim, *On Art and the Mind* (Cambridge, Mass.: Allen Lane and Harvard University Press, 1973). Copyright Oxford University Press.

ix

Introduction

> if often he was wrong and, at times, absurd,
> to us he is no more a person
> now but a whole climate of opinion
> under whom we conduct our different lives . . .
> (W. H. Auden, *In Memory of Sigmund Freud*)

Despite distorted understandings of Freud's views and despite periodic waves of Freud-bashing, Auden's assessment remains essentially correct. Freud's influence continues to be enormous and pervasive. He gave us a new and powerful way to think about and investigate human thought, action, and interaction. He made sense of ranges of experience generally neglected or misunderstood. And while one might wish to reject or argue with some of Freud's particular interpretations and theories, his writings and his insights are too compelling to simply turn away. There is still much to be learned from Freud.

The essays here collected focus on some of Freud's masterworks and some of his central concepts, trying to bring out the structure of his arguments and contributions to our self-understanding.

Freud was born in 1856 in Freiberg in Moravia, but after his family's move when he was four years old, he passed almost all of his long life in Vienna. The story of his life is the story of his thought. The great events were most often the occasions of his discoveries and speculations. After his childhood move, the rest of his life can be viewed as a tale of four cities, the psychogeography of which is explored by Carl Schorske. Vienna, embroiled in anti-Semitism, was the ambivalent scene of Freud's professional advances and defeats as well as home to his contented family life. London was, from the beginning until his flight there from Hitler in the last months of his

I

life, capital of the land of hope and order, ideal site of the liberal ego. Paris, on the other hand, place of his early studies of hysteria with Charcot, provided the romantic center for his imagination, offering the attractions of the dangerous and alluringly irrational id. And finally Rome, embodying layers of history through which the archeologist can dig just as the depth psychologist can excavate the buried past, was the unapproachable city of his youthful ambitions and adult dreams, and it became the locus for a fitful reconciliation of polarities.

Some of the episodes of Freud's childhood are later recalled in the *Interpretation of Dreams*, largely the record of the analysis of his own dreams. For Freud, dreams eventually came to be regarded as "the royal road to a knowledge of the unconscious" (1900a, V, 608); and how they served as both a source of insight and a kind of confirmation for his theories is considered by James Hopkins. Hopkins's main concern, however, is how Freud's interpretation of his dreams can be seen as an extension of commonsense models of explanation (by motive). Additional defense of Freud's approach can be found in David Sachs's discussion of Adolf Grünbaum's *Foundations of Psychoanalysis*, the most influential recent philosophical critique of Freud. While Sachs's essay takes the form of a review, it in fact constitutes an independent discussion of questions of evidence in Freud, going into particular detail about *The Psychopathology of Everyday Life*. That book, along with the *Interpretation of Dreams*, is one of Freud's many forays beyond the psychology of neurosis into the realm of general psychology. But it was with the neuroses that psychoanalysis received its start.

Freud's earliest psychoanalytic theorizing concerned cases of hysteria, a disorder involving organic symptoms with no apparent organic cause. Freud rejected the fashionable explanations of his time, which appealed to malingering, heredity, and the peculiarities of women (Freud in fact demonstrated the existence of cases of male hysteria), and came instead to propose a "seduction theory," which traced hysterical symptoms to traumatic prepubertal sexual asaults (typically by fathers). While Freud's views developed, he initially believed the assaults were experienced as neutral at the time they occurred, and that it was only later, after the intercession of puberty with the addition of new energy and new understanding, that the original experience was retroactively traumatized and defended against. It was thus no accident that sexuality was crucial in the understanding of pathological defense: It was only in the sphere of the sexual (with its presumed delayed onset) that a memory could have more force than an original experience, so the ego might be taken by surprise and rendered incapable of normal defense. But ultimately, to explain the character of the original experience and the repetition of symptoms (if the energy of an external trauma was what was crucial, why wouldn't the symptom successfully use up that energy and so clear itself up?), Freud had to postulate sexual energy in the child. And he came to abandon his seduction theory in favor of a theory that gave greater importance to internal conflict than external trauma. This has become a matter of controversy in recent years, some even suggesting that Freud abandoned his seduction theory because of the unpopularity of drawing attention to child molestation. The suggestion is ludicrous, if only because Freud replaced the theory with even more unpopular ideas (in particular involving the postulation of infantile sexuality and so the denial of the presumed innocence of childhood). The suggestion also misunderstands the move: Freud did not come to believe that children are never molested, that all such charges are the result of fantasy (his own cases compelled him to believe otherwise); his discovery was not that children are never in fact assaulted, but that they could develop hysterical symptoms later in life even if they had not been. Psychic reality was as important as material reality. And there were sufficient theoretical reasons for the shift, reasons that are traced by Gerald Izenberg.

Izenberg also argues for the importance of clinical experience and theoretical insight in producing the hypotheses that Freud used his self-analysis to test, including the hypotheses of infantile sexuality and the Oedipus complex. Freud's self-analysis, begun in the summer of 1897 (shortly after his father's death), can be taken as one of the turning points in the history of self-understanding. Exactly how its role in the development of Freud's thought should be understood, however, is controversial. In contrast with the confirmatory role argued for by Izenberg, Simon and Blass suggest that Freud's self-analysis was in fact the origin of the central ideas involved in the Oedipus complex. And they caution that such self-discovery requires justification before its results can be generalized. But this may get the confirmation situation backward. Freud himself insisted that "I can analyze myself only with the help of knowledge obtained objectively (like an outsider)" (1985 [1887–1904], 281). This suggests his understanding of the Oedipus conflict began with its discovery in his patients. Thus, his self-analysis would have been used to confirm the existence of the Oedipus complex (after all, if it was truly universal, it had to be present in him too), and was not the source of its discovery. That would explain why he wrote to Fliess "I have found, in my own case *too*, [the phenomenon of] being in love with my mother and jealous of my father, and I now consider it a universal event in early childhood" (p. 272, italics added, cf. p. 250 where it is already noted in others). Again the matter, like many discussed by the authors in this volume, is controversial and properly the subject of argument. The particular tension raised by the relation of conditions of discovery to conditions of confirmation emerges repeatedly. Nancy Chodorow, for example, brings attention to it in the course of her division, survey, and exposition of Freud's views on women.

It is also a tension relevant to a problem sometimes pointed to in connection with the contrast (already mentioned in passing) between the psychology of neurosis and normal psychology. It is sometimes suggested that it is in some way illegitimate to generalize from the study of "abnormal" cases to an understanding of the "normal." But such generalization is in no way peculiar to psychoanalysis. Certainly it is a standard feature of much medical argument (it was the study of scurvy among sailors on ships without fresh fruit that led ultimately to the understanding of the normal need for vitamin C in the diet). There need be no real problem, so long as one remains aware of the difference between the conditions of discovery and the conditions of confirmation. Indeed, as Freud argues, using the analogy of a crystal the breaking of which reveals its otherwise hidden structure, "pathology, by making things larger and coarser, can draw our attention to normal conditions which would otherwise have escaped us" (1933a, XXII, 58–9). In fact, I believe (and argue in my discussion, "Freud and perversion") that the theory of infantile sexuality that emerged from Freud's struggles with the seduction theory is only fully intelligible in the light of Freud's understanding of adult perversion as presented in his *Three Essays on the Theory of Sexuality*. Freud was not the first to note that children suck their thumbs, but it was his new conceptual understanding of the sexual instinct (as made up of components analyzable in terms of source, object, and aim) that enabled him to argue persuasively that such activity should be seen as an early manifestation of that instinct, as a form of infantile sexuality. The complex intertwinings of theory and observation (of self and other, of normal and abnormal), and their relation to evidence and confirmation, emerge again and again in this book.

There is also still much to be learned from Freud in relation to issues in contemporary philosophy of mind, moral, and social theory. Hopkins's discussion of the interpretation of dreams ties it to modern models of explanation by motive, which are of concern in recent philosophy of action. The special characteristics of unconscious mental states, including their relation to the states ascribed by commonsense psychology, are further explored by Sebastian Gardner. His discussion of the unconscious also connects with recent questions concerning the divided or multiple self. Clark Glymour discusses how Freud's early theorizing grew out of his medical, and specifically neurological, training. He then argues that the model of the mind in Freud's *Project for a Scientific Psychology* adumbrates significant features of recent computational models in cognitive psychology, and that his approach may still have much to teach us. For example, if Freud's explanations – like many modern ones – are often homuncular (accounting for the actions of an agent by the actions of littler internal agents), Freud's hypothetical basic units must be seen as having very complex capacities rather than as the simpleminded equivalents of on–off switches. The model, Glymour suggests, comes from politics rather than computers and has useful implications for puzzles about the relation of reason and the will: forms of irrationality that emerge in self-deception, ambivalence, weakness of the will, and the like, as well as in neurotic symptoms.

The shaking of the Cartesian picture of a unitary consciousness brings with it metaphysical and epistemological issues; it also promises to clarify the workings of our ordinary conflictual moral experience. Jennifer Church emphasizes distinctive features of primary process thinking and aspects of internalization in relation to moral development. As she presents it, the power and appeal of Freud's account of the superego can be found in its ability to make naturalistic sense of the dutiful selflessness that Kantians and others regard as characteristic of morality. The question remains whether that account can be detached from Freud's views on the specifically sexual character of our early relationships with our parents. Can castration anxiety be ignored, and the desirability of power substituted, when explaining the motivation for internalization? Freud's views on the character of our early relationships with our parents are traced in Bennett Simon and Rachel Blass's "The development and vicissitudes of Freud's ideas on the Oedipus complex"; and the distinctive features of the development of women according to Freud and problems connected with those views are further explored by Nancy Chodorow. The importance of ambivalence in the formation of conscience is discussed by John Deigh.

Some of the wider applications and implications of Freud's theories are considered in the final essays in the book. With Richard Wollheim's discussion, we can see how in his writing about Leonardo and others Freud uses psychoanalytic biography to illuminate the place of the infantile, especially infantile sexuality, in mature achievement. In some of his studies of art, we can see the pervasiveness (in transformed, sublimated form) of the forces that Freud had uncovered in explaining neurotic symptoms, dreams, jokes, and the like. But the motivations of art are complex, and in other of Freud's studies the focus is on the character of the subject in a work of art, on how the deepest mental layers in a representation are revealed. The carryover from Freud's clinical theorizing to other fields is considered further in Robert Paul's reading of Freud's anthropology, which emphasizes cultural analogues of obsessional neurosis in the context of Freud's developing thought about the nature of instincts. These analogues, he suggests, may help us understand the cross-cultural but enigmatic fact of gender inequality. The fantasy schemas of individual psychology help illuminate how we and our societies make ourselves who we are. The psychological place of religion in particular is also considered by John Deigh, who looks to Freud's changing theory of instincts to understand the deepening pessimism in his social thought between *The Future of an Illusion* and *Civilization and Its Discontents*.

What is presented here is, inevitably, a selection. Whole topics are neglected – for example, the role of transference (the patient's feelings toward the analyst, distorted in the analytic setting by projection based on earlier figures) in psychoanalytic theory and therapy, the problematic nature of Freud's theories of pleasure and of the death instinct, and the elaboration and reconstruction of Freud's views by Klein, Lacan, and others – and even for the topics addressed, there is of course more to be said. Ultimately, one should return always to Freud's own texts. While Freud was certainly not *right* about everything, he *thought* – provocatively – about everything.

1 Freud: The psychoarcheology of civilizations

In his last decade of life Sigmund Freud turned once more to a question that had troubled him ever since he published his conception of the psyche in *The Interpretation of Dreams* in 1900: What were the implications of individual psychodynamics for civilization as a whole? His mature reflections on that subject he set forth in *Civilization and Its Discontents* (1930a). Its somber conclusions have, of course, become part of our self-understanding: that the progress of our technical mastery over nature and the perfection of our ethical self-control are achieved at the cost of instinctual repression in the "civilized" man – a cost so high as not only to make neurotics of individuals, but of whole civilizations. An excess of civilization can produce its own undoing at the hands of instinct avenging itself against the culture that has curbed it too well.

One might expect that, in making a point so historical in its essence, Freud would have reached out to propose a scheme of civilization's march toward the organization of nature and the collective development of the superego. Such was not Freud's way. He approached his problem not historically but analogically, proceeding from an analysis of the individual psyche, its structure and experience, to the functioning and future of society. Yet to introduce his reader to the difference between the psyche and history, he had recourse to an ingenious historical metaphor. "We will choose as an example," he says, "the story of the Eternal City" to represent the nature of mental life. Freud asks the reader to consider Rome as a physical entity, from its earliest beginnings as a fenced settlement on the Palatine through all its many transformations until the present day. Imagine that all the buildings known to the archeologist and the historian stand simultaneously in the same

8

urban space with their modern survivors or successors: "On the Piazza of the Pantheon," Freud explains, "we should find not only the Pantheon of today as bequeathed to us by Hadrian, but on the same site also Agrippa's original edifice; indeed, the same piece of ground would support Santa Maria sopra Minerva and the old temple over which it was built." Freud wishes us to struggle with this multifaceted vision of the simultaneity of the noncontemporaneous, the Eternal City that is the totality of its undiminished pasts. (With eyes trained by Picasso and the Cubists, it is easier for us to visualize than for him.) But this, he acknowledges, is not possible either in space or time. ". . . Destructive influences . . . are never lacking in the history of a city," he grants, "even if it has had a less chequered past than Rome, and even if, like London, it has hardly ever suffered from the visitations of an enemy." Only in the *mind* can what is past survive, after it has been, at the level of consciousness, displaced or replaced; and there, it is "rather the rule than the exception" for it to do so (1930a, XXI, 69–72).

Here Freud lets the metaphor of the city as total history drop, turning our attention to the individual mind, the psyche. In the mind of each of us, it is civilization itself – not the pillaging enemy – that destroys the traces of past experience, burying the personal life of instinct under the weight of its censorious denials and demands. But the psychoanalyst can, like the archeologist, recover what is buried and, by restoring a personal history to consciousness, enable us to come to terms with its traumas and even to build it anew.

Is Freud suggesting that, if we could reconstitute the Eternal City in our minds as he has asked us to picture it, with all its pasts laid bare, we would redeem it? He would make no such claim; he only points to the need to recognize that those "immortal adversaries" that inhabit the depths in each of us, Eros and Thanatos, are active and/or repressed in the collective life too, and that the earthly city must deal with them. The model of the individual psyche helps Freud to diagnose the collective life, but not to formulate a social therapy.

Freud's use of Rome in *Civilization and Its Discontents* is highly abstract and literary, as an image of an unattainable, condensed *summa* of Western historical life. Forty years earlier, when he was *nel mezzo del camin'* and at work on *The Interpretation of Dreams,*

Freud had to conjure with Rome in a quite different way, as a central problem of his self-analysis, what he called his "Rome neurosis." Within his dreams of Rome at that time, he excavated in his psychoarcheological dig an earlier Rome that belonged to the days of his childhood. The *via regia* to his discovery of the unconscious life led through the Eternal City. Once he had conquered Rome, Freud returned to it again and again. It was the city most strongly related in Freud's mind with psychoanalysis and the one that resonated most fully with all his contradictory values and desires, compacted like the simultaneous totality of historical Romes that he had suggested to the readers of *Civilization and Its Discontents.*

I

Before there was psychoanalysis, before Freud confronted Rome and exhumed it, he was drawn to two modern civilizations – the English and the French. He saw each through the stereoptic lenses of his time and social class. Like many another Austrian liberal, Freud was a passionate Anglophile from his youth. His family experience confirmed his social prejudice. When the Freud family fortunes sustained reverses in the late 1850s, Sigmund's older half brothers emigrated to build successful careers in Manchester, while father Jacob removed the rest of his family from Freiberg in Moravia to a life of economic hardship in Vienna. After graduation from Gymnasium in 1875, Freud made his first visit to his relatives in England, a visit that left an indelible impression on him. In 1882, newly engaged but deeply frustrated about his career, England surfaced in his consciousness as a kind of land of hope. In a letter to his fiancée, Martha Bernays, Freud gave passionate voice to a longing to escape from Vienna and the shadow of "that abominable tower of St. Stephen" – symbol of Catholic reaction. "I am aching for independence," he wrote, "so as to follow my own wishes. The thought of England surges up before me, with its sober industriousness, its generous devotion to the public weal, the stubbornness and sensitive feeling for justice of its inhabitants, the running fire of general interest that can strike sparks in the newspapers; all the ineffaceable impressions of my journey seven years ago, one that had a decisive influence on my whole life, have been awakened in their full vividness."[1]

The "decisive influence" of his early visit to England, if we are to believe a letter Freud wrote to his closest friend immediately on his return in 1875, embraced both professional and intellectual values. England, as the land of "practical works," inclined him away from pure science toward medical practice. "If I wanted to influence many people rather than a small number of readers and co-scientists, then England would be the right country." At the same time, the young freshman bore witness to the impact of English scientific thought: "The acquaintance which I have made with English scientific books will always keep me, in my studies, on the side of the English for whom I have an extremely favorable prejudice: Tyndall, Huxley, Lyle, Darwin, Thomson, Lockyer and others."[2]

In 1882, in his mood of discouragement, Freud fanned the smoldering embers of Anglophilism that remained from his visit with reading of a wider kind. "I am taking up again," he reported to his Martha, "the history of the island, the works of the men who were my real teachers – all of them English or Scotch; and I am recalling again what is for me the most interesting historical period, the reign of the Puritans and Oliver Cromwell." One might have expected that the future liberator of sexuality would have defined his interest in the Puritans negatively. Not at all, for his eye was seeking civic virtue.

"Must we stay here, Martha?" Freud wrote of Vienna. "If we possibly can, let us seek a home where human worth is more respected. A grave in the Centralfriedhof is the most distressing idea I can imagine."[3] Although he seems often to have entertained the idea of emigrating to England in the 1880s, Freud could not shake off his attachment to hated Vienna as the scene of his professional self-realization. It was only Hitler that caused him finally to leave for London, in the end to be buried there rather than in the Centralfriedhof.

In his devotion to England as an ideal society, Freud only shared an attitude widespread in the Austrian liberal bourgeoisie before World War I. Indeed, when the Great War broke, Freud, who would soon give "all my libido . . . to Austria-Hungary," hesitated in his allegiance. As he wrote to Carl Abraham, "I should be with it (Austria-Hungary) with all my heart, if only I could think England would not be on the wrong side."[4]

Within the larger whole, however, there were different kinds of Anglophilism. Most of Freud's contemporaries among the intellectuals admired England for producing a human type who fused bourgeois practicality with aristocratic grace, business, and high style. The writer Arthur Schnitzler portrayed in a novel an Austrian Jew who, making a new life in England, embodied the typical Englishman as Austrians of the *fin-de-siècle* saw him: cool and gray-eyed, courteous, and self-possessed. The poet Hugo von Hofmannsthal and his friends in the higher bureaucracy wanted to establish a public school on the English model in Austria to breed such personalities. Theodor Herzl's Jewish state too would cultivate such aristocratic realists *à l'anglais.* Adolf Loos, architect and critic of Austria's visual culture, when he founded a journal called *Das Andere (The Other)* "to introduce Western culture into Austria," exalted the gentlemanly values of sobriety and practicality reflected in English clothing, interior decor, and use-objects.

Freud's Anglophilism showed none of these aristocratic-aesthetic features. He drew his image of England from an older, more militant midcentury liberalism, hostile to aristocracy and to the Catholicism associated with it in Austria. Parliamentarism was what they prized in English politics; philosophic radicalism was their lodestar in culture. Freud studied philosophy under Franz Brentano, a leading protagonist of English positivism in Austria. Under the editorial guidance of Theodor Gomperz, a classicist who, following George Grote, embraced the Sophists and radical democrats as the finest flowers of Athens, Freud worked on the German edition of the complete works of John Stuart Mill. (He translated "On the Subjection of Women," "Socialism," "The Labor Movement," and "Plato.") Though he does not speak of a debt to Bentham, Freud's early theory of instincts, with its duality of pleasure principle and reality principle, resonates with echoes of Bentham's hedonistic system. From the seventeenth to the nineteenth century, those whom Freud claimed as his "real teachers – all of them English or Scotch," were the protagonists of libidinal repression and the advocates of postponed gratification – whether as Puritan foes of aristocratic squandering and the Church of Rome or as secularized utilitarian moralists. They were builders, stern and rational, of the liberal ego which, for Freud, made England the classic land of ethical rectitude, manly self-control, and the rule of law.

Freud named all his children after his teachers or their wives – except one. Oliver, his second son, he named for Cromwell. Thus the great sex theorist paid tribute to the public virtues of private repression and the special achievement of English political culture.

II

It has become a commonplace of Freud scholarship to identify Paris with the impact of Jean-Martin Charcot, the great theorist and clinician of hysteria, on Freud's intellectual development. Justly so. Freud went on a fellowship to the Salpetrière Hospital for Women in 1885 as a neurologist exploring the organic basis of nervous disorders. Charcot turned him in a new direction, toward the study of hysteria, especially hysterical paralysis, as a disease that behaved "as if there were no anatomy of the brain."[5] He also opened Freud's mind, even if only in informal discourse, to "*la chose génitale*," the sexual component in the etiology of hysteria. When Freud returned to Vienna to open his own practice, it was as a neurologist still, but one with a special interest in "nervous cases" that others found tiresome: patients who did *not* suffer from organic lesions of the nervous system.[6] Thus returning from Paris with a pronounced predilection for what we would now call neurotics, Freud set out for the first time, boldly if only half aware, on the *via regia* to the unconscious.

Freud's letters to his fiancée during his half-year in Paris make it clear that the city itself, or more accurately, his encounter with it, both prepared and reinforced the impact of Charcot.

England was good order, morality, and liberal rationality, appealing to Freud as a possible refuge from the social inequities and professional frustrations of Austria. Paris was the very opposite: a city of danger, of the questionable, of the irrational. Freud accepted, but richly elaborated, Paris as the wanton, the female temptress; he approached it in a spirit of adventure at once thrilling and terrifying.

Until he went to Paris in 1885, there is, as far as I could find, no reference to the city in his writings, either as fact or as symbol. More than a decade later, however, in *The Interpretation of Dreams*, he tells the reader cryptically that "Paris . . . had for many long years been the goal of my longings; and the blissful feelings with which I first set foot on its pavement seemed to me a guarantee that others of my wishes would be fulfilled as well" (1900a, IV, 195). What wishes? Freud does not say. In the beautiful letters he wrote to his fiancée and her sister during his Paris *Lehrjahr*, however, the intense and impressionable young Freud seems to have opened himself to the whole world of forbidden *fleurs du mal* that Freud the Anglophile and liberal Jew had until then rejected or avoided: the Roman Catholic Church, the bewitching power of the female, and the power of the masses. As London was the city of the ego, where the whole culture supported one's independence and control, Paris was the city of the id, where instincts erotic and thanatal reigned.

Two months after his arrival in Paris, Freud could still write of it, "I am under the full impact of Paris, and, waxing very poetical, could compare it to a vast overdressed Sphinx who gobbles up every foreigner unable to solve her riddles."[7] Freud chose his image well, for the Sphinx united beauty and the beast, challenging natural law with her composite being and rationality with her fateful riddle that only brilliant, perverse Oedipus could solve.

Mindful of the bitter lifelong disgust and mistrust in which Freud held Catholicism, recalling his yearning to escape from the shadow of "that abominable tower of St. Stephen" to England in 1882, we are stunned to watch his reaction to Notre Dame. "My first impression was a sensation I have never had before: 'This is a church.' . . . I have never seen anything so movingly serious and somber, quite unadorned and very narrow." What Freud reported of the companion with whom he paid his first visit to Notre Dame must have been true of himself: "There he stood, deeply lost in wonder."[8]

Freud associated himself not only with the beauty of the cathedral, but with its beastly side as well. He later recalled that the platform of Notre Dame was his "favorite resort" in Paris. "Every free afternoon, I used to clamber about there on the towers of the church between the monsters and the devils." When Freud in a dream of omnipotence identified himself with Hercules, he discovered behind the dream Rabelais' Gargantua, avenging himself on the Parisians by turning a stream of urine on them from the top of Notre Dame (1900a, V, 469).

As for the people of Paris, they simply frightened Freud. They struck him as "uncanny." To be sure, political turbulence marked the months of Freud's stay, a period of governmental instability (the so-called *valse des ministères*) following the fall of Jules Ferry, stormy elections, and the rise of Boulangisme. Freud rarely identified the objectives of political demonstrators; what he saw was mob behavior as such, something to become all too familiar again in

Vienna a decade later: "The people seem to me of a different species from ourselves; I feel they are possessed of a thousand demons. . . . I hear them yelling 'A la lanterne' and 'à bas' this man and that. I don't think they know the meaning of shame or fear. . . . They are people given to psychical epidemics, historical mass convulsions, and they haven't changed since Victor Hugo wrote *Notre-Dame*."[9]

To the awe of the church and the fear of the feverish crowd one must add one more perspective to triangulate Freud's Paris: the theater, and especially its women. Freud went to theater first in hopes of improving his French, found he understood little, but returned ever again for other reasons. Freud devoted one of the longest of his long letters to a scene-by-scene account of Sarah Bernhardt's performance in Victorien Sardou's melodrama, *Théodora*.[10] He was utterly bewitched by her portrayal of the Byzantine heroine, a prostitute become Empress: ". . . Her caressing and pleading, the postures she assumes, the way she wraps herself around a man, the way she acts with every limb, every joint – it's incredible. A remarkable creature, and I can imagine she is no different in life from what she is on the stage."

"For the sake of historical truth," Freud continues, "let us add that I again had to pay for this pleasure with an attack of migraine." The tensions of the Paris experience, his new receptivity, sensual as well as intellectual, to the realm of instinct were doubtless related to Freud's long separation from his Martha. He cheerfully admitted to her his frequent recourse to cocaine to keep his tensions down or his spirits up. While he surely concealed no actions from her, he revealed one fantasy – that he might marry the attractive daughter of Dr. Charcot and thus in one stroke solve his problems of power – professional, social, and sexual – that evidently evoked a nettled response from Martha, who could not take it as lightly as Freud tried to present it.[11] One suspects that the decorous Freud could not and did not reveal the full extent of his newfound feelings. They are perhaps better expressed in a joke he delighted to record at a later time, when he had discovered that jokes contain the expression of repressed wishes: A married couple is discussing the future. The man says to his wife: "If one of us should die, I shall move to Paris" (1900a, V, 485).

In one of Freud's remarkable Paris letters, the very imagery he used seems to bring all the dimensions of his Paris experience into

relation to the impact of Jean-Martin Charcot: "I think I am changing a great deal. . . . Charcot, who is one of the greatest of physicians,
and a man whose common sense borders on genius, is simply wreck-
ing all my aims and opinions. I sometimes come out of his lectures
as from out of Notre Dame," our militant anti-Catholic continues,
"with an entirely new idea of perfection. . . . It is three whole days
since I have done any work, and I have no feelings of guilt," the
erstwhile Puritan adds. "My brain is sated as after an evening in the
theater. Whether the seed will ever bear fruit, I don't know; but I do
know that no other human being has ever affected me in the same
way. . . . Or am I under the influence of this magically attractive and
repulsive city?"[12]

Surely it was both. Paris, and Freud's rather stereotyped perception of it, provided the ideal setting to receive from Charcot a doctrine that opened the way to that questionable province of the psyche where neither body nor conscious mind seemed in control.

Before Freud left Paris for home he cemented his relations with
Charcot by volunteering as translator of a volume of his *Leçons sur
les maladies du système nerveux*, including his lectures on hysteria.
Thus Freud's tribute to English thought in his translation of John
Stuart Mill's essay on the subjection of women found an appropriate
French equivalent. Freud carried the symmetry into his family too:
He named his firstborn son Jean Martin for Charcot, as he would
soon, in tribute to Puritan England, name his second son Oliver,
after Cromwell. Thus Freud's personal exemplars of English ego and
Parisian id each had their namesakes among his children.

When Freud returned to Vienna he entered practice as a doctor of
nervous diseases. He chose Easter Sunday to publish this good news
in the *Neue Freie Presse*. Thus the Jewish admirer of Notre Dame
combined an announcement of his own resurrection and new life
with a defiance of Catholic sensibilities worthy of a Puritan prophet.
Such were the extreme polarities that entered into the genesis of
psychoanalysis.

III

By this time, you must be wondering whether the pictures that I
have drawn of Freud's London and Paris justify my subtitle, "The
Psychoarcheology of Civilizations." Since they antedate Freud's in-

terests in either the depths of the psyche or in archeology, our materials thus far have dealt with conscious ideas and values, not with buried ones; with the day-world, not the night-world. What is striking is the sharpness of the contrast between Freud's images of the two cultures. He not only kept their identities separate and antithetical but sought in neither any trace of the features he saw in the other. The Puritan-rationalist spectacles he wore when he looked at England allowed him to see there nothing of the cathedrals, crowds, or women that so caught his eye in France; nor did he remark the gracious, aristocratic side of English life and manners. In France, on the other hand, the image of the female and the Sphinx so dominated his perception that the positivist, rationalist, masculine side of French bourgeois society scarcely entered his field of vision. Finally, Freud made no attempt to establish any relationship between the contrasting values that attracted him in English and French culture. This he was to accomplish only indirectly in his encounter with Rome, where male and female, ethics and aesthetics – in short, the ego-world of London and the id-world of Paris – converged in bewildering conflation.

Rome had engaged Freud's fancy on and off since childhood. Not until the 1890s, when Freud was in his forties, while at work on *The Interpretation of Dreams*, did he conceive a truly passionate interest in the Eternal City. As in the early 1880s, when he had contemplated escape to the refuge of England, he entered in the mid-1890s another, deeper professional crisis. Where the impasse of the 1880s applied only to his career opportunities, the new one involved, by virtue of the very depth of his frustration, Freud's personal identity and intellectual direction as well.

I have elsewhere tried to show how the seething crisis of Austrian society, in which liberalism lacked the power to sustain itself against the rising tide of Catholic and nationalist anti-Semitic movements, affected Freud.[13] It drove him into social withdrawal as a Jew, into intellectual isolation as a scientist, and into introspection as a thinker. The more his outer life was mired, however, the more winged his ideas became. In his fundamental work, *The Interpretation of Dreams*, Freud transformed the poison of social frustration as Jew and as scientist into the elixir of psychological illumination. Essential to his procedure was to plumb the depths of his own personal history, thus to find a universal psychological structure, a key to human destiny that would transcend the collective history which until then had seemed to shape man's fate. Freud devised psycho-analysis as a counterpolitical theory in a situation of political de-spair. Where he had once been tempted to withdraw to England, he now turned inward into himself, to face and overcome the conflicts between his wishes and his hostile environment, by means of psy-choanalysis as *theory*. As he did so, he also resolved, by means of psychoanalysis as *therapy*, the conflicts between his wishes and his values.

It was in working through this intellectual and personal crisis that Freud's interest in antiquity and in Rome arose. He hit upon the analogy between his own procedure of digging into his own buried past as depth psychologist and the work of the archeologist. Soon his mild interest developed into an insatiable passion. He eagerly read the biography of Heinrich Schliemann, who fulfilled a childhood wish by his discovery of Troy. He began the collection of ancient artifacts that soon graced his office in the Berggasse. And, especially rare in those days of his social withdrawal, Freud made a new friend: Emanuel Löwy, a professor of archeology. "He keeps me up until three o'clock in the morning," Freud wrote to his dearest friend; "he tells me about Rome."[14]

What could be more natural than that Freud, an inveterate trav-eler, should pursue his newfound interest by visiting the Eternal City? But he found he could not. Five times Freud journeyed to Italy between 1895 and 1898, without ever reaching Rome. Some inhibi-tion held him back. At the same time, the yearning to visit it grew ever more torturesome. Rome became literally the city of his dreams, and Freud began to speak of his longing for Rome as "deeply neurotic."[15] As such, he incorporated it into his self-analysis and into *The Interpretation of Dreams*.

Freud explored fully only one dimension of his Rome neurosis in *The Interpretation*, that which bore on his relations with his father. But in it he revealed also the centrality of the Jewish problem and Austrian politics in his own life. He recalled from his school days his hero worship for Hannibal.

Like so many boys of that age, I had sympathized in the Punic Wars not with the Romans, but the Carthaginians. And when in the higher classes I began to understand for the first time what it meant to belong to an alien race, and anti-semitic feelings among the other boys warned me that I must take a definite position, the figure of the semitic general rose still higher in my esteem. To my youthful mind, Hannibal and Rome symbolized the conflict between the tenacity of Jewry and the organization of the Catholic church.

Freud then recaptured an episode from his childhood where his father told him of having been insulted by Christians, without fighting back. Freud resented his father's "unheroic conduct." He remembered having wished that his father had enjoined him, as Hannibal's had, "to take vengeance on the Romans." Ever since that time, Freud reported, Hannibal had had a place in his fantasies. In the face of the newly threatening power of anti-Semitism in the 1890s, Freud interpreted his longing for Rome as "actually following in Hannibal's footsteps. Like him, I had been fated not to see Rome" (1900a, IV, 196–7).

Two aspects of Freud's interpretation of his Hannibal identification deserve notice: First, that he had the same attitude toward Christian Rome that the English Puritans had had, as the hated center of Catholic power; second, that he had taken on the paternal burden of defender of Jewish dignity, which, despite his anger at his father's impotence, he was himself now powerless to realize. Freud's Rome neurosis, his inability to reach the city, was from this perspective the consequence of guilt, of an undischarged obligation at once filial and political.

Yet Freud's actual dreams of Rome in the years 1896 and 1897 spoke a different language, one more akin to the seductive allure of his Paris than to the Puritan probity of his England. All of them suggest fulfillment rather than conquest. All conflate images of Catholic Rome with Jewish ideas and situations (1900a, IV, 193–8).[16] In one dream Rome appears as "the promised land seen from afar," implying Freud to be in the same relation to Rome as Moses to Israel. The vision, though Freud does not say so, seems to express a forbidden wish: a longing for an assimilation to the gentile world that his strong waking conscience – and even his dream-censor – would deny him. He also identifies Rome with Carlsbad, Bohemia's equivalent of our Palm Springs, a city of pleasure, rest, and cure; in short, an earthly city of recreation (re-creation), of resurrection. Freud compares himself in the analysis of this dream to a poor, gentle Jewish character in one of the Yiddish stories he loved so well. Because the little Jew did not have the train fare to Carlsbad, the conductor beat him up at every station; but, undaunted, he continued on his *via dolorosa* (the expression is Freud's). Thus the lofty vision of Moses-Freud seeing Israel-Rome "from afar" had its lowly analogue in the picture of the little-Jew-Christ-Freud reaching Carlsbad-Rome on a *via dolorosa*. A third dream reinforces the Christian theme but telescopes it into that of ancient, pagan Rome. From a train window Freud sees across the Tiber the Castel Sant'Angelo, at once papal castle and Roman imperial tomb. Tantalizingly, the train moves off before he can cross the Bridge of the Holy Angel to reach the castle – a house of both buried paganism and Christian salvation.

How different is the Rome of Freud the youth of the 1860s and 1870s – forbidding, hostile, bureaucratic – from this Rome of the dreaming man in the 1890s: the first an object of hate, to be destroyed, the second an object of desire, to be entered in love! Surely in the second of these Romes, we can descry the positive features of Freud's Paris: the awesome but glorious feminine Catholic spirit of Notre Dame, the allure of the city of pleasure (Carlsbad-Paris-Rome); in short, Mother and temptress at once. Indeed Freud provided the materials to connect the lure of Rome to his surrogate mother, a beloved Czech Nanny of his childhood. She had taught him about her Catholic faith and taken him to church on Easter Sunday. In contrast to his father, she had given him "a high opinion of my own capacities." As the Rome of Hannibal was masculine, connected by Freud with his social duty and his oedipal conflict, so the Rome of Nanny was feminine, that of Mother Church, of tabooed oedipal love.[17]

While Freud in his psychoarcheological report analyzes only the first, pagan Rome, identifying with Hannibal and his wish "to take vengeance on the Romans," he gives us a clue that opens still another road that leads, like that of Nanny, to a Rome more consonant with the dream-wishes to enter it in love and fulfillment. The clue lies in a quotation from a German author which occurred to Freud in the course of wrestling with his Rome neurosis: "Which of . . . two [men] paced his study in greater excitement after forming his plan to go to Rome: Winckelmann or Hannibal?" Freud unequivocally answered for himself, "Hannibal," for he had been "fated not to see Rome." But Winckelmann would correspond to the other side of Freud's dream-truth, the one he failed to analyze for us. For Winckelmann, the great archeologist and art historian, had much in common with Freud: his poverty; an acute sense of low social origins; failure to find for many years a congenial position or professional recognition; a series of intense male friendships with homosexual overtones; hatred of political tyranny; hostility to organized religion; and a generativity crisis at the age of forty that resulted, like Freud's, in a "first work" of a new and revolutionary kind. Above all, Winckelmann, a Protestant, overcame his scruples and embraced Catholicism in order to enter Rome, to be able to pursue his passion for classical antiquity. He conquered his conscience for the sake of his science, his *amor intellectualis* for Rome.

Was not Freud more scientist than general – and a "soft" scientist at that? Was he not, on his journey to Rome, following in Winckelmann's footsteps rather than in Hannibal's? Freud's passionate cleaving to the friendship of Wilhelm Fliess as sole intellectual confidant during these years of crisis had homoerotic overtones that speak for Winckelmann too. Fliess was even more radically committed to the primacy of sexuality in psychic life than Freud. He advanced a radical theory of bisexuality that Freud seriously entertained. (Paris, where Freud espoused Charcot's theory that males too could suffer from the woman's malady, hysteria, had prepared him for that.) Freud called their series of meetings *à deux* "congresses"; he particularly longed for a congress on classical soil. When Fliess proposed in 1901 that they hold their congress at Easter, Freud replied that he was "powerfully gripped" (*mächtig gepackt*) by the idea; but since the friendship was then nearing its end, Freud declined.[18] He could not but admit to Fliess the pull of Rome as goal, as scene of resurrection: "In the midst of this mental and material depression, I am haunted by the thought of spending Easter week in Rome this year. Not that there is any justification for it – I have achieved nothing yet." Or again: "I shall no more get to Rome this Easter than you will."[19]

Of course, Freud was not ready to go the course of Winckelmann, to join the Church of Rome. The Hannibal and the Cromwell in him – the Jewish, liberal, and Anglophile values that furnished his conscience by day and censored his dreams by night – assured his capacity to resist any such apostasy. But the temptation that Winckelmann had embraced in Rome, so like the one that Freud had encountered in Paris – the affective power of Eros with which Catholic Rome was associated – Freud recognized as a deeper reality in his own psyche. It was his glory to exhume it painfully in himself and then to put it to work in building his dynamic psychoanalytic system.

After Freud finished his self-analysis and *The Interpretation of Dreams* in 1900, the gates of Rome opened to him at last. He entered the city not "to take vengeance on the Romans," nor to yield to the temptation of Holy Mother Church, but as an intellectual pilgrim. "It was an overwhelming experience for me, the fulfillment of a long-cherished wish," he wrote to Fliess. "It was also," he added, "slightly disappointing." Though he did not find all the strata of Rome's symbolic meaning for his psychic life simultaneously present, as in the metaphor with which this essay began, Freud could distinguish three Romes clearly, by historical period. Taking them in inverse order, the third Rome, modern Rome, was "hopeful and likeable." The second, Catholic Rome, with its "lie of salvation," was "disturbing," making him "incapable of putting out of my mind my own misery and all the other misery which I know to exist." Was not his misery the result of the powerful attraction of the Catholic world of Notre Dame, and the temptation of professional salvation through conversion after the example of Winckelmann – all of which conflicted with his Old Testament conscience and his ethnic fidelity? But beneath these, there was the first Rome, the Rome of antiquity. It alone moved him to deep enthusiasm: "I could have worshipped the humble and mutilated remnants of the Temple of Minerva."[20]

Minerva? A true brainchild of her father Jupiter, she was at once the goddess of disposing wisdom and protectrix of the polis. Her statue was just then (1902) being placed before Vienna's Parliament building, as the belated symbol of the liberal-rationalist polity. Minerva was also a phallic female, an antierotic goddess, who repelled her enemies with her spear, her snaky aegis, and her gorgon-studded shield. She unified in her ascetic bisexuality and rational cool the civic spirit that had so attracted Freud to masculine England with the female beauty and irrational power that had so moved him in Paris. In the deepest, pagan layer of the Eternal City, where he found the mutilated remnant of Minerva, Freud the psychoarcheologist could celebrate his own achievement: to reconcile in thought the polarities of male and female, conscience and instinct, ego and id, Jewish patriarchy and Catholic maternalism, London and Paris – all in the name of science. Freud's solution to his own problem with many-layered Rome brought with it the restoration of his own ego, endowing it with the capacity to comprehend a contradictory and nonhomogeneous reality and thus to find a way to live with it.

NOTES

1 Quoted in Ernest Jones, *The Life and Work of Sigmund Freud,* 3 vols. (New York, 1953–57), vol. 1, pp. 178–9.
2 Ronald M. Clark, *Freud: The Man and His Cause* (New York, 1980), pp. 38–40.
3 Jones, *Freud,* vol. 1, p. 179.
4 Ibid., vol. 2, p. 171.
5 Ibid., vol. 1, p. 233. For an able discussion of Freud's relation to Paris and Charcot somewhat at variance with mine, see Léon Chertok, "Freud in Paris (1885/86)," *Psyche* 5 (1973): 431–48.
6 Marthe Robert, *The Psychoanalytic Revolution,* trans. Kenneth Morgan, paperback ed. (New York, 1968), p. 72.
7 Sigmund Freud to Minna Bernays, Paris, 3 Dec. 1885, *The Letters of Sigmund Freud,* ed. Ernst L. Freud, trans. Tania and James Stern, paperback ed. (New York, Toronto, London, 1964), p. 187.
8 Freud to Martha Bernays, Paris, 19 Nov. 1885, *Letters,* p. 183.
9 Freud to Minna Bernays, Paris, 3 Dec. 1885, *Letters,* pp. 187–8.
10 Freud to Martha Bernays, Paris, 8 Nov. 1885, *Letters,* pp. 178–82.
11 "Now just suppose I were not in love already and were something of an adventurer; it would be a strong temptation to court her [Mlle. Charcot], for nothing is more dangerous than a young girl bearing the features of a man whom one admires." Ibid., 20 Jan. 1886, pp. 196–7; 27 Jan. 1886, pp. 197–8; 2 Feb. 1886, p. 201; 10 Feb. 1886, pp. 206–7.
12 Ibid., 24 Nov. 1885, pp. 184–5.
13 Carl E. Schorske, *Fin-de-siècle Vienna, Politics and Culture* (New York, 1980), ch. 4. Unless otherwise indicated, what follows is based on the materials there presented.
14 Freud to Wilhelm Fliess, Vienna, 5 Nov. 1897, Sigmund Freud, *The Origins of Psycho-analysis: Letters, Drafts and Notes to Wilhelm Fliess, 1887–1902,* ed. Marie Bonaparte, Anna Freud, Ernst Kris, trans. Eric Mosbacher and James Strachey, paperback ed. (Garden City, N.Y., 1957), p. 232.
15 Ibid., 3 Dec. 1897, p. 129.
16 One later Rome dream, in which the city is the setting of grief, is not included here. This dream's bearing on Freud's problem of ambivalence as a Jew has been interestingly demonstrated by Peter Loewenberg in "A

Hidden Zionist Theme in Freud's 'My Son, the Myops . . .' Dream,"
Journal of the History of Ideas 31 (1970): 129–32.

17 Freud to Fliess, Vienna, 3–4 Oct. 1897; Vienna, 15 Oct. 1897, *Origins*,
pp. 221–8. The most comprehensive treatment of the Nanny and Freud's
Rome neurosis is Kenneth A. Grigg, " 'All Roads Lead to Rome,' The
Role of the Nursemaid in Freud's Dreams," *Journal of the American
Psychoanalytic Association* 21 (1973): pp. 108–26.

18 Freud to Fliess, Vienna, 23 March 1901, *Origins*, pp. 315–6.

19 Ibid., 30 Jan., 15 Feb. 1901, pp. 328–9.

20 Ibid. [Vienna], 19 Sept. 1901, p. 336.

2 Seduced and abandoned: The rise and fall of Freud's seduction theory

For many years, Freud's "seduction theory" of neurosis was seen as an erroneous if initially plausible step on his way to the mature theory of psychoanalysis, and his account of his rejection of the seduction theory was taken essentially at face value. More recently, with the increasing appreciation of child sexual abuse, classical psychoanalysis has been criticized for dismissing childhood reality as infantile fantasy, interest in the seduction theory has been revived, and Freud's motives for abandoning it have been sharply questioned. The story of the rise and fall of the seduction theory thus takes on new interest and significance. Perhaps its most crucial lesson is the importance of theory in psychoanalysis. Theoretical presuppositions played a major role in creating the theory, in causing Freud to abandon it, and in helping him produce a replacement. Theoretical considerations also explain why, though Freud never ceased believing in the reality of sexual abuse in childhood, he could not find a causal role for it once he had adopted his new theory.

The climax of the story is well known. In his letter of September 21, 1897, Freud announced to Wilhelm Fliess, "I no longer believe in my *neurotica*" (1985 [1887–1904], 264), the seduction theory he had tenaciously defended for the two preceding years. His reaction to this event seemed paradoxical even to him. It was, he wrote, "the collapse of everything valuable" in his recent theoretical efforts, yet he had "more the feeling of a victory than a defeat (which is surely not right)." But it was. The famous letter was as much birth announcement as obituary. Less than two months later, Freud sent Fliess with mock fanfare the first outline of his theory of infantile sexuality and its role in the formation of neurotic symptoms in adulthood.

25

Freud offered Fliess four reasons for rejecting the theory that all neuroses were caused by traumatic incidents of seduction, or as he himself frequently called it, sexual abuse, in early childhood. (1) He had not brought a single therapy to a fully successful conclusion using that hypothesis. The patients who had seemed most gripped by analysis left therapy prematurely, and his partial successes seemed explainable in other ways. (2) Patients' reports of abuse had increasingly come to implicate perverse acts by their fathers. The frequency of hysteria – which implied an even greater frequency of perverse assaults, since not all of them produced hysteria – thus entailed the existence of an improbably large number of sexually abusive fathers. (3) It was difficult to tell the difference between truth and fiction in patients' emotion-laden stories of abuse. (4) Even in the spontaneous deliria of psychotics, hidden childhood experiences did not break through into consciousness; it was unlikely that this could happen in the treatment of (presumably better-defended) patients who were less ill.

A number of writers have attacked both the cogency and the sincerity of these reasons. The most serious criticisms are themselves tainted by a priori assumptions and faulty logic: They assert, without argument, that the abuse theory is basically right and Freud's later theory wrong, so that the reasons he gave Fliess for rejecting it *could not* have been his real reasons.[1] Yet these critics raise a real issue. Freud himself had apparently met most of the objections he raised to Fliess in articles published in 1896. With regard to therapeutic incompleteness and failure, for example, Freud claimed to have carried out "a complete psychoanalysis in thirteen cases of hysteria. . . . In none of these cases was an event [of sexual abuse in earliest childhood] missing" (1896a, III, 152). He even asserted that in some of these cases no success at all had been obtained *until* the analysis had come to its "natural" end with the uncovering of the earliest traumas (1896c, III, 206). Against possible criticisms that hysterics fabricated their accounts of seduction, Freud pleaded the fact that patients only produced them with the greatest reluctance, and with visible signs of violent distress. Furthermore, their stories had so many crucial features and details in common that one would have to hypothesize some sort of patient conspiracy if they were to be taken as fictions (ibid., 204, 205). And on the issue of frequency, Freud was emphatic in his insistence that "our children are far more often exposed to sexual assaults than the few precautions taken by parents in this connection would lead us to expect," citing, for support – admittedly at second hand – contemporary publications by pediatricians on the frequency of sexual abuse of children by nurses and nursery maids (207). In fact, Freud felt that he had to answer the argument that sexual assaults happen to children *too* often for them to have etiological importance, because their incidence was much greater than that of hysteria (1896b, III, 164; 1896c, III, 207) – the very argument he dismissed in the letter of September 1897 as highly improbable. Finally, the sincerity of his conviction of the reality of abuse seems underscored by the rhetoric of genuine moral outrage, not only at the physical cruelty of the perverse sexual attacks but at the psychological cruelty inherent in the adult's violation of the responsibility of superior strength: "[The adult] armed with complete authority and the right to punish . . . can exchange the one role for another to the uninhibited satisfaction of his moods . . . [while] the child . . . in his helplessness is at the mercy of this arbitrary will, . . . is perversely aroused to every kind of sensibility and exposed to every sort of disappointment. . . ." (1896c, III, 210).

It being unlikely that Freud forgot what he said in these articles or that he was trying to deceive Fliess, who after all had read them even before publication, he must obviously have changed his mind about the cogency of his previous arguments. The facts are somewhat more complicated. Freud was not simply repudiating the claims of the 1896 articles; important changes had taken place in the clinical theory since their publication. It was not until December of 1896, for example, that Freud fixed on the father as the universal abuser in cases of hysteria. But generally it can be said that by September 1897 Freud's belief in the intermediate steps of his theory – the credibility of his patients' accounts of abuse and hence its universal occurrence in the neuroses – had been undermined. He was only condensing a longer story when he offered his revised conclusions about the shakiness of the theory's building blocks as the reason for rejecting the whole construct. It is not necessary to appeal to factors outside Freud's clinical and theoretical work to explain why he changed his mind. What needs to be understood is the process by which he came to do so.

In fact Freud had sounded much more assured and emphatic about the seduction theory in his published articles than he did in private. The correspondence with Fliess reveals doubt almost from the very beginning. On November 29, 1895, for example, just over a month after he first announced the theory to Fliess, he expressed skepticism about his theoretical psychology, and uneasiness about the clinical theory: "The clinical solution of the two neuroses [hysteria and obsessional neurosis] probably will stand up, after some modification" (1985 [1887–1904], 152). The severity of his doubt increased after he narrowed the abuser down to the father: "so far," he wrote on January 3, 1897, "not a single case is finished. . . . As long as no case has been clarified and seen through to the end, I do not feel sure and I cannot be content" (218). A month later, with the news that his own father was responsible for the hysteria of his brother and several younger sisters, he added, "The frequency of this circumstance often makes me wonder" (231). And in May of the same year he reported a dream of "overaffectionate feelings" toward his daughter Mathilde, which he interpreted as "of course . . . the fulfillment of my wish to catch a *Pater* as the originator of neurosis and thus put an end to my ever-recurring doubts" (May 31, 249). These overt passages actually understate the degree of Freud's uncertainty for the period before he fixed on the father as the abuser. For during that time Freud was constantly raising questions about the correctness of what he called his "metapsychology," and these bore directly on his clinical theory as well. The fact is that the clinical seduction theory itself was based to a considerable extent on metapsychological assumptions, and it collapsed in the face of new clinical evidence equally theory-laden.

Freud began with two assumptions central to an understanding of his mode of theorizing. In the first place, he initially took for granted (as did medicine and psychiatry generally at the time) that the behavioral symptoms of neurosis were not meaningful emotional responses or actions. Their unintelligibility and irrationality meant that, a priori, they had to be explained by nonpsychological factors.[2] Thus, in an early definition of hysteria, Freud wrote, "Hysteria is based wholly and entirely on physiological modifications of the nervous system and its essence should be expressed in a formula which took account of the conditions of excitability in the different parts of the nervous system" (1888b, I, 41). This physicalistic approach, however, also reflected an even more fundamental presupposition about the relationship between mental and physical phenomena. Freud held a version of the doctrine of "psychophysical parallelism," which defined the psychological or mental as a "dependent concomitant" of the physical.[3] While psychological phenomena could legitimately be characterized in the autonomous descriptive terms of desire, intention, and belief, the ultimate explanation of psychic events according to this doctrine was always to be found in the physical realm. For Freud the final distinction between psychic and physiological processes – that is, between motivated action and reflex behavior – was their different location in the brain; the first were processes in the cerebral cortex and the second in the subcortical substance (1888–9, I, 84). The tendency to physical explanation was powerfully reinforced by the denial of psychological status to symptoms; it was the combination of the two that led Freud originally to search for a "physiopathological formula" for hysteria.[4]

True, certain clinical discoveries about hysteria enabled Freud to produce a first level of purely psychological theorizing. He had learned from Breuer's case of "Anna O." that hysterical symptoms could be relieved by uncovering unconscious ideas, and from Charcot that they could be induced by them (that is, by suggestion under hypnosis); and he concluded from these discoveries that it was necessary to "look for the causes of hysteria in unconscious ideational life" (1888b, I, 56). But this prescription did not yet mean that Freud thought hysterical symptoms were meaningful, if unconscious, actions – that is, that symptoms were produced by unconscious desires. The function of unconscious ideas had to be sought in a form of causality outside the sphere of intention. And in any case the hypothesis of unconscious ideas supplied Freud only with a rough first-level theory that had to be further grounded in a theory of the nervous system. This meant that he would be pursuing a three-track solution to neurosis: clinical, causal-psychological, and "metapsychological," or physical.

Freud's first theory of neurosis shows clearly the operation of all three levels of theorizing. In *Studies on Hysteria*, hysterical symptoms were seen as the "residues" of traumatic events that had been suppressed. The initial repression of the trauma was described in purely intentional terms as a conscious effort to ward off unpleasant events: "It was a question of things which the patient wished to forget, and therefore *intentionally repressed* from his conscious thought" (1893a, II, 10). But the *effect* of the repression was couched in causal-psychological terms. "Hysterics," Breuer and Freud wrote in their famous formula, "suffer mainly from reminiscences" (ibid., 7). "Suffering from reminiscences" was not engaging in psychological action; there was no motive for it, it was something that *happened to* the self. The proper explanation for it was referred to the abreaction theory, which was based on a set of mechanistic assumptions about the functioning of the nervous system. Psychic events represented a buildup of energy in the nervous system that had to be discharged in appropriate reactions to keep the sum of excitation constant (1940d [1892], I, 153–4). Hysterical symptoms were not meaningful actions but blocked discharges, the results of "accretion[s] of excitation in the nervous system, which the latter has been unable to dispose of adequately by motor reaction" (1892–4, I, 137). This type of explanation also extended to the workings of defense, for while Freud understood the *purpose* of defense against trauma as a conscious motive, he could not conceive of the *process* of neurotic defense in psychological terms because of the bizarre ways it functioned, that is, because of the symptoms that it produced. Attempting to explain the "displacement" of guilt feelings to inappropriate objects in "The Neuro-Psychoses of Defence" Freud wrote:

The splitting of the content of consciousness is the result of an act of will on the part of the patient; that is to say, it is initiated by an effort of will whose motive can be specified. . . . [But] between the patient's effort of will, which succeeds in repressing the unacceptable . . . idea, and the emergence of the obsessional idea . . . yawns [a] gap. . . . The separation of the . . . idea from its affect and the attachment of the latter to another . . . idea – these are processes . . . [whose] existence can only be presumed but cannot be proved by any clinico-psychological analysis. *Perhaps it would be more correct to say that these processes are not of a psychical nature at all, that they are physical processes whose psychical consequences present themselves as if what is expressed by the terms "separation of the idea from its affect" and "false connection" of the latter had really taken place.* (1894a, III, 46, 53; italics added)

I have of course omitted a major element of the clinical theory of *Studies in Hysteria*. Freud had come to the conclusion that the traumas that produced hysteria were exclusively sexual in nature. This hypothesis was partly derived from clinical findings – the memories uncovered in the process of therapy – but the issue is more complicated. Arguably, not even all the cases in *Studies in*

Hysteria dealt with explicitly sexual traumas; "Lucy R.," for example, had repressed the idea that she was in love with her employer. Moreover, Breuer, who contrary to what Freud sometimes said, did believe in, and publicly endorsed, the importance of sexuality in hysteria, differed with Freud primarily on the issue of its universality; he thus read the significance of their joint clinical evidence differently.[5] Freud's insistence on a single causal factor was the result primarily of his greater theoretical rigor and consistency. All nineteenth-century medicine and psychiatry operated within a Darwinian framework that viewed the human being as an organism powered by the instincts of self-preservation and preservation of the species. For explanatory purposes, all ordinary-language descriptions of human wants were theoretically squeezed into or reduced to these basic drives.[6] In Freud's basic mechanistic model, the internal sources of energy whose impingement on the organism initiated the discharge necessary to keep the level of energy constant were the biological needs of hunger and sex. It was Breuer who by the theoretical standards of the day waffled in refusing to generalize from the clinical material to the monocausality of sexual trauma.

But if the combination of clinical findings and theoretical categories virtually entailed a sexual etiology for hysteria, it certainly did not entail the conclusion that sexual trauma had occurred in childhood. Of all the cases in *Studies in Hysteria* only "Katharina" involved a prepubertal sexual assault. That case went back two years before *Studies* was written (1985 [1887–1904], August 30, 1893, 54), but in the book Freud drew no theoretical conclusions about childhood seduction from the timing of the assault on the girl. Freud did not in fact hit upon the theory until after *Studies* was finished, in the summer of 1895, and did not mention it to Fliess until the letter of October 8, 1895 (141).[7] Much more theory-based than the hypothesis that only sexual traumas caused hysteria was the hypothesis that all traumas that caused hysteria took place in childhood.

What led Freud to the childhood-abuse theory was his effort to solve what he regarded at the time as his biggest theoretical puzzle – the pathological form of defense that produced neurotic symptoms.[8] It was that puzzle which drove him to embark on the *Project for a Scientific Psychology* in the summer of 1895. The idea of psychological defense itself was not problematic; it was a normal operation of the human mind faced with unpleasant events or memories. But normal defense did not generally lead to total forgetting: Though usually absent from consciousness, unpleasant memories could be recalled by fresh perceptions (1950a [1887–1902], I, 351–2). Pathological defense, on the other hand, paradoxically involved both a total repression of the original unpleasant event and a residue of alien "reminiscences" in the form of physical symptoms of unmotivated guilt. So even while *Studies in Hysteria* was still in galleys, Freud turned to a new "hobbyhorse," as he called his theoretical psychology, "tormented" by the need for "clear assumptions about normal mental processes" upon which to base "a satisfactory general conception of neuropsychotic disturbances" (1985 [1887–1904], May 25, 1895, 129).

Though the *Project* has been extensively discussed, certain points relevant to the origins of the seduction theory need to be repeated here.[9] Building on the work of Theodore Meynert, Freud attempted to extend a mechanistic model of reflex functioning to voluntary and learned behavior. The crucial bridge between the two was the "experience of satisfaction," which, according to Freud, made learning possible – and necessary. In reflex behavior, energy impinging on the nervous system through an external stimulus (e.g., a hot object) was automatically discharged in a reflex movement that also removed the source of the stimulus (withdrawing the hand). But mere reflex behavior (e.g., sucking) could not put an end to a stimulus coming from internal needs such as hunger; an appropriate operation on the external world (sucking on breast or bottle) was necessary. When such an operation was performed, it left memory traces both of itself and of the resulting "experience of satisfaction." Subsequent influxes of energy would activate these memory traces and cause the organism to initiate the appropriate action. More consistent in his mechanism than Meynert, Freud hypothesized that in early stages of infantile development, fresh influxes of internal energy from hunger would at first cathect the memory traces of the experience of past satisfaction with enough quantity to produce "the same thing as a perception – namely a *hallucination*" (1950a [1887–1902], I, 319). Thus the primary tendency of the organism would be toward hallucinatory gratification or fantasy wish-fulfillment. Only the continuing unpleasure of the undischarged energy would "teach" the organism to inhibit the flow of energy to the memory trace of the previous experience of satisfaction and use it instead to initiate a search for "indications of reality," the presence of a real object in the external world suited to furnish a real experience of satisfaction.

One unexpected application Freud found for this model based on the idea of hallucinatory experiences of satisfaction was a theory of the meaning of dreams. For dreams were in fact verifiable hallucinatory images, images that "meet with belief" when they appear to consciousness (ibid., 339). Freud thus came to the momentous conclusion in the *Project* that "Dreams are the fulfillments of wishes – that is, hallucinatory fulfillments following experiences of satisfaction" (340). The hypothesis was entirely theory-based.

But Freud was much less successful in using the model to give a mechanical explanation of pathological defense – its primary intended purpose. In fact its account of normal defense made pathological defense even harder to understand than before. Whenever the ego suffered a trauma, a network of memory traces was laid down that included both the trauma and the events signaling its end. When a subsequent perception cathected the memory-image of the trauma, the resultant threat of pain caused the ego, in a diversionary move, to redirect the energy of the stimulus to the memory traces of the event signaling the end of the trauma (322–4). Thus, successful defense depended precisely on "signal unpleasure" from the original traumatic memory. But this idea made the total repression of memory in hysteria inexplicable from the mechanical point of view (352).

Simultaneously, however, the metapsychological difficulty suggested a modification of *clinical* theory. The deployment of normal defense at the recall of a trauma depended on the intensity of its original unpleasure. If the initial event in hysteria were not very intense, no defensive paths of diversionary memories would be prepared against it. But if that event somehow became intense retroactively, that is, only when remembered later, the ego would be overwhelmed by the influx of energy because there would be no diversionary pathways available in advance. It would then be subjected to uncontrolled random displacements of energy – exactly what symptoms appeared to be. The only sequence of events that fit this possibility was sexual development, as then conventionally understood. Before puberty, a sexual "event" would not be accompanied by much energy because of the asexuality of childhood. Only after puberty would there be available sufficient energy to generate a sexual response. If a sexual stimulus after puberty aroused the memory of a mildly unpleasurable sexual event dating from before puberty, it would generate a much greater quantity of unpleasurable feeling than had accompanied the original event, and would release an uncontrolled defensive maneuver resulting in the displacement of ideas.

In the *Project* Freud gave the example of a woman who could not enter a shop alone. As a girl of twelve, she had entered a shop to buy something and ran away in fright when she heard two shop assistants laughing at her clothes; she was also aware that one of them was sexually attractive. Further investigation revealed that when she was eight, she had entered a shop to buy candy and the shopkeeper had grabbed at her genitals through her clothes. She had not, however, remembered this episode at the time of the later one; all that remained in her consciousness with heightened intensity after the second episode was the idea of clothes.

Anxiety about being laughed at for her clothes, Freud argued, could not account for her inability to enter a shop unaccompanied. It was really the fear of being sexually attacked that inhibited the girl, but that memory was repressed and the idea of clothes substituted during the second incident at age twelve. As Freud explained,

If we ask ourselves what may be the cause of this interpolated pathological process, only one presents itself – the *sexual release*, of which there is also evidence in consciousness. This is linked to the memory of the assault; but it is highly noteworthy that it [the sexual release] was not linked to the assault when this was experienced. Here we have the case of a memory arousing an affect which it did not arouse as an experience, because in the meantime, the change [brought about] in puberty had made possible a different understanding of what was remembered. (356)

Freud called the concept that he advanced here "deferred action." The childhood event became a trauma only when the child could experience and understand it as a sexual attack, that is, only retroactively, after puberty, and its memory would be repressed only if it had become a trauma by deferred action, because there would be no prepared defenses. The theoretical possibility of pathological defense thus depended wholly on the asexuality of childhood.

Freud started tinkering with this clinical explanation virtually from the start. In contrast to hysterics, obsessional neurotics displayed guilt rather than just revulsion and fright. Freud linked this fact with his finding that obsessionals had experienced sexual pleasure in their childhood sexual experiences. He therefore hypothesized that an initial seduction could arouse a precocious sexuality in a child, who might then in his turn become an abuser. One passively experienced sexual attack thus gave rise to hysteria; continued sexual activity on the part of the abused child gave rise after puberty to obsessional neurosis.

Necessary as this modification seemed, Freud recognized that it exacerbated difficulties in the theory that he had initially ignored. What, for example, was the source of the unpleasure in hysteria? It could not be the original assault itself, which was posited as at most only a minor annoyance or fright. Furthermore, if sexual energy sufficient to initiate defense was possible only with the advent of puberty, why should that sexual feeling be experienced as unpleasure? But there was also a question about the source of the prepubertal sexual pleasure in obsessional neurosis. If childhood was asexual, how was such pleasure possible? As early as November 2, 1895, Freud recognized the weak link in his argument. "I have begun to have doubts about the pleasure–pain explanation of hysteria and obsessional neurosis which I announced with so much enthusiasm," he wrote Fliess (148). And a few months later: "As long as there is no correct theory of the sexual process, the question of the origin of the unpleasure operating in repression remains unanswered" (Draft K, January 1, 1896, 164).

Throughout 1896, Freud made little progress on such a theory. His letters do show an increased preoccupation with the element of active sexual desire in adult hysteria. While such desire did not seem to affect the childhood etiology, since all the instances he discussed dated from after puberty, it made Freud much more aware of the element of conflict in hysteria between sexual wishes and forces opposing them. The ongoing case of Emma Eckstein played an important, though not exclusive, role in this development.[10] Freud found evidence that she had been a hysterical bleeder since puberty, and was only too happy to send the evidence to Fliess in implicit exculpation of Fliess's near-disastrous bungling of her operation (May 30, 1896, 186).[11] But it is obvious that Freud was after bigger game than Fliess's acquittal. The Eckstein material gave him new theoretical insight into the nature of symptoms. Her episodes of bleeding both in puberty and during her treatment with Freud seemed connected with wishes to gain the attention of doctors to whom she was attracted. So symptoms were not just to be seen as random displacements of energy; they were, Freud concluded, "almost all *compromise* formations" between desire and repression (189). This was an important new formulation; it brought symptoms closer to the model of meaningful human action. "There is no doubt," Freud wrote Fliess on June 4, 1896, "that Eckstein's hemorrhages were due to wishes" (191–2).

For the next few months, Freud's letters were preoccupied with the final illness of his father, who died on October 23. Jacob's death affected him deeply, though it is difficult to know whether it had any effect on his work. He did report a dream whose major theme was self-reproach for not having done his duty to his dead father (October 26, 1896, 202). And shortly afterward, on December 6, he announced two new conclusions. The first reinforced and tightened the seduction theory. "The essential point of hysteria," he asserted, "is that it results from *perversion* on the part of the seducer and . . . that heredity [in hysteria means] seduction by the father. . . . hysteria is not repudiated sexuality but rather *repudiated perversion*." If Freud was tending in this direction during his father's last months, it might well account for the guilt he expressed in his dream.

The letter's second conclusion, however, moved in the opposite direction. The perverse attacks that produced hysteria, Freud noted, involved not only the genital organs but other parts of the body, whose stimulation the abused child apparently found pleasurable. This evidence enabled him to push further the idea that desires caused symptoms: "A hysterical attack is not a discharge but an *action*, and it retains the original character of every action – of being a means to the reproduction of pleasure. . . . [Symptoms] are aimed at *another person* – but mostly at the prehistoric unforgettable other person who is never equaled by anyone later." It should be noted that his definition of the "original character of every action" as "a means to the reproduction of pleasure" came straight from the theory of the *Project*.

At this point, then, Freud had a two-act theory of hysteria. In the first, the child was the passive victim of sexual abuse at the hands of her father, which she experienced as somehow both mildly painful and pleasurable. In the second, the adult (or older child) actively, if unconsciously, reproduced the memory of the seduction in order to relive the pleasurable contact with the beloved father. In some ways, this theory sounds strikingly contemporary, at least in its validation of both the reality of abuse and of the child's longing for the parent. But for Freud it was highly unstable because its basic premises were contradictory. The explanation of the production of neurotic symptoms still depended on the theory of the deferred action of childhood abuse, a theory possible only on the assumptions of childhood asexuality and random energy discharge. But the notion of reactivating memory to relive pleasure contradicted just these assumptions, based as it was on sexual pleasure in childhood and active wishes to reexperience it. What in retrospect might seem to current practitioners a desirable synthesis was for Freud theoretically untenable.

The factor that ultimately exploded the unstable equilibrium was the presence of fantasy in neurotic symptoms, to which Freud now began paying close attention. Fantasies offered the first real clue that his patients' memories were not to be fully trusted. That some "memories" were unreal was easy enough to discern in the obviously fantastic material that drew Freud's initial interest. Patients reported memories of events that sounded like the stories of possession and torture in medieval witchcraft. Here again Emma Eckstein played a leading though not exclusive role. She reported a "memory" of the devil sticking needles into her fingers and placing a candy on each drop of blood (1985 [1887–1904], January 17, 1897, 225). For a time, the existence of such fantasies did nothing to shake Freud's belief in the reality of the crucial memory of seduction; he continued to explore fantasies while simultaneously trying to find evidence to confirm paternal abuse. Indeed, many of the fantasies, Freud thought, derived from things children overheard at an early age but only understood subsequently, an interpretation based on the asexuality of childhood (April 6, 1897, 225). On May 2 he further tightened the connection between fantasies and actual events. Fantasies were indirect reproductions of scenes of abuse; the purpose of the fantasy was both to embellish the facts, reliving them, and to defend against them, but in the crucial sense, "all their material is of course genuine" (239) – that is, they refer to real events.

But the notion of fantasy as reliving undercut the idea that the *memory* of the assault was the crucial repression. "The psychic structures which in hysteria are affected by repression," Freud continued, "are not in reality memories – since no one indulges in memory activity without a motive – but *impulses* that derive from primal scenes [i.e., of seduction]." The fantasies were in part "psychic facades produced in order to bar access to these memories," but that meant that they were a "protective weapon against [the patient's] own libido" (1985 [1887–1904], Draft L, 240, 242). A few weeks later, in the very letter containing the dream about his daughter that he interpreted as his wish to incriminate fathers, he clinched the notion that fantasies were related to impulses rather than memories. "Remembering is never a motive but only a way, a method. The first motive for the formation of symptoms is, chronologically, libido. Thus symptoms, like dreams, are the *fulfillment of a wish.*" These wishes, Freud had also discovered, included hostile impulses toward parents, typically death wishes for the parent of the same sex. Freud's theory had become an action theory that utterly reversed his initial premise of the meaninglessness of symptoms. Indeed, he went on to elaborate, symptoms were the fulfillment of not one but two wishes. "Wish fulfillment must meet the requirements of . . . unconscious defence. This happens if the symptom is able to operate as a punishment (for an evil wish or because of a lack of trust in one's ability to hinder [sexual desire]). The motives of *libido* and of *wish fulfillment as a punishment* then come together" (Draft N, 250–1).

In the light of this conclusion, germinating for months, it is hardly any wonder that Freud was so plagued with doubts about the father-etiology. The wish-fulfillment theory of symptoms had in principle doomed the seduction theory. For, if symptoms were largely fantasies, that is, hallucinatory wish-fulfillments, the metapsychological model of the *Project* demanded that they have been preceded by prior experiences of gratification. And such childhood experiences in turn required a conception of infantile sexuality. Freud could not have retained an etiological role for seduction because for him it was indissolubly linked with the hypothesis of childhood asexuality. Moreover, once he had arrived at the notion of sexuality in childhood, he not only did not need seduction as a causal theory but he could not see how to integrate theoretically such seductions as he believed had actually happened.

Freud however, was still unable to take the final step. He went through what he called "some kind of neurotic experience" that resulted in intellectual paralysis. "Something from the deepest depths of my own neurosis set itself against any advance in the understanding of the neuroses, and you have somehow been involved in it," he wrote Fliess on July 7. "For my writing paralysis seems to me designed to inhibit our communication" (255). The last step, Freud apparently feared, might occasion a break with Fliess. Just why and how can only be guessed. Certainly the abandonment of the seduction theory threatened to destroy the clinical accomplishment on which he had for so long based his claim to Fliess's admiration, but it would also be the beginning of his liberation from the need for the close relationship with him. And the replacement theory had its own problems; it implicated Freud himself as harboring both libidinal and death wishes, not only against his father but against his surrogate, Fliess.

Freud thus had ample motive to start on his own analysis by the summer of 1897. Tracing the historical development of Freud's ideas enables us to better understand the role of his self-analysis. The work blockage unquestionably stimulated it and perhaps even made it necessary. But it was made *possible* because of his new theory of wish-fulfillment. He could now turn to himself as a sort of experimental subject to test his hypotheses. Once impulses were involved as the neurosogenic agents, the theory became universal and self-referential. Freud turned to self-analysis to test a hypothesis he had already worked out on other grounds. A month after reporting its beginnings to Fliess (August 14, 261) and after his return from a vacation in Italy, he announced the abandonment of the seduction theory.

William McGrath, following a suggestion of Ernst Kris, has argued that a piece of Freud's self-analysis, carried out while he was on vacation that summer but reported only later in *The Interpretation of Dreams*, made this final step possible. During his travels Freud made a plan for the following year's vacation, which would again bypass Rome as he had that summer. The plan made him think of the Carthaginian (and Semitic) general Hannibal, who had, like him, failed to reach Rome. The thought triggered the memory of a boyhood episode that had also involved Hannibal. Jacob Freud had recounted an episode of backing down from some anti-Semitic bullies; the young Sigmund had immediately thought of and identified with the Semitic general Hannibal as an expression of anger at his father and a resolve to avenge the shame of his cowardice. McGrath further relates the political consciousness of these vacation memories to an intensification of Freud's political impulses in the spring and summer of 1897, the result of a series of political blows that affected him personally and as a German-Jewish liberal. Among them were his rejection for a promotion in January, which he feared had been blocked by anti-Semitism, and later the confirmation of the anti-Semitic Christian Socialist leader Karl Lueger as mayor of Vienna by the emperor, who had held out for two years despite Lueger's electoral victories but now gave in, sealing the political triumph of anti-Semitism and antiliberalism in Austria.[12] These events reignited Freud's youthful political interests and heightened his unconscious anger at his father, anger that, according to McGrath, helped sustain Freud's hypothesis of the abusive father as cause of hysteria. The self-analysis over the summer helped overcome his anger. "Once he had consciously regained the memory of the adolescent incident on which his Hannibal fantasy rested, that memory began to lose some of the driving force it had possessed in its repressed state, and hence much of the need to blame the father implicit in the episode began to dissipate."[13]

This reconstruction of the vacation event is plausible, though the whole mode of explanation tends to overweight the importance of political factors in Freud's theorizing in general and the story of the seduction theory in particular. Freud hardly commented on the political events whose significance McGrath emphasizes, and his theorizing, as the present account shows, is in any case much more self-contained than externalist accounts in general allow for. Political and psychological factors seem most relevant where Freud's self-analysis was involved in the process of discovery, and Freud himself testified to the fact that in the spring of 1897, the process was neurotically blocked. But we have also seen that surrendering the seduction theory meant giving up the possibility of a metapsychological understanding of pathological defense as well as an etiology based on the recognizable causal model of a discrete causal event.

The causal role of Freud's self-analysis in the process of discovery must be reduced, and even its reduced role remains ambiguous. When he gave up the seduction theory, Freud toyed with the possibility that there was no childhood etiology at all: "It seems once again arguable," he wrote in the September 21 letter – *after* the beginning of his analysis – "that only later experiences give impetus to fantasies, which then hark back to childhood" (265). This possibility was definitively answered for Freud by a theoretical consideration. It was true that the original rationale for placing the basic causal event in childhood – the need to give a theoretical account of pathological defense – was no longer compelling if the clinical evidence for the occurrence of such an event could not be trusted. However, the theoretical entailments of the concept of hallucinatory wish-fulfillment equally demanded that fantasies with a content of infantile pleasure be preceded by experiences of infantile gratification. Freud certainly did not rely on the childhood memories of his self-analysis alone to establish the importance of childhood events in neurosis; the letters of the fall of 1897 show him most concerned to verify his memories by tests of internal consistency and by inquiries of his mother about their accuracy (October 15, 271–2). And in any case, by itself, the evidence of the self-analysis was highly problematic. It was less the originator of material than the verification of material derived from patients. "I can analyze myself only with the help of knowledge obtained objectively (like an outsider)," he wrote plaintively on November 14; "True self-analysis is impossible: otherwise there would be no neurotic illness" (281). Even the Oedipus complex, not yet so called, was discovered first in his patients and then confirmed in himself. "I have found in my own case *too* being in love with my mother and jealous of my father," he wrote on October 15, 1897, "and consider it a universal event in early childhood" (272, italics added).

Nevertheless, all was not clear sailing for the new theory. Freud could not shake off the seduction theory completely. On December 12, 1897, for example, he wrote surprisingly that his "confidence in paternal aetiology has risen greatly" (286). Thereafter odd statements in Freud's work continually acknowledge the occurrence, and occasionally even the frequency, of sexual abuse in childhood (e.g., as late as 1940a [1938], XXIII, 187). Freud even insisted on retaining the idea that sexual abuse could play a causal role in the etiology of neurosis (1896b, III, 168, footnote added in 1924 edition).

But he never explained how. The problem was that he had no way of accounting for its role in hysteria once he laid out his theory of childhood sexuality more fully. In the letter of November 14, 1897, he put forward the hypothesis that various parts of the body are capable of generating sexual excitement in childhood but are "extinguished" in normal development. Memories of excitations of these zones can reanimate impulses from them in adult life – a variation and extension of the theory of "deferred action" that originally explained neurotic symptom formation. But these zones, particularly the anus, have meanwhile become associated with a natural, biologically based, sense of disgust. It is this disgust that is the source of unpleasure that causes repression. Freud had finally come up with an explanation of the source of unpleasure in sexuality that had so long eluded him. "To put it crudely," he wrote Fliess, "the memory actually stinks just as in the present the object stinks" (1985 [1887–1904], 280). But with repression now organically rooted, Freud had no way to theorize the impact of acts of abuse except insofar as they contributed to the fixation of childhood sexuality. This was not the result of a personal failing but an implication of Freud's biologically based drive theory. So long as drives and the forces opposing them are seen as purely internal and triggered by a purely biological developmental timetable, there is indeed no way of thinking about sexual abuse in a clinically useful way. Only the concept of narcissism, which though Freud was not aware of it, exploded the bounds of drive theory,[14] and its extension in British "object relations" theory and Heinz Kohut's self-psychology, with their theoretical incorporation of the impact of the nurturing environment on self-esteem and selfhood, could furnish the kind of clinical theory necessary to make sense out of the effects of child abuse on neurotic disturbance.

NOTES

1 See in particular J. M. Masson, *The Assault on Truth: Freud's Suppression of the Seduction Theory* (New York, 1985), pp. 110ff., p. 144; M. Krull, *Freud and His Father* (1979, trans. A. J. Pomerans, New York, 1986), pp. 69–70.

2 See G. N. Izenberg, *The Existentialist Critique of Freud: The Crisis of Autonomy* (Princeton, N.J., 1976), ch. 1, "Freud's Theory of Meaning," esp. pp. 22–32, for a more extended discussion of Freud's conceptualizing of symptomatic behavior. The present essay develops a number of themes from the earlier work with particular attention to the problem of the rise and fall of the seduction theory. The 1976 book was written before the full version of the Fliess letters was available.

3 *Ibid.*, p. 62. See also F. J. Sulloway, *Freud: Biologist of the Mind: Beyond the Psychoanalytic Legend* (New York, 1979, 1983), ch. 2.

4 Izenberg, *Existentialist Critique of Freud*, p. 32.
5 Sulloway, *Freud*, p. 62.
6 Izenberg, *Existentialist Critique of Freud*, p. 57; Sulloway, *Freud*, p. 91.
7 In the light of Masson's argument that Freud abandoned the seduction theory largely in order to exculpate Fliess from responsibility for the botched nasal operation he performed on Emma Eckstein, which nearly led to her death from hemorrhage because of the gauze Fliess had left inside the nasal cavity, it should be noted that Freud did not even arrive at the seduction theory until months after the operation and its sequelae (February–March, 1895).
8 Izenberg, *Existentialist Critique of Freud*, p. 36; Sulloway, *Freud*, p. 123.
9 The best historical discussion is still P. Amacher, *Freud's Neurological Education and Its Influence on Psychoanalytic Theory, Psychological Issues*, vol. 14, no. 4, (New York, 1965). See also Ernst Kris's introduction to the first (partial) English translation of the Fliess correspondence, which includes the *Project, The Origins of Psychoanalysis: Letters to Wilhelm Fliess, Drafts and Notes: 1887–1902*, (New York, 1954); Izenberg, *Existentialist Critique of Freud*, p. 36ff, and Sulloway, *Freud*, ch. 2, with its extensive bibliographical references.
10 See, for example, the case of Mrs. P. J., Freud's letter to Fliess, Draft J, 155–8.
11 See note 6.
12 W. J. McGrath, *Freud's Discovery of Psychoanalysis: The Politics of Hysteria* (Ithaca, N.Y., 1986), p. 175ff.
13 Ibid., p. 212.
14 Izenberg, *Existentialist Critique of Freud*, pp. 197–200.

3 Freud's androids

A recent essay in *Science* compares Freud's work with contemporary "cognitive science." The comparison is rather to Freud's disadvantage, and to the disadvantage of Freud's contemporaries: *Our* contemporaries have a conception of the mind as a computational system. Some of their theories posit a quantity, "activation," that is responsible for aspects of mental functioning. Some of their theories postulate "parallel processing" through a network that is analogous to the connected system of nerve cells in the human nervous system. Unlike Freud, the story goes, our contemporaries have an experimental tradition that supports their theories. The result is that we now have a powerful and distinctive science of both the unconscious and the conscious, a science whose theories have led to new experiments "that tentatively reveal a tripartite classification of nonconscious mental life that is quite different from the seething unconscious of Freud."[1]

In a general way, these perceptions are widely shared, not only among academic psychologists, but among philosophers of mind, philosophers of science, research administrators, and increasingly, the educated public. They have the impression that contemporary cognitive psychology with its computer simulations of mind is onto something new and scientific that was at best only dimly foreshadowed in earlier psychologies. My purpose is to argue the contrary. A big part of contemporary cognitive science is pretty much what you would expect to get if Sigmund Freud had had a computer.

I thank Jerome Neu for helpful comments on this essay.

I

While the popularity of cognitive science, the digital computer, and
the formal theory of computation are all relatively new, most of the
basic ideas of contemporary cognitive science are *not* new. They
appeared nearly in their present form in the late nineteenth century
in the work of a group of neuropsychologists and neurophysiologists: Hermann Helmholtz, Theodor Meynert, Ernst Brücke,
Jean-Martin Charcot, Pierre Janet, Carl Wernicke, Sigmund Exner,
Joseph Breuer, and others. One of the others was Sigmund Freud. As
an intellectual community, they were at once unified enough in
theme and different enough in details to represent almost every
fundamental idea of our own contemporary cognitive psychology.
Freud and his contemporaries lacked the notion of a digital computer, of course, and of computation theory, and they also lacked the
specific algorithms that have been proposed in the last thirty years
to explain specific cognitive capacities. But they did not lack the
idea that the brain is a biological machine that executes algorithms,
nor were they without ideas about the computational architecture of
that machine, nor did they lack the several conceptions of psychological explanation that are at work in contemporary sciences of the
mind. Freud, especially, did not lack any of these things.

The neuropsychology of the late nineteenth century does not just
anticipate our own; on the major conceptual issues it is quite as
developed. Freud and his contemporaries understood the value of
tying psychology to physics and biology, and they disputed among
themselves the value of locating the mechanisms of thought in particular regions of the brain. Freud and his contemporaries understood the brain as a computational device, and they hypothesized a
"language of thought" analogous to what we would nowadays call a
"machine language" for a computer. They understood the elements
of what we now call "connectionist" computation, and they made
proposals as to how, using thermodynamic principles, connectionist
devices can learn. Freud himself introduced much of the equivocal
character that besets contemporary accounts of mental states as
functional states. He employed a conception of homuncular explanation that anticipated contemporary modes of explanation in econom-
ics and political science, and that is philosophically unexception-

able. Freud's understanding of mental representation derived as much from the arts as from biology, and the arts provided him with a view about representation and rationality that has implications for contemporary discussions of the relation between rationality and analog computation.

Freud tended to exaggerate every intellectual issue, and, especially in his more youthful work, tended to look for unequivocal, radically general, and uncompromising formulations of fundamental hypotheses about the mind. A certain extremism is one mark of a philosophical intellect, for it tends to make issues stark and simple and as general as possible, the way philosophers like them. The result is that Freud's writings contain a philosophy of mind, and indeed a philosophy of mind that addresses many of the issues about the mental that nowadays concern philosophers and ought to concern psychologists. Freud's thinking about the issues in philosophy of mind is often better than much of what goes on in contemporary philosophy, and it is sometimes as good as the best. Some of it is dated, of course, by the limits of Freud's scientific knowledge, but even when Freud had the wrong answer to a question, or refused to give an answer, he knew what the question was and what was at stake in it. And when he was deeply wrong, it was often for reasons that still make parts of cognitive psychology wrong.

These claims may seem mysterious. Why, if Freud was a spokesman for a movement that almost fully anticipated contemporary cognitive psychology, is that fact not already recognized? And how did Freud come to be seen as the source of a movement, psychoanalysis, pretty much orthogonal to contemporary cognitive psychology? Cognitive psychology is a new discipline even if it is not a new subject. The parts of Freud's work that most clearly develop and illustrate the foundational issues in cognitive psychology were written before the turn of the century; they are unread by most academic psychologists, and they do not include any of Freud's most popular writings. It was in his early years, while still directly under the sway of the neuropsychological and neurophysiological communities, that Freud formulated the basic themes with which we shall be concerned. Psychologists, like almost everyone else, know Freud principally from a later period of his life; without the contrast of the earlier period of Freud's work, the issues that concern us are less vivid and more difficult to discern.

Sigmund Freud entered medical school at the University of Vienna in 1873. His medical education, which continued for eight years, was divided by two attachments. One, to Franz Brentano, the defrocked Catholic priest who had come to the University of Vienna as Professor of Philosophy the semester after Freud had begun his studies, occupied the first two years of Freud's career as a medical student. The other, to Ernst Brücke, Professor of Physiology, continued for the rest of Freud's student days and for some while after. Two other men, Theodor Meynert, Professor of Psychiatry at the University, and Josef Breuer, one of the most eminent Viennese physicians, also had powerful influences on Freud in his student years. Brentano on the one side, and Brücke, Meynert, and Breuer on the other, framed the understanding of mind and matter that Freud endorsed. The views of the two sides were very different in some important respects, alike in others, and where they differ Freud's opinion came to rest with Brücke's side rather than Brentano's.

Brentano gave Freud all the formal philosophical tutoring he was ever to have. Freud learned logic – Aristotle's theory of the syllogism – from Brentano, and he learned the strategems of philosophical argument. In 1874, while Freud was studying with him, Brentano published *Psychology from an Empirical Standpoint*, and the contents of that book gave Freud one vision of what psychology should seek to know, and of what methods it should use. Brentano's views of the goals of psychology were simple and rather traditional. Everyone has private access to one's own mental phenomena, to thoughts and dreams and images and pains and pleasures. To deliberately recollect one's own mental phenomena is to *introspect*. By introspection, properly conducted, everyone can collect facts about one's own mental life. The facts revealed to different people will of course be different, but according to Brentano there must be regularities revealed in any one person's mental life, and the regularities will be the same from person to person. Those regularities are the laws of mental life, and to find them is the proper goal of empirical psychology.

Brücke, along with Emil Du Bois Reymond and Hermann Helmholtz, had studied physiology with Johannes Müller. Müller was a sort of vitalist, who held that the workings of the body could not be entirely explained on physical and chemical principles. He must have wanted either in charm or persuasiveness, for history has it that his three most distinguished students allied themselves against his doc-

trines. Their views were essentially those of the great French physiologist Claude Bernard, who in 1865 popularized scientific materialism
in his *Introduction to the Study of Experimental Medicine.*

The essential doctrine shared by Brücke, Du Bois Reymond,
Helmholtz, and Bernard is what philosophers nowadays call the doctrine of *supervenience.* The idea is that one set of properties determines another set in every possible circumstance. Property P su-
pervenes on a set S of other properties provided every pair of possible
circumstances that are alike with regard to S are also alike with
regard to P. The physiologists held that all properties supervene on
the physical properties; same physics, same everything else. They
also held to a strict physical determinism, by which they meant that
if two systems should be in the same physical circumstances at
corresponding moments, then those systems would also be alike in
their physical states at subsequent, corresponding moments. The
doctrines of physical determinism and supervenience evidently together imply that determinism holds for all properties of all things,
not just for physical properties. Determinism and supervenience together promoted a contempt for statistical methods in science.

Brücke, Freud's most influential teacher, was a physiologist, and so
were Du Bois Reymond and Helmholtz, his compatriots in the nation
of materialism. Freud did anatomy with Brücke, chiefly neural anatomy, which was also one of Meynert's specialties. In Brücke's laboratory physiology and anatomy were one subject pursued by different
methods. Physiology, like any other science, is many things. Traditionally it is the study of *functional structure* in living organisms.
Theories of functional structure are really special kinds of *decomposi-
tions* of capacities. Humans live; how do they do it? They do it by
eating and breathing and excreting. And how do they breathe? They
do it by inspiring air into the lungs, absorbing part of it into the blood
through the lungs, and expiring the remainder of the air and gases
received from the blood. And how are these things done?

Physiological explanations do several things at once. They focus
on a capacity to be explained, they decompose it into component
capacities that together are supposed either to *constitute* the capacity to be explained, or to have it as an *effect.* But the component
capacities are produced by specific *physical structures* within the
organism. Breathing involves the nose and mouth, the larynx, the
lungs, the diaphragm. In physiology, the analysis of functional struc-

ture is concomitant with the analysis and description of physical components that carry out the component functions or capacities. The connection of function and physical structure permits the order of questions to be reversed. When a new, discrete anatomical structure is discovered, one can ask what its function is, which is only a way of asking what capacities are based on the anatomical part.

Now the materialist school of physiologists held that the analysis of capacities ought to end in physics and chemistry. The capacity to breathe is analyzed into the capacity of the lungs to inspire, expire, and to exchange gases with the blood. The capacity to exchange gases with the blood is analyzed into changing physical conditions, namely the volume, pressure, and chemical composition of the gases in the lungs, the concentrations of various chemicals in the blood, the mechanical effects of increased air pressure in the alveolae, and the laws of thermodynamics and diffusion. In the end, nothing remains in any instance but physics and chemistry.

Materialist physiology, the sort of physiology advocated by Brücke and the other members of the Helmholtz circle, must inevitably be extended to a materialist psychology as well. The analysis of biological capacities must at many points appeal to capacities of the brain, and to *cognitive capacities*. Processes that appear to be under "voluntary" control must, according to Brücke and his colleagues, be analyzable into capacities that are finally explicable in physical and chemical terms. The cognitive capacities include the ability to recognize things, to locate them in space and to manipulate them, the ability to remember, to learn and solve problems, and above all, the ability to converse and communicate. Language seems a crucial case. If the capacity to communicate in language could be analyzed into component capacities, and ultimately into physical and chemical structures and processes, one of the great challenges to materialist physiology would be met.

How even to begin to construct a cognitive physiology? In ordinary physiology there are specific tissues involved, and one can use essentially physical experiments to examine the causal properties of those structures in order to discover the component capacities. But with cognitive capacities there is only one structure, the nervous system, and it is difficult to get at and to manipulate. Without such manipulation, it would appear that one can only guess at the component capacities that make up the capacity to converse.

Traditional philosophical psychology analyzed the mind into a collection of "faculties," the Will, the Imagination, Reason, Judgment, and so on. The faculties form a kind of organizational chart of the mind, with each faculty given a set of powers or functions. Faculty psychology is like physiology *without* physics. Two of the most powerful ideas in the theory of mind developed in the nineteenth century are that the traditional faculties are the wrong way to decompose human capacities, and that the right ways, the correct subcapacities, are based on specific tissues within the brain and nervous system. Francis Gall advocated the localization of faculties in regions within the skull, but the real advance in the idea of localization turned on novel analyses of the capacity for language.

In 1861, Broca claimed to have located a region of the cortex responsible for the *production* of speech. Stimulated by Broca's work, Theodor Meynert and his student, Carl Wernicke, began a kind of physiology of the mind whose signal triumph was announced in 1874, the same year in which Brentano's book was published, and the second year of Freud's medical studies.

Wernicke's triumph was the discovery of a region responsible for the *comprehension* of speech. The work was a combination of neuroanatomy and clinical psychiatry. Patients with linguistic *incapacities*, aphasias, were classified by the particular sort of incapacity they exhibited, and when the patients died their brains were examined for lesions. The location of the lesion identified the region of the cortex responsible for the patient's aphasia, and hence a region necessary for the corresponding linguistic subcapacity.

Meynert and Wernicke decomposed the capacity for speech into a set of subcapacities: the capacity to hear, the capacity to interpret sounds as speech and understand the speech, the capacity to reason and think, the capacity to produce speech. They supposed each of these capacities to have a physical locale in the brain; special tissues, the fiber tracts of the brain, convey the output of one capacity from its locale to the locales of other capacities. The mind has an organizational chart, indeed, and it is a chart of capacities and subcapacities, but it is at the same time a chart of mental organs that are specific physical tissues inside the skull.

Meynert and Wernicke were not just pluggers, too absorbed with biological and clinical detail to concern themselves with the overall structure of mind. Meynert published a textbook on psychiatry in

1884, in which the general idea of a neurophysiology of the mind was developed. Wernicke wrote a series of books and essays with the same aim, including in 1879 an essay on consciousness. In 1894 another of Brücke's students, Sigmund Exner, who was only slightly senior to Freud, wrote a speculative neuropsychology in much the same spirit. In several ways, Exner's book provided the framework for Freud's early thinking about the mind and the brain.

Brentano and the neurophysiologists agreed that psychology should have exact laws, and that the goal of psychology should be to find such laws. They disagreed about everything else, and for the most part Freud's views reflect those of Brücke and Meynert, not the view of Brentano. Brentano held that there are exact laws that refer only to the mental, and do not need to appeal to physical circumstances. Brücke and Meynert and Wernicke held that the exact laws concern physical properties or concern the relationship of physical features to mental capacities. The exact lesions that will incapacitate people to produce speech may not be known, just as the exact mass of hydrogen may not be known. But it is a perfectly general law that if all of Broca's area is destroyed, the capacity for speech will be lost. Brentano, unfortunately, had no laws of any interest to propose, and while his *Psychology from an Empirical Standpoint* contains lively criticism, when it turns to producing "results" from Brentano's method the product is deadly dull and nearly vacuous. Wernicke's accomplishment in producing a new psychophysical hypothesis correlative with a new analysis of the capacity for language stands in stark contrast to Brentano's rather lame effort. Any scientific reader of both Brentano's and Wernicke's work, and Freud was surely such a reader, could not have failed to notice the extraordinary difference in clarity, detail, and accomplishment in the positive parts of the two books, even if, as Freud came eventually to do, one disagreed with Wernicke's theory of language capacity.

Freud was reared to think that *psychology should be a neurophysiology of the mental* in which the explanation of capacities in terms of subcapacities proceeds in pace with the identification of parts of the brain essential for the component capacities, and the explanation of the component capacities eventually becomes a matter of physics and chemistry upon which all other properties supervene. That way of thinking about the project of psychology is one thread in contemporary cognitive science. Freud learned this way of thinking about psychology, but for two reasons it does not describe quite how he thought about the matter, even from early days in his professional career.

There is the problem of the contents of consciousness. Although it is true that the kidneys cleanse the blood, a materialist physiology need not give an account of the property of "cleansing" in general, because there is no such property. But one cannot say the same for the contents of consciousness, for the taste of pineapple, for the desire to have sexual relations with another, for the stomachache. The properties of each of us revealed immediately through consciousness seem real enough (indeed so real that we cannot bring ourselves *not* to believe in them), and the phrases that describe them cannot be dismissed as terms of convenience, useful but signifying nothing. A neurophysiology of the mental has a further obligation, and that is to explain what the contents of consciousness are and how they come about. Wernicke and others realized as much, even if they did not know how to provide such an explanation.

And, for Freud, like many other students of neurology of the time,[2] there is the further complexity that he did not quite believe Wernicke's localization schemes, nor was he sure that *any* localization scheme is possible for cognitive capacities. Nor was he quite sure of the contrary, which is why, over nearly fifty years, he often said one thing and then another about the place of thought.

Freud took his medical degree in 1881. For the next four years he worked in laboratories and hospitals in Vienna, until in 1885 he received a traveling scholarship that took him to Paris to study with Charcot, the great French neurologist. He won the scholarship in part through Brücke's lobbying, and it was in the way of compensation: Brücke had told Freud he had no prospects of an academic career. Returning from France, Freud again took up work in hospitals and clinics until, in 1887, he began private practice as a neurologist. Although he was no longer doing anatomical research, and after he began private practice had neither time nor morgues for research on the localization of cognitive functions, Freud remained fully informed of developments in mental physiology through the middle of the 1890s. In small ways he even contributed to those developments.

Freud's style of argument in the 1890s was framed by the empiricist scientific standards of John Stuart Mill (some of whose social essays he translated for Theodor Gomperz's German edition of Mill's works). In private, in his manuscripts and in his correspondence with his friend Wilhelm Fliess, Freud developed a broad, speculative conception of mind and of the enterprise of psychology. That conception can be found in his letters and manuscripts, especially around 1895. Its major statement is a document later entitled *Project for a Scientific Psychology*; it was evidently originally intended for publication, but Freud was uneasy with it, and seems to have submitted it to no one but Fliess. Late in his life Freud attempted unsuccessfully to have the manuscript destroyed. Commentators since have been struck by how much of the *Project* echoes through Freud's later work; we find pieces of its formulations in *The Interpretation of Dreams*, in "Instincts and Their Vicissitudes," in *The Ego and the Id*, in Freud's posthumous *Outline of Psycho-Analysis*, and we find its terminology throughout Freud's subsequent writings.

The *Project* really was Freud's project; it states the understanding both of mind and of the aims of psychology that governed his work in the 1890s, and that remained a part of his conception throughout his life. In major respects, Freud's conception was that of many cognitive psychologists of our own time. Once again, Freud was not singularly prescient; his perspective was shared by many of his teachers and colleagues, and his *Project* is largely an adaptation of their views. The similarity between Freud's enterprise and enterprises of our own day is less a cause for wonder than an aid in understanding both him and us.

I have argued that at least in the early part of his career, Freud conceived of himself as doing mental physiology, and that he shared the enterprise with many of the neuropsychologists of his day. The *Project for a Scientific Psychology* is his clearest and bravest attempt at a physiology of the mind. The most striking difference between that enterprise and contemporary cognitive science is that we possess the computer, and the computational pictures of how the mind works that the computer has provoked. To see the connections between what Freud was about and what contemporary cognitive psychologists are up to, we must consider the analogies between physiology, on the one hand, and computer science on the other. Freud aside, the analogies are essential to what cognitive science is supposed to be about. Once the analogies are briefly described, we will return to the details of Freud's mental physiology, and see how profoundly our novelties are echoes too.

II

Computing machines have an architecture or structure, just as the human body does. One can do a physiology of computers as well as (indeed more easily than) a physiology of the brain. Part of my digital computer is machinery for input and output; part of it is random access memory; a physically distinct part of it is memory storage; part of it is a central processing unit that performs operations in binary arithmetic; part of it is buses that connect the pieces. The different pieces of hardware have different functions, and can be functionally described, just as parts of my car can be, and parts of my body.

Computers have a physical structure, and the physical parts have functions. Without a program, those functions cannot be performed. In conventional computers a program is a set of instructions that is stored in the machine memory and then carried out, sequentially, when the computer is given an appropriate input. We usually specify the instructions in a "high-level language" such as PASCAL or LISP; in a proper machine, instructions written in such languages are translated into instructions that cause the physical parts of the machine to act appropriately. The program, the LISP code or the PASCAL code or the machine code into which it is translated, determines a sequence of computational stages for every possible input. The program determines a function from inputs to outputs, but because the sequence of computational stages may be infinite for some inputs, the function may not be defined on all possible inputs. The partial functions so determined are ipso facto computable functions. This way of looking at things enables us to ignore the physical details and consider simply the abstract structure of a method of specifying programs. Any such method, such as LISP or PASCAL, or a machine language code, is a *programming system*. Ideal programming systems permit the expression of programs for every computable function, and in fact an infinity of different programs in the same programming system will compute one and the same computable function.

There is an infinity of different programming systems that are equivalent in defining programs that will compute exactly the same class of computable partial functions. Programming systems have a kind of formal or mathematical structure quite aside from any physical implementation. Each one of them represents a way of organizing computing, an "architecture," if you will. The study of the structure of programming systems is not computational physiology because the study of formal structure need not be concomitant with a study of physical structure. We can get a little closer to physiology if we consider the notion of a *machine model* which I, perhaps idiosyncratically, take to be the combination of a programming system and a story. The story says what *kinds* of physical pieces might realize the programming system. A universal Turing machine is a familiar machine model. There is a programming system, which could be given as a finite mathematical object, and there is a story about how the programming system might be realized. In the story, there is a tape with squares upon which elements of the input vocabulary may be written; there is a movable "head" that is always at one square or another and can read what is written on that square and can also write something else in its place; there is a machine table that contains "states" that tell the head what to write and how to move and determines the subsequent state. The Turing machine story does not describe any particular physical object, but it describes an imaginable *kind* of physical object with separate parts having specific computational functions and relevant capacities, and it connects that kind of physical object with a programming system. The result is that we can see how objects of that kind could carry out computations.[3]

A machine model is not a piece of computer physiology, but it is exactly the sort of *theory* we could use in doing computational physiology. If one wanted to understand how it is that a device one thinks might be a computer is indeed a computer, one would want to identify the physical parts of the object with the parts of a machine model and to show under that identification that the physical object goes through a sequence of states corresponding to the stages of the associated programming system. Identifying a physical object, or a class of physical objects, as instances of a machine model is clearly an inductive task; the identification represents an empirical claim, and evidence consists of observations of the internal and external behavior of objects in the class. Not only is it an empirical task to identify an actual physical object as a computer that realizes a particular computational model, in the worst case it is a daunting empirical task. The class of possible theories to be considered is enormous; there is an infinity of different programming systems, and the number of machine models is therefore bounded only by the possibility of telling physical stories to go with the programming systems. We can imagine Turing machines that have not just one but any number of tapes. We can imagine that there are addressable registers rather than tape squares. We can imagine physical processes, such as cellular automata, that are very remote from our usual notion of machinery, but that still represent machine models. Sometimes the story comes first, the programming system second; we may have a physical idea about how computation could be carried out without having a fully articulate formal understanding of the associated programming system. We may sometimes know what particular physical arrangements ought to compute without knowing quite how to classify things more generally. In science, intuition and theory play leapfrog.

Now the very idea of contemporary, computational cognitive psychology is that *we* realize some machine model or other; the goal of cognitive psychology is to do computational physiology *on us.* There may be no one thing that contemporary cognitive scientists believe, but there are characteristic theses. Cognitivists hold that the brain is a system that computes, and that its computations produce the phenomena of learning, perception, memory, language, imagination, and so forth. They begin to differ when one asks what sort of computer the brain is, and how and what exactly it computes. Some say that the brain is a *symbolic* computer, which sounds utterly redundant, since a computer that computed something other than symbols would be a factory. But they mean something more than that; they mean, at least, that the brain is a computer that encodes propositions and images in physical variables and states. The analogy is with machine states in a digital computer. Physical configurations in the machine encode propositions or imperatives that can be expressed in programming languages. Physical configurations in the brain encode propositions or imperatives or images that can be stated in English, or psychologese, or PASCAL, or can be depicted. The brain is a computer with a *language,* the language of thought.[4]

III

Many cognitive psychologists see the brain/computer as having a physical structure that is computationally relevant, and that realizes some programming system, in just the way that a real physical computer has a physical structure that is relevant to its computational functions. Of course they do not regard the brain as a computer organized in just the way IBM now designs them, but they do think of the brain as having specialized, physically distinct pieces that have particular causal and computational roles in producing various human capacities such as visual memory, or visual image formation, or speech recognition, and so on. They think of the brain as executing procedures, not necessarily serially. Sometimes a more or less explicit programming system is proposed by psychologists, but more often the suggestions are partial and fragmentary and focus on the functional roles of hypothetical pieces in some not yet fully explicit machine model. The theory of computation forms the theoretical backing for the enterprise of cognitive psychology, but the particulars of the formal theory are rarely used. Which is, in part, why contemporary work is so much like the enterprise of nineteenth-century neuropsychology. Freud and his contemporaries had no glimmer of the notion of a programming system, but they certainly thought of the brain as a biological machine that manipulates symbols, and they certainly thought that particular physical pieces or aspects of the brain have special roles in those manipulations. Although Freud could not have known it, his speculations about mental physiology are as much speculations about the machine model of mind as are the theories of our contemporaries. The differences between Freud's contemporaries and ours are largely in manner of speech, not in manner of thought. To see just how close the thoughts are, let us consider two contemporary approaches to the computational physiology of the mind.

There are two main contemporary views of the computational structure of the brain, although each view has many variants, and there are many attempts at compromise. Those who follow one main line in cognitive psychology regard the brain as executing instructions serially; the instructions, in turn, are stored somehow within it. There is another, apparently quite different, computational picture of the brain. The initial idea was to take more seriously the superficial anatomy of the brain, and to build machine models that have some faithfulness to it. The brain's structure is cellular, and the cells connect through the synaptic connections structure of the nerve cells. This suggests a network, or more precisely a graph, whose vertices are the cells and whose edges represent synaptic connections. Exactly this picture was suggested during the days of cybernetics by McCullough and Pitts. It has been revived in recent years under such titles as "Parallel Distributed Processing" or "Connectionist Machines." The network and the algorithms for modifying its characteristics can, if one insists, be viewed as a kind of fixed, hard-wired program, but the algorithms or instructions for such networks specify the behavior of individual network nodes and links more or less separately; each node or link executes the instructions pertinent to it alone.

A variety of connectionist devices have been proposed; one example will have to suffice. Consider a network in which each vertex can have only one of two states, *on* or *off*. Suppose, further, that every edge in the network has a numerical weight, either positive or negative, attached to it. Think of the state of each vertex as a random variable, and suppose that the probability at any moment that a particular vertex v is *on* depends *only* on the vertices adjacent to it that are *on* at the same moment, and the weights of the edges connecting those vertices with v. If we start such a network in some state, then the state will change over time, as vertices flash *on* and *off*. If we let the network run for a long while, there will be a long-run frequency with which any particular vertex is *on*, and there will therefore also be a long-run frequency with which each possible state of the system (that is, each possible assignment of values 0 or 1 to every vertex) occurs. So there will be a long-run or "equilibrium" probability distribution over the states of the system. Now it turns out that associated with any state of the system there is a function determined entirely by that state and the weights of the edges in the network, and that function looks formally very much like the energy function of statistical thermodynamics. The equilibrium probability distribution over the states of the network is in turn a function of the energies of the states. In fact, on simple assumptions, the equilibrium probability distribution looks like the Boltzmann distribution of statistical thermodynamics. Put simply, networks of this kind tend toward the lowest entropy states available to them.

Boltzmann machines can be made to learn. More accurately, procedures can be described that alter a Boltzmann machine until it computes some independently specified function. Boltzmann machines learn by a kind of analogue to facilitation in which future behavior is altered by the previous occasions in which the internal nodes of the system have been activated. In practice, Boltzmann machines learn very slowly. In addition to Boltzmann machines several other kinds of distributed processors, or connectionist machines, have been described, with a variety of different learning procedures.

Connectionists cite Karl Lashley and Donald Hebb as their sources. In the 1920s Lashley, an American-born-and-educated physiological psychologist, emphasized the holistic character of brain processing. Hebb, in 1939, suggested that learning takes place in the brain by facilitation, and in particular that the more frequently a neural pathway is activated the more probable it is that it will be activated on subsequent occasions. Lashley and Hebb no doubt deserve their credit, but contemporary connectionists would be more accurate if they traced their sources to Hermann Helmholtz, Sigmund Exner, and Sigmund Freud. While the algorithms will not be found in the writings of Freud and his contemporaries (nor in Lashley or Hebb, for that matter), all of the other elements of connectionism are there, including even the notion that analogues to thermodynamic principles govern the processes of the connection machine that is the brain, and the idea that learning takes places by neural facilitation. Freud himself anticipated both the views of Lashley and Hebb, and presented them in detail that is more congruent to current thinking. In 1891, in his book on aphasia, Freud embraced a holistic account of brain functioning that is essentially the same as Lashley's. By 1894 he had mixed that picture with the views, championed by Meynert, Wernicke, Lichtheim, and others, that the brain contains physically distinct processing modules. The result was theoretically of a piece with the kind of work we find published by many contemporary cognitive psychologists.

Freud and his contemporaries already knew enough of neural anatomy and physiology to make many of the same general guesses about how the brain computes that are made by our contemporaries.

In particular, exactly like the cognitivists of our day, Freud held the brain to be a machine, and although he did not use the word, a machine that computes, and whose computational processes explain our behavior and our experience. Further, like many of our contemporaries, Freud held there to be a private, innate language of thought in which propositions are expressed and which acts as the fundamental coding in the brain.

Freud's machine model was a collection of neurones joined together at synapses like the vertices of a graph. He held the computations of the system to be governed by quasi-thermodynamic principles, and in particular by the principle that the system seeks the lowest energy state. Again like many contemporary connectionists, Freud held that learning takes place by facilitation. And finally, we will not much misunderstand Freud's enterprise – not just in his secret *Project,* but also in *The Interpretation of Dreams, The Ego and the Id,* and elsewhere – if we take him to have been seeking a machine model of the mental functioning of the brain. In none of this, save in some of his hypotheses about the structure of that model, was Freud particularly original.

Freud's *Project* begins with these words:

The intention is to furnish a psychology that shall be a natural science; that is, to represent psychical processes as quantitatively determinate states of specifiable material particles, thus making those processes perspicuous and free from contradiction. Two principal ideas are involved: [1] What distinguishes activity from rest is to be regarded as Q, subject to the general laws of motion. [2] The neurones are to be taken as the material particles. (1950a [1887–1902], I, 295)

The picture of the nervous system we obtain from Freud's *Project* goes roughly like this. The nerve cells are connected at synaptic junctions; they pass something among them that changes their physical energy state. Denote this something, whatever it may be, by "Q," for quantity. There are two ways in which Q might increase in the nervous system: through stimuli from the external world, and through "internal stimuli" from the cells of the body, which is to say through the internal chemical mechanisms of the instincts of hunger, thirst, sex, and so on. The amount of this quantity in the nervous system is not constant but can be increased or decreased by internal and external causes. The nervous system, as Freud conceives it, behaves like any other physical system; it tends to the lowest possible energy states, and the state transitions have a psychological correlate. Increase in energy, or Q, is painful, decrease is pleasurable. The organism is so structured that it reacts automatically to avoid the increase of Q from external stimuli by automatic motions, or reflexes. But Q from internal sources cannot be avoided by reflex motions. To shut off the internal sources of excitation requires rather definite physical situations and the motion of the organism must therefore be directed toward realizing them. The hungry baby, for example, must find the mother's breast. Freud supposed that such motions are carried out by a kind of computational process in which energy is stored up in the nerve cells temporarily. That store constitutes thought and desire and plan, and the nervous system tolerates it only because it leads, in the long run, to lower internal excitation than would otherwise occur. Freud calls the store of energy in a nerve cell "cathexis."[5] When a collection of nerve cells and their energy state represent the memory of a thought, Freud says the thought (or the "idea") is cathected.

Freud supposed that the cells of the nervous system are not all of one sort with regard to their changes of energy state. Some cells, he supposed, are unaltered by the passage of the unknown Q through them, while another class of cells is changed in a quasi-permanent way. The second class, the psi neurones, are responsible for memory, planning, goal-directed movement, and so on, but their processes are not *conscious*. They can have their energy states raised and kept raised; Freud says they are cathected. For Freud, learning is fundamentally adapting an energy distribution among the psi neurones, and it is accomplished by *facilitation* and cathexis. For example, if a is a nerve cell connected with cells b, c, and d, and a and b are cathected, then proportionately more Q passing though cell a will move to b than will move to c or to d. Moreover the passage of Q along any path is subject to a threshold; unless the difference in Q values is high enough, no Q will pass at all. So the cathexis of cells a and b inhibits passage of Q from cell a to cells c or d. If cell c is what Freud calls a "key" neurone, one that controls somatic cells generating Q, then because of the facilitation between a and b, the passage of Q through a is likely not to stimulate c; the facilitation between a and b prevents Q from increasing in the system.

This much of Freud's *Project* is in the same spirit as contemporary

work on connectionist models of mind, and it is motivated by much
the same picture of the mind and much the same level of anatomical
and physiological detail. Connectionists propose that the brain is a
computational network that functions to minimize entropy and that
learns by facilitation. Freud has no algorithms, and his usage is not
entirely consistent, but he says something analogous. *The economic
viewpoint, the pleasure principle, really is Freud's computational
model.*

Freud's general conception of connectionist learning is different
from the framework of our contemporaries in one important respect. In that respect Freud's view is novel and deserves technical
attention – attention that it will not be given here. Contemporary
connectionist learning algorithms are essentially static; they modify a network to approximate a fixed probability measure. Freud's
conception is more genuinely dynamic. The energy of the network
is viewed as *potential energy* that the system tends to minimize;
the network is not isolated but is instead subject to energy shocks.
The energy shocks depend on the response the network gives to
externally imposed inputs, and the effect of any shock is to add
energy to the network. Freud thinks the system learns by adjusting
weights (and more or less fixed *on* or *off* values for certain network
nodes) that will tend to minimize the energy shocks in the long
run. The network learns through psychological Darwinism; those
network arrangements are fittest that minimize the long-run energy shocks, and the fittest survive. Essentially, the nervous system
is represented as a subcomponent of a larger, constant energy system; energy transfers in and out of the subcomponent must occur
through specific nodes. Energy inputs to the subcomponent are
determined by some externally imposed schedule, and the problem
is to find an algorithm for adjusting the subcomponent's weights
on node links that will minimize the expected energy of the subcomponent for every externally imposed schedule. Just how the
adjustment takes place Freud does not say. Freud's conception of
how the nervous system learns is a kind of compromise between
contemporary connectionist algorithms, of which the Boltzmann
algorithm is one example, and contemporary "genetic" learning
algorithms, that also use Darwinian ideas.[6]

Connectionist psychologists of our day sometimes want to superimpose upon their computational picture a notion of computation in which there is a language of thought; Freud did the same, although he did not write of languages but rather of "ideas." Freud supposed that a collection of cathected neurones constitutes a "memory image" of an object or circumstance. These memory images are the objects of propositional attitudes: They may be desired, or wished, or feared, or believed. Freud makes it clear that they have a *linguistic* structure. Thus when writing about "Cognition and Reproductive Thought" in his *Project* Freud says:

> Let us suppose that, quite generally, the wishful cathexis relates to neurone a + neurone b, and the perceptual cathexis to neurone a + c. Biological experience will teach here once again that it is unsafe to initiate discharge if the indications of reality do not confirm the whole complex but only a part of it. A way is now found, however, of completing the similarity into an identity. The perceptual complex, if it is compared with other perceptual complexes, can be dissected into a component portion, neurone a, which on the whole remains the same, and a second component portion, neurone b, which for the most part varies. Language will later apply the term *judgment* to this dissection and will discover the resemblance which in fact exists between the nucleus of the ego and the constant perceptual component and between the changing cathexes . . . [of desire]; it [language] will call neurone *a* the *thing* and neurone *b* its activity or attribute – in short its *predicate.* (327–8)

Freud had only subject and predicate, and none of our programming systems, but he most certainly had the notion of a language of thought. Moreover, it is perfectly clear that Freud regarded the language of thought as preceding all natural language and in a way independent of it. Thus babes have wishes, perceptions, and judgments whose content is represented in the language of thought even before they have the language of their mothers. So too, the representation of words and the representation of "ideas" are distinct, and one of the mechanisms for evading repression is, according to Freud, to bring an idea and a corresponding word or description in natural language into association.[7]

Freud's view is that we are biological machines; we compute and learn by means of the pleasure principle, and we change our state according to physical law. Our nervous states include energy distributions that are representational and have a linguistic structure that arises spontaneously, before any natural language is learned. Hear how Freud continues his theory of the mechanisms of wish and judgment, and how they produce motion:

If neurone a coincides [in the two cathexes] but neurone c is perceived instead of neurone b, then the activity of the ego follows the connections of this neurone c and, by means of a current of Qn along these connections, causes new cathexes to emerge until access is found to the missing neurone b. As a rule, the image of a movement [a motor image] arises which is interpolated between neurone c and neurone b; and, when this image is freshly activated through a movement carried out really, the perception of neurone b, and at the same time, the identity that is being sought, are established. Let us suppose, for instance, that the mnemic image wished for is the image of the mother's breast and a front view of its nipple, and that the first perception is a side view of the same object, without the nipple. In the child's memory there is an experience, made by chance in the course of sucking, that with a particular head-movement the front image turns into the side image. The side image which is now seen leads to the head-movement; an experiment shows that its counterpart must be carried out, and the perception of the front view is achieved. (328)

To see how close Freud's conception is to contemporary views, or, if you prefer, to see how little we have progressed, it is useful to compare these passages with a contemporary discussion of distributed processing:

The very simplest distributed scheme would represent the concept of onion and the concept of chimpanzee by alternative activity patterns over the very same set of units. It would then be hard to represent chimps and onions at the same time. This problem can be solved by using separate modules for each possible role of an item within a larger structure. Chimps, for example, are the "agent" of the liking and so a pattern representing chimps occupies the "agent" module and the pattern representing onions occupies the "patient" module.

The authors go on to give the following description:

In this simplified scheme there are two different modules, one of which represents the agent and the other the patient. To incorporate the fact that chimpanzees like onions the pattern for chimpanzees in one module must be associated with the pattern for onions in the other module. Relationships other than "liking" can be implemented by having a third group of units whose pattern of activity represents the relationship.[8]

While Freud suggests that activation of individual neural states represents subjects and predicates, and a pattern of activation represents a judgment or wish, these contemporary connections instead suggest that patterns of activation among groups of neurones represent subjects and predicates. The differences are not large. In many other connectionist models, just as in Freud's model, individual nodes represent subject and predicate.

In Freud's *Project*, the infant is described more or less as an android run by a connectionist computer. If the details are a little hazy, and perhaps if we press even incoherent, still I think there is little doubt that Freud's conception of psychology and of the functioning of the mind is much the same as that of our contemporaries. I say again that there is not much new in it, and Freud is but a window to his time. Brücke and Wernicke had speculated, and so had Meynert, and in 1894, the year before the *Project* was written, Sigmund Exner, who had worked with Freud in Brücke's laboratory, published his *Entwurf zu einer physiologischen Erklärung der psychischen Erscheinungen*, which Freud's *Project* imitates in some detail. Of course Freud is original and peculiar in certain ways; between investigating belief and investigating desire, Freud always preferred desire, and his psychology is more a theory of wishing than of learning.

Freud's problems are our problems. Consider only the question of consciousness. The evident phenomenal fact is that consciousness is serial and in normal people unified. Freud's French contemporaries, and others taken by the phenomena of multiple personalities, were happy to hypothesize parallel consciousnesses in one and the same brain, but Freud did not. There is one unified consciousness, and in it one thing happens after another. We can recall not only what we have done, but in most circumstances the sequence of our actions. We view our own actions – at least our recent actions – as our own, not as the actions of a stranger. But Freud's machine model is not serial, it is a parallel distributed processing model in which there is no innate control unit, and nothing intrinsic to guarantee coordination. Each nerve cell does its thing, affected only by those cells that synapse with it. Thus for Freud the unconscious, or what he later called the id, is a collection of nerve cells with independent representations; as thoughts, the representations corresponding to the cells of the id may be inconsistent, they are not subject to logical processing, and they do not *occur* serially the way conscious thoughts do. Freud says the id is not subject to time, and he claims thereby to refute Kant. Freud's picture of the id is just the sort of thing we might naively expect from connectionist computation. It is just the sort of thing we do not find in consciousness. Somehow, if the connectionist picture is right, serial computation (or something that looks and feels like it) must emerge from the connections. Freud had no serious idea as to how, nor do we. His only suggestion is that consciousness is due to wave properties of the physical energy of the nerves, and that some nerves are specially equipped to detect the wave properties. The proposal is physically jejune, but even if we suppose it we obtain no explanation of the unity and serial character of consciousness.

Freud's conception of psychology in the middle of the 1890s is of a physiology of the mind in which the description of function, capacity, and physical structure and process are concomitant and inextricable. In the next decades Freud began to extricate them, and thus created a body of questions that apply as much to contemporary cognitive psychology as to psychoanalysis.

IV

Between 1885 and 1898, or thereabouts, Freud labored to stay abreast of developments in neuropsychology. Freud's book on aphasia, published in 1891, is evidence of that attempt. The private *Project* shows as much; its neurophysiology is up to date, and in many ways it simply copies the ideas of Sigmund Exner's *Entwurf*, which had appeared the year before. But in the long run Freud could not hope to continue making contributions to neuropsychology. He lacked both laboratory and morgue to do original work. Still, while he could leave neuropsychology, he could not leave the general conception of the mind and of psychological science upon which he had been reared. What he could do is separate and qualify its pieces, and he tried.

In physiology the analysis of function goes hand in hand with the identification of organic structures and the determination of their causes and effects on one another. In their different ways, Wernicke's work on aphasia and Freud's *Project for a Scientific Psychology* attempted to do the same thing for the mind. But when Freud turned to private practice he was confined to clinical evidence, to the evidence of his patient's behavior, their histories, their memories, their errors; he could not get at their brains. The result was that he began to attempt to characterize the functional structure of mind without a concomitant physical basis, without the organs of function (the ego, for example, or the dream censor) having any identification as specific tissues, without their causes and effects identified as specific kinds of physical changes.

So it happened that in the years after 1898, Freud often described mental processes and entities in terms of their *functional role:* in terms that is, of what they do to one another and to behavior, not in terms of physical characteristics. The mechanisms of defense, repression, the dream work, and later the id, the ego, and the superego are characterized by what they do to one another, and by how they together determine behavior.

Now in fact what I have just written is a half truth. It is half true that after 1898 Freud characterizes the mind functionally without concomitant physics. In fact, he is radically inconsistent, as though, depending upon your point of view, either he could not shake old bad habits, or he could not escape the fundamental soundness of his earlier physiological approach to the mind. Throughout the rest of his career, Freud explained behavior by appeal to the "libido," which in one reading is nothing other than his term for whatever part of the real physical psychic energy is due to sexual sources. In *The Interpretation of Dreams* there is a last chapter taken principally from the unpublished *Project.* Freud warns the reader that the elements of the theory are not to be assumed to have discrete and distinct physical locations, but he also makes it clear that the "systems" he describes and the processes among them are thought somehow to be realized in the brain by "neuronal excitations." In 1914, in his paper on the unconscious, Freud renounced a physiological significance for his theory "at least for the present." But he could not stay away from physiology and anatomy for long; much of his 1915 essay "Instincts and Their Vicissitudes" comes directly from the *Project,* and in the last decade and a half of his life he repeatedly gave his functional structures a physical locale. Thus in 1917, in the last chapters of his *Introductory Lectures,* Freud offered hypotheses about the physical location in the brain of various functions. *Beyond the Pleasure Principle,* published in 1920, was, like the *Three Essays on Sexuality* fifteen years earlier, a biological tract based on psychoanalytic evidence, and it made again many of the points made in the *Project*, and made them in the same language. Parts of this book, and passages in *The Ego and the Id* as well, are unintelligible unless we read Freud's theory as in part a theory of the physical partitioning of the brain's functions. In Freud's last works, *Moses and Monotheism* and *An Outline of Psycho-Analysis*, the anatomical localizations conjectured in the *Project* are again asserted.

So it seems fair to say that Freud thought he could characterize a *functional structure* for the mind without at the same time identifying the physical basis of that structure, that he thought the functional structure was somehow realized by the excitations of the brain cells, and that he could not keep himself from intermittent speculations about the physical locales of some of these functions. Cognitive psychologists nowadays attempt to describe the procedures by which cognitive capacities are exercised. Save for the cognitive neuropsychologists, they usually do so without much or any regard for the physical basis or locale of the procedures. Now and then an anatomical or physiological speculation will slip in. They have voluntarily embraced the separation of substance and function to which Freud was driven by necessity, and philosophers have made the separation into a metaphysic. Many psychologists, and philosophical commentators, avoid talking of machine models altogether, and prefer instead to claim their goal is the discovery of the "functional architecture" of mind. Of course, there is no harm in using different words, but the words are chosen to a point. The point is partly, I suspect, to avoid reference to the formal theory of computation, which many psychologists do not understand and do not much care about; but more important, the point is to emphasize the thought that the story that goes with a machine model is not, contrary to my usage, a story of *physical* kinds. In this view, the story given in a machine model does not describe a physical kind but instead describes something that is different in principle, a *functional* kind.

V

A homuncular explanation accounts for the actions of an agent by the actions of littler agents that compose it. Homuncular explanations have traditionally been despised on the grounds that they are circular; they appeal not just to events that are as puzzling as the events to be explained, but worse, to events that are puzzling for the very same reasons as the events to be explained. If Judith's action in insulting Hermione is explained by postulating an entity within Judith that wished to insult Hermione and that makes Judith move, nothing is explained, at least not according to the philosophers.

Cognitive science has helped to make homuncular explanations seem more like genuine explanations. The very idea of functional analysis is to decompose capacities into relationships among subcapacities; if the means by which the subcapacities are effected remain for a while mysterious and the subcapacities can be described in terms of belief and desire, then for that while they can be thought of as homunculi. The decomposition is paralleled in the strategy of the computer programmer, who writes "big" functions initially in terms of names of slightly simpler functions, leaving for later a specification of those simpler components. Even with homuncular subcapacities, a functional analysis may enlighten us, contribute to our understanding, and do something explanatory.[9] Daniel Dennett says that homuncular explanations really explain provided the homunculi are stupider than is the agent whose actions they are to explain, stupider in that the homunculi have a more limited set of cognitive capacities than does the agent they compose.

Freud held a far more generous conception of the value of homuncular explanations, and I believe he was right to do so. In a sense, Freud's homunculi, at least some of them, can be smarter than the agent they compose, not stupider. Freud's conception of homuncular explanation derives from a more general strategy, namely to see the internal devices of the mind mirrored in the devices of social intercourse, in politics, in literature, in the theater. Freud grew to maturity in a time when Austria was in political and social turmoil; he had for a while liberal, even radical, political views, and took a keen interest in Viennese politics. His education was classical, and he maintained throughout his life a lively interest in the arts and their devices.[10] Those devices, made internal, became for Freud part of the strategems of mental representation.

Freud's views contain a kind of anticipation of the results of political and economic theories of our own time, and by transforming observations about collective decision making into a theory of mind, Freud created a homuncular theory that does genuinely – whether or not correctly – explain features of human action. More than that, Freud's theory provides the framework for *one* sort of explanation of a variety of phenomena that have concerned philosophy since Plato: actions that require an apparently paradoxical failure of will or reason, including self-deception, weakness of will, or acting against one's own better judgment, and weakness of reason or failing to consider in evidence or consequence what one knows to be relevant.

In the right contexts homuncular explanations genuinely explain. If we open Judith up and find within her a little person who through the magic of electronics causes Judith to move, and the little person tells us it wished to insult Hermione, we will conclude that the homuncular explanation was no pseudoexplanation at all, but a genuine and correct explanation. In this case, the right context is *physics;* Judith's interior is a piece of physics, and it is the physical and literal construal of the homuncular explanation of Judith's insult that makes the explanation explanatory. If the explanation were instead that there is no little man inside Judith, but rather Judith insulted Hermione because she was in a *functional* state *like* that of having a little man inside her who wished to insult Hermione, we might have a *real* pseudoexplanation. Construed literally and physically, the homuncular explanation is a real enough explanation, although not the sort we expect to be correct. Construed metaphorically, the homuncular explanation looks to be a pseudoexplanation for reasons like Molière's: it seems to say that Judith insulted Hermione because Judith was in an insulting-Hermione mental state. But are there cases besides little men in heads in which homuncular explanations genuinely explain and might even be reasonably regarded as correct?

Politics provides a context in which homuncular explanations are familiar, and their familiarity suggests that they provide some genuine satisfaction to the understanding. Some of the events in our world are events in which states do things, and governments take actions. How do we explain the actions of governments? Almost always, I think, in homuncular fashion. We explain the actions of governments through the beliefs and interests and desires and weaknesses of the people whom we say *compose* the government, and through the "functional" relations of those persons in their roles as parts of the government. We may even explain the actions of governments in terms of intermediate homunculi, such as coalitions or interest groups or corporations or the armed forces. We explain the actions of supernational bodies, such as the General Assembly of the United Nations, in terms of the beliefs and desires of homuncular agents that are governments. The popular press is full of such explanations, it invents them even when they are not appropriate: I am not arguing that a homuncular explanation is always the *best* explanation.

Homuncular explanations of the actions of a government or other social entity are especially useful when those actions taken together are irrational in the sense that an action taken to achieve one goal has that goal defeated by an action taken to achieve some other goal, and the incompatibility is part of the doctrine of the government, part of what it believes, or a trivial inference from its doctrine. That is commonly the case with governments, and explanations are therefore often sought. How do we explain the fact that the government of the United States, under the administration of Ronald Reagan, wished to reduce spending on social welfare including aid to dependent children, felt obligated to continue minimum support for indigent mothers and their children, yet reduced or eliminated abortion and birth control services for the poor, even while the government recognized that the absence of those services could only increase the numbers of children who required public support? The collection of beliefs and actions is puzzling because it is so palpably irrational, so straightforwardly *stupid*. No matter what consistent things you might desire, you would not do as Reagan's administration did. We give a homuncular explanation of the government's irrationality: The government acts in accord with the interests of different groups on different issues, even though the government knows that those interests and actions are logically and causally connected, and that the connections make for incompatibilities; one group dominates on one occasion and one issue, other groups on other occasions and issues. So we might say: Those who oppose birth control and abortion create sufficient political pressure[11] to undo government support for these activities; the middle class and the upper middle class, who for the most part favor or are indifferent to birth control and abortion, strongly favor a reduction in taxes and of the use of taxes to provide aid for the poor, and they create pressure upon the government to adopt such goals; everybody knows that sex causes pregnancy and pregnancy causes babies. Each of these groups *could be*, although I rather doubt they are, rational in the sense of having a consistent set of preferences. None need be diminished in its cognitive capacities in comparison with the government, although the government's *power* is greater.

Our time has made the irrationality of collective choice into mathematical theorems of various sorts. The original theorem was Arrow's.[12] The theorem says that under various technical assumptions, if there are at least two agents and three alternatives, then the only rule that will determine a consistent collective preference ordering of the three alternatives for every possible pair of preference orderings of the agents is a rule in which the collective preference ordering is, in every case, exactly the preference ordering of *one* of the agents. In understanding the theorem, the "rules" for determining collective choice need not be thought of as voting schemes; they can just as well be jousting tournaments or arm wrestling contests. Arrow's theorem is a result about political homunculi. If for the moment we think of rationality as requiring consistent preferences and nothing more, the theorem could be read this way: Unless one homunculus dominates in every possible case, an agent whose preferences are determined by the preferences of rational homunculi must, for some possible circumstances, be irrational.

Brentano taught Freud the doctrine of the unity of self. Freud did not believe it. According to Freud what produces action is not a unified self, but a collection of agents. The self is a collective fiction, like the government. The agents that compose a person have an identity through time and circumstance and they have a set of relations to one another; that identity and those relations, and nothing else, determines the identity of the person through time and circumstance. The homuncular agents differ in their desires and preferences. The actions of the person reveal a social choice, in something like Arrow's sense, determined from the preferences of the component agents by causes, by forces, rather than by voting procedures.

We know Freud's agents as the ego, the id, and the superego, but that classification appeared late in Freud's career, and is in any case too crude. Freud held the ego to be divided into a conscious and an unconscious part, which act in certain respects as agents with independent preferences. The conscious ego is rational and deliberate, something like the Mr. Spock of the society of the mind. It has detailed preferences about actions and thoughts. The unconscious ego has a funny set of preferences; it prefers to keep out of consciousness those thoughts that, were they to become conscious, would create enormous (conscious) pain. About everything else it is indifferent. The conscious ego, in a way, shares the preferences of the unconscious ego, but it cannot *think* them without agony, so (thanks to the unconscious ego) it does not think them. The id contains conflicting and inconsistent desires for the satisfaction of instincts, but it is indifferent to how those desires are fulfilled. The conscious ego cares a great deal about how, if at all, the id's desires are fulfilled, and so does the superego. The superego, the agent of conscience, has preferences over actions and thoughts, preferences more restrictive than those of the ego. Action results from the resolution of these conflicting preferences.

Freud's homunculi show many of the strategems of voters and voting blocks, and the life of the mind he assumes could, one thinks, be treated as a game of strategy played by several parties. Freud's agents try to conceal their preferences from one another; some agents censor the information that other agents attempt to send to one another. Freud's agents negotiate and make compromises and settle for their second and third choices when they cannot have their way. Of course, underneath all of this talk of agents and their wishes and compromises, Freud sees ultimately an entirely physical set of forces, compromising, if you will, by vector addition. Like a computer programmer, Freud starts with the big pieces, and tries to say what they do to one another, leaving as yet to be explained the mechanics by which they do it. The strategy is just the one Dennett describes, save that in an obvious sense Freud's homunculi need not be in the least stupider than the person they compose. If rationality is consistency of preference, then Freud's homunculi are more rational than persons. We may be equivocal, self-deceptive, suffer weakness of will, have inconsistent desires, but on Freud's account the homunculi within us need not.

I do not know whether Freud's homunculi are *necessary* to give a social explanation of individual irrationality, and the general question seems worthy of some attention. If an agent has an irrational (e.g., intransitive) set of preferences, what is the least number of rational homunculi into which he may be decomposed, such that the agent's preferences may be seen as collective preferences formed on the basis of the preferences of the homunculi? One would guess that in the absence of further constraints two homunculi suffice. If so,

Pierre Janet's psychiatry, which explained neurosis by a "second consciousness," would seem more economical than Freud's. But of
course the question may have more interesting answers if constraints
are imposed on the preferences of the homunculi or on the rules by
which the conflicting desires of homunculi may be accommodated.

Are Freud's homunculi physical or fictional or "functional"? The
answer is a little equivocal. Most often, although certainly not always, Freud treats the ego, or at least the conscious ego, as a specific
suborgan of the brain, usually the frontal cortex. The id is more
vaguely characterized spatially, but Freud often writes as though it
has some specific location. The unconscious ego lies between the
two. The superego is characterized functionally rather than spatially. They are homunculi, but they are not *just* functional homunculi, they are (generally) also physical homunculi. Some of the
homunculi, the ego for example, are *rational* agents, more rational
than the person they compose. Even the id, if its conflicting preferences are regarded as the preferences of subhomunculi, could perhaps be thought of as a collection of rational agents. Or could it?
What is required in order to gather together a group of desires and
beliefs and call it an *agent*? What is going on when Freud separates
our desires into the desires of distinct *agents* within us?

One story is that agency is what is required to explain and predict
patterns of behavior, and there is nothing more to being an agent
than exhibiting a pattern of behavior that can be explained by supposing there is a unified, more or less rational system of belief and
desire.[13] On this view thermostats are agents quite as much as people, but it is not clear that Freud's homunculi will count. For the
separate homunculi exhibit no "behavior" in the usual sense; all of
their interactions are with one another, and the behavior of the
individual they compose is not the behavior of any of the person's
homunculi, but the effect of their negotiations and compromises.
One might try somehow to extend the notion of behavior to include
the goings-on internal to the mind, but within Freud's picture it
would, I think, be a large undertaking to separate events that are
explained as the actions of a single homunculus. More likely, we
could extend the picture to something like this: To be an agent is to
be a unified, more or less rational system of belief and desire that,
together with other agents, explains a pattern of behavior. Some

people would add then the system of beliefs and desires must be very large, and much like our own, but Freud would not.[14]

This does not explain what ties a collection of beliefs and desires together to make an agent. I cannot take one of your beliefs, one of mine, some of Saul Bellow's desires, and so on, and form a collection of beliefs and desires that is an agent. Why not? One insufficient reason is that the beliefs and desires are not localized in space, in the same head. Spatial distribution of beliefs and desires does not itself imply that the beliefs and desires are not those of one agent, as science fiction writers and philosophers both remind us.[15] In any case, the suggestion would only help Freud a little, since he is so equivocal about the existence of distinct spatial locations for his homunculi within the brain. A better explanation is that agency must bear a causal relation to action. A system of beliefs and desires taken from many people does not produce any actions; neither does it provide the reasons for any actions. The beliefs and desires of a normal, rational person both cause his action and provide reasons for it; not all beliefs and not all desires one has have a causal role in each action one undertakes, but virtually any belief and any desire are connected in forming possible reasons and possible causes for some potential action. In Freud's case none of the homuncular agents (save perhaps on some occasions the ego) are exclusively responsible for any action of the individual, and so this rather standard conception of agency does not straightforwardly apply. It does apply, more or less, if we socialize it. Roughly, what makes a system of beliefs and desires an agent is that they collaborate in almost every circumstance; they represent a vote in the society of mind, a society in which, to be sure, not all votes are equal. A collection of beliefs and desires forms a homuncular agent if the beliefs and desires are consistent and rationally combined to form preferences that are accommodated in the social determination of collective preferences and in the consequent determination of action by the whole individual.

Whether or not one believes in Freud's homunculi, Freud provides a *form* of explanation of action that is perfectly genuine, and might in appropriate applications even be correct. Freud's typical applications of his social theory of mind are to the explanation of irrational actions, especially the actions of neurotics, but the kind of explanation he provides also addresses ancient philosophical chestnuts.[16]

Reason and the will present puzzles that still feature large in the philosophy of mind. The puzzles concern familiar psychological phenomena whose reality we all recognize, but whose very description seems paradoxical.

We all recognize that people sometimes deceive themselves about their feelings, their desires, their reasons for action, even their beliefs. But self-deception seems to require that one and the same agent both know something and not know it at the same time, or both desire something and not desire something at the same time. And that seems not just unlikely, but *logically* impossible.

Ambivalence presents something of the same difficulty. Sometimes people seem to have analytically incompatible attitudes toward the same object. Their behavior rapidly alternates between animosity and affection toward the same person. We are inclined sometimes to say that a woman both loves and hates a man, or a man a woman. But to love is by its very meaning not to hate, and to hate is by its very meaning not to love, and so our common assessment of ambivalence seems inconsistent.

Weakness of will occurs when someone believes that, all things considered, a certain action is for the best, but succumbs to temptation and does not perform the action. With plausible assumptions the circumstance becomes paradoxical. Assume in addition only that agents want to do what they judge it best to do, and that if they do either of a pair of actions intentionally, they will do the action they want to do when they believe themselves free to do it, and we have a contradiction.[17]

There are weaknesses of reason that are at least as perplexing. Sometimes a person will sincerely want a certain outcome and sincerely believe that a certain action is necessary to obtain that outcome, and believe himself able to perform the action, and yet to all appearances deliberately fail to perform the action. Thus the infamous Professor Blondlot presumably knew what sort of experiments needed to be conducted in order to convince his contemporaries that his "N-Rays" were the real McCoy, but he did not conduct them, even though, historians seem to say, Blondlot was no mountebank. Sometimes a person will have evidence relevant to a conclusion, know it is relevant, and yet fail to use it, and draw an erroneous conclusion. Sometimes a person will know that a proposition is a consequence of what is believed, and yet fail to believe the consequence or to revise the beliefs of which it is a consequence.

It may be that not all of these difficulties are distinct, and that there is a reduction or commonality of pattern or explanation. Whatever the case, moral philosophy, and more lately philosophical psychology, have been concerned to explain these perplexities, or to explain them away, to show how they are possible, and why they are sometimes actual. It is straightforward to remove the apparent paradox in one or another of these cases by supposing the situation has in some way been misrepresented. For example, when someone has evidence that P is not the case, and knows it is evidence, and then ignores the evidence and asserts that P is the case, one need not be believing that what one believes to be disconfirmed is confirmed. We might instead explain the action by a kind of inward decision theory: The agent will choose to believe P or not according to which action has the greatest expected utility; believing P brings satisfactions if P is true, less satisfaction if P is false, but even though P is less probable than not, the expected utility of believing P is greater than the expected utility of not believing P. Pascal understood this sort of thing.

For Freud failures of rationality, or apparent failures, were the keys to the structure of mind, just as failures of speech were to Wernicke the keys to the functional structure of the brain. The interesting thing about Freud's social theory of mind is that it provides a mechanism for explaining not just one, but all of these paradoxes of will and reason. Moreover, the explanation is so obvious as to be almost irresistible, although not, I think, logically inevitable and certainly not necessarily complete. Freud did not seriously claim that his mode of explanation is exhaustive, and that such phenomena cannot arise in other ways.

A Freudian explanation of self-deception turns on the fact that the self is a collection P of agents, that what is known to one of these agents may not be known to another of them, and what is desired by one may not be desired by others, or be any of the desires attributable to the individual as a whole. What the id knows the conscious ego does not; what the id wants, the ego may not; what you want may not be what your id wants or what your ego wants. Any explanation of self-deception that supposes that we are composed of separate memory stores and that thought can occur while drawing from some of these stores but not from others, will be a Freudian explanation in spirit, whether or not the separate stores have the particular features Freud postulated. Sometimes accounts of this sort seem entirely plausible as an account of the phenomena of self-deception. A Freudian explanation of certain weaknesses of reason is of the same form. How is it that someone can neglect to consider evidence that is relevant to a conclusion, evidence that the agent knows about and whose relevance is also known, and evidence of a kind the agent is competent to evaluate? Easily enough if the agent has separate memory stores, and some of those stores are or can be made to be inaccessible to ratiocination. Freud's original examples are unconscious memories, but he expanded the framework, and the applicability of the explanatory strategy, to include the "preconscious."

Ambivalence is explained by supposing multiple agents with reasonably fixed but contrary preferences, and by supposing that no one of the agents always dominates. Freud's explanation of ambivalence in the Rat Man case goes like this: Conscious love and conscious hatred of one and the same object are possible provided neither is intense. When both become sufficiently intense they are incompatible and one emotion must become unconscious, generally the more painful emotion. Perhaps Freud can be understood as follows. One and the same agent cannot both love an object and hate that same object at the same time. But one agent can love *aspects* of an object and hate other *aspects* of an object. When attitudes toward aspects of objects become sufficiently intense, they become detached. They become attitudes toward the objects, not just toward aspects of the objects, and they therefore become incompatible. The rejected attitude becomes the attitude of some other agent within the self and helps determine the preferences of that agent. When the ego loves what the id hates there will be inconsistent preferences each of which will be revealed in varying circumstances, and there will also be sometimes a kind of indecisiveness. The phenomena of ambivalence are accounted for.

Weakness of the will is no more than ambivalence in action. One agent's reasons may be causes, but not reasons, for another agent.[18] One agent may decide that, all things considered, it is best not to have a further drink; the preference of another agent may intervene, and the drink taken. If one of the agents gives reasons and expresses regrets, while the other is silent, we say the person was impulsive, that he gave in to temptation, that he had a weak will. Acts of incontinence betray an irrational whole that emerges from parts, homunculi, that may be more rational.

These are the ways Freud goes about explaining irrationality. His explanations may or may not be correct, but they are surely *explanations*. If that is doubted, consider that in each of the kinds of cases considered, whether ambivalence, weakness of will, self-deception, or weaknesses or reason, there are analogous phenomena in public life, and we routinely and sometimes correctly give Freudian explanations of these phenomena when they appear in the actions of governments, corporations, and other social entities. In the case of governments we know the homunculi exist, and who they are, and we can more directly verify the explanation offered. Freud's explanations of the self are less secure; they are not less genuine.

VI

Showing and saying have always been deeply entangled enterprises that somehow reach similar ends by disparate means. Saying has linguistic structure, logical structure, grammar; showing, to all appearances, has not. Showing is saying without chains. Every now and then there is an attempt to reduce one of the pair, saying and showing, to the other, or to establish the primacy of one to the exclusion of the other. In the early part of this century Wittgenstein, and the logical atomist movement generally, sought to reduce saying to a kind of showing. Later an heir of the movement, Nelson Goodman, sought to explain showing as a kind of saying. Several recent essays attempt to show the primacy of saying in the life of the mind, and psychologists continue to debate the autonomy of showing in mental life. Showing is certainly a way of saying, but since it lacks grammar and its objects lack grammatical categories, showing does not permit us our usual analyses of what is said. For most pieces of language we can give accounts of how they contribute to the truth value of sentences in which they occur; we do so by giving truth definitions that make the truth or falsity of sentences functions of the semantic properties of their component pieces. With pictures, with illustrations, with bits of theater, we can do no such thing. There are parts and uses of language that behave more like pictures than like sentences, and exactly this feature makes them puzzling and challenging for philosophical analysis. Demonstratives, thises and thats, can be used to show by saying, and for that reason they resist analysis by truth definitions. Metaphors and similes are refractory in the same way, and for the same cause; they are ways of asserting a showing.[19]

For Freud, who took his hypothetical forms of mental representation as much from the arts as from logic, the homunculi communicate both by image and by language, both by saying and by showing. Freud's accounts of the battles of the ego and the id and the superego read like little internal melodramas, and they are. The theater, above all art forms, is the place in which a complex thought can be both illustrated and said. Yet for Freud the theater of the mind is a kind of puppet show, controlled by purely physical forces that carry out computations; the show is the manifestation of the computations. Which brings us, implausibly, to Freud's views of the relations between computation and mental representation, and how the mind can work both by showing and by saying.

Connecting the *Project* with Freud's *Interpretation of Dreams*, published only four years later, we can extract a view about analog computation that bears on contemporary debates. The exercise has a certain ahistorical character, but historians of philosophy do not hesitate to offer Aristotelian, or Humian, or Leibnizian treatments of contemporary philosophical issues; I see no reason not to do the same for Freud.

Early in his career Freud, along with Breuer, thought of the symptoms of neurotics as a kind of aberrant reflex. Freud taught that behavior that seems aberrant and without rational structure may often have such a structure nonetheless, even if it is not evident. Freud's examples often concern the behavior of psychoneurotics. Thus his patient Dora, for example, will not give voice to the thought that she wants a family friend, Herr K., to make love to her, but Freud thinks she says it by playing with her reticule, and by her loss of speech when Herr K. is away. The actions are not speech, but Freud takes them to express a thought, usually by constituting an instance of the thought, or by being a little allegory. It is the same with Freud for internal actions as for external actions, for thoughts as for behavior. Dreams often seem to have no rational structure, but Freud insists that underneath, they do. The dream is usually an image or a sequence of images, proceeding as an inner theater of the absurd. But each play has, according to Freud, a message that it does not say explicitly but shows instead. The showing may be by pun, or by showing the opposite, or by excessive literalism, or by any of the other tricks of the theater. A woman in love with a conductor whom she regards as a towering figure dreams of a conductor in a tower above her.

The deepest novelty of *The Interpretation of Dreams* is the thought that literary and theatrical devices for representing meaning – the devices of parody, allegory, irony, exhibition, and depiction – may also be internal devices used in mental representation. The fundamental semantic insight is that the categories of proof and model theory are not mutually exclusive. One can imagine systems of expression in which some things are *said* by being *modeled*, and even systems in which things are said partly syntactically and partly by being modeled. In a way, the idea is easy and familiar. Almost everyone has seen children's books written partly in words and partly in pictures, with the pictures inserted in a line in place of a word or phrase, or sometimes in place of a syllable. Freud's thought is that mental representation works in a roughly similar way, in combination, of course, with irony and other devices.

If the difference between analog and digital computers is roughly the difference between proof relations and model relations, as I suggest, then one observation follows, an observation that might in any case be given other grounds: The class of computers cannot be partitioned into analog and digital. A computer can be both, or have features of both. A digital computer can be used to produce images, and the images can be used in analog computation. In principle, the analog output could be used to cause the input to another digital process, and so on.

Our usual formal systems, logics, make us think of accounts of inference as specifications of rules. Reasoning, ideally, is producing a sequence of sentences in accord with the rules. Syntactic rules permit the derivation of assertions based on the combinatorial properties of their syntactic components. There are notions of "semantic rule" in the philosophical literature, but they do nothing quite like what syntactic rules do. "Semantic rules" are usually, depending on the philosopher, either very general axioms (e.g., 'Everything colored is extended') or metalanguage statements about the *interpretation* of syntactic components. They are not analog inference rules. But I think we can imagine a *system of inference* that mixes proof theory and model theory, and contains analog rules of inference. Tracing out the derivation of a conclusion in such a system would amount to giving reasons for the conclusion, and some of the reasons would correspond to analog computations.

Our usual rules of inference for formal systems are combinatorial. Analog rules of inference cannot be. They must instead state general features of models that can be inferred to be features of the things modeled. We can imagine a language for talking of observable objects in the night sky. Let the language have the usual form of the predicate calculus, but let pictures of the sun, moon, shooting stars, comets, planets, and fixed stars also serve as individual names. Let the language be sufficiently interpreted that certain monadic predicates signify color terms: red, yellow, blue, and so on. Let the pictures come in various colors and suppose we add to the language the rule:

> From any well-formed formula S, if p is a picture symbol occurring in S, and p has color r and R is a color predicate interpreted as r, infer S & R(p).

In a system of inference that mixes proof and model theory, one can infer that the moon is yellow from premises that contain no color predicates but instead contain a depiction of the moon. (That color is modeled by color is of course irrelevant to the philosophical point.) An automaton that used such a system of inference would do some analog processing, and yet its conclusions about the colors of objects in the night sky would be "cognitively penetrable" in the sense that the processing would provide reasons for the conclusions. Perish the thought that there could be no such automaton, since something noncombinatorial must be done to apply the rule, namely it must be determined that p has color r. The detection of color can be done mechanically, as with spectroscopes, and our automaton can carry out derivations that accord with the rules of the system provided the automaton has some device for determining such physical properties of its representations. No homunculus is necessary for analog computation, any more than for digital computation.

One might object that in such an automaton the workings of the spectroscope would not be reasons, and that is so. The workings of the spectroscope would *cause* certain representations and certain inferences to occur, but they would not themselves be reasons. And yet the workings could be woven into a process of inference so centrally that physical features of the spectroscopic process – such as the time it takes – become physical features of the reasoning process. More important, the physical output of the spectroscope could affect inference in a way that is cognitively penetrable. If, for example, what is inferred is a probability (e.g., of yellow) function of features of the measured spectrum, then that probability could be combined with prior probabilities in standard ways; the resulting inference to the conclusion that something is yellow will be determined both by the physical measurements and prior beliefs.

There is no difference in the philosophical point if the spectroscope is inside an automaton's head or in a physical laboratory. When a physicist looks at a spectrum, physical features of the spectrum combine with the physicist's prior beliefs to lead to a conclusion about the color of some object. Ordinary perception is a process in which "analog" features interact with digital features to produce reasoning; we have done no more than imagine that some of the analog features are themselves in the head.

The moral of the argument is that we can conceive of analog computation that, given an appropriate interpretation, forms part of a system of reasons for conclusions. A corollary, obvious in its own right, is that pieces of analog computation within a system that simulates rational behavior do not require special homunculi, and need not introduce special mysteries. I suppose the corollary has some practical bearing on disputes over mental imagery, but I do not mean to propose that our brains do actually implement analog inference rules of the sort I have considered. It would be charming if Freud were right after all, and if we worked by a mixture of syntactic representations and models, mixing digital and analog computation in our reasoning, but for all I know that may be altogether the wrong way to look at ourselves.

NOTES

1 J. Kihlstrom, "The Cognitive Unconscious," *Science* 257 (1987): 1445–52.
2 For example, Paul Mobius and Hughlings Jackson.

3 Compare J. Hopcroft and J. Ullman, *Introduction to Automata Theory, Languages and Computation* (Reading, Mass.: Addison-Wesley, 1979).

4 Compare J. Fodor's *The Language of Thought* (New York: Crowell, 1979). Fodor maintains that the brain has an innate, unconscious, utterly private *language*, a machine code if you will, in which thought finds expression.

5 The common translation from the German *besetzen*. Freud took the term and the idea from T. Meynert's *Psychiatry* (1884).

6 See J. Holland, *Adaptation in Natural and Artificial Systems* (Ann Arbor: University of Michigan Press, 1975).

7 Colin McGinn in *The Character of Mind* (Oxford: Oxford University Press, 1982) objects to the very idea of a language of thought that what is expressed in language may be expressed *insincerely*, and whatever the sort of "language" for thought supposed by cognitivists, it does not include insincere expression. While cognitivists in general can safely ignore this rebuff, it does not apply to Freud at all.

8 G. Hinton, J. McClelland, and D. Rumelhart, "Distributed Representations," in D. Rumelhart, J. McClelland, et al., *Parallel Distributed Processing*, vol. 1 (Cambridge, Mass.: MIT Press, 1986), pp. 82–3. Anyone who doubts the claim that much of contemporary connectionist cognitive psychology is reasonably viewed as nineteenth-century neuropsychological explanation plus the computer would do well to compare this volume with Exner's book and Freud's *Project*.

9 The best description of functional analysis is in R. Cummins, *The Nature of Psychological Explanation* (Cambridge, Mass.: MIT Press, 1983), but an earlier, vivid statement of the idea and the connection with homuncular explanation is to be found in D. Dennett's *Brainstorms* (Cambridge, Mass.: Bradford Books, 1978).

10 It is probably no accident that in the late 1890s plays about the unconscious meanings of dreams appeared in Vienna. For a discussion of the political background of Freud's youth, see W. McGrath, *Freud's Discovery of Psychoanalysis* (Ithaca, N.Y.: Cornell University Press, 1986).

11 Note how much the idiom is like Freud's, who speaks similarly of the "pressure" of instincts, or the "pressure" of repression.

12 K. Arrow, *Social Choice and Individual Values*, 2d ed. (New York: Wiley, 1963).

13 This view of agency is, I think, central to D. Dennett's *The Intentional Stance* (Cambridge, Mass.: MIT Press, 1987).

14 Compare Richard Rorty's "Freud and Moral Reflection," in J. Smith and W. Kerrigan, eds., *Pragmatism's Freud: The Moral Disposition* (Baltimore: Johns Hopkins Press, 1986).

15 See Dennett, "Where Am I?" in *Brainstorms*.

16 For an entirely contrary assessment whose arguments I find unpersuasive, see Irving Thalberg's "Freud's Anatomies of the Self," in J. Hopkins and R. Wollheim, eds., *Philosophical Essays on Freud* (Cambridge: Cambridge University Press, 1982).

17 These conditions are a paraphrase from Donald Davidson's "How Is Weakness of the Will Possible?," in *Essays on Actions and Events* (Oxford: Oxford University Press, 1980). For the second conjunct to be plausible, "believe themselves free to" must be read as "believe themselves able to."

18 See Donald Davidson's insightful "Paradoxes of Irrationality," in Hopkins and Wollheim, *Philosophical Essays on Freud*. Save for the phrasing in terms of homunculi, my account of Freud's treatment of irrational action means to be in accord with Davidson's. Compare also D. Pears, "Motivated Irrationality" in the same place, and his book *Motivated Irrationality* (Oxford: Oxford University Press, 1984).

19 Compare N. Goodman, *Languages of Art*, 2d ed., (Indianapolis: Hackett Publishing, 1976); D. Kaplan, "D-That" in P. Cole, ed., *Syntax and Semantics*, vol. 9: *Pragmatics* (New York: Academic Press, 1978), pp. 221–43; and P. Machamer, "Problems of Knowledge Representation: Propositions, Procedures and Images," preprint, University of Pittsburgh.

4 The interpretation of dreams

The Interpretation of Dreams is often regarded as Freud's most valuable book, and it was pivotal in his work.[1]

Freud began his psychological investigations by following up an insight of his senior colleague Joseph Breuer. One of Breuer's patients was a very intelligent and articulate young woman diagnosed as hysterical. Breuer inquired into her symptoms in great detail, and discovered that they were connected with her emotional life in a number of ways.

In particular, she and Breuer could often trace the beginning of a symptom to an event that had been significant to her but that she had forgotten. Where this was so, moreover, the symptom itself could be seen to be connected with feelings related to this event, which she had not previously expressed. Such symptoms thus had a meaningful connection with events and motives in the patient's life. And they were relieved when she brought these events to consciousness and felt and expressed the motives connected with them.

She was, for example, afflicted for some time with an aversion to drinking, which persisted despite "tormenting thirst." She would take up the glass of water she longed for, but then push it away "like someone suffering from hydrophobia." Under hypnosis she traced this to an episode in which a companion had let a dog – a "horrid creature" – drink water from a glass. She relived the event with great anger and disgust; and when she had done so, the aversion ceased, and she was able to drink without difficulty.

Thus, apparently, this particular symptom owed its origin to this

I should like to thank Tom Petaki and Jerry Neu for readings of the first draft of this chapter which helped me to avoid serious mistakes and to improve it at a number of points.

episode (and also, of course, to the background, including motive, which the patient brought to it). The causal link between episode and symptom seems marked in the content of the symptom itself, since both were concerned with such topics as drinking water, disgust, anger, and refusal. So the symptom could be seen as expressing memories or feelings about something of which the patient was no longer conscious.[2]

Freud repeated Breuer's observations in other cases, and extended them by investigating the psychological background and significance of symptoms of other kinds. This meant that he asked his patients about their lives, motives, and memories in great detail.

Freud was a probing and determined questioner. He found, however, that the most relevant information emerged when his patients followed the spontaneous flow of their thoughts and feelings. So he asked them to describe this as fully as possible, and without seeking to make their passing ideas sensible, or indeed to censor or control them in any way. No one had previously sought so fully to relax the rational and moral constraints upon one person's description of thought and feeling to another, and this proved a valuable source of information. The drift of thought, once undirected and unimpeded, led by itself to the topics Freud had previously found important through questioning, and to others whose significance he had not suspected. Freud called this process of self-description "free association."

Freud had kept records of dreams for some years. He soon found that these too could be understood as linked with memories and motives that emerged in the course of free association. In investigating these connections, moreover, he could use his own case as well. So he began the same kind of psychological study of himself as he conducted on his patients, centered on the analysis of his dreams.

As this work progressed, Freud realized that his and Breuer's previous findings about symptoms were better represented in terms of the model he was developing for dreams.[3] He thus framed an account of symptoms and dreams that was relatively simple and unified. Moreover, as he soon saw, this could be extended to other phenomena in which he had taken an interest, including slips, jokes, and works of art. *The Interpretation of Dreams* thus sets out the paradigm through which Freud consolidated the first, pathbreaking phase of his psychological research, conducted as much upon himself as upon his patients.[4] In what follows we will try to understand the nature and role of this paradigm.

I. MOTIVE, MEANING, AND CAUSALITY

Our most basic and familiar way of understanding the activities of persons – either our own, or those of others – is by interpreting them as actions resulting from motives,[5] including beliefs and desires. In everyday life we do this naturally and continuously. Thus we see someone moving toward a tap, grasping a glass, and so on, and interpret this in terms of his wanting a drink, and so moving because he takes this to be the way to get one. Again, we hear certain sounds, and take these as someone's asking for a drink, and so regard them as ultimately derived from a desire to do this, and a belief that making those sounds is a way of doing so.

This is a fundamental kind of psychological thinking, and one that partly defines our conceptions of mind and action. It is at once interpretive and explanatory. It is interpretive because, as such examples illustrate, assigning motives enables us to make sense of what people say and do. It is explanatory because we take the motives we thus assign to be causes within persons which prompt their actions, and which, therefore, serve to explain them.[6]

As we shall be seeing, Freud cast light on dreams and symptoms also by relating them to motives. In this he stressed both the hermeneutic and causal aspects of commonsense thinking. He spoke of the interpretation of dreams, and of finding the sense of dreams and symptoms. Finding the sense of something, however, meant showing that it stood in an intelligible connection with a motive or system of motives, and hence locating it in an order of interpretable psychological causes. And Freud took this to be part of the causal order of nature generally.[7]

The hermeneutic and causal aspects of explanation by motive are, in fact, deeply interwoven and closely coordinated. We can begin to see this – and to appreciate its significance – if we focus on the way that our capacity to use our commonsense psychology of motive is linked with our knowledge of language.

The close connection between language and motive shows in the fact that motives characteristically have, or can be given, what we may call *linguistic articulation*.[8] For example, as we may put it, we do not merely desire, hope, or fear; we desire, hope, or fear *that S*, where "S" admits of replacement by any of a great range of sentences of our language.

In virtue of this motives can be said to have a kind of content, which sentences (as well as single words and phrases) are used to specify. For example, if we say that John believes (hopes, fears, or whatever) that Freud worked in Vienna, we thereby articulate John's motive by using the sentence "Freud worked in Vienna." This means that the content of the motive is that Freud worked in Vienna. The content is that given by the sentence.

A sentence contained in an ascription of motive in this way serves to describe the mind of the person to whom we ascribe the motive. But the sentence also, and at the same time, relates to reality. The usual purpose of the sentence is to specify how things are in the world, if it is true; and this is understood by all who know what the sentence means. In describing motives in this way, therefore, we represent our minds as engaged with the world – with the situations or states of affairs that would render the articulating sentences true. Where a desire, hope, or fear is *that S*, the situation that would render "S" true is also that which would satisfy the desire, realize the hope or fear, and so on.

This is part of what is sometimes called the intentionality, or object-directedness, of the mental. The mind of someone who believes that Freud worked in Vienna can be said to be directed on that man, and that city, and on his working there. Likewise if someone desires that he himself work in Vienna – again he is concerned with that person, that place, and so forth. The matter is the same, again, if he fears being poor, or the dark. The description tells us what object, situation, or aspect of reality he has (as we say) in mind.

Thus we can say that each motive of the kind we are considering has a corresponding phrase or sentence, which is tailor-made for it, and which shows its intentional content, that is, how it relates to the world. Such sentences specify conditions in reality, to which motives are related in characteristic ways, according to their type. Thus beliefs are related by such sentences or phrases to the conditions in which they would be true;[9] desires, to the conditions in which they would be satisfied; hopes and fears, to the conditions in which they would be realized; and so forth, through the sorts of motives whose contents bear on how things are.

In this way the language we speak, and the motives we ascribe in mutual understanding, fit together as if designed for each other (as, presumably, they were by evolution). An important consequence of this, I think, is that our capacity to understand the one serves also for the other. That is, we are able to understand motives, in good part, through understanding the sentences that articulate them.

In understanding a language we are able to understand an unlimited number of sentences, on the basis of the words in them and the way they are put together. For we understand sentences that are new to us, generally without effort, provided we know their grammar and the words in them.

When we understand an indicative sentence, we know how to relate it to the world, in the sense that we know the situation in which it would be true. Thus in understanding "Freud was a scientist" we know that it is true just if Freud was a scientist. We may miss this because it is so obvious that it goes without saying. But it is real knowledge, which relates that sentence and the world; and it goes without saying precisely because we do understand the sentence, and so already grasp the relation in question.

Again, in understanding, say, "All scientists are fallible" we know that it is true just if all scientists are fallible. Clearly there is a pattern here. We can indicate it by saying that for many a sentence "S" which we understand, we know something of the form:

"S" is true just if S.

Because in knowing a language we understand indefinitely many such sentences, this pattern picks out indefinitely many things we thereby know, or can become aware of.

As well as knowing the conditions in which sentences which we understand are true, we know how they relate to one another by implication. Someone who understands both "Freud was a scientist" and "All scientists are fallible," for example, will know that if both are true, so is "Freud was fallible." Clearly, again, we know, or can readily acknowledge, relations of this kind among countless sequences of sentences. We can put this by saying that often in knowing how one pair (triple, etc.) of sentences relates to the world, we are thereby able to know how another sentence does. This knowledge can be said to be of the form, for example:

If S_1 and S_2 are true, so is S_3.

Here also such relations coincide with ways in which we naturally think. Someone who is capable of knowing the above implications, for example, and who believes that all scientists are fallible, will tend to believe that Freud was fallible, if he believes that Freud was a scientist. Or again, if he thinks that Freud is infallible, he may change his mind about the fallibility of scientists, or deny that Freud was one. Whichever of these ways he thinks, he does so in accord with this pattern of implication, which links the truth of the first two sentences to that of the third. Each sentence we understand naturally links with others, and takes us to still others, and likewise for our thoughts, as our attention, interests, and the like direct.

Now as is familiar, almost everyone is capable of understanding sentences and their relations of implication on the basis of words. This seems to be a basic, and perhaps innate, human capacity. And this, it seems, goes with something like psychological understanding, of the motives that we articulate by sentences.

For, clearly, if we understand the "S" in an instance of "Jones fears that S," then we thereby know the situation Jones fears. And in knowing this we are thereby able to apprehend something about what things are like for Jones in his fear. Also, we know something about how this fear will interact with his other motives, and how this will bear on his behavior. For the impact of his fear will depend upon how Jones thinks about the situation he fears; and we know much about this in knowing the patterns of implication connecting the sentence that describes his fear with those in terms of which the rest of his motives are described. If I know that someone fears that he will wind up in poverty, but believes that if his friends stand by him this will not happen, then I know of further beliefs about his friends and what they will or will not do, that may comfort or alarm him. And the pattern of my thought is naturally poised to extend itself through this network of possibilities along with his, and will do so if he gives me a clue. Thus, it seems, understanding the sentences that articulate motives at once puts us *en rapport* with the minds of others, and enables us to grasp the interactive role, which these motives play as causes. Knowledge of meaning, for articulated motives, yields apprehension of situation, and of causal role, as one.

This, I think, illustrates the way in which our system of commonsense psychological explanation is one in which our understanding of linguistic meaning and motivational cause work in natural harmony. Motives, as their name implies, are psychological causes. The phenomenon of articulation, however, makes clear that these are causes whose working is encoded in language – causes, that is, whose working is sensitive to, or coordinate with, the meanings of the terms standardly used to describe them. Hence we find that causal relations in the field of motive are mapped by relations of meaning in the field of language. In particular, as we see above, causal relations among motives are mapped by relations of implication among sentences, and causal relations between motive and reality by those between sentence and situation. Commonsense psychology thus shares the system and structure of language, so that hermeneutic understanding, and grasp of the causes of behavior, form a unity.

Part of this coordination of meaning and causality shows clearly in the basic case of desire. Desires are commonly described in terms of what they are desires for, that is, the things that would satisfy them. These, however, are precisely the actions or situations that desires serve to bring about, when they are acted on. (A desire to get a drink, e.g., if someone acts on it intentionally, should produce an action of getting a drink.) So, plainly, the linguistic articulation (or content) of a desire serves to describe it as a cause, in terms of an effect which that cause is supposed to produce when it operates in a certain way. In understanding the description of a desire, therefore, we already know a central feature of its causal role, that is, what it is supposed to do.

Only realistic desires can be satisfied, so desires are constantly informed by beliefs. Thus if someone desires to get a drink, and believes that the way to do so is to ask for a drink, he will ordinarily form a desire to ask for a drink. We form desires from other desires and beliefs in this way naturally and without reflection – the process is an instance of the natural interest-directed thinking mentioned above. This thinking too involves a pattern of implication, which we can grasp as holding among terms or sentences: We move from desire (to A) and belief (the way to A is to B) to further desire or action (to B). So here again our understanding of the contents of desires and beliefs, and the patterns that relate them, goes with an intuitive grasp of the way they work. The dynamics of motive, that is, are again encoded in the linguistic roles of the terms and sentences that describe their contents.[10]

Now we can see something more about the commonsense link between content and causality by drawing on another closely connected idea. We regard many causes as bearers or transmitters of a kind of causal order, which we describe in terms of information. We speak of the structured groove on a gramophone record,[11] for example, as containing information about sound. This, in turn, can be taken as information bearing on either the past or future – as about a particular performance sounded, or again about how this record will sound, if played. This is because the record owes its structure to that of the events of the past performance, and in virtue of this structure can be used to shape events in a related way in the future.

When a desire causes an action, it also shapes and informs that action, in the sense that the desire determines and orders the parts and properties of the action. If I sing the national anthem because I want to, my desire will be responsible for my singing certain words and notes, making certain quite particular sounds and movements in a certain order, and so on. Surely in this case also there is again a transfer of order, or information; from desire as cause to action as effect. We mark successful transfer of this kind by describing the action as we describe the desire. Actions that go right are those that go as desired; and this means that they can be described in the same terms as (the content of) the desire that prompted them.

This means that the functioning of desires can be described in another way. A desire transmits an order to actions that is partly described by the content of the desire. So we can see the description of content itself as a description of the kind of order, or information, that is passed from desire to action. We can see desires that is, as *causes that transmit content to their effects*. And for causes that do this, it seems, we mark the causal connection hermeneutically, by a connection in (description of) content between cause and effect.

The same holds for belief. We have seen that beliefs are described in terms of the conditions that would render them true. This marks the fact that beliefs are supposed to bear information about reality, and so are meant to be shaped to accord with it. Beliefs are thus supposed to derive their content from reality, just as actions derive theirs from desires. Beliefs are thus shaped by the world in perception. Roughly, to perceive that S is to have reason to believe that S, which is caused in an appropriate information-transmitting way by the situation that renders "S" true. So here again there is an information-bearing causal line, which we mark in terms of transmitted content.[12]

Likewise, again, for the shaping of desire by belief. Where an agent's desire is informed by his beliefs, the content of the beliefs is transmitted to the desires, and thence to action. This kind of transfer, as we saw above, fits a characteristic pattern, which links truth and satisfaction. By the pattern, the truth of an agent's belief (the way to A is to B) entails that the satisfaction of his final desire (to B) will secure that of his initial one (to A). So the pattern indicates not only how desire and belief naturally interact, but also how this is a function of the relations to the world that their articulating sentences specify (how the truth-conditions of beliefs are supposed to shape, or enter into, the satisfaction-conditions of desires). This in turn marks the way in which reality informs thought, one thought informs another, and thought informs action.

The case is similar with other motives. If someone decides to avoid what he fears, the content of his fear will enter that of his desires in a particular way – as specifying the situations he now wants to keep away from; likewise, again, if he accepts that he must honor an obligation, perform a duty, and so forth. The mark of the operation of motive is thus the transmission of content: The production of further motive or behavior with content that is the same as that of the cause, or appropriately derived from it. This being so, we can trace the operations of motive by the interpretation of content. Our language of motive is a natural system for the hermeneutic grasp of psychological causal role.

This means that our commonsense psychology of motive uses our mental capacities in a particularly concentrated and effective way. By describing motives by way of the words and sentences we use for describing the world, we harness both the full descriptive range of natural language for specifying similarities and differences among the causes of behavior, and the full synthesizing and projecting power of linguistic understanding for grasping the import of these specifications. This use of cognitive resources makes this everyday way of thinking a uniquely flexible and efficient mode of psychological explanation. It is not just that we have no alternative that affords comparable insight or predictive power[13] (although of course we do not). Rather, it seems unclear that any such alternative is possible – that anything else could enable us to process such important information about ourselves, or to do this so well. For no description of our psychology that did not thus embed our description of the world could so directly reflect the way we are engaged with it, and hence the ways in which our attitudes toward worldly situations move us.

The underlying causal situation of course admits of description in other terms. Thus one might suppose that desires are in fact realized by inner representations or models of potential movements and actions, which function to shape the actions they produce.[14] (Such a model would be one sort of cause that could form its effect in the appropriate content-transmitting way.) A belief could likewise be said to involve a representation, shaped to model the situation to which it relates, and operating to form others, namely those in desires and other beliefs. The content-related causal role of other aspects of commonsense psychology could also be described in this way; and there is no barrier to thinking of the relevant representations or models as structures in the brain. But the remarkable thing about commonsense thinking is precisely that it *does not* present such mechanisms in such terms, but rather only via their linguistic articulation. For this gives them in a form that enables us to grasp their causal role in thought and action so naturally, rapidly, and intuitively that we need not even realize we are doing so.

These considerations suggest that there can be no conflict, but rather a natural and pervasive harmony, between the hermeneutic activity of interpretation and the causal explanation of behavior. We interpret one another by finding the right words or meanings – in effect by assigning sentences to motives, and hence ultimately to behavior. But this is also understanding one another in terms of causes that pass content to their effects and have conditions of satisfaction that they operate to secure. The finding of sense or meaning, the articulation of object- and satisfaction-directedness, and the establishing of commonsense causal order, are one and the same.

And so, as it happens, our natural criteria for sound interpretation, based on content, are at the same time criteria for good causal explanation. Thus for example the better a particular pair of instances (desire and action, say) match in content, the better we take the former to explain the latter. Thus we take a desire to sing the national anthem to be particularly well suited to explain someone's singing the national anthem; for here, as in other cases, desire and action overlap in content. So generally, ascribing a desire will provide the best explanation we can manage for the complex, ordered sequence of events involved in an action. We can readily understand this in causal terms. The comprehensive matching shows that the cause has the features required to explain those of the effect; and each point of comparison renders the alternative, that the two are merely coincidentally related, less likely.

Also, we seek explanations relating to contents that are deep – in which factors like significant desires or emotions, or traits of character, are derivationally related to a whole range of behavior. This is partly because the derived items are thereby shown to share, and hence to have been shaped by, a common requirement as to conditions of satisfaction. An ideal, so far as these criteria are concerned, would be the derivation of the greatest possible range of behavior from the fewest motives, by steps between each of which there was the greatest possible interlocking of content. This, we can now see, is also an ideal of economic, comprehensive, and reliable causal explanation.

Freud's topic in what follows is interpretation, and the hermeneutic demands he makes on the reader are great. So it may be worth bearing in mind that these are demands for sensitivity to a certain sort of presentation of causes. Nor, despite its complexity, can interpretation be dispensed with in any case. No discipline can give us a grasp of phenomena that is surer than our understanding of the language in which they are couched. And this understanding is continuous with that of motive, and created and sustained in the commonsense interpretive practice whose nature and extension we are now considering.[15]

II. DREAMS AND MOTIVES

One of the main claims of the *Interpretation* is that dreams are wish-fulfillments. It will prove worth seeing what is involved in this as clearly as possible. So let us begin with one of Freud's simplest examples. Freud noticed that frequently when he had eaten anchovies or other salted food he would dream *that he was drinking delicious cool water.* Then he would wake up, find himself thirsty, and have to get a drink (1900a, IV, 123). This is a familiar and, it seems, transparent sort of dream.

Clearly there is a content–content relation between Freud's motives and his dream. One of his motives is that he is thirsty, and his dream is that he is slaking his thirst. It can be no coincidence that a person should have this sort of dream when thirsty, so we assume that the thirst caused the dream. This is another instance of the fit between content and causality. The relation in content is evidence that here – as in the case of desire and action – thirst is working as a cause that transmits content to an effect. If we are to understand the dream in this way, however, we need the cause to have the requisite articulation: We must regard the thirst as focused on a particular kind of satisfaction, the cool drink that appears in the dream. Accordingly, Freud assumes that the thirst gave rise to a wish to drink, which the dream represents as satisfied.

This is in fact the ascription of a new motive, a dream-wish. It seems to implement the simplest possible hypothesis about the transmission of content from thirst to the dream – namely, that the thirst gave rise to an intermediary with a content that was realized in the dream. Such a hypothesis assimilates the production of the dream to the kind of transmission familiar from wishful thinking or imagining, in which desires or wishes cause representations of their own satisfaction. Hence the dream can be called a wish-fulfillment.

This is closely analogous to a very basic commonsense understanding of an action. If someone is thirsty and gets a drink, we will assume that he is doing what he wants. Here also we introduce an explanatory item – a desire to get a drink – which arises from the thirst and constitutes an articulation of it, and which we take to shape, and thus to determine the content, of the action we observe. This is precisely the role of the dream-wish; except, of course, that it shapes a dream, rather than an action, of drinking.

This difference is also important. In the case of desire and action, transmission and satisfaction go together – the content-bearing effect really satisfies the motive that shapes it. In the case of wish and dream this is not so. The satisfaction of a wish to drink cool water would be an actual drink, not a dream; and in fact the dreamer's real underlying thirst remains unslaked. The process of wishful imagining generally produces only representations of satisfaction, and not real satisfaction. So while acting on a desire is a paradigm of rationality, representing the satisfaction of a wish in this way is not.

Indeed, wish-fulfillment can be seen as a paradigm of irrationality. To the dreamer, it seems as if he is active and satisfying his thirst; in reality, he is supine, and (so to speak) merely fobbing himself off, with a hallucination that, however pleasant, can at best bring temporary relief. So in a sense the dreamer is self-deceived, both about how things are with him (his motives and their gratification), and about how things are in the world (what he is actually doing). The illusion of which he is the author may, moreover, actually work to prevent his acting rationally; for so long as he imagines that he is drinking, he may be impeded from forming, or acting on, a real desire to drink.

Thus Freudian wish-fulfillment can be seen in two ways: as a marginal kind of satisfaction, in which a motive is allowed only imaginary gratification (although this may be the best that is possible for some motives); or as a kind of frustration, in which its form of expression actually prevents a motive from influencing action directly. This last feature makes clear that the role of dream-wishes is very different from that of desires, despite their having the same kind of content, in the sense of real conditions of satisfaction.

We generally speak of wishing rather than wanting where we take real satisfaction to be out of the question. Hence we may wish that we were younger, or that the past had been different, but do not take ourselves to desire such things. And since the role of wishes is not to produce actions, but rather to be related to imaginings or other expressions, we do not require that wishes be reasonable, sensible, or consistent.

Yet precisely for this reason, wishes can be especially informative. They are derived from motives, and articulate them, but are not realistically constrained. So, arguably, they can show what the conditions of satisfaction of the motives underlying them would be, if those motives could operate without hindrance from reality and rationality. This can be illustrated by the dream of drinking. The dream-wish is aimed at a drink that is particularly delicious, cool and satisfying – such, in fact, as occurs only in a dream. Freud may never have had such a drink, and this will not be the kind of drink he seeks when awake. Nevertheless, it seems, the dream may tell us something about his underlying motives, which his mundane realistic desire does not. It may indicate something about the kind of drink he would really like, if freed from the constraints of reality.

Freud gives other examples concerning motives that are simple and basic and, hence, show themselves in a way we can understand with no difficulty. Thus there are dreams of children, such as his little nephew and daughter. The boy had reluctantly handed Freud a birthday gift of cherries, and awoken the next morning exclaiming "Herman eaten all the chewwies"; and the two-year-old Anna, forbidden to eat for a day because of vomiting supposedly owed to strawberries, had called out excitedly in her sleep "Anna Fweud, stwawbewwies, wild stwawbewwies, omblet, pudden." Here, it is natural to think, the children's wishes for forbidden food can be read directly from their dreams (or, rather, probable dream-reports), which represent these wishes as satisfied (1900a, IV, 130).

The interpretation of dreams dealing with more complex motives is naturally more complex. To see this, let us turn to a fuller example, that of the specimen dream Freud first analyzed, and with which he begins his exposition of his theory, the dream of Irma's injection (1900a, IV 106–21). Part of the content of this is as follows:

> I said to [Irma] "If you still get pains, it's really only your fault." She replied: "If you only knew what pains I've got now in my throat and stomach and abdomen – it's choking me." I was alarmed and looked at her. . . . I thought to myself that after all I must be missing some organic trouble. I took her to the window and looked down her throat. . . . I at once called in Dr. M., and he repeated the examination and confirmed it. . . . a portion of the skin of the left shoulder was infiltrated . . . M. said: "There's no doubt it's an infection, but no matter; dysentery will supervene and the toxin will be eliminated." . . . We were directly aware, too, of the origin of the infection . . . my friend Otto had given her an injection. . . . Injections of that sort ought not to be made so thoughtlessly. . . . And probably the syringe had not been clean. (ibid., 107)

This dream, unlike the previous ones, does not *seem* wishful. Irma was a young patient with whom Freud and his family were on very friendly terms. Although the dream was not a distressing one, much of it treats of two anxieties: that Irma was seriously unwell and that Freud had failed to see that her illness was organic, not psychological. In the dream Freud was alarmed about this.

Such a dream can be understood, Freud held, only in the light of the dreamer's associations to it, that is, what the dreamer thinks of, if he lets his thoughts flow without censorship, in connection with the elements of the dream. As noted, Freud had already found that material which emerged in this way enabled him to understand much about symptoms. In using the same procedure for self-analysis, he would write down what occurred to him in connection with elements of his dreams as it did so, even where this at first seemed senseless or irrelevant.

Some of the most straightforward material yielded by association concerns the events of the day that influenced the dream and that are in one way or another shown in it. Freud held that such "day residues" were to be found in almost every dream. Often one is simply reminded of the connected material as one contemplates the dream. In the case of the Irma dream, this information was at hand.

The doctors M. and Otto, who appear in the dream, were long-standing friends and colleagues of Freud's. M. was a leading figure in Freud's circle (probably in fact Breuer). Otto had recently been visiting Irma's family, and had been called away to give an injection to someone who was unwell. The day before the dream Otto had reported, on the basis of this visit, that Irma was looking "better, but not quite well." Freud had felt vaguely reproved by this comment on a mutual friend, and had in consequence written out Irma's case history on the night of the dream, in order show it to M., so as to justify himself.

Taken against this background of motive, the apparent anxieties of the dream can be seen to have a further significance. For Freud saw that wishes related to his desire not to be culpable for Irma's illness, and not to be at fault, seemed prominent both in the dream and in his associations to it. Thus in the dream he had said to Irma "*If you still get pains, it's really only your fault.*"

I noticed, however, that the words I spoke to Irma in the dream showed that I was specially anxious not to be responsible for the pains she still had. If they were her fault they could not be mine. Could it be that the purpose of the dream lay in this direction?

The wish that Freud took to be operative emerged shortly later. He writes the relevant part of the dream in italics, and then describes his associated thoughts.

I was alarmed at the idea that I had missed an organic illness. This, as may well be believed, is a perpetual source of anxiety to a specialist whose practice is almost limited to neurotic patients and who is in the habit of attributing to hysteria a great number of symptoms which other physicians treat as organic. On the other hand, a faint doubt crept into my mind – from where I could not tell – that my alarm was not entirely genuine. If Irma's pains had an organic basis, once again I could not be held responsible for curing them; my treatment only set out to get rid of *hysterical* pains. It occurred to me, in fact, that I was actually *wishing* that there had been a wrong diagnosis; for if so, the blame for my lack of success would have been got rid of.

This hypothesis – that he was wishing for a misdiagnosis, so as to be relieved from responsibility for Irma's pains – fits with material in the rest of the dream. For it shortly emerges that the illness which Freud had failed to diagnose was caused by Otto's injection. Thus the conclusion of the dream is that Freud was not responsible for Irma's pains, but that Otto was. The reproach that Freud had felt in Otto's remark was thus dreamed as deflected back onto Otto, via the injection that Otto had given someone else.[16]

Freud cites many further details of the dream and associations that cohere with this hypothesis, and even critical commentators have found it compelling. Let us, therefore, take its initial plausibility as granted, and concentrate rather on its implications.

A first point is the character of the wishes that are represented as fulfilled. From the vantage point of the *Interpretation* as a whole, these are relatively straightforward and superficial dream-wishes, unearthed by only a first layer of associations and memories. Nonetheless they already stand in striking contrast to motives from waking life. By everyday standards, for example, these wishes are egoistic, ruthless, and extreme. We should regard someone who acted on *desires* with these contents – who to escape an imagined reproach arranged for his friend and patient to be seriously ill, and for revenge threw the blame for this on another friend, the author of the supposed reproach – as criminal or worse. Likewise the way of thinking shown in the dream is radically defective: The reversal of Otto's reproach, for example, seems like a transparently childish "It's not *me* that's bad – it's *you*."

As well as extreme, these wishes are sharply at variance with

Freud's other motives. In consequence, the representation of their fulfillment seems alarming rather than pleasant, and the acknowledgment of them, even as mere dream-wishes, is not entirely easy. Thus take the wish that Irma be physically ill. Since she was Freud's friend and patient, this would have been a source of considerable distress in real life; and the situation was one of some alarm in the dream. Accordingly, in acknowledging the wish Freud says that he "had a sense of awkwardness at having invented such a severe illness for Irma simply in order to clear myself. It looked so cruel. . . ."

In light of their content we can readily imagine someone denying that he could possibly have such motives, even as dream-wishes. Yet Freud's self-ascription of them is clearly consistent with his being a decent enough man, physician, and so on. For evidently the desires that guide his actions have other contents and draw on other sources. (What Freud actually did to justify himself, for example, was to go over Irma's case, and write up a report to check with someone.) So here the difference between wish and desire, already apparent in the dream of drinking, becomes more significant.[17]

I mentioned earlier the idea that wishes give information about the nature of the motives that give rise to them, by providing what can be regarded as an unconstrained articulation of their content. This naturally applies also to the present example.

Here the idea would be that the motives engaged in Freud by Otto's remark found two expressions. One was Freud's fleeting and unclear feeling of annoyance at Otto, and his activity in writing up the case to show to a colleague whom he particularly respected. The other, which analysis has brought to the fore, was the imagined situation in which Irma was physically ill, and the same respected colleague observed that the blame for this was to be placed on Otto's malpractice.

In light of the second expression, on this view, we can see that Freud's underlying motives are to be regarded as considerably different than the first expression alone, or even Freud's sincere account before analyzing the dream, would suggest. The analysis reveals motives that are more extreme, less coherent, and possessed of further contents than could previously have been acknowledged. Thus even this first example, if typical, would suggest the possibility of considerable revision of our everyday understanding of motive.

This revision seems, moreover, to be prompted by reasoning with a discernible pattern, which Freud used in other cases. It will be important to assess this; so let us try to describe it as carefully and fully as possible.

In the instances we have been considering, three sorts of elements – motives, wishes, and dreams – are hypothesized to fit a causal pattern.[18] As a first approximation, the pattern can be written as follows:

$$\text{Motive}(C_m) \rightarrow \text{Wish}(C_w) \rightarrow \text{Dream}(C_d).$$

(Here the arrow indicates a causal connection, and C_m, C_w, and C_d are supposed to stand for the contents of motive, wish, and dream, respectively.)

In typical instances of this pattern, as we have seen, the motive and dream are introduced, and their contents assigned, by previously accepted criteria. The wish, by contrast, is introduced by hypothesis, or inference to the best explanation, in the way we have been describing.

The series of inferences that lead to this pattern seem roughly to be the following: We begin with a dream-report, and memories or associations that support the ascription of motives in the normal way. So we have

(1) Motive (C_m), Dream (C_d),

for example, simplifying,

Motive (thirst), Dream (drinking); or
Motive (no responsibility), Dream (organic illness);
Motive (annoyance at Otto), Dream (Otto's malpractice);
etc.

We now notice that C_m and C_d are related in content, in such a way as to lead us to suppose that the one has influenced the other.[19] This is, clearly, an important aspect of the inference. So letting R stand for this relation, and symbolizing as before, we can write this as:

(2) R (C_m, C_d); therefore, $M(C_m) \rightarrow D(C_d)$.

This now appears as an instance of causal transmission of content, which we already take to be the mode of operation of motives. At this stage, however, the apparent connection still requires to be elucidated. We can see that there is good reason to take C_m and C_d to be causally related; but we do not yet see just how they are related. So

the observed connection in content and the presumed causal connection are still in need of explanation.

Next we notice that this can be taken as an instance of a familiar
pattern, that of the commonsense phenomenon of wishful imagining. This, however, means interpolating a further element, the
dream-wish, in the way described. So this interpolation is an inference that serves to explain two phenomena. It at once elucidates the
connection between motive and dream, and also thereby provides a
more detailed explanation of the content of the dream. Thus we get,
as above,

$$(3) \quad M(C_m) \to W(C_w) \to D(C_d).$$

This formulation now needs to be qualified, to indicate that the
inference to it includes claims about the mode of causality, or mode
of transmission of content, connecting the elements. The motive
gives rise to the wish by, say, wish-instigation, and the wish to the
dream by wish-fulfillment. Wish-instigation, we assume, produces
an articulation of motive that is less realistically constrained than
those seen in action; and wish-fulfillment as it were reverses the
sign on this articulation, representing it as fulfilled. So we have

$$(4) \quad M(C_m) - [wi] \to W(C_w) - [wff] \to D(C_d).$$

This registers constraints on the contents that may figure in this
kind of pattern. The C_m must be related as required by what we are
calling wish-instigation to the C_w; and the C_w must likewise be
related as required by wish-fulfillment to the C_d.

These are significant requirements, which bear directly on the
double explanatory role performed by the introduction of the dream-
wish. The final elucidation of the initial connection between motive
and dream is gained by seeing the dream as the result of the combined and complementary processes of wish-instigation and wish-
fulfillment.

This is not arbitrary, because each of these processes has a characteristic effect on content, and the combination of these effects seems
to be just what is to be observed, in the initial difference between
motive and dream. (The difference seems relatively precisely accounted for, by what we know about the two kinds of transmission
involved in the explanation.) And this in turn entails a more ade-

quate account of the content of the dream, by reference to a wish with the requisite content and mode of transmission. Also, this means that the content of the explanatory hypothesis is fixed by what it is introduced to explain. Because the hypothesis represents the content of the dream as derived from that of the wish, the content of the hypothesis is read, in part, directly from the dream.

This seems also to be the pattern we find in Freud's examples of the dreams of little Herman and Anna.[20] The exaggeration of motive in Herman's having eaten *all* the cherries (none for the old man to whom they were originally given), or in the ampleness of Anna's menu, again seem instances of what we are calling wish-instigation, which have then been passed on to the dream by wish-fulfillment. In these cases, however, the original motives are inferred on different, more circumstantial, grounds, in which the dream itself plays a role. And this too, I think, strikes us as having a degree of cogency worth getting on with.

Collecting these ideas, we can represent the kind of inference with which we are concerned as

From: $M(C_m)$, $D(C_d)$, such that R (C_m, C_d)
 To: There is a $W(C_w)$, such that
      $M(C_m) - [wi] \rightarrow W(C_w) - [wff] \rightarrow D(C_d)$

This is clearly only a preliminary specification, but it admits of some discussion as it stands. As we have already seen, this is a kind of inference that has apparently cogent instances. The cogency, in turn, seems owed to the relatively precise explanation that an inference provides for the phenomena upon which it is based, namely the particular relation of content that obtains between C_m and C_d. So there is reason to take this as a form of inference to the best explanation of the phenomena upon which it is based. (In this also it appears to cohere with commonsense psychology, since motives seem in general to be introduced as the best explanation for what they cover.)[21]

Because this seems a potentially cogent sort of reasoning, and one of a familiar general kind, it is hard to see how there could be a methodological objection to its use, provided of course that the conditions that account for its cogency are adhered to. Of course there can be bad interpretations of this kind – one does not have to read far to find them. But in these, I think, we can see that the appropriate conditions of cogency are in fact not met, and that this accounts for their weakness.

These conditions include, at the outset, the accurate ascription of base motives, and also a degree of connection between motive and dream that is significant enough effectively to rule out coincidence. Hence, in general, a dream cannot be cogently interpreted without this kind of background. (The case is different where we take the wish-fulfilling character of the dream to be clear. So far as we accept that a dream is a wish-fulfillment, and also can read the wish in it, then we can omit further recourse to the background, because we already see the base in the dream, wishfully transformed. This is nearly the case, perhaps, with Herman and the cherries.)

As well as possessing a degree of internal cogency, this kind of inference can be tested in other commonsense ways. A person's motives for one action are characteristically linked in content with those for other actions. So, generally, we cross-check our ascription of motive in one case by comparison with others. Ascriptions with contents that repeatedly figure in explanation are thus borne out, while others that do not fit tend to be revised, or dropped altogether. This helps to ensure that the total account of motive that we build up as we come to know a person maximizes the kind of coherence of content that marks good causal explanation, as sketched here.

The kind of ascriptions Freud is dealing with here clearly admit of this kind of checking. We should certainly expect the kind of concern shown in this dream with *not being responsible for illness* to show up elsewhere in a doctor's life and thought, so that the role ascribed to it elsewhere could be compared with that hypothesized here.

The introduction of psychoanalytic interpretation, moreover, means that we can cross-check ascriptions not only as among motives explaining actions, but also in relation to those shown in dreams, symptoms, and so forth. Psychoanalysis thus strengthens commonsense psychology as it extends it, by adding to the materials that figure in confirming and disconfirming ascriptions of motive. And since psychoanalytic ascriptions are thus subject to our commonsense kind of cross-checking, the maximum use of this is also a condition of their cogency.

In this instance we can see that Freud's further analysis of the dream both confirms the conclusions reached so far, and places them in a new context that amplifies and explains them further. So let us go into some of the rest of the material that emerged in his associations, starting with the next but one.

In associating to the part of the dream in which he *took Irma to the window* Freud remembered that the way Irma stood by the window in the dream came from a real scene he had witnessed, in which Dr. M had examined another woman by a window, and pronounced that she had a diphtheritic membrane. The woman was a friend of Irma's, who suffered from hysterical choking.[22] Thus, Freud saw, the Irma in the dream was a sort of composite figure, who had been given her friend's position by the window, as well as her cough, and infiltrated membrane.

The diagnosis by M of a diseased membrane, which was both remembered from this scene and reproduced in the dream, was in turn linked[23] with other things Freud remembered, and which he had deep feelings about. His daughter Mathilde had been seriously ill, and diphtheria and diphtheritis had been considered in her case. Also, Freud had recently heard that membrane tissue from the nose of one of his patients had been killed off, as a result of her following his own example, in using cocaine for nasal treatments.[24]

Freud had been a very enthusiastic advocate of the medical use of cocaine, which he had taken as his own therapeutic discovery. This enthusiasm, as he now recalled, "had brought serious reproaches down on me." Also it had, as he said, "hastened the death of a dear friend." The friend suffered from incurable nerve pain, and was addicted to the morphia he used to relieve it. Failing to grasp that cocaine was also addictive, Freud suggested he use it instead. His friend was soon dependent on increasing doses of cocaine, and died six years later.

Moreover this death, it seemed, was connected in Freud's mind with another, which again involved injections, for which he would wish not to be responsible. For he now associated as follows:

I at once called in Dr. M., and he repeated the examination. . . . This reminded me of a tragic event in my practice. I had on one occasion produced a severe toxic state in a woman patient by repeatedly prescribing what was at that time regarded as a harmless remedy (sulphanol), and had hurriedly turned for assistance and support to my experienced senior colleague. . . .

My patient – who succumbed to the poison – had the same name as my eldest daughter . . . Mathilde.

We can thus see from Freud's associations that the question of responsibility for Irma was linked in his mind with other cases, which were more serious and painful. His enthusiasm as a would-be therapeutic pioneer, when directed to cocaine rather than psychoanalysis, had harmed one of his patients, and hastened the death of a friend by injections. In the case of Irma he was now thinking of justifying himself by seeking the opinion of M. This, however, was what he had done in the case of another patient who was not doing well, and whom he had actually killed by injections.

It seems clear that these associated memories also influenced the dream. They suggest, for example, that M's claim that *the toxin will be eliminated* refers back to the episode with the patient Mathilde, in which Freud, in consulting with M, must have hoped that the toxin that he had injected would not prove fatal. And they enable us to see more of the significance of the deflection on to Otto, made via the notion of injection. Here are Freud's final associations, as they drift toward what is most significant for understanding this aspect of the dream.

Injections of that sort ought not to be made so thoughtlessly. Here an accusation of thoughtlessness was being made directly against my friend Otto. I seemed to remember thinking something of the same kind that afternoon when his words and looks had appeared to show that he was siding against me. It had been some such notion as: "How easily his thoughts are influenced! How thoughtlessly he jumps to conclusions!" – Apart from this, this sentence in the dream reminded me once more of my dead friend who had so hastily resorted to cocaine injections. . . . I noticed too that in accusing Otto of thoughtlessness in handling chemical substances I was once more touching upon the story of the unfortunate Mathilde, which gave grounds for the same accusation against myself. . . .

And probably the syringe had not been clean: This was yet another accusation against Otto, but derived from a different source. I had happened the day before to meet the son of an old lady of eighty-two, to whom I had to give an injection of morphia twice a day. At the moment she was in the country and he told me that she was suffering from phlebitis. I had at once thought it must be an infiltration caused by a dirty syringe. I was proud of the fact that in two years I had not caused a single infiltration; I took constant pains to be sure that the syringe was clean. In short: I was conscientious. (1900a, IV, 117,118)

In light of this material we can begin to see, among other things, why Otto's remark, and the topic of responsibility for Irma, should have acquired the significance shown in the dream. As we might put part of the point: Freud was so sensitive on the topic of Irma, partly because she was linked in his mind with sources of guilt of whose bearing he was unaware, until he had analyzed the dream. And if *such* guilt was to be linked with Irma and her pains, then better to have misdiagnosed her from the start and not bear responsibility at all.

The dream treats these deeper issues, it seems, with the same wishful irresponsibility as Irma's illness itself. Otto's supposed thoughtlessness in describing Irma's health has, in the dream, been transformed into a version of the very thoughtlessness – about injections, cocaine, and so forth – with which Freud would reproach himself. But since in Freud's dream it is Otto who makes thoughtless (and dirty) injections the question of Freud's own guilt does not arise. Thus the infantile "it's *you*, not *me*" produced by Otto's remark emerges both as further reaching, and more violently irrational, than was first apparent.

This is all the material from this dream we will consider. (For a partial survey, see the accompanying diagram of Freud's dream of Irma's injection.)

Clearly the topics or concepts in this material are closely interconnected, and woven in with the motives that seem to be engaged. For example the initial connections between Irma, her friend, Freud's daughter, and his other female patient, are made partly in terms of the notion of *infiltration*, or damage to a membrane, which Irma suffers in the dream, as did these other figures in real life. In the dream Irma's infiltration is connected with a toxin, and so links Irma with the patient whom Freud injected with a toxin. Otto's injection of the toxin in the dream thus links him not only to Irma there, but also to Freud's other female patients, as well as the friend who died after cocaine injections. Also, however, the causing of infiltrations was something that Freud, with his care as to syringes, could take himself to be beyond reproach about – he had thought just the other day about how some *other* physician might have caused an infiltration in a patient he regularly injected. (Not *me* – *him*.) So despite their variety, the uses of infiltration and related concepts here also show a unity in their working below the surface

FREUD'S DREAM OF IRMA'S INJECTION

Dream

| Irma, friend and patient: Freud says if you still get pains it's your own fault; Irma at window choking, organically ill | M called in, repeats examination, finds infiltration, toxin | Otto has given thoughtless injection, syringe not clean |

Associations (i)

| | Freud annoyed by Otto's remark | wants to justify himself via M. thinks alarm ungenuine; dream speech shows he wants not to be responsible, wishing Irma's illness |

Associations (ii)

Diphtheritic infiltration discussed in case of Freud's daughter Mathilde	M examining Irma's friend at window, hysterical choking, diphtheritic infiltration	M also called in case of patient Mathilde killed by Freud's toxic injections
	Patient follows Freud's example, uses cocaine, gets nasal infiltration	Friend follows Freud's advice, dies addicted to cocaine injections
	Otto's remark was thoughtless, Freud is conscientious about injections, always uses clean syringes, never causes infiltrations	

Inferences

From dream, Associations	(i)	Freud wishing Irma organically ill, to avoid responsibility; wishing to get back at Otto Fulfilled as Irma organically ill, Otto's fault
	(ii)	Freud wishing to avoid responsibility for friend's and patient's deaths related to injection; wishing to get back at Otto. Fulfilled as Otto gives thoughtless dirty injections
	(iii)	Both (i) and (ii) related to guilt.

of the dream. They serve both to *collect* the instances of guilt and blame with which the dream is partly concerned, and also to *shift* this guilt and blame away from the dreaming Freud and on to his accuser Otto.

III. THEORY AND TERMINOLOGY

We have gone over some of Freud's first data, so let us sketch how these relate to the theoretical terms that Freud introduces in the *Interpretation*.[25] For this purpose I shall italicize terms while mentioning related material.

We have seen how Freud's interpretation of a dream proceeds from a connected field of material that arises by way of association to the dream and that includes motives and memories we can see reflected in it. Freud called the content of the dream as experienced and remembered its *manifest content,* and the material that had given rise to the dream, as shown in association, its *latent content.*

This terminology registers the fact that Freud took the motives that had given rise to the dream as fixing its content, just as we take the motives that give rise to an action as fixing how it is to be described. That is, Freud now describes dreams, like actions, in terms of their psychological roots, as well as their manifest and visible parts. (Thus in a dream, as well as in an action, the latent content of a kiss can be betrayal.) This seems reasonable in light of the kind of analysis we have discussed, for surely our sense of the content of the dream has changed, so that we now regard the representation of Otto as marked by Freud's latent wish to avoid responsibility.

Freud's interpretation of a dream proceeds from a comparison of manifest and latent content, and represents the manifest as a *transformation* of the latent. This is reflected in the rule of inference sketched above, which can also be taken as specifying a transformation, as between latent motive and manifest realization. Freud spoke of such transformation as effected by *dream-work,* which combined the latent elements and provided for their representation in manifest form. This has a number of further aspects, also apparent in the material discussed.

Irma is shown in the manifest content with features that relate her in various ways to figures in the latent content. This reflects the fact that she shares significance with these figures, as one for whose condition Freud has concern and responsibility, and hence the potential for guilt. And Freud's wishful absolution from blame in the manifest content evidently relates to feelings involving these latent figures also. Thus the Irma of the dream has a composite significance, which Freud describes as follows:

> The principal figure in the dream-content was my patient Irma. She appeared with the features which were hers in real life, and thus, in the first instance, represented herself. But the position in which I examined her by the window was derived from someone else. . . . In so far as Irma appeared to have a diphtheritic membrane, which recalled my anxiety about my eldest daughter, she stood for that child, and, behind her, through the possession of the same name as my daughter, was hidden the figure of my patient who succumbed to poisoning. In the course of the dream the figure of Irma acquired still other meanings. (1900a, IV, 292)

In light of this it appears that the transformation of latent to manifest content involves something like a channeling of representation and significance, from a number of latent figures and situations, onto a single manifest one, who as it were carries the wishful burden of the rest. Freud observed that something similar held in almost every dream he analyzed. He compared the process to the production of a composite photograph, and called it *condensation.*

Freud also observed that the latent content is often characterized by certain emotions or feelings, which appear differently, or not at all, in the manifest dream. Freud called the process that yielded this result *displacement.* Thus in the Irma dream Freud seems to have felt a significant latent guilt, toward the dead or damaged figures for whom Irma stood. In the transformation from latent to manifest content this guilt would seem to have been displaced. The deeper guilt appears at the surface, if at all, only as anxiety that Irma has been misdiagnosed; and this is a step toward absolution. Guilt itself seems almost entirely deflected, via the use made of the fact that Otto gave an injection while at Irma's, onto the figure of Otto himself.[26]

Freud also noted that the processes of condensation and displacement work in part by connection with language and other modes of symbolism. This has already been illustrated. We saw previously how the concept of infiltration served both to collect instances relating to concern and guilt, and to shift these away from the dreaming Freud. Here the collection via this term or concept corresponds to the condensation of significance in the figure of Irma, and the shift to the displacement of guilt.

We saw in Section II that wish-fulfillment itself involved a two-fold denial of reality. Freud's notion of displacement adds to this a further, and distinct, vector of *distortion*.

Freud evidently found his thoughts and feelings about his responsibility for the deaths of his patient and friend painful. For this reason, it would seem, these figure in the manifest dream only in a form that would not remind him of them. They are touched on only indirectly, by allusions to toxin, injections, and the like. Death is not mentioned, and the patient Mathilde is the last of the series of figures to be found hidden behind the manifest Irma. Where things are made explicit, they are at the same time rendered unrecognizable. For example we could scarcely find a clearer expression of painful self-reproach than the exclamation that *injections of that kind ought not to be made so thoughtlessly* formulated at the close of the dream. But in the manifest content this is made to serve as a denial, rather than an acknowledgment, of the latent guilt that it nonetheless expresses.

This suggests a quite systematic process of disguise and distortion of things that are painful or otherwise unacceptable to the dreamer. Freud found this to be a very common feature of dreams, and likened it to the (Russian) *censorship* of his day. Thus although Freud's wish to avoid guilt for causing death is not rationally constrained in the means by which it is (represented as) satisfied, as we can see from the treatment of Irma and Otto, still it is very thoroughly censored, so that its representation arouses little discomfort.

Hence, as we may put it, Freud's wish not to bear responsibility in these cases is represented as fulfilled via both Irma's illness and Otto's malpractice, but without its main topic – Freud's own involvement in death – being clearly or explicitly represented at all. So this dream is also an instance of the *disguised* fulfillment, of a wish that is itself *kept from consciousness* in the dream.[27]

Among the things regularly kept from awareness in this way, Freud found, were motives that aroused great anxiety, and upon which it would be irrational and dangerous to act, such as the sexual and aggressive motives that Freud took to arise in early childhood, and so be first directed toward the parents. So Freud took it that these were subjected to a process of *repression*, which rendered them incapable of influence on action – they were, as it were, taken out of the workings of everyday thinking, and relegated to another system, the *Unconscious.*

Motives in this system operated in accord with *primary processes* of mental functioning, including the condensation and displacement we have already seen. These, Freud hypothesized, allowed motives to gain a sort of primitive additive accumulation of strength (cf. again the collection and wishful shift of significance) which resulted in their sole form of expression, that of wish-fulfillment. Such motives thus have a form of organization that is prerational. They are cut off from the *secondary processes* involved in purposive, verbal, and realistic thought, and affect them only indirectly.

Freud noted that dreams commonly use *symbolism*, particularly in the representation of sexual matters. Since this is not particularly salient in the material we have covered, let us illustrate it by another example. Freud cites the dream of a man who had just received a young girl to live in his household. He felt attracted to her, apparently imagining *coitus a tergo;* and he thought she had given him the impression that she would accept an approach. That night he dreamed that:

Standing back a little behind two stately palaces was a little house with closed doors. My wife led me along the piece of street up to the little house and pushed the door open; I then slipped quickly and easily into the inside of a court which rose in an incline. (1900a, V, 397)

The connection between house and girl was made clearer by the fact that the house, as the dreamer realized, was remembered from the girl's place of origin.

Freud's conception of symbolic sexual wish-fulfillment is regarded by many as the most controversial part of his work. In practice, however, it is the most thoroughly exploited. Symbolic expression serves simultaneously to communicate and to obscure a sexual content. So it can be used to arouse sexual fantasy, or to associate it with one thing or another, without unacceptable explicitness. Hence images of the kind Freud took to be natural expressions of wish-fulfillment are now commonly produced deliberately, so as to make use of their sexual content. For example Freud noted that in men "flying dreams usually have a grossly sensual meaning" (1900a, V,

394). Now, of course, airline tickets are sold by advertisements that feature attractive air hostesses, who smile and say "Fly me."

Freud noted that such use of symbolism often served as a disguise that protected the feelings of the dreamer about his own motives, and so passed the censorship spoken of above. This may have been so in the case of the dream of entry to the house, for the helpful role attributed to the dreamer's wife suggests a denial of conflict and guilt. Something similar seems to hold in culture. Certainly the meaning of many advertisements would be less acceptable if put straightforwardly.

Symbolism has, moreover, a broader role, as a kind of natural metaphor, or mode of comparison. The dream of Irma's injection, for example, begins with the question of her having accepted Freud's "solution" to her problems; and in the rest of the dream this is elaborated with a host of comparisons, involving the taking and putting of substances of various kinds in various ways. Thus Irma's failure to accept Freud's interpretations is shown as her choking on what has been put into her, this as one chemical or another, and so on throughout the dream.

This is not just disguise, but an independent form of information processing, or symbolic thought. And we can take this kind of thinking to encompass much that we have been explicating. In metaphorical thinking we juxtapose two or more things, and so regard each in light of the other. Freud's analysis suggests that his dreaming mind was occupied in a form of comparison of Irma with a whole range of other figures, present and past, and that such unconscious comparison plays a far-reaching role in our mental life.[28]

IV. EXPLANATORY SCOPE, STRUCTURE, AND
ACCUMULATION

We have begun to see how the data of free association, and the kind of reasoning that Freud applied to them, might serve to extend commonsense understanding of motives and their working. We can judge relatively little of this on the basis of the material we can cover here. Still it seems that Freud's reasoning, as sketched, has notable potential for both scope and power.

As regards scope, we can see that such reasoning need not be limited to dreams. It turns upon relations of content. So it would seem potentially applicable to a whole range of phenomena with representational content, provided the right information could be collected about the representations and their relations to motives. Hence Freud applied this reasoning widely. In *The Interpretation of Dreams* he uses it to elucidate symptoms as well. Thus he takes the example of a young female patient who was

most surprisingly dressed. For though as a rule a woman's clothes are carefully considered down to the last detail, she was wearing one of her stockings hanging down and two of the buttons on her blouse were undone. She complained of having pains in her leg and, without being asked, exposed her calf. But what she principally complained of was, to use her own words, that she had a feeling in her body as though there was something "stuck into it" which was "moving backwards and forwards" and was "shaking" her through and through. Sometimes it made her whole body feel "stiff." My medical colleague, who was present at the examination, looked at me; he found no difficulty in understanding the meaning of her complaint. (1900a, V, 618)

Here we see the same sort of reasoning as above, but applied to a seemingly physical complaint. The symptom can be understood as a representation of the satisfaction of a wish derived from a (perhaps unconscious) desire to have sexual intercourse. And of course this explanation might be cross-checked with others, as Freud's description suggests.

Also, reasoning of this kind is capable of gaining power through use, in two connected ways. First, such reasoning creates inductive support for the kind of conclusion that it is used to draw. So far we have considered examples whose wish-fulfilling character could be established more or less directly by reference to memory and association. But the regular finding of such examples might lend inductive support to the view that most dreams, symptoms, or phenomena of some other kind, were similar in this respect. Again, such examples might support the view that motives like guilt, or mechanisms like distortion, were common features of wish-fulfillments. In this case the judgment that a particular dream was a wish-fulfillment, or provided grounds for the ascription of particular wishes, might have a degree of support external and additional to the features of the instance.[29]

Moreover, what analysis reveals is not just a single latent motive, but a characteristic structure. We find levels of association, which correspond to layers of motive. Thus with the Irma dream the first level of association takes us to events and motives of the day before the dream and enables us to relate some of the contents of the dream to these. The next takes us to earlier events and to deeper motives. These are closely related to those of the previous layer – there is Freud's wish to avoid responsibility for Irma, and then the guilt that underlies it – and also cast light on further features of the manifest dream; and so on.[30] The accumulation of instances of good explanation, therefore, lends inductive support to the ascription of a latent framework, within which elements can fit at a number of interlocking places. This in turn enables additional evidence to be brought to bear in a variety of ways.

In addition, inference of the kind we are considering is cumulative in another way. It operates upon motives in virtue of their content, and yields further motives and specifications of content. It naturally tends, therefore, to supplement the base on which it operates. Each inference adds information about motive and content, which is available to serve as a basis for the next inference, and for further inferences in future.[31]

The fuller the base, the greater the possibility of seeing more of the kind of noncoincidental connection between contents with which such reasoning begins. Also the more an element of the base is used in good explanations, the better it is confirmed by its explanatory role, and by its interlocking with other elements so confirmed. So the use of such reasoning might supplement and strengthen its base in such a way as to prompt still further and surer inferences; and these in turn might yield further such supplementation; and so on.

These considerations suggest that experience might give us good reason for an extension of commonsense psychology that was both sound and radical. We might proceed, that is, by a series of inferences that were grounded in common sense, and had strong support at each step, to an understanding of dreams, symptoms, and actions cast finally in terms of motives quite different from those that were commonsensically acknowledged at the outset.[32] This is, I think, the possibility that was realized in Freud's work. Since this kind of extension depends on the taking of many instances, we cannot hope to show it convincingly here. Still, the following may serve as an illustration. A man dreamed he had a secret liaison with a lady whom someone else wanted to marry. He was worried in case this other man might discover the liaison and the proposed marriage come to nothing. He therefore behaved in a very affectionate way to the man. He embraced him and kissed him. (1900a, V, 398–9)

The dreamer in fact had a secret liaison with a married woman, who was the wife of a friend; and he did think that his friend might have noticed something. This situation seems reflected in the dream, so that the friend could be identified with the "other man."

The dream, however, omitted something that was particularly important in the situation. The dreamer was expecting this friend to die from illness, and so was consciously occupied with his intention to marry the widow after the death. And also, the dreamer's associations to his hypocritical affectionate behavior in the dream traced it to a source quite different from the friend with whom he was consciously concerned: It came, rather, from his memory of his own relations with his father in childhood.

Now if we take this dream to have the same structure as that of Irma's injection, the dreamer's friend and his father will stand behind the other man of the dream, in the way that Freud's injured patient, his dead patient, and others stood behind Irma. On this account, that is, the other man will be a composite figure, formed by condensation, and deriving his role as unsuccessful rival from the dying friend, but his capacity to make the dreamer's liaison come to nothing from the father. The figures in Freud's dream were linked by his attitudes of concern, responsibility, guilt, and so on. Here, by contrast, the links would appear to pertain to sexual rivalry, hypocrisy, and guilt.

On this interpretation the dreamer's liaison would thus represent his enjoying also the object of his father's desire, and his hypocritical affections in the dream would refer also to those to his father, from which they were actually derived. The dreamer's father, in turn, would be represented not only as a rival, but also as one expected to die, and upon whose death the gratification of the dreamer's desires depended. Thus by finding in this dream the same structure as before, we should arrive at an interpretation of it in terms of the Oedipus complex. And as in Freud's dream, the topic of the dreamer's involvement with death, which figures clearly in the material that seems to have influenced the dream, would seem to have been censored out.

This interpretation turns on the comparability of the motives relating the figures from which the dream is derived. Three aspects of the dream seem to bear on this. First, we obtain what seems to be a straightforward derivation of manifest from latent content, if we assume that the latent motive is a wish to be a successful rival to the father. This also brings the motives relating to the dreamer's father into greater congruence with those bearing on his friend and rival, with which they are linked by association. In addition, taking the father as the object of the wish also serves to explain the representation of the other man in the manifest content as a potentially frustrating rival, as opposed to a temporary hindrance. Finally there is the relation of motives in the latent content itself. The dreamer's rivalry in love with his friend must have been a source of conflict to him, since he was betraying, and perhaps wishing the death, of someone for whom he also had real affection. This would seem similar in structure to oedipal rivalry.

We obtain the greatest fit between associated figures and motives if we take the dreamer to have a similar ambivalence and rivalry to his father. This seems the conclusion toward which the comparison registered by the dream points. Nonetheless this conclusion remains lacking in support, because no further justification appears in the material reported.

Still the conclusion admits of further support. More features of the case might home in on the motives toward which the dream so far only points suggestively. The dream might be linked with further feelings or memories about the parents, or the transference of these onto the analyst. Or it might, again, be one of a series, each of which indicated the same pattern of feelings, and some of which made enmity to the father clearer. Also there might be evidence from other cases: that dreams generally were wish-fulfilling, that layers of motive revealed in association were highly congruent, that the oedipal constellation of motives was very widespread, and so on. Any of these things would add something to our reasons for taking this dream as bearing on oedipal interpretation, and a combination of many, such as psychoanalysis is supposed to provide, might add notable weight. And if this is so, there is surely also the possibility that we might have registered this supporting material before we encountered this dream and its associations, and so been able to see the dream in this light on first acquaintance.[33]

Finally, let us consider some thinking that has been influential in psychoanalysis since Freud. The grounds for Freud's account of childhood included adult memories of sensual and aggressive feelings toward the parents, as well as the reliving of these in the transference, and the further evidence provided by associations, dreams, and the like. However extensive or comprehensive such evidence becomes, it remains indirect, and remote in time from the events upon which it is supposed to bear. Freud took it, however, that there was no better source of information, since children did not in the main act on their oedipal motives, and indeed lacked the concepts and ways of thinking required even to put them into words. Hence also, although children often have symptoms and difficulties analogous to those of adults, Freud did not try to apply analytic therapy to them, except in special circumstances, and then in a very limited way.[34]

But in addition to speaking, children constantly represent things in play – with, for example, dolls, toys, clay, paints, and games of make-believe. Later analysts, and in particular Melanie Klein,[35] realized that these representations, like dreams, could be seen as showing very articulate contents, which reflected the children's motives and mental states, and embodied their wish-fulfilling fantasies. This made it possible to analyze disturbed children, and hence to learn more about their mental life.

To take an example from a child playing a game of make-believe in which she had the part of a queen: When she

as queen, had celebrated her marriage to the king, she lay down on the sofa and wanted me, as the king, to lie down beside her. As I refused to do this I had to sit in a little chair by her side and knock at the sofa with my fist. This she called "churning" . . . immediately after this she announced that a child was creeping out of her, and she represented this scene in quite a realistic way, writhing about and groaning. Her imaginary child then had to share its parents' bedroom and had to be a spectator of sexual intercourse between them. If it interrupted, it was beaten . . . If she, as the mother, put the child to bed, it was only in order to get rid of it and to be able to be united with the father all the sooner.[36]

Freud noted that the parents are frequently represented in dreams as king and queen. If we take this child's real parents so to stand behind the figures she represents here, we can see this game as concerned, among other things, with her feelings about their sexual relations. So these are feelings that the child can play out fairly fully, even if she cannot put them into words.

The representation of her parents' relations – as lying together with something knocking something, or "churning" – has elements that could be taken as symbolism or metaphor in adult dreams. In such a dream these elements could be connected by association to articulate sexual thoughts, as in the example of the house, door, passage, and so forth earlier. Since the child thinks about such things less articulately, the meaning of a representation has to be shown in other ways, such as the structure of the play of which it is part (e.g., by the fact that the knocking or "churning" took place after the king and queen lay down together, and was followed by the birth of the child). This can nonetheless be relatively clear; and in some instances things are shown more explicitly. Thus, for example, when this little girl masturbated, as she did openly, both at home and in her analytic sessions, she would play what she called "the cupboard game," in which she would pull at her clitoris, saying she "wanted to pull out something very long."

Although we cannot go further into the matter here, it seems reasonable to hold that such representations in play can be related to the kind of infantile sexual and aggressive motives that Freud hypothesized. (For example in this material there may be: a wish to be the queen; to lie down beside the king; to do "churning," with something knocking at something; to alter the situation of being a child excluded from the parental bed; to make another child suffer the same situation; to have something very long in, or perhaps as, her genital; and so on.[37]) Accordingly, many analysts have taken conclusions drawn on this basis to support, and to extend, those of Freud.

We noted at the outset that Freud's work on dreams provided a paradigm in terms of which he could consolidate both previous findings and future investigations. This seems reflected in the range of application of the reasoning we have considered, which allowed Freud's thinking, and that of his successors, to relate to a wide variety of bases and sources in a similar way. There is, unfortunately, no space here for a fuller account of these matters, which would treat also of the limitations of this theorizing, particularly as compared with that of physical science. Still, the tendency in philosophical and methodological discussions is almost always to emphasize purported weaknesses rather then strengths in Freud's thought. To obtain a correct view it is necessary to lean against this long prevailing wind.

NOTES

1 The judgment of value was Freud's own, in his final preface, and commentators have tended to agree. Richard Wollheim, for example, regards the book as Freud's "masterpiece"; and Frank Sulloway takes it to be the "greatest" of the series of early works which "places Freud among the most creative scientific minds of all time" (*Freud: Biologist of the Mind*, [New York: Basic Books, 1979], p. 358).

    For some recent philosophical criticism of Freud on dreams see Clark Glymour, "The Theory of Your Dreams," in R. Cohen and L. Laudan, eds., *Physics, Philosophy, and Psychoanalysis* (Dordrecht, The Netherlands: Reidel, 1983, and Adolf Grünbaum, *The Foundations of Psychoanalysis: A Philosophical Critique* (University of California Press, 1984). I think these criticisms are based on misunderstandings, which I have in turn criticized in "Epistemology and Depth Psychology: Critical Notes on *The Foundations of Psychoanalysis*" in Peter Clark and Crispin Wright, eds., *Psychoanalysis, Mind and Science* (Oxford, Basil Blackwell, 1988). The present essay continues the argument of that paper.

    On the general methodology of Grünbaum's critique, see also note 21. On the contra-Freudian theory in J. A. Hobson's interesting recent book *The Dreaming Brain* (London: Penguin, 1990) see note 27.

2 For this instance see 1895d, II, 34ff. The connection of such material with Breuer and Freud's early theory, that *"hysterics suffer mainly from reminiscences"* (II, 7) is relatively clear. Also, however, the same symptom can be construed as fulfilling a wish not to drink, originating in this scene. This illustrates how the data that led Freud to frame his first hypothesis also fit the second.

3 Thus in 1899 Freud wrote to his friend Wilhelm Fliess that "the dream schema is capable of the most general application . . . the key to hysteria as well really lies in dreams" (1985 [1887–1904], 338). And in his first preface he describes the theoretical value of the dream as that of "a paradigm" that is "the first member" of a class of phenomena including "hysterical phobias, obsessions, and delusions" (1900a, V, xxiii).

4 For this last reason the book establishes a notable relation between author and reader. In presenting his own dreams Freud asks his reader "to make my interests his own for quite a while, and to plunge, along

with me, into the minutest details of my life" (1900a, IV, 105–6). Although he reveals much, Freud still wants to keep his secrets. At the same time his purpose is to provide new ways to understand the material he presents and leaves hostage to his reader's penetration. So his methods point beyond what he says, to further conclusions about his life and feelings.

Freud's findings about symptoms could be replicated only by other physicians, and with a great deal of perseverance. Many people, by contrast, could follow his example and investigate dreams. Such attempts, moreover, could be informative without going deep. The partial analysis of just a few dreams, for example, may acquaint someone with such novelties of Freud's approach as free association and that to which it leads, in a way that importantly supplements reading. Thus through the *Interpretation* Freud began to gain a wider audience, who understood something of the nature of his work.

D. Anzieu provides detailed discussion of Freud's analyses of his own dreams, and references to a number of further works on Freud's dreams, in *Freud's Self-Analysis* (London: Hogarth Press, 1986). As Anzieu notes, Freud very often provides clues so that persevering readers can work out things left obscure.

5 In what follows I shall be using "motive" in a broad way, for almost any of the psychological causes by which we ordinarily explain behavior, as in "He did it because . . . ," "He did it out of . . . ," and so forth. Thus, for example, love, hatred, jealousy, envy, greed, and lust are motives, as well as the more fully articulated instances derived from them, such as conviction as to the rightness of one's own conduct, desire to harm one's rival, and so forth.

6 This kind of explanation, and particularly its causal nature, has been explored by Donald Davidson in a classic series of essays beginning with "Actions, Reasons, and Causes" (see his *Essays on Actions and Events* [Oxford, Clarendon Press, 1980]), to which I refer the reader in search of a deeper and more detailed treatment.

7 Freud emphasized the connection of his thought with commonsense explanation by motive in saying, for example, that as opposed to Breuer he "was inclined to suspect an interplay of forces and the operation of intentions and purposes such as are to be observed in normal life" (1925d, XX,23). And he says that in speaking of "the sense of a psychical process we mean nothing other than the intention it serves and its position in a psychical continuity. In most of our researches we can replace 'sense' by 'intention' or 'purpose' " (1916–17, XV, 40). Freud's word translated by "purpose" here is *Tendenz*, which according to Strachey might be better translated by "trend." I think that part of

Freud's idea is that brought out below, in terms of the characterization of intentionality.

8 This notion of articulation was introduced by Wittgenstein, who stressed its importance for psychology. (See his *Philosophical Remarks* [Oxford: Blackwell, 1975], p. 70: "I call only an *articulated* process a thought. . . . Salivation, no matter how precisely measured, is not what we call expectation.") Articulated motives are the "propositional attitudes" spoken of by Russell in his introduction to Wittgenstein's *Tractatus Logico-Philosophicus* (London: Routledge and Kegan Paul, 1922) and thenceforward in analytic philosophy. They might better be described, as Wittgenstein takes them in that book, as attitudes toward situations or states of affairs.

9 As I shall be using these terms, the truth-condition of "Snow is white" is that snow is white, of "Grass is green" that grass is green, and so on, ad infinitum. The notion is used for motives by way of the sentences that articulate them. Thus the sentence that articulates the motive of belief in "John believes that snow is white" is "Snow is white." The truth-condition of this sentence, and hence of the belief itself, is that snow is white.

Similarly, I take it that the satisfaction condition of the hope that snow is white is that snow is white. The condition of satisfaction of the desire that snow be white (for snow to be white, etc.) is that snow be white; this condition, however, is met if snow is white, so again the condition can be cast in the indicative, as that snow is white. The case is similar, despite grammatical variations, for the other motives with which we shall be concerned.

The condition of satisfaction, realization, or whatever, of a given motive stands in a relation to that motive that is logical or conceptual. It is a norm or rule, given in language, that having a drink of water satisfies a desire to have a drink of water, or that a belief that grass is green is true if grass is green. Wittgenstein makes the point in a parallel case by saying that "It is in language that an expectation and its fulfillment make contact" (*Philosophical Investigations* [Oxford: Blackwell, 1963], p. 445).

Also Wittgenstein stresses that "the fact that some event stops my wishing does not mean that it fulfils it. Perhaps I should not have been satisfied if my wish were satisfied" (p. 432). Of course it is true that a desire is normally extinguished or altered when its condition of satisfaction is known to obtain. This, however, is part of the rational working of desire, and so part of the parallel between meaning and the causal role of motives that we are discussing.

10 This encoding is accomplished, I think, by our use of our language for

describing the world *within* our language for describing motive. I discuss
this more fully in my essay in Hopkins and Savile, eds., *Psychoanalysis,
Mind, and Art: Essays for Richard Wollheim* (Oxford: Blackwell, forthcoming).

11 Wittgenstein compares the representational or information-bearing role
of thought to that of a gramophone record at *Tractatus* 4.014. Since he
takes the record to be an abstract model, this is part of his account of
mind and language in terms of mental models. On this see also note 14.

12 The "direction of fit" of desires and belief is thus the direction of the
flow of information that they register. And the role of transmission of
information is not accidental here. In many cases it is clear that a belief
will not count as a belief that S, unless linked in an appropriate content-
transmitting way to the situation that would render "S" true, or to the
objects and properties that figure in this situation. (This does not of
course mean that innate beliefs are impossible, since, among other
things, they may be shaped in the appropriate way by evolution.)

Ruth Garrett Millikan's *Language, Thought, and Other Biological
Categories* (Cambridge, Mass.: Bradford Press, MIT Press, 1984) contains
a most illuminating account of the determination of content by evolution. Although these matters are beyond the scope of the present paper, I
think that Millikan's account may enable us to understand the thinking
described in psychoanalytic accounts of fantasy, primary process, and so
forth, as a form of processing of biologically significant information.

13 Interpretation is connected with a kind of prediction that we could
make by no other means, as when we are able to predict various things
about the remainder of a person's pattern of action (that he will put his
hand *there*, or next move *there*) on the basis of interpreting part of it.
Nonetheless our interpretive understanding goes well beyond our ability
to predict; for we are built to be able to use others as sources of information regarding things that are beyond our ken and out of our control.

14 As note 12 indicates, this seems to be the psychology implicit (but not
fully worked out) in Wittgenstein's *Tractatus*. Wittgenstein sought to
explain our capacity to think and act in reference to things in the world
in terms of inner pictures or models, which were used by the mind (or
brain) in thought, and hence exercised causal control over behavior. (See
also, for example, his claim that "Language must have the same multiplicity as a control panel that sets off the actions corresponding to its
propositions," and that "Our expectation anticipates the event. In this
sense it makes a model of the event" in *Philosophical Remarks* (Oxford:
Blackwell, 1975), pp. 58, 71; and also *Zettel* (Oxford: Blackwell, 1967)
pp. 236, 444.

Wittgenstein often returned to this theory, but could not see how to free it from objection, and finally let it go. The account in Millikan, cited above, is at a number of points comparable to it. Mental models and their connection with content are also illuminatingly discussed in Colin McGinn's *Mental Content* (Oxford, Basil Blackwell, 1989).

15 I should like to thank Gabriel Segal for discussing the ideas of this section with me and making a number of comments that were clarifying and prompted improvements in exposition.

16 Freud summarizes his interpretation as follows:

> The dream fulfilled certain wishes which were started in me by the events of the previous evening (the news given me by Otto and my writing out of the case history). The conclusion of the dream, that is to say, was that I was not responsible for the persistence of Irma's pains, but that Otto was. Otto had in fact annoyed me by his remarks about Irma's incomplete cure, and the dream gave me my revenge by throwing the reproach back on to him. The dream acquitted me of the responsibility for Irma's condition by showing that it was due to other factors – it produced a whole series of reasons. The dream presented a particular state of affairs as I should have wished it to be. *Thus its content was the fulfillment of a wish and its motive was a wish.* (1900a, IV, 118–9)

Agreement on the cogency of this extends to Grünbaum and to Glymour, cited above, who describes this part of Freud's account as "enormously plausible." It should not, however, be supposed that Grünbaum or Glymour would accept the overall account that follows, which contrasts sharply with theirs.

17 To say that wishes can conflict with the motives that govern our actions is to say that they need not accurately reflect what we value, when we take things more fully into account, as we do in deciding how to act. Thus the wishes that Freud finds here conflict with something he presumably values considerably, and might in reality make serious efforts to preserve, that is, the welfare of a family friend and patient.

This enables us to see that Freud's account of dreams is consonant with the fact that many dreams are connected with alarm or anxiety. The representation of the fulfillment of motives that clash with what we value greatly is, surely, an appropriate source of anxiety. So such feelings in dreams are not paradoxical, on Freud's account, but rather a consequence of something familiar. If we accept that human beings have seriously conflicting motives, then we must allow that their wishes – or indeed in some cases their desires or voluntary actions – can be a source of distress, anxiety, or whatever.

18 I do not mean to imply by this that wishes are not motives. Rather, they are distinguished from other motives here, because they have the particular role of mediating the production of representations.

19 Freud often takes it that connection in content among psychological

elements provides grounds for inference as to causal connection (see, e.g., 1900a, V, 528). This idea was taken up and explicated by Schmidl in "The Problem of Scientific Validation in Psychoanalytic Interpretation," *International Journal of Psychoanalysis* (1955). (I owe this reference to the researches of Frank Cioffi.) It is, I think, strengthened by consideration of the systematic relations of content and causal role in commonsense psychology indicated in the text.

20 There is a question as to whether we should represent these instances as of the pattern in the Irma dream, since there is so little in the way of independent grounds for ascribing the motives that we take to give rise to the wishes behind them.

The same question arises for reasons. We sometimes know an agent's desires and beliefs in advance, and infer merely that he is now acting on them; and sometimes we infer the contents of previously unsuspected desires or beliefs from what the agent does. Should we take ourselves to use the same pattern of inference in both cases?

The sense in which the pattern is the same is that the conclusion of such inference always imposes the full desire–belief–action pattern onto the material interpreted, even if only some parts of the full pattern are *introduced* in the instance of inference. Likewise in this case, where the conclusion actually involves the full motive–wish–dream pattern.

We thus have differences among instances of the same pattern, regarding the number of elements taken as part of the base for inference, and the number introduced in the inference itself. In general the more added, the greater the chance of error, and the greater the relevance of crosschecking. Also, the more added, other things being equal, the less *internally* cogent the inference; for the instance accomplishes less explanatory unification of already given material.

As we shall see in the final section of this essay, the taking of many instances of inference of this kind might enable us to accumulate a basis for inference that would enable us to see a wide range of representations as wish-fulfilling, and (perhaps) to read the wishes in them more readily and directly.

21 Adolf Grünbaum, in his critique *The Foundations of Psychoanalysis*, argues that psychoanalytic causal claims must be taken as answerable solely to Millian inductive canons, saying, for example, that "the establishment of a causal connection in psychoanalysis, no less than in 'academic psychology' or medicine, has to rely on modes of inquiry that are refined from time-honored canons of causal inference pioneered by Francis Bacon and John Stuart Mill" (p. 47).

Grünbaum thus apparently does not allow that psychoanalytic claims are supported in any such way as is sketched here. He devotes almost a third of his book to arguing against hermeneutic approaches to psycho-analysis, and does not acknowledge that hypotheses about motive can be supported by explanatory considerations.

His methodology thus makes no room for the kind of interpretive thinking that we already take to establish the working of motive, and extend in psychoanalysis. The Millian modes of inquiry that he endorses, moreover, seem inapplicable to motive.

These are, roughly, correlational and eliminative methods: They are applied to items or properties that are observed to go together, to determine whether this co-occurrence is causal or accidental. So they are applied to A's and B's that are already given, to investigate whether the A's actually cause the B's, as opposed, say, to accompanying them by chance.

Now as noted in the text it seems that we should not construe ourselves as simply *observing* that motives co-occur with the actions or wish-fulfillments that we take them to cause. Rather, surely, we are better represented as *hypothesizing* the various motives, in order to explain what we observe in terms of them. We thus treat motives as a species of unobserved causes, introduced to explain observed effects. This has two consequences. First, the putative causes and effects are not of the same observational status, as Millian methods presuppose. And second, the pair of items in question are already understood as cause and effect, and on non-Millian grounds.

So far as claims as to the working of motive are understood in this way, it follows that they neither admit nor require certification by Millian or Baconian modes of inquiry. They do not admit of it, because you cannot verify whether a cause that you are taking as beyond observation actually is a cause by observing how it co-occurs with its putative effect. And they do not require it, because the hypotheses by which they are introduced already acknowledge their causal status, and are in turn supported in other ways, and via their explanatory consequences. Because psychoanalysis is a psychology of motive, the Millian methodology that Grünbaum advocates seems radically inappropriate to it.

The danger, moreover, is not merely that such modes of inquiry do not adequately register support for interpretive hypotheses as to the role of motive. Rather, they are also likely to represent true claims as false. For Millian and Baconian methods are meant to serve a sieving or eliminative function – to eliminate the A's and B's that might mistakenly be taken as connected, but are not. And methods that sift out A's and B's that are not strongly correlated are also liable to sieve out causes that, like motives, play a special or restricted role.

Mill's First Canon, for example, allows us to infer that A is not the cause of B, if A occurs without B. (Cf. the "we may reason thus: b and c are not effects of A, for they were not produced by it in the second experiment . . ." in *John Stuart Mill's Philosophy of Scientific Method* [New York: Hafner, 1970], p. 212.) This would enable us to reason as follows: people who are hungry (even desperately hungry) sometimes do not eat, and people who are thirsty sometimes do not drink; so hunger and thirst do not, as one might have supposed, cause eating and drinking. This, clearly, provides no explication of the role of motive, save that it is not that of sole sufficient condition; so the use of such a criterion is tantamount to an ignoring of the actual causal role of motive. This is not Grünbaum's intention, but he provides no account as to how Mill's canons are to be used so as to avoid such results.

Their difficulties show in further ways: Millian canons are on the face of it insensitive to the vast range of connections and distinctions of meaning and logic by which information about the working of motive is carried in commonsense psychology, and so unfit to detect or certify it. Also, they commonly require repeated instances to be used upon, whereas motives constantly vary, in response to need, experience, and thought, and so rarely satisfy the same description from instance to instance. (Motives are, however, very rich in the kind of causally connected content, with which commonsense and psychoanalytic reasoning works.)

Clearly it would be an error to conclude that motives do not perform significant explanatory and causal work, because they do not stand still for certification by Millian methods, which would in any case fail to record their labor. But it remains unclear, where the basic roles of motives are concerned, what other conclusions these methods are suited to draw. Hence, of course, their suitability as a vehicle for criticism of Freud.

As noted in the text, commonsense psychological practice involves the cross-checking of ascriptions of motive from action to action, and psychoanalytic practice extends this. If we construe motives as causes whose role is reflected in their content we can see our commonsense causal/hermeneutic thinking as performing a function of integration of instances, positive and negative, in relation to causal hypotheses, which is partly analogous to that of inductive methods as used elsewhere. The lesson to be drawn from this, however, is not that commonsense or Freudian thinking is unsupported without Millian testing, but rather that it is already (to some degree) supported by a kind of testing that is analogous and appropriate to it.

22 The association is

> *I took her to the window.* . . . The way in which Irma stood by the window suddenly reminded me of another experience. Irma had an intimate woman friend of whom I had a very high opinion. When I visited

this lady one evening I had found her by a window in the situation reproduced in the dream, and her physician, the same Dr. M., had pronounced that she had a diphtheritic membrane. The figure of Dr. M. and the membrane reappear later in the dream. It now occurred to me that for the last few months I had every reason to suppose that this other lady was also a hysteric. Indeed, Irma herself had betrayed the fact to me. What did I know of her condition? One thing precisely: that like my Irma of the dream she suffered from hysterical choking. So in the dream I had replaced my patient by her friend. (1900a, IV, 110)

23   The linkage also goes via further elements of the dream – a white patch, and scabs, which Freud saw in Irma's throat when he examined her – which are not discussed here. (They pretty clearly have to do with the sexual aspect of the dream.)

24   The relevant part of the association is

I was making frequent use of cocaine at that time to reduce some troublesome nasal swellings, and I had heard a few days earlier that one of my women patients who had followed my example had developed an extensive necrosis of the nasal mucous membrane. I had been the first to recommend the use of cocaine, in 1885, and this recommendation had brought serious reproaches down on me. The misuse of that drug had hastened the death of a dear friend of mine. (1900a, IV, 111)

25   These matters are treated elsewhere in more adequate detail. Freud provided his own concise introduction to them in *On Dreams* (1901a, V, 633–86). There is a clear and philosophically informed account in ch. 3 of Richard Wollheim's *Freud* (London: Fontana Modern Masters, 1971). The introductory account in ch. 6 of Paul Kline's *Psychology and Freudian Theory* (London: Methuen, 1984) includes a survey of empirical work on dreams, and references to the literature in academic psychology.

26   This is not an example that Freud gives, although it seems a reasonably clear instance of the phenomenon as he describes it elsewhere. I am inclined to think that this is because he did not at this time give sufficient attention to the role of guilt. Also his concept of displacement, like that of condensation, has many complexities not touched on here. See 1900a, IV, 305ff.

27   It is thus worth noting that these few data from Freud's initial specimen dream, analyzed only this far, tend to confirm what J. Allan Hobson calls Freud's "disguise censorship" model of dreams, and thus to disconfirm the rival "transparency" alternative recently proposed by Hobson himself. (See *The Dreaming Brain* [London: Penguin, 1990].)

Hobson's book has been highly praised, and the work on the physiology of dreaming and its relation to psychology that he presents seems valuable and illuminating. Nothing in the scientific material, however, supports his contention that dreams are transparently related to the motives that influence them. Physiology is at best silent on this point. And since physiological mechanisms are opaque to consciousness, their acknowledgment tends rather to support the view that what moves us in acting or imagining need *not* be transparently revealed.

It is hard to see why dreams should be supposed to have a transparent relation to motives, when actions do not; and hard to see why Hobson should now insist on this idea, in the face of the many examples to the contrary that Freud and others have long been providing. Hobson does not, however, discuss these. (He does say, somewhat surprisingly, that "Freud's *Interpretation of Dreams* . . . is devoid of either detailed descriptions or illustrations of actual data. . . . There are no verbatim dream reports. . . ." p. 90.) One readily understands objection to Freudian interpretations that are very complex or farfetched. But on this point simpler and plainer data seem already to suffice.

Hobson's insistence on transparency seems to affect his consideration of data generally; in accord with it he seems happy to disregard associations and focus on manifest dream content alone.

This is surely a retrograde step. For by ignoring associations and memories Hobson fails to avail himself of data that could enrich his hypotheses, and against which they could be tested. For example, when he comes to consider the role of memories in the dreams of his subject the "Engine Man" Hobson holds, like Freud, that the dreamer goes "back, back (into his memory file)," in search of material connected with the themes of the dream (278). But because he does not consider actual memories that this dreamer links with the material of the dream, his ideas about the role of memory remain unconstrained by real data from memory, and hence speculative. In the analysis of the Irma dream, by contrast, we find data with clear bearing on many hypotheses about the "memory files" that the dreamer opens (information about significant actions and persons, significant motives, and so on.)

Hobson attempts to justify his procedure by urging, for example, "With such rich manifest content to work with, why delve deeper?" (234). One answer would be that it is preferable for scientific hypotheses to take account of all relevant data, so far as possible, even if some have to be got by delving. Where hypotheses about memory and dreams are concerned, the dreamer's own actual memories, and the way they are shown in association, seem clearly relevant.

Hobson does say that "it will be important to verify biographical surmises in living subjects whose dreams are interpreted within the transparency framework." In this way, he holds, we need not be "throwing out the psychodynamic baby with the psychoanalytic bathwater" (281). But if interpreting "within the transparency framework" means avoiding data of association that disconfirm the framework, this is not good scientific practice. It is one thing to see what you can get on the basis of manifest content alone, or manifest content and physiology; it is quite another to hold that conclusions reached in this way should supplant those based on fuller data. Hobson appears to be claiming that his "transparency framework" should replace Freud's ("the psychoanalytic bathwater"), while systematically ignoring evidence that confirms Freud's and disconfirms transparency.

Also, the methodological considerations that Hobson takes to guide his own approach seem actually to fit better with Freud's. Hobson stresses that he seeks to anchor psychological thinking in physiological knowledge, by assuming or hypothesizing an isomorphism between physiological and psychological levels. He calls this the "principle of isomorphism," and illustrates it by "such a bottom-up hypotheses as: if the brain's visual centers are active in REM [rapid-eye-movement] sleep, then dreams will be characterized by visual sensation; similarly, if the brain's motor centers are active in REM sleep, then dreams will be characterized by intense imaginings of movement" (p. 158).

Accordingly, Hobson urges that "the sensorimotor hallucinosis of the dream experience is the direct and necessary concomitant of the specific activation of sensorimotor brain circuits" (p. 210), evidence for which he describes with admirable lucidity. This is certainly plausible, and clearly in harmony with Freud's psychological findings. The stress on motor neurons and bodily movement, for example, coheres well with the partial analogy between dream and action emphasized in the text.

There is, however, further relevant brain activity, which Hobson does not omit to mention. He notes that in REM sleep "the penis of the male and the clitoris of the female are both periodically engorged through the night in concert with changes in the brain" (p. 138); and he hypothesizes that dream sleep provides maintenance and development of the brain circuitry involved in sexual activity, and also perhaps "genetically determined behavior rehearsal" (p. 294) for it. As he says, "the fixed-action patterns that constitute the sexual act itself have a life of their own. They are, apparently, in constant readiness. REM-sleep erections and wet dreams are the outward sign that at least part of this theory must be correct" (p. 295).

But then what about the "direct and necessary concomitant" of the nightly activation of brain circuits in this case? Consistent application of his principle of isomorphism would suggest that Hobson should here reason as above. The parallel would be: If the brain's "sexual activity" circuits are active in REM sleep, then dreams will be characterized by sexual imaginings. This would be a significant application of iso-morphism, because it would yield a "bottom-up hypothesis" that was genuine and risky, as opposed to those cited, in which the principle is used to derive only what is antecedently well known.

And taken thus seriously, Hobson's principle of isomorphism, and the data he cites concerning REM sexual arousal, cohere with Freud's inde-pendent finding that dreams are frequently characterized by sexual imag-ining, which is, however, disguised or symbolic. Because Freud's claim was based on associations and did not employ the notion of iso-morphism, this provides evidence of the utility of the principle from a distinct source, and also some indication that it extends to association and memory as well.

On the other hand the data and principle seem again to conflict with "the transparency framework." Hobson reports no sexual dreams from the Engine Man, for example; but presumably his circuits and patterns too were refreshed several times a night. On the other hand, Hobson does report, for example, that "The Engine Man also flies, magically, as in this account. . . ." (p. 244).

28 Metaphor is discussed in connection with Davidson's work in Marcia Cavell's "Metaphor, Dreamwork, and Irrationality" in E. LePore, ed., *Truth and Interpretation: Perspectives on the Philosophy of Donald Davidson* (Oxford: Basil Blackwell, 1986). The notion also plays a signifi-cant role in Lacan's explication of Freud. See, for example, *Ecrits* (Lon-don: Tavistock, 1977) ch. 5.

Symbolic thought can also be seen as enabling unconscious motives to influence the overall course of action, so that patterns of wish-fulfillment and rational action are more closely interwoven than might appear. A possible example is mentioned in note 34.

29 Compare the way that someone who checks his visual estimate of dis-tances by pacing them off acquires inductive evidence that his visual estimate is accurate, and thereby increases the confidence he can rightly accord to cases in which he judges by vision alone.

30 Freud's conception of analysis is thus connected with an ideal of explana-tory conpleteness: An analysis would be complete, in theory, when we had gone as deep in motive, and as far back in time, as was required to collect all the latent material operative in producing the manifest.

In the case of the Irma dream Freud continued his analysis well be-yond the associations reported in the *Interpretation* and found sexual motives bearing on the women represented in it. See his reference to "sexual megalomania" in Freud and Abraham, *A Psychoanalytic Dia-logue* (London: Hogarth, 1965).

31 Thus Freud's first interpretation puts *avoidance of responsibility* clearly

into our base for interpreting his wishes; and this paves the way for the deeper interpretations about avoidance of responsibility relating to other cases, and the guilt that would explain it, which follow. Because these cohere with the original ascription, they tend to confirm it; and these in turn clearly pave the way for more.

32 This is a possibility that Grünbaum seems disinclined to acknowledge. He has written the following in a personal communication to the analyst Marshall Edelson, quoted in the latter's *Psychoanalysis, A Theory in Crisis* (Chicago: University of Chicago Press, 1988), p. 330:

> I no more think that psychoanalytic theory is an *extension* of common-sense psychology than I think theoretical physics is an extension of common-sense "physics." What commonsense man believes a table is mostly *empty* space between particles?? . . .
> If psychoanalysis were the extension of commonsense you depict, why did it encounter so much disbelief? . . . It is *utterly* incredible commonsensically that horror dreams should be wish-fulfilling.

In these remarks Grünbaum seems not to take account of the idea that an extension can go far from its commonsense basis, but by steps each of which is cogent in light of what has gone before. Strictly speaking, only the first such step needs to accord with unmodified common sense; and that step may itself take us beyond it. This seems to be how it is with the Irma dream.

As to Grünbaum's other points: A theory based on common sense but going well beyond it would be expected to encounter disbelief precisely where those to whom it was presented had not traversed sufficiently many of the steps supporting the extension. But we surely need not go very far to accept the possibility that a person's own motives (or indeed his own actions on occasion) may have aspects that are horrible to him, so that he finds their unconstrained realization a nightmare.

33 Here also the oedipal motives might serve to explain the dreamer's situation in a deeper way. It might be that he was drawn to a liaison with the wife of a friend partly *because* he linked this situation with his father. In this case the liaison itself would be wish-fulfilling, and so a sort of symbolic or metaphorical gratification of repressed motives.

34 As he said, "too many words and thoughts have to be lent to the child, and even so the deepest strata may turn out to be impenetrable to consciousness" (1918b, XVII, 9). He did, however, direct the therapy reported in "Analysis of a Phobia in a Five-Year-Old Boy" (1909b, X, 5ff).

Little children can of course make some use of concepts related to sexual motives. Thus consider the following exchange recorded by Melanie Klein, from a conversation in which she had tried to explain to a little boy how babies are made.

Fritz listened with great interest and said, "I would so much like to see how a child is made inside like that." I explain that this is impossible until he is big because it can't be done until then but that then he will do it himself. "But then I would like to do it to mama." "That can't be, mama can't be your wife, for she is the wife of your papa, and then papa would have no wife." "But we could both do it to her." I say, "No, that can't be. Every man has only one wife. When you are big your mama will be old. Then you will marry a beautiful young girl and she will be your wife." He (nearly in tears and with quivering lips) "But shan't we live in the same house together with mama?"   *The Writings of Melanie Klein* (London: Hogarth Press, 1975), vol 1, pp. 34–5.

35 I have discussed some of Klein's theories, comparing them with Piaget's and relating them to some experimental work with babies, "Synthesis in the Imagination: Psychoanalysis, Infantile Experience, and the Concept of an Object," in James Russell, ed. *Philosophical Perspectives on Developmental Psychology* (Oxford: Basil Blackwell, 1987). Her work is also discussed in Richard Wollheim's *The Thread of Life* (Cambridge: Cambridge University Press, 1984).

36 *The Writings of Melanie Klein*, vol II, pp. 39, 40.

37 Other phenomena can be observed here, such as the child's attempt to identify with certain figures and feelings, by taking their part herself, or to distance herself from others, by assigning them to the partner in play. Also this play indicates how some forms of representation come quite close to the phenomena that they represent (the lying down together), while others remain at greater distance.

5 The unconscious

Psycho-analysis regarded everything mental as being in the first place unconscious; the further quality of "consciousness" might also be present, or again it might be absent. This of course provoked a denial from the philosophers, for whom "consciousness" and "mental" were identical, and who protested that they could not conceive of such an absurdity as the "unconscious mental." There was no help for it, however, and this idiosyncrasy of the philosophers could only be disregarded with a shrug. Experience (gained from pathological material, of which the philosophers were ignorant) of the frequency and power of impulses of which one knew nothing directly, and whose existence had to be inferred like some fact in the external world, left no alternative open. It could be pointed out, incidentally, that this was only treating one's own mental life as one had always treated other people's. One did not hesitate to ascribe mental processes to other people, although one had no immediate consciousness of them and could only infer them from their words and actions. But what held good for other people must be applicable to oneself. Anyone who tried to push the argument further and to conclude from it that one's own hidden processes belonged actually to a second *consciousness* would be faced with the concept of a consciousness of a thing of which one knew nothing, of an "unconscious consciousness" – and this would scarcely be preferable to the assumption of an "unconscious mental." . . . The further question as to the ultimate nature of this unconscious is no more sensible or profitable than the older one as to the nature of the conscious.

(1925d [1924], XX, 31–2)

Reasons for believing in the existence of the unconscious are of course empirical, but the question as to what most fundamentally distinguishes Freud's conception of the unconscious is conceptual. I shall be concerned primarily with the nature of the unconscious in broad, philosophical terms, rather than with the fine detail of Freud's characterization of it. I mean to offer a brief defense of the coherence of the concept, and at least to sketch, without exploring in any depth, some of the issues that would be involved in a fuller treatment of the subject.[1]

1. Some very general things about Freud's characterization of the unconscious should first be stated. It will be taken that Freud believed the following true of his concept of the unconscious: that the "descriptive" sense of "unconscious" (the criterion for which is simple awareness) is to be distinguished from the "dynamic" sense, and that the defining preoccupation of psychoanalysis is with the dynamic unconscious; that the dynamic unconscious is a source of motivation, specifically motivation that is actually or potentially a cause of mental conflict, and that it makes little or no positive contribution to cognition; that its hypothesis is specifically conceived with reference to the clinical phenomena of resistance and transference; that it is, however, in one complex and qualified sense, directly manifest in dreams; that it is closely related to, as a failure and cause of disturbance of, the faculty of memory; that at an earlier stage, that of the "Project" (1950a), it is embryonically envisaged as a neural level; that it is first properly conceptualized as *Ucs* on the first topography; that it is first formulated in such close relation to the concept of repression that the unconscious appears at that stage as approximately coextensive with the repressed; that the hypothesis of the unconscious is different from, and excludes (relative to any given explanandum) the hypothesis of a second consciousness; that it is sharply distinguished from the preconscious, (*Pcs*), which is unconscious in the merely descriptive sense; that *Ucs*, although it corresponds to a special kind of neural feature ("free cathectic energy"), is autonomous relative to the anatomy of the brain; that, although it is immediately proximate to instinctual life, "ideas" (or "instinctual representatives"), rather than instincts themselves, are its primary content; that in addition to ideas it is also necessary to speak, if only in highly qualified terms, of emotions as unconscious; that the behavior of its elements is characterized by a set of largely semilogical or syntactically characterizable features, including absence of negation and indifference to time,

which are described by Freud as constituting "primary" process, a condition that is closely related to the prevalence in the unconscious of the pleasure, as opposed to the reality principle; and that the unconscious as *Ucs* is on the second topographical (called "structural") model of the mind distributed across the entirety of the id and the major portion of the ego.[2]

To these characterizations an obvious first remark can be added regarding the epistemology of the unconscious. Knowledge of the unconscious is fixed in two connections: (i) by reference to the behavior of the analysand – here the unconscious state is identified by a definite description which is constructed out of reports of the analysand's behavior (as "the motive that caused the analysand to forget x, to misrepresent y, etc."); and (ii) by reference to dreams, fantasies, and symptoms, which give an indirect but nevertheless privileged insight into the content of unconscious states – here the unconscious state is identified in terms of its intrinsic representational content.

None of these attributions is likely to be thought contentious. The following three basic questions are however left open: Does it make sense, and if so on what grounds, to talk at all of unconscious states? What kind of a thing is the unconscious? Of what kind are the states that compose the unconscious? These questions will be dealt with in turn in the three following sections, most time being devoted to the first.

2. *Is the concept of unconscious mentality cogent and unobjectionable?* The order of argument in this section will roughly parallel Freud's own in his "Justification for the concept of the unconscious" (1915e, XIV, pt. I).

"Unconscious mentality" does not involve a straightforward *contradictio in adjecto:* It is not a plain analytic truth of any kind that all mentality is conscious.[3] There are roughly three grounds on which it might nevertheless be held that the notion of unconscious mentality involves a conceptual absurdity: antiabstractionism, dependence for causal power, and redundancy. These will be explained in turn. Antiabstractionism: The objection is that the notion of unconscious mentality involves a conceptual extrapolation from conscious mentality of a kind that is objectionable, as an illegitimate "abstraction" from known reality. Dependence for causal power: The objection is that because mental states are dependent on their being conscious for their possession of causal power, any notion of unconscious mentality will necessarily be epiphenomenal, and hence impossible to motivate by considerations of explanation. Redundancy: The objection is that it can be established in advance that any adduction of unconscious mentality as an empirical explanatory hypothesis will be redundant relative to other available and preferable empirical hypotheses. In most negative treatments of the concept of unconscious mentality these points are not separated out.[4]

If we now consider these objections in turn, it may be readily granted in the first place that we start from a view of the mind that contains a central place for consciousness. But necessarily connected to the ordinary conception of consciousness is the practice of describing mental states as being either "in" or "not in" consciousness. We employ this distinction to make sense of miscellaneous cognitive shortcomings and failures of self-knowledge: When we say, for example, that something, a piece of knowledge or the thought of an object, is at some point not in mind ("She failed to bear it in mind that . . ."; "The thought that . . . was far from his mind"), or that a person fails to realize something that she knows, or that a belief is in some sense buried (the truth about which a person deceives himself, the akrates' knowledge of what it is best to do).

Now (to introduce a philosophical distinction) the sense in which mental items may be said to be *in* consciousness is not the same for all kinds of mental state: What it is for a pain to be in consciousness is not what it is for a belief to be in consciousness. The first, we might say, is just for all of the *being* of the mental state to be laid out under the subject's mental gaze. The second, by contrast, consists in the occurrence of episodes (episodes of thought) in which the belief is, in various ways and to varying degrees of clarity, with room made for errors of various kinds, *manifested.*[5]

The corresponding senses of what it is for items of each kind *not* to be in consciousness are also not the same. What it is (or would be) for a pain not to be in consciousness is not the same as what it is for a belief not to be in consciousness. What the former is (or would be), is something that arguably presents a serious difficulty for the ordinary conception of mind; whereas what the latter consists in is already understood on the ordinary conception of mind (it is in fact the same as what Freud calls descriptive unconsciousness).

The qualified spatialization of consciousness that can be located in ordinary thought about the mind thus provides a source of motivation, and one free from conceptual confusion, for Freud's topographic characterization of the consciousness; we may then suggest that Freud's conception of the mind in topographic terms is a continuous extension of the ordinary conception of the mind.

The foregoing analysis of what it is to be in consciousness has further importance for the concept of unconscious mentality, in the following way. If the equivocal nature of the notion of a mental state's being in consciousness is overlooked, and all mentality is taken to be in consciousness in the strong sense appropriate only to such items as pains, then we will of course arrive immediately at a highly skeptical view of Freud's concept of unconscious mentality – which does indeed then look as if it involves "abstraction," an illegitimate extrapolation from everything with which we are familiar. When, however, we recall that there is in ordinary thought a way of describing mental states' relation to consciousness that unequivocally supports a distinction between mental states and the consciousness that there is of them, we break with strong idealism, as it might be called, about mentality:[6] We suppose that mental states like beliefs do not exist solely by virtue of consciousness of them. Freud's notion of unconscious mentality is arrived at by pressing the distinction of mental states from consciousness and combining it with explicit topographic characterization, in which psychological locales are spoken of as existing independently from their members at any given moment.

It may be acknowledged that a *weak* form of the claim that mental states depend upon consciousness nevertheless remains an option, in terms of what has so far been argued, to the extent that it may still be thought that the existence of an individual mental state remains *dependent* upon corresponding *possibilities* of manifestation. But to break with this weaker view it would be necessary only to find specific, well-articulated reasons for thinking that mental states can and do exist in the absence of the usual possibilities of manifestation. It is of course the defining claim of psychoanalysis that such reasons exist; as Freud says in the prefatory quotation, we have to look at "pathological material," of which philosophers are ignorant insofar as they do not appreciate the specific needs for explanation that such empirical material creates, in order to grasp these reasons.

It is not easy to conceive of an argument for thinking that this defining claim of psychoanalysis is false a priori, and that the reasons adduced in support of psychonanalytic claims cannot pull their weight – by, for example, ruling out unconscious mental states on the grounds that mental phenomena are to be identified outright with dispositions to utterance – which is not also objectionably reductive.

Nevertheless, the claim for dependence needs to be examined. There are in fact two forms of dependence to consider: causal and conceptual dependence. Could the dependence be causal? It is, once again, very hard to see what argument there could be for the unrestricted universal law "If something is a mental state, then it must be able to cause manifestations of itself" that would not simply beg the question against psychoanalysis.

Could the dependence be conceptual? A more fundamental objection can be made to this proposal. Such a view would be ultimately indistinguishable from a kind of "phenomenalism" about the mental; that is, it would amount to an *identification* of mental states with either actual or possible manifestations. By saying that conceptual dependence is in this context ultimately indistinguishable from a kind of phenomenalism, it is not of course meant that "X's are conceptually dependent on Y's" is logically equivalent to "X's are actual or possible Y's." Rather, what is meant is that, *in the present case*, if conceptual dependence is alleged to be sufficiently strong to rule out unconscious mental states, no reason can be given by anyone who wishes to hold the claim of dependence for not also accepting the second, reductionist claim; the motivation for the two are equivalent, and the second claim is more economical than the first.

Without taking up the issue of whether phenomenalist paraphrases for the mental can be made out with any plausibility, two observations can be made. First, whatever motivation there may be for phenomenalism with regard to the physical world (such as epistemological security) carries over very poorly to the mental. Second, phenomenalism with regard to the mental makes it much more difficult to see how the mental can still be thought of as a system of causally interrelated states; indeed, it seems to require the further, highly unexplanatory thought that consciousness is a creator *ex nihilo* of mental states.

So the question of whether there exist mental states that are independent of possibilities of manifestation appears to be open to empirical determination. Is there, however, some way in which we could know in advance that there can be no empirical need for the unconscious?

In William James's *The Principles of Psychology*,[7] the concept of unconscious mentality is considered in terms of its role as a necessary concomitant of what James calls "mind-stuff" theories, by which he means theories that regard mental states as empirically analyzable compounds. James considers that we might be inclined to introduce unconscious mental states to account for habitual action, for the nonreflective exercise of complex competences, and for the capacity to make associative connections between ideas nonreflectively. Also included by James, as inviting the postulation of unconscious mentality, are those numerous explananda – such as mental confusion in its many forms, the component of suffering in desire and disquiet, and unattended sense-awareness, where something is sensed but not noticed, which is happening all the time – which include some of the considerations that led Leibniz to postulate *petites perceptions* (perceptions too small, brief, unintense, or lacking in novelty or variation, to appear in consciousness).[8] A genuine puzzle is constituted by such explananda for anyone who wishes to view psychological attribution as a form of causal explanation. It is in fact highly arguable, following Leibniz, that the existence of the unconscious in this descriptive sense of the term is, for anyone who does take a causal-realist view of ordinary psychology, neither inferred nor a contingent matter but a necessity. All, however, that James is able to do when faced with this problem is to refer either to the possibility of making the brain occupy the relevant role, or to suppose that we instantaneously (in some peculiarly extended sense of the term) "forget" many of our "feelings." So long as we do not see sufficient reason to pass the task of explanation on to neurophysiology, James's first proposal is not relevant, and it is obvious that his substitution of "forgotten feelings" for "unconscious mentality" does nothing to provide a clear or adequate means of handling the class of explananda under consideration.

The following replies may now be made to the original grounds for dissatisfaction with the concept of unconscious mentality. Antiabstractionism: It has been suggested that the ordinary concept of a mental state like a belief already extrapolates or "abstracts" from conscious experience in the relevant sense, sufficiently so to make room for the stronger notion of unconscious mentality that Freud employs. Dependence for causal power: Similarly, it does not seem to be any part of the ordinary view of the mind either that only the manifestations of mental states like beliefs are causally efficacious, or that such mental states are only causally efficacious in so far as they are manifest; that is, we ordinarily take it that beliefs and desires do their work in the mind *not just* because there is consciousness of them. (This holds for at least the central range of their effects. There are of course *some* kinds of effect – such as those that are bound up with deliberation – for each of which it is true that a mental state must be conscious in order to achieve those effects.) The ordinary conception of consciousness does not make conscious status a precondition for possession of causal power, but instead makes causal power transcendent of the consciousness that there is of it. Redundancy: James's alternative proposal fails to achieve a clean victory, so it remains an open question whether or not there are good empirical reasons for adducing the Freudian unconscious.

At the point where we attempt to introduce mental states that cannot be manifested, we will be saying one of two things: either that there are mental states that are *accidentally* unmanifestable, or that there are mental states that are *nonaccidentally* unmanifestable. The distinction of accidentality rests on a notion of *kinds* of mental state, or in other terms, of what is and is not due to the intrinsic nature of a mental state.

It will now be helpful if we spell out more precisely various conceptions of the psychoanalytic concept of the unconscious in terms of successive degrees of independence from the concept of consciousness:

(a) The unconscious as entirely composed of ideas that *were conscious* and have been repressed; this would meet what we could call the "Lockeian" condition on mentality (that there can be nothing in the mind that has not previously been in awareness).[9]

(b) The unconscious either as entirely composed of, or at least as including some ideas that were not originally conscious but that *could become conscious.*

(c) The unconscious as either entirely composed of, or at least as including some ideas that were not originally conscious and that *could not become conscious.*

The first and second conceptions employ the notions of accidental unconsciousness, the third that of nonaccidental unconsciousness.

The last of these conceptions matches the unconscious in the writings of Melanie Klein and W. R. Bion, but it is also, most probably, attributable to Freud. There is evidence that Freud allowed for, and to a certain extent employed (c), even if he did not pursue its possibilities as far as certain of his successors have done. This evidence is not, however, supplied by his description of instincts as things that are innate and that cannot possibly become objects of consciousness, since these were regarded by Freud not as mental, but rather as physical (1915d, XIV, 148 and 1915e, XIV, 177). The evidence comes instead from Freud's explicit statements that the concept of the unconscious is *broader* than that of the repressed, together with his further admission of a phylogenetic heritage and of the existence of primal fantasies.[10]

A further question should now be raised regarding the various strengths of conception: Is there any good *conceptual* reason for preferring to confine the concept of the unconscious to strength (b) or even (a)? The Lockeian condition, which would at first glance have such a consequence, seems compatible with realism about unconscious mental states, and to add only a genetic condition on their existence. But there is, it may now be observed, something objectionably *arbitrary* about the Lockeian condition: If an idea can become unconscious at a later time, why can it not be originally unconscious and later *become* conscious? What is the rationale for the temporal asymmetry in the Lockeian condition? The only possible rationale for the Lockeian condition would seem to lie, once again, in a view to the effect that the *creation* of a mental item somehow involves consciousness as a genetic ingredient. But this notion – which seems to demand that consciousness be regarded as a *creative cause* – is certainly not to be found in common sense, and it is very hard to see what sort of philosophical backing, compatible with

ordinary psychological realism, could be provided for it. (Th
tions to the Lockeian condition here recapitulate the earl'
tions to phenomenalism with regard to the mental.)

If this is right, then it would be unjustified to hold the concept of
the unconscious at (a): Ordinary psychological realism leads straight
to (b). And the further move from (b) to (c) is, as we have already said,
made by subtracting the possibility of manifestation. What then
licenses this further move?

The rationale for denying that (at least some) psychoanalytic unconscious states are of a kind that can be manifested lies in the
difference between their fundamental features and those of mani-
festable mental states. These features are the "special characteristics of the system *Ucs*" (1915e, XIV, pt. V). They explain their states'
nonmanifestability, in that these states are sufficiently different *in
internal constitution* from states that can be manifested so as not to
be such as to possibly appear, except in distorted and indirect forms,
and under special conditions (such as dreaming), in consciousness.
In Kleinian theory this kind of rationale is greatly elaborated, as
unconscious states are identified with fantasies, whose objects constitute an inner world, the apprehension of which does not engage
the same psychological powers as are exercised in awareness of external reality.

How, in view of all this, the concept of the unconscious should be
coordinated with that of repression – whether the connection is conceptual or ultimately contingent – depends, in the first instance,
upon how broadly we conceive of repression. There is a narrow
understanding of the concept of repression (that which is most
closely aligned with the model of hysterical "forgetting") according
to which it denotes a particular species of psychic defense (on which
reading its importance in Freud's writings steadily declines, and the
concept is virtually eliminated in Kleinian theory). On a broader
reading of the concept, whether or not there is also a use of the term
to denote a particular species of defense, repression, although it is
never equivalent to "unconscious defense," remains involved, if
only implicitly, as a *component* of all forms of unconscious psychic
defense.[11] So, the repressed narrowly construed can be regarded as
coextensive with the unconscious of strengths (a) and (b), but not (c);
for the unconscious according to conception (c), the narrow concept
of repression will be necessary to account for at most some uncon-

scious contents. On the broader reading, by contrast, repression is part of the causal explanation of all unconscious processes.

In a restricted sense, then, it may be held that whereas for (a) and (b), the concept of the unconscious *derives* from that of repression, which is a view that some of Freud's remarks suggest,[12] for (c) this is not the case. We should, however, beware of misunderstanding this statement as implying that (c) involves a conceptual jump, as if with (a) and (b) we are working with a concept of the unconscious that can be logically derived from inside ordinary thought, and with (c) we are not. The bare concept of unconscious mental existence is *constant* throughout (a) to (c). What changes is just the *explanation* of nonmanifestability. So (c) does not represent a radical conceptual departure from common sense, and does not require any other, special *conceptual* condition to be met for its intelligibility to be vouchsafed.

A different question now requires attention. It had been supposed, in line with the prefatory quotation from Freud, that positive reason to believe in the existence of the unconscious may come, and does in fact come, from empirical quarters. Is there a single and unified way of characterizing the *kind* of reason that Freud thought warranted the adduction of the unconscious? Freud wrote: "It [the unconscious] is *necessary* because the data of consciousness have a very large number of gaps in them" (1915e, XIV, 166).[13] The terms of this suggestion may seem to rub up against an important philosophical and intuitively appealing view, to the effect that consciousness is characterized by a special kind of unity, on account of which it can not logically tolerate "gaps" of any kind. But we do not need to challenge this doctrine in order to understand Freud's assertion. We can interpret Freud's notion in terms of *gaps in self-explanation.* These gaps are as such fully *psychological in nature* – they occur at points where we would ordinarily expect an intentional psychological explanation to be available – and in this way they stand apart from other, merely nominal gaps in ordinary psychological explanation (such as, for example, the impossibility of explaining in intentional terms *how it is* that one ordinarily remembers something).

We are, however, left with the following puzzle: What relation holds between the existence of a mental state and consciousness of it? An anxiety surfaces at this point, which is that, if it is so much as conceded that there *could be* such a thing as a mental state without consciousness, and on that account we break a strong definitional connection of mentality with consciousness, then, because no way exists of showing how mentality can *imply* consciousness, the admission of an unconscious will have inadvertently ousted us altogether, qua our conscious existence, from reality (this was a worry, and a line of objection to psychoanalysis, of Sartre's[14]). Now, it is no doubt true that psychoanalytic theory heightens our intellectual awareness of general problems of mind, in particular of the problem of securing causal-explanatory value for the mental without making the particular feature of consciousness seem epiphenomenal; but, in the terms set up over the course of the preceding discussion, it has already been indicated in what way the anxiety may be allayed.

It is not the case that the very idea of unconscious mentality implies that conscious status is only an epiphenomenal property, or that it is only ever an accidental property of mental states. This consequence is in fact blocked by the fact that we *introduced* the concept of the unconscious by reference to that of consciousness, and did not do so in a way that implied that consciousness is epiphenomenal. This manner of introducing the concept of the unconscious establishes a broad (and, from the psychoanalytic point of view, wholly acceptable) conceptual dependence of unconscious on conscious mentality. A *general* dependence of the concept of a mental state on that of consciousness does not entail the possession by each *species* of mental state of the feature of consciousness: Psychoanalytically attributed states can lack manifestability and yet not be conceptually independent of consciousness, for the reason that they are necessarily parts of *the mind*, the concept of which *is* connected with that of consciousness.

Psychoanalytic theory thus has no need to deny that, if there were no phenomenon of self-consciousness, there would be no unconscious, or that – for a large range of mental states – the feature of consciousness is highly causally significant. Indeed, the claim for the efficacy of psychoanalytic therapy (although this is not as straightforward a matter as is often supposed) *requires* such supposition.

This is as true for the second topography as it is for the first. Although the second topography does not have explicitly marked out on it a particular place called consciousness, it does not *exclude* such an identification: *Cs* can readily be mapped onto appropriate parts of the ego. And the concept of a mental state that is employed on the second topography is philosophically no more independent from the concept of consciousness than is the concept of a mental state employed on the first topography. The difference consists in just the fact that, on the second topography, the characterization of unconscious mental states in terms of their (in)susceptibility to manifestation, because this feature is no longer supposed to correlate in a reliable way with those causal properties of mental states most significant for psychoanalytic theory, is no longer built into the model. So again, the second topography does not, just because it has no fixed or explicit locale for consciousness, imply its elements' conceptual independence from that concept.

Without being able to explain the nature of the relation between mentality and consciousness, psychoanalytic theory can nevertheless be relieved of some of the burden, and protected against the ravages of, philosophy.

3. *What* kind *of entity is supposed by speaking of the "unconscious"?* In particular: What significance is borne by Freud's nominalization, "*the* unconscious" (which may seem to pointedly mark a certain distance from any commonsense view of the mind)?

We might initially think it appropriate to try to read "the unconscious" as elliptical for an expression that would read in full something like, to take an obvious example, "unconscious mind." Whether or not Freud always intended the expression to be read in this way, which seems unlikely, the important philosophical question is in any case the following: What sortal, or more general term, does the unconscious fall under? What *sort* of a thing is the unconscious?

Now it is clear that in considering this issue we are at the same time brought up against the crucially important question of to what extent Freud envisaged the hypothesis of the unconscious as showing that we are in some novel, or unanticipated, or counterintuitive sense constitutionally "divided" or nonunitary kinds of being ("multiple selves," as it has been suggested we should call the products of Freudian and similar speculation[15]).

The question of the magnitude or severity of the division of personality envisaged by Freud can be put into focus more sharply by asking the following, more formal question: Is the sortal under which the unconscious falls one that is distinct from, and not logically subsumable under, the sortal that is employed in, at a fundamental level, individuating a person? To this question there will be three kinds of answer: a negative answer, and weak and strong versions of an affirmative answer.

The *negative* answer will be to the effect that the concept of the unconscious may either be formally compared to such concepts as that of the memory or the will, terms that designate faculties or functions, pitched at a level of description clearly compatible with the strongest views of the unity of the person; or (although this second view is not exclusive of the first) it should be understood as referring simply to the set of mental states that are unconscious and in other ways possessed of special features that make them worth distinguishing as a unitary mental phenomenon.[16]

The *weakly divisive* answer will be to the effect that the introduction of the unconscious does introduce a new sortal, one not even latently available in pretheoretical views of the mental, but whose employment does not involve any radical inconsistency with those views.

The *strongly divisive* answer, by contrast, will be to the effect that the concept of the unconscious does involve the introduction of a sortal whose use is inconsistent with, and controverts, ordinary views of the unity of the person. This view will be held by anyone who thinks that the unconscious falls under a sortal of a kind that is in fact given application at the basic point at which a person is individuated, from which it will follow that Freudian theory shows us to be *multiples* of that of which we previously took ourselves to be single instances.

It is important to make explicit what would be two *bad* reasons for taking Freud to be committed to a person-divisive view. First, Freud is not committed to such a view by his claim (in the passage quoted at the beginning, and elsewhere – 1915e, XIV, 169 and 1933a [1932], XXII, 70) that knowledge of the unconscious is grounded in a similar way to knowledge of another person's mind. For the use of such a ground is just as compatible with the view that what is ascribed in speaking of the unconscious is just a further set of mental states, as it is with the view that what is ascribed is a second mind in a person-divisive sense. Second, he is not so committed by his description of the mind on the topographic model as "built up of a number of *agencies* or *systems*" (1925d [1924], XX, 32), for these are terms used in a special way, and it is a further question what precisely Freud took them to signify.

In support of the negative answer, it may be pointed out that, as Richard Wollheim notes,[17] conflictual relations between conscious and unconscious systems do not ever hold between them merely by virtue of their difference as regards the (un)conscious status, understood descriptively, of their elements: such a difference does not *of itself* engender conflict. Consciousness and unconsciousness are not intrinsically inimical properties, and *Cs-Pcs* and *Ucs* are not *intrinsically* antagonistic to each other; conflict occurs between them only because of the particular character of the contents of *Ucs* and their consequent connection with repression.

Does the picture change, however, when we move to consider the second, "structural" topography? The second topography only provides an explicit expression of facts already recognized on the first, while reversing its order of priority, by making the identification of the place of a mental item independent of the identification of its descriptively (un)conscious status. There is then, again, no fundamental conceptual shift involved in the transition to the second topography,[18] a point that is also shown by the fact that Freud's later forms of description explicitly combine the second topography with the first.[19] Given that the first topography is not metaphysically person-divisive, and that the second is contained immanently in the first, it would be inconsistent to view the second but not the first topography as metaphysically person-divisive.

It is, furthermore, important to bear in mind the distinction between constitutional conflict and metaphysical person-division as defined earlier: The latter is not implied by the former. Constitutional conflict is indeed built into the second, as it is not into the first, topography; but this is because the two topographies employ different kinds of characterization of mental parts (for which reason they are in principle compatible), and not because the transition from the first topography to the second necessarily involves a heightening of personal division. Whether the fact that the psychological structure of a person implies conflict divides the person in a metaphysical sense depends on the further character of the constitutionally conflicting parts.

It is to be stressed that Freud exhibits the functional interdepen-

dence, as much as he does the conflict, of the parts. They are on the
second topography related to one another as different stages in psychological processing, where 'process' is defined with respect to a
single whole organism. It is indeed *because* this is so – because they
each require one another in order to constitute a human organism,
and because a whole human organism is presupposed for their
existence – that intrapsychic conflict is inevitable. It is also to be
observed that much important psychic conflict on the second topography occurs *within* the ego, indicating that Freud's intrapsycho-
logical criteria of individuation were not exclusively guided by facts
of conflict. The ego, id, and superego, as parts of the soul, do war, but
they are not each of them warring souls.[20]

Sartre's well-known criticism of Freud, which focuses on Freud's
notion (in the theory of dreams) of the censor mechanism, took Freud,
however, to be committed to the strongly divisive answer. Sartre
claimed: "By the distinction between the 'id' and the 'ego,' Freud has
cut the psychic whole into two. I am the ego but I am not the id. . . . By
rejecting the conscious unity of the psyche, Freud is obliged to imply
everywhere a magic unity."[21] Sartre went on to locate paradox in such
a conception of the person. Is Freud committed to a metaphysically
person-divisive view of the kind that Sartre identifies as his target,
albeit, perhaps, contrary to his own intentions?

What the question ultimately hangs on, it may be suggested, is
this: Is it necessary, as Sartre in fact supposes, to think of the unconscious, or any distinct entity required by the characteristic form of
psychoanalytic explanation, to take possession of the beliefs of the
person and to execute intentions directed toward the person's mind,
in such a way as to manifest a point of view of its own, one that is
not the same as that of the person in whole? If that were so, it would
be true that the person is deeply divided, for there would then be
contained within him or her something that ill-deserves being described as a "mechanism" and in fact amounts to a "proto-person."
A problem would then arise regarding the causal genesis of this
mental part, and the suspicion would form that the hypothesized
mental part is nothing but the person in whole under another name
(indicating some sort of deep logical confusion in psychoanalytic
theory).[22]

By way of defusing this criticism, a first important comment is the
following: Psychoanalytic theory is entitled to use the concept of a

disposition, in a sense that does not imply the presence of intentions within the mind, and in its developed form psychoanalytic metapsychology in fact does so (in, to take a central case, the theory of signal anxiety; 1926d [1925], XX, 125–6), in a way that makes the activation of a disposition take over the work done in Freud's earlier theoretical account by the censor mechanism.

The adequacy of replies to Sartre of this general kind turns, however, on another question, which concerns how much we have to use the unconscious to explain. What ultimately decides the issue between Freud and Sartre is how much *rationality*, or capacity for *strategic thought*, is invested by Freud in his account of the unconcious: If rationality, marked by the capacity to formulate *intentions*, is involved in unconscious thought, then the unconscious approximates to a proto-person, but if it is not involved, then it need not be so conceived.

Although it might perhaps be argued on Sartre's behalf that there is reason for thinking that, in the case histories, Freud ought to have conceived the unconscious as capable of manipulative intent, there is conclusive evidence that he did not aim to do so. Freud is categorical that in all the cases of unconscious motivation with which psychoanalytic theory is concerned, a firm distinction is to be drawn between the influence of the unconscious proper, *Ucs*, whose operation is always conceived by way of extrapolation from the *non*-strategic model of wish-fulfillment, as a process in which representations of needed but unavailable objects are formed in direct response to frustration, without any mediation by thought; and the operation of desires in *Pcs*, which may have a strategic character, in such a way that the latter is dependent on the former. So any phenomenon that emerges in psychoanalysis that appears to exhibit strategicality is to be regarded as issuing directly from *Pcs*, not *Ucs*, and there will be an expectation that a corresponding wish can be located in *Ucs*, one that lends force to and that is (in a sense that does not imply strategicality) subserved by, the desire in *Pcs*.[23]

We can now see why there is a difference in principle, and not one in name only, between Freud's concept of the unconscious and alternative attempts to conceptualize the same set of facts in terms of a second consciousness, or a dissociated or (in Pierre Janet's phrase) *désagrégé* part of the mind,[24] which do have person-divisive implications. Freud's alternative is more conceptually conservative than

Janet's, and thus requires less philosophical defense. (Also, it does not confront the objection that no explanation is given for the existence of isolated pockets of mental life.)

The conclusion of this section is that psychoanalytic theory can protect itself against all of the embarrassments that Sartre attempts to create for it, and return at most a weakly divisive, and probably only a *negative* answer to the original question of person division, by construing itself in a way that leans on the attribution of *nonintentional* mental processes.

4. *What is the nature of the states attributed by psychoanalysis?* More specifically: Given the distinguishing "special characteristics of the system *Ucs*," how *like* conscious mental states, conceptually, are unconscious mental states?

The question will be taken up here with respect to only four of the many possible respects of comparison.

(i) Are unconscious mental states *propositional?* That they are, is something that might well be doubted, in view of the connection between the concept of a propositional attitude and the idea of the mind as a system that is tied down, by way of the truth-directedness of its beliefs, to how things really are in the world. Unconscious states are insensitive to reality and do not cause action in such a way as to reflect a grasp of reality. Unconscious states are not directly tied down to external states of affairs in the way that beliefs are, nor are they tied down indirectly in the way that desires are, by virtue of being the natural and logical companions of beliefs: Unconscious states do not pair with beliefs to form reasons for action. Freud writes: "Belief (and doubt) is a phenomenon that belongs wholly to the system of the ego (the *Cs*) and has no counterpart in the *Ucs*" (1950a [1887–1902], I, 255).

If unconscious states are not strictly propositional attitudes, they nevertheless have content: We describe them in terms of objects and states of affairs that we take them to somehow represent, and we take them to explain action by supposing that they somehow purposefully cause action that in some sense "projects" the state of affairs that they represent. How might one envisage the nature of their content? We might decide to call such states "prepropositional." This would not entail that they are (as "information" in cognitive psychology is ordinarily conceived to be) "subpersonal," any more than calling the content of a visual representation such as a painting nonpropositional would commit one to saying that its content was therefore not the topic of a person's understanding. The model of visual representation seems to provide us with just the right analogy, and it invites us to say that (at a minimum) unconscious states have representational content just in the sense that they impinge upon persons in such a way as to introduce thoughts of specific states of affairs into their minds, and thereby bear on the content of persons' full-fledged propositional attitudes. This proposal also accords with the Kleinian conception of the unconscious as incorporating an inner world, conceived as a scene of fantasy.

(ii) Do unconscious states have a *phenomenological character?* The question of the existence of unconscious phenomenology naturally takes off from the case of unconscious emotions. Freud made a special case for emotions, devoting to them the third section of his 1915 paper on the unconscious. He however did not think that emotions could be unconscious in an unqualified sense, because he took emotion to involve awareness (1915e, XIV, 177).

It is questionable whether Freud was right to take such a conservative view of unconscious emotion, especially given that he also spoke of the unconscious as a locale of pleasure and unpleasure (1920g, XVIII, pts. I–III). An argument for the possibility of unconscious emotion might proceed by reiterating the argument for basic psychological realism in Section 2: We do not ordinarily take it that it is the aspect of an emotion that consists in its appearing to consciousness (which is what we might ordinarily call the "feeling") that has causal power, but rather that the appearing is *of* something with causal power (separating the emotion from the feeling of it in the same way as the belief and its manifestation in a thought-episode are separated). By again subtracting the fact of manifestation, we arrive at the idea of unconscious emotion.

Can we still talk of an unconscious emotion as being efficacious *by virtue of how it feels?* We can, so long as it is granted – which is plausible – that there is *a* concept of feeling that does not imply explicit conscious awareness. Then we can say that what in part ordinarily gives an emotion its causal power is the phenomenological property that it is apprehended as having when a feeling manifests it. This makes room for the claim that there are unconscious emotions in the strong sense that they are states whose causal power derives in part from their phenomenology (which are effective in certain directions and not others because of how they feel).

The suggestion that there are full-fledged unconscious emotions has a general importance, in that phenomenological properties (unconscious pain, pleasure, and anxiety) seem to be required as *crucial determinants* of the course of unconscious processes.[25] That phenomenological properties have a heightened causal value in the unconscious is of course just what one would expect, given its instinctual, infantile, fantastic, and so forth character.

(iii) Are unconscious states *theoretical* states? The fact that we speak of "psychoanalytic theory" does not of course by itself bind us to viewing psychoanalytic attributions as attributions of theoretical states, any more than speaking of a theory of colors commits us to viewing colors as theoretical properties. It might seem however that Freud's opening statement that psychoanalytic theory "regard[s] everything mental as being in the first place unconscious" chimes in with the view that the states attributed by psychoanalysis are theoretical, simply because theoreticality does not create an expectation of (and perhaps does not even allow for) consciousness.[26]

Four considerations inveigh, however, against this suggestion.

One is that the conceptual materials required for understanding introducing psychoanalytic concepts are (as the second section tried to emphasize) readily available in ordinary talk about the mind.

A second consideration is that unconscious states are, it has been suggested, imbued with phenomenological properties, and these are properties of a kind notoriously difficult to incorporate in the theoretical framework. Whereas paradigm *rational* action explanations can arguably omit references to phenomenological properties, or be reconstructed in ways that make reference to only *beliefs* about phenomenological properties, none of this is true for psychoanalytic explanations.

A third consideration is this: Insofar as we adopt an outlook governed purely by theoretical considerations, we will be led to postulate states defined by causal role, in response to demands formulated in exclusively third-person terms, and not constrained by experience in any nontheoretical sense. There can be no guarantee that what we are led in that way to postulate will bear the right kind of intimate, resonant relation to experience that we rightfully expect from psychological language and that psychoanalytic language seems to possess in full.[27]

The fourth, and most compelling consideration follows on from the third, and it concerns the manner of our knowledge of the unconscious. Is it in fact the case that just because the unconscious *is* (in the descriptive sense) unconscious, that it can only be epistemically fixed in the two third-person connections referred to in the first section, and that experience is unable to play a direct, nontheoretical role in constraining our thought about unconscious mentality? The data of clinical practice, both implicitly and explicitly, suggest quite the opposite: The unconscious can *also* be epistemically fixed through something that we could call the "quasi-manifestability" of unconscious states. To *some* degree the unconscious is introspectable: People who have undergone analysis for a certain length of time come to be able to recognize events in their unconscious – activations of impulses, onsets of fantastic activity, and so forth – as they occur. They are then aware of these movements of their mind in such a way that they can identify their content and direction, and can perhaps do something to hinder them, but without being able to fully control (let alone initiate) them.

Certainly quasi-manifestability is not an autonomous epistemic route to the unconscious; it is conditional upon the analysand's prior adoption of a third-person perspective on himself or herself in the psychoanalytic context. Only in this way can psychoanalytic concepts be acquired. We should thus modify the earlier definition of unconscious mentality as mental states lacking in possibilities of manifestation; rather, they allow for manifestation in a finer and conditional sense.

We may then suggest that the psychoanalytic concept of the unconscious appears to fit best with a realistic view of psychological language. Freud's statement (in the prefatory quotation) that the "question as to the ultimate nature of this unconscious is no more sensible or profitable than the older one as to the nature of the conscious" may be understood as implying that a shift into a theoretical gear is not needed in order to make sense of unconscious mentality.

(iv) Are unconscious states *"owned by" the person* to whom they are attributed, in the way that conscious states are? If we break connections with manifestation (even just the usual ones, rather than all), by virtue of what can states attributed to a person still be considered to *belong to them*, in the ordinary pretheoretical sense of that expression, rather than be thought of as part of their "sub-personal" constitution? We are left with a tough question that is again bound up with the metaphysical identity of persons.

The worry is that on the spectrum between a paradigmatic self-ascribed state of pain, and a state ascribed in cognitive psychology, psychoanalytic states, by virtue of their unavailability for self-ascription without a process of conceptual education, fall too close to the latter to be considered properly the person's. What then can hold them in place, properly attached to the person?

The reasons for continuing to regard unconscious states as owned by the person are surely the following: They have none of the hard-edged scientific character of the attributions of cognitive psychology; they participate intimately in the person's mental, particularly emotional life, and provide the wellsprings of motivation; and they are quasi-manifestable.

One might be satisfied with quasi-manifestability and the other features as sufficient conditions for the personal status of mental states. But one might, instead, either deny that there is quasi-manifestation, or reject it as sufficient for personal status. There is indeed natural room for doubt as to whether unconscious states are properly owned, given that – being in such a radical sense *unchosen* – they appear not to meet one of the obvious conditions for topics of personal responsibility. But perhaps, although we are not logically compelled to take responsibility for unconscious states and their immediate effects, and may without strict inconsistency refuse to identify with them, it can still be urged that *less distortion* is involved overall in so doing than would result from dissociating oneself from one's unconscious states by denying ownership of them; it appears easier, and more intuitively sound, to extend the bounds or responsibility so as to accommodate the unconscious than it does to contract the category of psychological ownership in such a way as to exclude states of a kind with such patent significance for the ways in which we react toward and engage with a person.[28]

We converge then, tentatively, on the following view of Freud's concept of the unconscious: as a set of states with representational

content distinguished by special features, which need not be regarded as propositional attitudes, characteristically endowed with
phenomenological properties, attributed in a spirit of plain psychological realism, and at least some of which cannot be manifested in
the ordinary sense, but which there is not sufficient reason for refusing to consider as properly owned by the person; composing an entity the supposition of which is consistent with ordinary views of
personal unity.

NOTES

1 The principal texts of Freud's in which the concept of the unconscious is
   discussed are "A Note on the Concept of the Unconscious in Psycho-
   Analysis" (1912g, XII), "Repression" (1915d, XIV), "The Unconscious"
   (1915e, XIX), "Some Elementary Lessons in Psycho-Analysis" (1940b
   [1938], XXIII) and The Ego and the Id (1923b, XIX, pt. I). I have relied
   heavily on Richard Wollheim, Freud (Glasgow: Fontana, 1971), ch. 6 and
   the succinct entry "Unconscious" in Jean Laplanche and J.-B. Pontalis's
   The Language of Psycho-Analysis, trans. Donald Nicholson-Smith, International Psycho-Analytical Library, vol. 94 (London: Hogarth Press and
   the Institute of Psycho-Analysis, 1983).
2 Sources of reference illustrating these features of the unconscious are, in
   order: descriptive versus dynamic senses (1915e, XIV, 172–3); as source
   of motivation (1895d [1893–5], II, 293); related to conflict (1895d, II,
   121–4); resistance (1914d, XIV, 16); transference (1916–17 [1915–17],
   XVI, Lecture XXVII); manifest in dreams (1915e, XIV, 187); related to
   memory (1895d [1893–5], II, pt. I); as neural (1950a, I, 234); as Ucs
   (1915e, XIV, pt. II); repression (1915d, XIV); excludes second consciousness (1910a [1909], XI, 25–6 and 1910i, XI, 211–13); distinct from Pcs
   (1940a [1938], XXIII, pt. IV); corresponding neural feature (1920g, XVIII,
   34); autonomous (1925d [1924], XX, 32 and 1900a, V, 536); ideas and
   instincts (1915d, XIV, 148 and 1915e, XIV, 177); unconscious emotion
   (1915e, XIV, pt. III); primary process (1950a [1887–1902], I, 324–7 and
   1900a, V, 598–601); pleasure principle (1911b, XII); structural model
   (1923b, XIX, pt. II).
3 Freud describes the "equation" of what is conscious with what is mental
   as "either a petitio principii which begs the question whether everything
   that is psychical is also necessarily conscious; or else it is a matter of
   convention, of nomenclature" (1915e, XIV, 167). He says the same in
   1912g, XII, 260. Nevertheless, Freud thought of it as in some sense the
   accepted or natural view; see 1940b [1938], XXIII, 283.

4 William James for example speaks of the "unintelligibility" of the notion of unconscious mentality, and asserts that "we find that we can express all the observed facts in other ways" in *The Principles of Psychology*, vol.1 (1890) (New York: Dover, 1980), p. 175.

5 The term "manifestation" is taken from Wollheim, *The Thread of Life* (Cambridge: Cambridge University Press, 1984): see pp. 168–70. Note also Wollheim's coordination of the concepts of consciousness and unconsciousness, ibid, p. 45.

6 Of the kind expressed in James's statement that "the essence of feeling [by which James seems to mean any psychological state or event] is to be felt, and as a psychic existent *feels*, so it must *be*" (*The Principles of Psychology*, vol. 1, p. 163).

7 Ibid, ch. 6.

8 See *New Essays on Human Understanding*, trans. Peter Remnant and Jonathan Bennett (Cambridge: Cambridge University Press, 1981), pp. 53–6 and 164–7. Freud acknowledged the existence of this, or a highly similar, nonpathological puzzle (1940a [1938], XXIII, 157 and 1940b [1938], XXIII, 283–4).

9 See *An Essay Concerning Human Understanding* (1690), ed. Peter H. Nidditch (Oxford: Clarendon, 1975), I, iii, 20.

10 See Freud (1907a [1906], IX, 48; 1915d, XIV, 147–8; 1915e, XIV, 166; and 1923b, XIX, 18). A distinction between innate and acquired unconscious contents is made in 1940a [1938], XXIII, 163: The former include the id's "scarcely accessible nucleus." Phylogenetically innate primal fantasies are identified by Freud in the case of the Wolfman: see 1918b [1914], XVII, 120. See also 1921c, XVIII, 75 n1 and 1916–17 [1915–17], XVI, 368–71.

11 On repression, and this distinction, see the entry "Repression" in Laplanche and Pontalis, *The Language of Psycho-Analysis*.

12 "Thus we obtain our concept of the unconscious from the theory of repression. The repressed is the prototype of the unconscious for us" (1923b, XIX, 15).

13 See Wollheim, *Freud*, p. 159 and James, *The Principles of Psychology*, vol. 1, pp. 239–40.

14 See "Consciousness of Self and Knowledge of Self," 139–40, trans. Mary Ellen and Nathaniel Lawrence, in Nathaniel Lawrence and Daniel O'Conner, eds, *Readings in Phenomenological Psychology* (Englewood Cliffs, N.J.: Prentice-Hall, 1967).

15 Jon Elster, Introduction to *The Multiple Self*, ed. Jon Elster (Cambridge: Cambridge University Press, 1985).

16 This is in line with Wollheim's view: see "The Mind and the Mind's Image of Itself," in *On Art and the Mind* (London: Allen Lane, 1973).

17 Wollheim, *Freud*, pp. 174–5.

18 Ibid, p. 174.

19 See 1923b, XIX, pt. II; 1933a [1932], XXII, Lecture XXXI; and 1940a [1938]: XXIII.

20 See Brian O'Shaughnessy's discussion of this topic in "The Id and the Thinking Process," in Richard Wollheim and James Hopkins, eds, *Philosophical Essays on Freud* (Cambridge: Cambridge University Press, 1982).

21 *Being and Nothingness: An Essay on Phenomenological Ontology*, trans. Hazel E. Barnes (London: Methuen, 1958), pp. 50–3. The same criticism was made earlier by V. N. Vološinov in *Freudianism: A Critical Sketch* (1927), trans. I. R. Titunik, ed. I. R. Titunik and Neal H. Bruss (New York: Academic Press, 1976), p. 70.

22 It is a difficult question whether the theory of "sub-systems" in the writings on irrationality of Donald Davidson and David Pears returns the strongly divisive, or only a weakly divisive answer to the original question, and how it fares with Sartre's criticism. See Davidson, "Paradoxes of Irrationality," in Wollheim and Hopkins, eds. *Philosophical Essays on Freud*; "Deception and Division," in Elster, ed., *The Multiple Self*; and Pears, *Motivated Irrationality* (Oxford: Oxford University Press, 1984), ch. 5 and "Goals and Strategies of Self-deception," in Elster, ed., *The Multiple Self*.

23 A great many of Freud's clinical interpretations exemplify this structure. That *Ucs* is not capable of strategy is also shown very clearly by Freud's handling of ostensible cases of ratiocination in dreams (1900a, V, 418 and 445).

24 See Henri-Jean Barraud, *Freud at Janet: Étude Comparée* (Toulouse: Bibliothèque de Psychologie Clinique, 1971), ch. 7.

25 For particularly clear illustrations, see Wollheim, "The Bodily Ego," in Wollheim and Hopkins eds., *Philosophical Essays on Freud*, and Donald Meltzer, *Sexual States of Mind* (Perthshire: Clunie, 1973).

26 Statements that might be read as suggesting theoreticality are to be found in 1940a [1938] XXIII, 158–9 and 1925e [1924], XIX, 217.

27 See Wollheim, *Freud*, pp. 203–4.

28 See Freud's discussion of the question of moral responsibility for the content of dreams (1925i, XIX, (B), 131–4).

6 The development and vicissitudes of Freud's ideas on the Oedipus complex

The Oedipus complex lies at the heart of Freud's dynamic developmental theory. In the evolvement of psychoanalytic theory, this complex is associated with the entire range of feelings the child may experience in relation to his parents and interactions he or she may have with them. The love and hate of the Oedipus complex, the conflict, and the way in which the complex is resolved become at certain points the basis for the understanding not only of child development, personality trends, and psychopathology, but also of broader phenomena, such as the development of social institutions, religion, and morality.

Freud's ideas on the Oedipus complex emerge gradually; they change, the terminology is changed, the scope of what is to be considered oedipal is constricted and expanded. These developments and vicissitudes were influenced by a variety of factors. Freud's attempts to conceptualize intrapsychic material emerging from analyses of some of his patients, as well as from his self-analysis, his attempt to deal with opposing theories and their proponents, and the interaction of the oedipal complex with other focal theoretical issues, are among the major influential factors.

In the first section an outline of the basic stages in the evolution of Freud's ideas on the Oedipus complex is presented. In the second section we present some conjectures about events in Freud's personal and professional life that influenced the course of development of his ideas on the Oedipus complex.

EVOLUTION OF IDEAS ON THE OEDIPUS COMPLEX

Stage I: 1897–1909

This period is that of the pure positive oedipal dynamics. In his discussion of these dynamics the focus is on the love of the mother and the rivalry with the father. Loving and affectionate feelings toward the father are described by Freud. They are not, however, considered to be an inherent component of the oedipal drama. These affectionate feelings, which at times receive extensive attention by Freud, are, however, ascribed an important auxiliary role in relation to this drama. These feelings are seen to be the main motive behind repression of the hostility felt toward the father. The castration complex, later to be designated as *the* repressive force (1926d, XX, e.g., 108), is not yet central in this regard.

It is important to note here that throughout this period the adjective "oedipal" is reserved for the description of the basic unconscious tendencies that are revealed in the two criminal acts of the Greek king. A more encompassing term is employed to account for the more intricate matrix of feelings toward the father: the "father complex." Freud's frequent shifts from one term to the other tend, at times, to blur the distinction that he at this point seemed to maintain.

The myth of Oedipus Rex and the idea that the child's dynamic constellation corresponds to that of Oedipus (or in a later version of him as Hamlet) is first noted in Freud's letters to Fliess (1950a, I, e.g., 254–5, 253–66). There Freud was apparently sharing the products of his discoveries from his self-analysis. These insights are combined with other clinical data in his study of dreams (1900a, IV, e.g., 248–67). The major case studies of this period (Dora, 1905e, VII; Little Hans, 1909b, X; and the Rat Man, 1909d, X) all complement these studies by providing important illustrations of manifestations – normal and pathological – of the oedipal dynamics.

During this period of Freud's work the psychic development prior to the formation of the oedipal constellation was not systematically conceptualized. Freud's notions concerning early development were contained within the sketchy framework of stages of libido and the progression of the erotogenic zones. He is not precise on the ages of transition from anal to genital concerns, but oedipal strivings are noted well before age five or six. When Freud specifically conceptualized a preoedipal stage (see Stage VI), the framework of the drives and their vicissitudes was only loosely integrated with the dynamic oedipal and preoedipal constellation.

Stage II: 1909–14

This period is a turbulent one. It begins in 1909–10 with the crystallization and naming of the concept Oedipus complex as the central psychodynamic constellation. Three years, in which no mention of this complex or any other reference to Oedipus, follow. And it is concluded with *Totem and Taboo*, the book in which Freud presents a phylogenetic explanation of the oedipal complex.

One important factor that unites these years is Freud's focus on the boy's longing for his father. During the three-year interval in which the term "Oedipus" was neglected, Freud studied this longing through such concepts as the "father" and the "parental" complexes. In 1913 this idea of longing is gradually incorporated into the concept of the oedipal complex itself, and becomes an essential and important part of it.

In 1909 Freud briefly describes the oedipal dynamics discussed earlier, makes reference to the myth of King Oedipus "who killed his father and took his mother to wife" and proclaims that this complex "constitutes the *nuclear complex*" of every neurosis (1910a, XI, 47). It was only shortly later that the term "Oedipus complex" was coined and defined as a constellation of desire for the mother as a sexual object and hate of the father as a rival (1910h, XI, 171). Together with its characteristic defenses it becomes the central determinant of mental life, normal and pathological.

Despite the significance assigned to the oedipal complex in these years, no further reference to Oedipus is made until 1913. Freud, however, did not put aside the examination of the child's relationship to his parents. Most informative in this regard are Freud's careful studies of the lives of two public figures, Leonardo da Vinci and the Judge Schreber (1910c, XI; 1911c, XII). In both it is the special relationship of the boy to his father that is highlighted and further elaborated. At this juncture, the focus is on homosexual libido and affectionate feelings toward the father, issues that are not yet discussed in terms of the Oedipus complex per se.

It is in his book, *Totem and Taboo* (1912–13, XIII), that Freud reintroduces the Oedipus complex. With renewed vigor and a heightened sense of conviction, Freud restates his position that the oedipal complex is at the nucleus of neuroses and proceeds now to reveal its prehistoric mythical origins.

Throughout the work the father (and his predecessor, the primal father of the prehistoric myths) is described as combining in him all the loving and admirable characteristics of the fathers of Freud's case studies and at the same time as being a terrible, threatening and restrictive figure. For most of the book only the hatred of the rivalrous father is considered oedipal per se, with the loving feelings being assigned a role in the repression of the oedipal wishes, and the overall ambivalent and conflicted son–father relationship being referred to as the "father complex." Here Freud basically repeats the positions he presented in the case of little Hans, with perhaps a greater emphasis on the repressive force of the love. It is this love that is now seen to be at the basis of the development of a sense of *guilt* that restrains the hostile and incestuous impulses. In terms of what is oedipal, Freud's terminology seems to be identical to that of 1909. Toward the very end of the book, however, Freud's terminology undergoes a change. In the final pages of *Totem and Taboo* (pp. 156–7), Freud reiterates the centrality of the Oedipus complex and points to it as a source of religion, morals, society, and art. He then singles out a specific psychological problem in the ambivalence displayed toward cultural institutions and suggests that this is rooted in the father complex. Although not unambiguously stated, it is implied here that the father complex is now to be considered one aspect of the Oedipus complex – the latter being the all-encompassing complex and the ultimate foundation of all explanations. Thus, the son's ambivalence toward his father becomes an inherent factor in the Oedipus complex.

Stage III: 1914–18

During this period Freud's discussions of the oedipal complex focus primarily on instinctual and incestuous wishes. In addition to the two original oedipal wishes Freud now makes frequent note of incestuous strivings in relation to the father. This focus and addition are accompanied by a gradual decrease in the attention afforded to the affection and admiration the boy feels toward the father, the importance attributed to these, and the dyadic relationship that served as their context. The stage is set for the introduction of the negative oedipal complex.

This period begins with Freud's essay, "On the History of the Psycho-Analytic Movement" (1914d, XIV). There Freud, as he castigates Jung for his misinterpretation of the Oedipus complex, stresses that instinctual, incestuous impulses are the basic and essential components. He refers to the complex as "a conflict between ego dystonic erotic trends and self preservative ones" (62), and at one point even seems to exchange the term "Oedipus complex" with the term "sexual complexes." These references set the tone of this entire period.

The emphasis on instinctual, incestuous wishes in relation to the mother and on hostile ones in relation to the father persists throughout. In addition to these, Freud now makes several allusions to the possibility of an inverse or reversed triadic relationship; the father now becoming an object of incestuous wishes, and the mother a rival. During this period Freud does not, however, actually present the inverted Oedipus complex as a universal triadic relationship. In his analysis of the Wolf Man (1918b, XVII), Freud does come close to this. It is here, in fact, that the term "inverted Oedipus complex" is first introduced. And yet, it would seem that here the inverse relationship is seen to be reflective of early pathological interactions rather than a universal, normal constellation, and that the inversion pertains to the boy's relation to the father only, rather than to the triad. The early rivalry with the mother over the father here is absent.

Hand in hand with the focus on the instinctual wishes or impulses there is a noted deemphasis of the affectionate and admiring son–father dyadic relationship. As the idea that *all* such instinctual wishes belong to the Oedipus complex begins to emerge, the stage is set for the actual presentation of the triadic negative Oedipus complex.

Stage IV: 1919–26

This is the period of the "complete Oedipus complex." The complete Oedipus complex is first presented as such in 1923 and is further developed in several expository papers in the years to follow. In the few years immediately preceding its presentation Freud was working on two theoretical issues, bisexuality and identification, which were to provide both the theoretical basis for Freud's ideas on the inverted Oedipus complex and the extra support necessary for its inclusion into a triadic context.

A major question that Freud is confronted with at this point is whether the concept of "bisexuality" and its universality is to be considered to relate to the sexual desire for objects of both sexes (female and male) or to the feminine (passive) and masculine (active) components of sexual desire. Freud opts for the first alternative and thus grounds his proposition concerning the universality of incestuous wishes directed toward both parents.

As to identification, Freud was at this time in the process of conceptualizing ideas on the mechanism of identification and the nature of identificatory objects.

In terms of the Oedipus complex the major conclusion to be drawn from these conceptualizations was that the conflict inherent in the complex is to be resolved through an intensified identification of the boy with his father. Through such an identification (a) the boy can in an indirect and sublimated way *have* the mother, and (b) the "ego-ideal" (the precursor of the superego) is formed. Hence the father's prohibitions and threats are internalized and the incestuous wish is repressed. (See *Group Psychology and the Analysis of the Ego*, 1921c, XVIII.)

The development of Freud's ideas on identification had an additional important and yet indirect impact on the concept of the Oedipus complex. Though it was never overtly discussed, Freud was having difficulty explaining how the little boy would come to identify with his mother. That such identification was, in fact, taking place was apparent from the nature of the ego-ideal and the boy's character formation in a more general sense.

This difficulty was, it would seem, one of the determinants of Freud's postulation in 1923 of the universality of the complete Oedipus complex (*The Ego and the Id*, 1923b, XIX). The complete Oedipus complex refers to the simultaneous presence of both a positive oedipal constellation (i.e., in the case of the boy a rivalry with the father for the mother's love) and a negative or inverse Oedipus constellation (in the same boy a rivalry with the mother for the father's love). By presenting the inverse constellation as normative, a framework for the boy's identification with his mother is formed. Just as the resolution of the positive Oedipus complex leads to identification with the father, so the resolution of the negative complex will lead (as Freud assumed to occur in the girl's positive Oedipus complex) to identification with the mother. It is in this way that the boy's incestuous feelings toward the father, which in the reexamination of bisexuality was discovered in a dyad, are transmuted into a triadic relationship.

These theoretical developments also allowed Freud to address more systematically the question of the "dissolution of the Oedipus complex." Instead of a simple schema involving the transition from an oedipal period to a latency period (via repression of drives and a shift away from incestuous objects), a more complex and structured model emerges. This model centers on the processes of superego formation and on the different role of castration anxiety in boys and girls. For the little boy castration anxiety brings about the destruction of the complex by the time of latency, and for the little girl castration anxiety initiates her entrance into the complex. The discussion of female–male differences becomes highlighted in the last stage of Freud's writing (see Stage VI).

The complete Oedipus complex stays in the forefront for the remainder of this period, and appears in Freud's major theoretical works of that time (e.g., The Ego and the Id, 1923b, XIX; "The Dissolution of the Oedipus Complex," 1924d, XIX; "Some Psychical Consequences of the Anatomical Distinction between the Sexes," 1925j, XIX; "Inhibitions, Symptoms and Anxiety," 1926d, XX).

The predominance of the complete Oedipus complex in these writings is somewhat curious. Aside from the latent theoretical necessity that emerges from a very close study of Freud's remarks on identification, there does not seem to be any evidence compelling the postulation of parallel inverse triadic relationships. The idea of a universal mother–son rivalry for the father is not intuitively obvious; clinical data supporting it are not forthcoming; and even a hypothetical description of the specifics of such a rivalry is not presented by Freud or his analytic colleagues. It may at this point be wondered whether a nontheoretical factor is responsible for the peculiar broadening of the scope of the concept of the oedipal complex so that it may include the dyadic inverse relationships as well. Freud's references in this period (in 1920) to the Oedipus complex as "the Shibboleth that distinguishes the adherents of psychoanalysis from its opponents" (1905d, VII, p. 226n) is a springboard for speculation in this regard.

Stage V: 1926–31

During this period Freud takes a respite from the complexities of theory building in which he was so fervently involved in the previous period. The Oedipus complex as a given appears in these years in Freud's applications of psychoanalytic theory to issues of cultural, sociological, and literary significance. The major writings here are *The Future of an Illusion*, 1927c; *Civilization and Its Discontents*, 1930a; "A Religious Experience," 1928a; and "Dostoevsky and Parricide," 1928b (all in XXI).

It is interesting that in these applications of the Oedipus complex there is renewed emphasis placed on the boy's dyadic relationship with his loving father and on the role of this relationship in the formation of an internal moral system (i.e., the superego).

Stage VI: 1931–8

Freud's emergent ideas on female sexuality lead him in this period to the systematic presentation of the unique dynamics of the little girl's Oedipus complex. This brings in its course the conceptualization of the "preoedipal" relationship to the mother and, together with other theoretical developments, also results in the downplay of the boy's inverted Oedipus complex. At the conclusion of this stage the description of the male Oedipus complex is reminiscent of Freud's earliest view, in which the father is portrayed in the main as the aggressive rival for the mother's love.

Throughout the previous periods discussed, the entire question of female sexuality was shrouded in a great deal of obscurity. Accordingly, references to the Oedipus complex of the little girl were scarce and as a rule contained no more than a brief statement to the effect that the female complex may be assumed to be analogous (and inverse) to that of the male. In 1925 (toward the end of Stage IV) Freud acknowledged that this analogy was invalid. In his highly condensed and seminal paper on female sexuality, entitled "Some Psychical Consequences of the Anatomical Distinction between the Sexes" (1925j, XIX) Freud presents a formulation of the female Oedipus complex dynamically distinct from that of the male. This formulation and its implications are to be fully incorporated into the classical psychoanalytic theory of development only in 1931 ("Female

Sexuality," 1931b, XXI). This incorporation marks the beginning of the final stage.

In the various descriptions of the unique female Oedipus complex (1925j, XIX; 1931b, XXI; 1933a, XXII; 1940a, XXIII) the following is highlighted: The girl's first object of love is like that of the boy – the mother. It is here the abandonment of the mother and the concomitant turn to the father as a result of events that take place in the *preoedipal* period that leads to the triadic relationship referred to as oedipal. At some point in the preoedipal period, the girl, recognizing that she has been castrated, envies the male for having a penis, depreciates the mother for not having one, and also reproaches the mother for having brought her into the world inadequately equipped. It is only as a consequence of all this that the girl turns away from her original object of love. Normally the girl will then direct her affection toward the father, substituting the wish for a penis with a wish for a baby. The oedipal triad that emerges here, rather than being a conflictual state in need of resolution, appears as the desirable developmental outcome reflective of the normal female attitude that is to persist throughout life.

The ramifications of this formulation of the Oedipus complex were far reaching. Aside from this controvertible contribution to the understanding of female development in general, it turned Freud's attention to the structural dynamics of the preoedipal period. This period had over the years been dealt with sporadically and piecemeal. Freud formulated early development now in terms of narcissism, now in terms of the unfolding of libido, and now in terms of the dyadic relationships between the child and each of his or her parents. Freud did not develop a comprehensive framework for these various perspectives.

Freud's revisions of his theory of the Oedipus complex also raised critical theoretical questions necessitating a thorough reexamination of Freud's ideas on identification and bisexuality. This reexamination in turn, led to the development of a more sophisticated understanding of these constructs. Concomitantly the recognition that the inverse or negative male Oedipus complex cannot be assumed to be equivalent to the positive female Oedipus complex in its new form, ultimately led to the downplay of the "complete Oedipus complex."

As Freud in his final book (1940a, XXIII) summarizes the basic tenets of psychoanalytic theory, it is almost exclusively the positive constellations that are discussed in the context of the oedipal complex. Freud reiterates the position he presented at the beginning of this period concerning the girl's Oedipus complex. Regarding that of the boy Freud, it would seem, returns to focus on the view he presented in his very earliest works – the boy loves his mother and hates his father who, too, contends for her love.

EVENTS AFFECTING DEVELOPMENT OF IDEAS ON THE OEDIPUS COMPLEX

In our description we have suggested that Freud's ideas on the Oedipus complex changed *pari passu* with developments in other areas of psychoanalytic theory. Identification, bisexuality, superego, and revisions in the theory of anxiety, all interacted with his conceptualization of the Oedipus complex. His formulations of masochism, especially in women, were intertwined as well. It is also obvious that new clinical findings went hand in glove with these theoretical changes.

In this section our focus turns to additional factors that seem to have influenced the course of Freud's thinking on the Oedipus complex. These factors can be described as combining personal issues and issues pertaining to the psychoanalytic movement. Freud's descriptions of the passionate attachments and rivalries of the Oedipus complex clearly derive much of their vividness and force from his own attachments and rivalries. The following are some illustrations of major influences and are presented in the spirit of suggesting further lines of inquiry.

Freud's self-analysis

During the early years of what we have referred to as Stage I (1897–1909) Freud was intensely involved in the exploration of his own inner life, including his memories of his childhood experiences. The details of this exploration unfold in Freud's *The Interpretation of Dreams* (1900a, IV, V), and in his correspondence with Wilhelm Fliess (1985 [1887–1904]). The discovery of the Oedipus constellation was a major and perhaps *the* major outcome of these explorations. We would like to call attention to some possible implications of this mode of discovery for Freud's contemporaneous and subsequent theorizing.

Self-discovery as a process and a product of this introspective process lend a special sense of conviction to both. The generalizibility of the findings from the discoverer, Freud, to all of mankind (and later womankind) is in need of justification. The conviction derived from self-discovery may have to some extent blinded Freud to this necessity. The effect of this, for better or for worse, on the course of the development of Freud's theorizing may have been to make for a rather literal correspondence between the unfolding of unique personal experience and vicissitudes of theory. Freud saw himself in a very concrete sense as Oedipus. This is most dramatically illustrated in the oft repeated and now legendary incident in which Freud, when presented by his disciples with a medallion depicting Freud on one side and Oedipus and the Sphinx on the other, was shocked. He then reported that the inscription on the medallion, a Sophoclean description of Oedipus' greatness had been the very words that he, in a youthful fantasy had envisioned inscribed on a statue of himself.[1]

Thus, it could be the case that the theoretical formulations of the dynamics of the Oedipus complex were limited by Freud's perhaps idiosyncratic, personal experiences within his own family constellation and his memories of these experiences. Freud's self-analysis appears to pose another problem for theory construction. In this open-ended analysis, as is common in psychoanalyses in general, a rich congeries of memories and fantasies emerged. From our contemporary perspective these represent a mixture of oedipal and preoedipal material.[2] Both these kinds of material were viewed by Freud for a long time through the prism of the Oedipus conflict. This prolonged lack of distinction was associated with the downplay of the complexity and importance of the preoedipal.

Freud's analyses of Anna Freud

New information about Freud's analyses of his daughter Anna (1918–1922, 1924–1925) has recently come to light.[3] There is a temporal correspondence between Freud's emerging formulations on female sexuality and his analyses of Anna. There is also a correspondence between Sigmund Freud's and Anna Freud's ideas about "beating fantasies" and about jealousy and the implications of these for female psychosexual development. Young-Bruehl has claimed that Anna Freud is, in fact, one of the cases summarized in Sigmund Freud's paper on the "beating" fantasies. This leads us to suspect that the analysis of Anna with all its transference and countertransference complexities may have disproportionately influenced Freud's formulations on the centrality of female masochism and penis envy and their respective roles in the female Oedipus complex.

Freud's relationship with Jung

We have pointed out that immediately after coining the term "Oedipus complex" and asserting its centrality and ubiquity (1910) in the following three years Freud makes no mention of the term in his published writings. When reintroduced (1913) it is gradually expanded to include almost all familial and cultural dynamics. Freud's concern with the place of the boy's love for the father becomes a central dynamic feature during the years of absence of the term.

An examination of the Freud–Jung correspondence (1974a) augmented by material from the *Minutes of the Vienna Psychoanalytic Society*[4] during this period strongly suggests the following hypothesis. Freud's conflicted entanglement with Jung influenced the rhythm of the appearance, disappearance, and reappearance of the term as well as changes in what the term subsumes. It became clear to Freud that the Oedipus complex was becoming the core of contention between himself and Jung. It seems to us that Freud and Jung were enacting the ambivalent dynamics of the Oedipus complex in their scientific debates about the Oedipus complex. For instance, Jones[5] reports Freud's speaking both of his wish to break with Jung and his fear of breaking with Jung by publishing *Totem and Taboo*, a manifesto on the centrality of the Oedipus complex. Thus the lacuna in the use of the term "Oedipus complex" corresponds to a period of Freud's hesitation to attack Jung, and its reappearance is associated with the decision to launch a full attack. It is in this combative sense that by 1920 the Oedipus complex becomes the "shibboleth" of psychoanalysis.

What we have suggested here is that there may be limitations of the theory associated with the motives and conflicts of the theory maker, Freud. Nevertheless, to elucidate some of the personal motives is not to determine the truth value of the theory. For this task a variety of methods of verification are required. Freud's demonstration of the emergence of oedipal dynamics in the analyses of his many patients is a first step toward such verification. However, other methods and measures are required to control for "contamination" of the clinical findings by the clinician's theory. Further, for generalizations such as the innateness and universality of the Oedipus complex, let alone the details of the dynamic sequences and developmental processes, even more complex and elaborate methods of proof and disproof are needed. To date, each of these issues both within psychoanalysis and outside psychoanalysis has been called into question.[6] At present there are lively debates about what are the appropriate methods and even if such methods exist.

The first ninety years of psychoanalysis have not produced *conclusive* evidence justifying either detailed clinical propositions or the more sweeping generalizations. We are uncertain as to what will happen in the next ninety years, but it is fair to say that the consensus (not unanimity) among analysts about what is enduring in Freud's formulations is something like the following: The child has complex relationships with both his parents, and these relationships have a developmental history. He loves and hates the parents, wishes to be like them, and fears them. She will at times use one parent to gain what is needed from the other. These feelings of the child have a counterpart in a complex array of feelings in both the mother and the father, individually and as a dyad. Both parents were once children and there are complex reverberations between the feelings of the child and the residual childhood feelings of the parents. The complexity of these interactions are only barely analogized in the figure of the triangle. The development and expression of sexual feelings and fantasies are intrinsic to the complex and change in response to both internal and external (familial and cultural) pressures. Less agreement among analysts exists on the questions of how important is the Oedipus complex in the development of psychopathology and character, many regarding the crucial phases to be those prior to the emergence of this complex. Similarly there is less agreement on the centrality of the analysis of the Oedipus complex in the conduct of clinical psychoanalysis.

It is safe to predict that such debates will continue. They seem to be embedded in the very nature of psychoanalysis, the psychoanalytic movement, and its relationship to the founding father.

NOTES

1 E. Jones, *The Life and Work of Sigmund Freud* (New York: Basic Books, 1953), vol. 2, pp. 13–14.
2 Harold P. Blum, "The Prototype of Preoedipal Reconstruction," *Journal of the American Psychoanalytical Association* 25 (1977): 757–83.
3 Elizabeth Young-Bruehl, *Anna Freud* (New York: Summit Books, 1988).
4 Vols. III, IV, ed. Herman Nunberg, Ernst Federn (New York International Universities Press, 1974, 1975).
5 Jones, *The Life and Work of Sigmund Freud.*
6 Panel, "The Oedipus Complex: A Reevaluation." M. H. Sacks, reporter. *Journal of the American Psychoanalytical Association* 33 (1985): 201–16.

7   Freud and perversion

The first of Freud's *Three Essays on the Theory of Sexuality* is titled "The Sexual Aberrations." Why should Freud begin a book the main point of which is to argue for the existence of infantile sexuality with a discussion of adult perversions? (After all, the existence of the adult aberrations was not news.) I believe Freud's beginning can be usefully understood as part of an effective argumentative strategy to extend the notion of sexuality by showing how extensive it already was. Freud himself (in the preface to the fourth edition) describes the book as an attempt "at enlarging the concept of sexuality" (1905d, VII, 134). The extension involved in the notion of perversion prepares the way for the extension involved in infantile sexuality.

The book begins, on its very first page, with a statement of the popular view of the sexual instinct:

It is generally understood to be absent in childhood, to set in at the time of puberty in connection with the process of coming to maturity and to be revealed in the manifestations of an irresistible attraction exercised by one sex upon the other; while its aim is presumed to be sexual union, or at all events actions leading in that direction. (1905d, VII, 135)

But it quickly becomes obvious that this will not do as a definition of the sphere of the sexual. Sexuality is not confined to heterosexual genital intercourse between adults, for there are a number of perversions, and even popular opinion recognizes these as sexual in their nature. Popular opinion might wish to maintain a narrow conception of what is to count as *normal* sexuality, thus raising a problem about how one is to distinguish between normal and abnormal sexuality, but the more interesting and immediate problem is to make clear in virtue of what the perversions are recognized as sexual at all.

175

And it is here that Freud makes an enormous conceptual advance. He distinguishes the object and the aim of the sexual instinct (decomposing what might have seemed an indissoluble unity), and he introduces the notion of erotogenic zones (thus extending sexuality beyond the genitals), and is thus able to show that the perversions involve variations along a number of dimensions (source, object, and aim) of a single underlying instinct. Heterosexual genital intercourse is one constellation of variations, and homosexuality is another. Homosexuality, or inversion, involves variation in object, but the sexual sources (erotogenic zones, or bodily centers of arousal) and aims (acts, such as intercourse and looking, designed to achieve pleasure and satisfaction) may be the same. Thus what makes homosexuality recognizably sexual, despite its distance from what might be presented as the ordinary person's definition of sexuality, is the vast amount that it can be seen to have in common with "normal" sexuality once one comes to understand the sexual instinct as itself complex, as having components and dimensions.

Freud makes the complexity of the sexual instinct compelling by drawing on the researches of the tireless investigators of sexual deviation such as Krafft-Ebing and Havelock Ellis. He makes the complexity intelligible by distinguishing the few dimensions (source, object, and aim) of the underlying instinct that are needed to lend order to the vast variety of phenomena, providing an illuminating new classificatory scheme. Once each of the perversions is understood as involving variation along one or more dimensions of a single underlying instinct, Freud is in a position to do two things. The first is to call into question the primacy of one constellation of variations over another. The second is to show that other phenomena that might not appear on the surface sexual (e.g., childhood thumbsucking) share essential characteristics with obviously sexual activity (infantile sensual sucking involves pleasurable stimulation of the same erotogenic zone, the mouth, stimulated in adult sexual activities such as kissing), and can be understood as being earlier stages in the development of the same underlying instinct that expresses itself in such various forms in adult sexuality. Freud is in a position to discover infantile sexuality. To briefly retrace the steps to this point: Perversions are regarded as sexual because they can be understood as variations of an underlying instinct along three dimensions (somatic source, object, and aim). The instinct has components, is complex or "composite" (1905d, VII, 162). If adult perversions can be understood in terms of an underlying instinct with components that can be specified along several dimensions, then many of the activities of infancy can also be so understood, can be seen as earlier stages in the development of those components. But now I wish to focus on the newly problematic relation of normal and abnormal sexuality. Is one set of variations better or worse than another? The mere fact of difference, variation in content, is no longer enough once one cannot say one set of variations is somehow natural and others are not. Once one sees sexuality as involving a single underlying instinct, with room for variation along several dimensions, new criteria for pathology are needed. Moreover, insofar as variation is thought-dependent, rather than a matter of biological aberration, the question arises of whether there is such a thing as a pathology of sexual thought. Is there room for a morality of desire and fantasy alongside the ordinary morality governing action?

HOMOSEXUALITY

Freud initially distinguishes inversion from perversion. Inversion involves displacement of the sexual object from members of the opposite sex to members of the same sex. Inversion includes male homosexuality and lesbianism. Insofar as it involves variation in object only, it may appear less shockingly "deviant" than other sexual aberrations. But insofar as the point of singling out inversion is to contrast it with aberrations involving displacement in aim rather than object, it might as well include a wider range of aberrations, aberrations where displacement is to someone or something other than members of the same sex. From that point of view, bestiality, necrophilia, and so forth are more like inversion than like the other aberrations – and Freud in fact treats them together as "deviations in respect of the sexual object" (1905d, VII, 136). If we include these less common and more troubling variations in object, inversion may no longer seem a less problematical form of sexual aberration. Moreover, the distinction between inversion and perversion tends to collapse in the course of Freud's discussion of fetishism (is the deviation in object? in aim? – 1905d, VII, 153). And it should be remembered that homosexuality is itself (like heterosexuality) internally complex, encompassing many different activities and attitudes. I shall use "perversion" broadly, as Freud himself usually does, so that homosexuality counts as a perversion within Freud's classificatory scheme.

Is that a reproach? In the *Three Essays*, Freud states explicitly that it is inappropriate to use the word "perversion" as a "term of reproach" (1905d, VII, 160). But that is in the special context of exploring the implications of his expanded conception of sexuality. In the case of Dora, published in the same year as the *Three Essays*, he refers to a fantasy of fellatio as "excessively repulsive and perverted" (1905e, VII, 52). A reproach seems built into the reference. It could be argued that Freud is forced to use the vocabulary of the view he wishes to overthrow, and that it carries its unwelcome connotations with it. Indeed, he in the same place argues that "We must learn to speak without indignation of what we call the sexual perversions – instances in which the sexual function has extended its limits in respect either to the part of the body concerned or to the sexual object chosen" (1905e, VII, 50). Perhaps Freud's own feelings, about the term if not the specific acts referred to, are ambivalent. The important question is what the appropriate attitude is and whether Freud's theory offers any light. So, again, let us consider homosexuality. Supposing it is a perversion, is that a reproach? Is the fact that it counts as a perversion a reason for disapproving of it in others or avoiding it oneself?

One could take the high ground and claim that it is pointless to disapprove what is not in a person's control, and then argue that choice of sexual object or sexual orientation is not in a person's control. But this does not really take one very far. Perhaps one has no or only marginal control over whether one contracts diabetes, but this does not stop us from recognizing that diabetes is a bad thing (while it does compel us to regard diabetes patients as victims). Even if we had an etiological theory that assured us that homosexuality is not a matter of choice, and so perhaps not properly disapproved, that would not settle the question of whether it is a good or a bad thing (something we should avoid if we could). Moreover, even if sexual orientation is a given, outside the individual's control, what is given is a direction to desire. There remains the question of whether the individual should seek to control and suppress, or act on and express, the given desires.[1] Freud does not in fact take the high ground. His own etiological views seem to leave open the extent of biological and other dispositional factors in leading to homosexuality. Whether homosexuality is innate or acquired is for him an open and a complex question (1905d, VII, 140). And, to whatever extent it is acquired, the conditions of its acquisition are also complex (ibid., 144f.). The so-called choice of a sexual object is thus multiply obscure, and it is unclear to what extent the relevant causal conditions are within the individual's control (though one might also question whether and when control should be regarded as a condition of responsibility).[2] Freud nonetheless argues, on other grounds, that the "perversity" of homosexuality gives no reason to condemn it:

The uncertainty in regard to the boundaries of what is to be called normal sexual life, when we take different races and different epochs into account, should in itself be enough to cool the zealot's ardour. We surely ought not to forget that the perversion which is the most repellent to us, the sensual love of a man for a man, was not only tolerated by a people so far our superiors in cultivation as were the Greeks, but was actually entrusted by them with important social functions. The sexual life of each one of us extends to a slight degree – now in this direction, now in that – beyond the narrow lines imposed as the standard of normality. The perversions are neither bestial nor degenerate in the emotional sense of the word. They are a development of germs all of which are contained in the undifferentiated sexual disposition of the child, and which, by being suppressed or by being diverted to higher, asexual aims – by being "sublimated" – are destined to provide the energy for a great number of our cultural achievements. (1905e, VII, 50)

This passage actually contains at least two different types of argument. One is an appeal to universality across individuals, another an appeal to diversity across cultures. There is no doubt that sexual standards are culturally relative: Different societies approve and disapprove of different sexual activities. But one might still wonder whether some societies are perverse in a pejorative sense. There is no avoiding direct consideration of the question of the criteria for perversion. Do they allow for something more than culturally relative, or even individually relative (whatever pleases one), judgments of sexual value?

CRITERIA OF PERVERSION

Once one accepts Freud's view of the complexity of the underlying sexual instinct, the old content criterion for perversion and pathology must be abandoned. As Freud writes, "In the sphere of sexual life we are brought up against peculiar and, indeed, insoluble difficulties as soon as we try to draw a sharp line to distinguish mere variations within the range of what is physiological from pathological symptoms" (1905d, VII, 160–1).

It might seem simple enough to provide a sociological or statistical specification of perversion, but there are difficulties. For what precisely would the statistics reflect? One's questionnaires or surveys might seek to discover what the majority regards as perverse, but that would leave one wanting to know what perversion is (after all, members of the majority might in fact be applying very various standards). One might try to avoid direct circularity by, without mentioning the concept perversion, trying to elicit information revealing of which sexual desires the majority disapproves. But circularity reemerges on this approach because there might be all sorts of different grounds for disapproval (aesthetic, moral, religious, political, biological, medical, to name a few), and what one wants is to single out those desires and practices that are disapproved of as (specifically) perverse. It appears one's questions and evidence would have already to be applying some standard of perversion in order to achieve that singling out. Parallel and further problems would apply to surveys of actual sexual practices. (Are perversions necessarily rare? If a practice became popular, would it therefore cease to be perverse? And if a practice were rare, e.g. celibacy or adultery, would that necessarily make it perverse?) Surely perversion is meant to mark only a certain kind of deviation from a norm. And there is another difficulty. For whatever method one uses, it will turn out that what counts as perversion will vary from society to society, will vary over time and place, in short, will be culturally relative. So insofar as one's concern is wider than the views of a particular society or group, insofar as it is a concern with general psychological theory, with the nature of human nature, no sociological approach will do. Moreover, insofar as one's concern is personal, or perhaps even therapeutic (unless one's standards of therapy are simply adaptation to local and contemporary prevailing norms), that is, if one is concerned to know how one ought to live one's life (including one's sexual life), a sociological approach will not do. For one's society may be wrongheaded, prejudiced, misguided, or in other ways mistaken. One has only one life to live. It might be necessary to resist one's society's demands or even to leave it. So one must look further.

Perhaps perversion can still be defined in terms of content if we are willing to start (again) with the popular view of normal sexuality as consisting of heterosexual genital intercourse between adults: then, any sexual desire or practice that goes beyond the body parts intended for sexual union, or that devotes too exclusive attention to a form of interaction normally passed through on the way to the final sexual aim, or that is directed at an object other than an adult member of the opposite sex, might be regarded as perverse.[3] One might insist on this stand independently of what the members of any particular society happen to think. But as we have seen, once one accepts Freud's analysis of the sexual in terms of a single, but complex, underlying instinct, while it becomes clear why the sexual perversions count as sexual, it becomes unclear why they are perverse. What privileges heterosexual genital intercourse between adults? Is there some further criterion that transcends individual societal views?

One might consider disgust. That is, we might try to pick out sexual activities to be condemned as perverse on the basis of a, presumably natural, reaction of disgust. Extensions of sexual activity beyond the genitals, alternative sources of sexual pleasure, would be perverse if disgust at them were sufficiently widespread. So fellatio and cunnilingus might count as perverse were disgust widely felt at oral–genital contact (as Freud reveals it was in his society at the time of the Dora case). But disgust is itself generally culturally variable and often purely conventional. As Freud points out, "a man who will kiss a pretty girl's lips passionately, may perhaps be disgusted at the idea of using her tooth-brush, though there are no grounds for supposing that his own oral cavity, for which he feels no disgust, is any cleaner than the girl's" (1905d, VII, 151–2). Nonetheless, Freud seems to think that a content criterion can be preserved in certain extreme cases "as, for instance, in cases of licking excrement or of intercourse with dead bodies" (161). Perhaps some things, such as licking excrement, are thought to be objectively, universally disgusting. But perverse practices reveal that is not true, and Freud should know better.

Developmentally, children must learn to be disgusted at feces.

This fact may not be obvious, but Freud was well aware of it. During the period of his earliest speculations about anal erotism, Freud wrote a fascinating letter to his friend Fliess:

I had been meaning to ask you, in connection with the eating of excrement [by] [illegible words] animals, when disgust first appears in small children and whether there exists a period in earliest infancy when these feelings are absent. Why do I not go into the nursery and experiment with Annerl? Because working for 12 1/2 hours, I have no time for it, and the womenfolk do not support my researches. The answer would be of theoretical interest. (1985 [1887–1904], 230, letter of February 8, 1897)

(This letter reminds us how little Freud's theories about infantile sexuality were based on the direct observation of children. Which, to my mind, far from undermining his achievement – given its substantial confirmation by subsequent observations – makes it all the more remarkable. Freud was not the first person to observe that children suck their thumbs, but it was only with his conceptual innovations that he and others could see this and other infantile activities as sexual.) The answer to his question about excrement was well known to Freud by the time he wrote the *Three Essays.* Children will play quite happily with their little turds, and as Freud writes, the contents of the bowels "are clearly treated as a part of the infant's own body and represent his first 'gift': by producing them he can express his active compliance with his environment and, by witholding them, his disobedience" (1905d, VII, 186). And Freud elsewhere develops the analogy between feces and other valued possessions, such as gold (1908b).[4] Disgust at the excremental is itself in need of explanation.

Where the anus is concerned . . . it is disgust which stamps that sexual aim as a perversion. I hope, however, I shall not be accused of partisanship when I assert that people who try to account for this disgust by saying that the organ in question serves the function of excretion and comes in contact with excrement – a thing which is disgusting in itself – are not much more to the point than hysterical girls who account for their disgust at the male genital by saying that it serves to void urine. (1905d, VII, 152)

It is true that Freud singles out disgust as one of the triumvirate of "forces of repression" (disgust, shame, and morality – 1905d, VII, 162,178), and it may be that the forces of repression are ultimately instinctual and so present in every society, but that need not fix the content of the reaction. That is, it *may* be that everyone is necessarily (meaning biologically) bound to feel disgust at something, while still leaving room for variation in the objects of disgust. It should be no more surprising that the objects of disgust (as an instinct) are variable, than that the objects of sexual desire (as an instinct) are variable. So if the objects of sexual desire have no fixed or determinate content, neither do the objects of sexual disgust. We must look elsewhere if we are to find usable criteria for perversion and pathology.

Before looking elsewhere, we should note that there is another problem in a content criterion for perversion, which stems not from the variations we have been emphasizing, but from the universality we have mentioned only in passing. Freud points out that we can find apparently perverse desires not only in (otherwise admirable) other societies, but also within ourselves. In the case of homosexuality, he points out that our desires are responsive to external circumstances. Many will turn to homosexual pleasures given the appropriate favorable or inhibiting circumstances (e.g., "exclusive relations with persons of their own sex, comradeship in war, detention in prison. . . ." – 1905d, VII, 140). And even more strongly Freud concludes:

Psycho-analytic research is most decidedly opposed to any attempt at separating off homosexuals from the rest of mankind as a group of a special character. By studying sexual excitations other than those that are manifestly displayed, it has found that all human beings are capable of making a homosexual object-choice and have in fact made one in their unconscious. (145 n.)

There is a sense in which all human beings are bisexual. Moreover, the universality of perversions other than homosexuality is exhibited in the role they play in foreplay (210, 234). The prevalence of perversion (and the "negative" of perversion, neurosis) receives its theoretical underpinning in terms of the universality of polymorphously perverse infantile sexuality. But for now the point is to see that a simple content criterion for perversion will not do. Given the facts of variety in cultural practice and of uniformity in individual potential, it is difficult to see how any particular object-choice (to focus on one dimension) can be singled out as necessarily abnormal. The nature of the sexual instinct itself sets no limit, for as Freud concludes, "the sexual instinct and the sexual object are merely soldered together" (148).

An alternative criterion for perversion and pathology emerges in connection with Freud's discussion of fetishism. Freud characterizes fetishism in general in terms of those cases "in which the normal sexual object is replaced by another which bears some relation to it, but is entirely unsuited to serve the normal sexual aim" (1905d, VII, 153). (Note that the variation seems to affect both object and aim.) But he shows that it has a point of contact with the normal through the sort of overvaluation of the sexual object, and of its aspects and of things associated with it, that seems quite generally characteristic of love. He continues:

The situation only becomes pathological when the longing for the fetish passes beyond the point of being merely a necessary condition attached to the sexual object and actually *takes the place* of the normal aim, and, further, when the fetish becomes detached from a particular individual and becomes the *sole* sexual object. These are, indeed, the general conditions under which mere variations of the sexual instinct pass over into pathological aberrations. (154)

Freud spells out the general conditions in terms of "exclusiveness and fixation":

In the majority of instances the pathological character in a perversion is found to lie not in the *content* of the new sexual aim but in its relation to the normal. If a perversion, instead of appearing merely *alongside* the normal sexual aim and object, and only when circumstances are unfavourable to *them* and favourable to *it* – if, instead of this, it ousts them completely and takes their place in *all* circumstances – if, in short, a perversion has the characteristics of exclusiveness and fixation – then we shall usually be justified in regarding it as a pathological symptom. (161)

But this really will not do as a general criterion either, for reasons provided by Freud himself in a note a few pages earlier:

psycho-analysis considers that a choice of an object independently of its sex – freedom to range equally over male and female objects – as it is found in childhood, in primitive states of society and early periods of history, is the original basis from which, as a result of restriction in one direction or the other, both the normal and the inverted types develop. Thus from the point of view of psycho-analysis the exclusive sexual interest felt by men for women is also a problem that needs elucidating and is not a self-evident fact based upon an attraction that is ultimately of a chemical nature. (146 n.)

Once it is recognized that the instinct is merely soldered to its object, that there are wide possibilities of variation in the choice of object, then every choice of object becomes equally problematical, equally in need of explanation. Exclusiveness and fixation cannot be used to mark off homosexuality as perverse without marking off (excessively strong) commitments to heterosexuality as equally perverse. Thus, exclusiveness and fixation are no help if the point of a criterion for perversion is to distinguish the abnormal from the normal, and if heterosexual genital intercourse between adults is to be somehow privileged as the paradigm of the normal. We need some norm for sexuality if the notion of perversion is to take hold. From where can we get it? Is there any reason to suppose that it will take the form of the popular view of normal sexuality?

DEVELOPMENT AND MATURATION

Freud in fact, as we have seen, operates with multiple criteria for perversion and pathology. We have also seen that his own views provide materials for a critique of those criteria if one attempts to generalize them. But there emerges from within his theory yet another criterion, a criterion that is meant to be ultimately biological and so not culturally relative. As Freud puts it at the start of the third of his *Three Essays:* "Every pathological disorder of sexual life is rightly to be regarded as an inhibition in development" (1905d, VII, 208). Perverse sexuality is, ultimately, infantile sexuality. While consideration of the adult perversions prepares the way for the extension of our understanding of sexuality to infantile activities in the course of Freud's book, infantile sexuality prepares the way for both normal and perverse sexuality in the development of the individual.[5] It is through arrests in that development, or through regression to earlier points of fixation when faced by later frustration, that an adult comes to manifest perverse sexual activity. We can pick out sexual desires and activities that count as perverse if we have an ideal of normal development and maturation.

Freud's theory of psychosexual development, with its central oral–anal–genital stages, provides such an ideal. The dynamic is at least partly biological. At first, the infant has control of little other than its mouth, and in connection with its original need for taking nourishment it readily develops independent satisfaction in sensual sucking

(182). That the anus in due course becomes the center of sexual pleasure and wider concerns ("holding back and letting go") is not surprising in the light of a variety of biological developments: As the infant gets older, the feces are better formed, there is more sphincter control (so the child begins to have a choice about when and where to hold back or let go), and with teething there is pressure for the mother to wean.[6] Finally, there comes puberty and the possibility of reproduction and increased interest in the genitals. But one should not totally biologize what is at least in part a social process. There may be a confusion between the ripening of an organic capacity with the valuation of one form of sexuality as its highest or only acceptable form. The subordination of sexuality to reproduction, and the importance attached to heterosexual genital activity, is after all, a social norm. Freud does not claim that there is a biological or evolutionary *preference* for reproduction; the individual preference, if any, is simply for end-pleasure. Even if the preference for end-pleasure or orgasm over fore-pleasure (210–12) is biologically determined, the conditions for such pleasure are not. Whether end-pleasure takes place under conditions that might lead to reproduction depends on a wide range of factors, and whether it *should* take place under such conditions is subject to both circumstance and argument. Even if one attaches supreme importance to the survival of the species, other things, including sexual pleasure (which may in turn depend on a certain degree of variety) may be necessary to the survival of the species. And for most of recent history, overpopulation and unwanted conception have been of greater concern than maximizing the reproductive effects of sexual activity. Under certain circumstances homosexuality might have social advantages.[7]

In terms of Freud's instinct theory (not to be confused with standard biological notions of hereditary behavior patterns in animals), every instinct involves an internal, continuously flowing source of energy or tension or pressure. Freud adds, however: "Although instincts are wholly determined by their origin in a somatic source, in mental life we know them only by their aims"(1915c, XIV, 123). Given Freud's fundamental hypotheses concerning the mechanisms of psychic functioning, the aim is in every case ultimately discharge of the energy or tension. And given Freud's discharge theory of pleasure (or tension theory of unpleasure), the aim must ultimately be understood in terms of pleasure. Freud is well aware of the problems of a simple discharge theory of pleasure, especially in relation to sexuality (where, after all, the subjective experience of increasing tension is typically as pleasurable as the experience of discharge). (See 1905d, VII, 209f. and 1924c.) The point here, however, is that on Freud's view the essential aim of sexual activity (as instinctual activity) must be pleasure, achievable by a wide variety of particular acts (under a wider variety of thought-dependent conditions). Sexuality may serve many other purposes and have many other functions and aims from a range of different points of view. Among these are reproduction, multilevel interpersonal awareness, interpersonal communication, bodily contact, love, money.[8] Within Freud's theory, perversion is to be understood in terms of infantile, that is nongenital, forms of pleasure. This approach has its problems. For one thing, homosexuality, in some ways the paradigm of perversion for Freud, is not necessarily nongenital and so not obviously perverse by this criterion. Moreover, insofar as other perversions, such as fetishism, aim at genital stimulation and discharge, they too are not purely infantile (cf. 1916–17, XVI, 321). In practice, of course, Freud collapses the individual's experienced concern for genital pleasure together with the biological function of reproduction, so that the development and maturation criterion for perversion reduces to the question of the suitability of a particular activity for reproduction.

One should not confuse the (or a) biological function of sexuality, namely reproduction, with sexuality as such. Freud is at pains to point out that sexuality has a history in the development of the individual that precedes the possibility of reproduction. The reproductive function emerges at puberty (1916–17, XVI, 311). An ideal of maturation that gives a central role to that function makes all earlier sexuality of necessity perverse. The infant's multiple sources of sexual pleasure make it polymorphously perverse. And the connection works both ways. Sexual perversions can be regarded as in their nature infantile. As Freud puts it:

if a child has a sexual life at all it is bound to be of a perverse kind; for, except for a few obscure hints, children are without what makes sexuality into the reproductive function. On the other hand, the abandonment of the reproductive function is the common feature of all perversions. We actually describe a sexual activity as perverse if it has given up the aim of reproduction and pursues the attainment of pleasure as an aim independent of it. So . . . the breach and turning-point in the development of sexual life lies in

its becoming subordinate to the purposes of reproduction. Everything that happens before this turn of events and equally everything that disregards it and that aims solely at obtaining pleasure is given the uncomplimentary name of "perverse" and as such is proscribed. (1916–17, XVI, 316)

I believe Freud may well provide an accurate account of the link in our language between perversion and nonreproductive sex. On the other hand, I don't believe Freud's theory is committed to maintaining that link (the theoretically necessary aim is pleasure, not reproduction). Moreover, even if detachment from the possibility of reproduction is a necessary condition of regarding a practice as perverse, it cannot be sufficient: Otherwise sterile heterosexual couples or those who use contraceptives would have to be regarded as perverse. (More on these matters in a moment.)

In privileging heterosexual genital intercourse between adults, if only for the purpose of classifying the perversions, one is making a choice based on norms. Freud's discussion of reproduction reflected prevailing social norms, and so the fact that they were norms was perhaps concealed. The norms of the sexual liberationists, such as Herbert Marcuse and Norman O. Brown, are in some ways perhaps continuous with the standards built into Freud's model. Does polymorphous perversion include sadism? Should it? Contemporary debates over the appropriate ideals of sexuality cannot be decided by simple appeals to biology. "Regression" is doubtless an empirical concept, but it gets its sense against a background provided by social norms of development (not purely biological norms of development). In picking out the perversions we apply an external standard to sexuality. Which is not to say that we should not. It is to say only that we should be self-conscious about what we are doing and why. Calling perversions "infantile" may in fact describe them, but the immature is usually regarded as inferior. And if that judgment is to follow, one needs more grounds than those provided by biology. After all, if we live long enough, we eventually decay. Later does not necessarily mean better.

MORE ON HOMOSEXUALITY

Is homosexuality a perversion? On a content criterion, whether ultimately based on a reaction of disgust or something else, the answer will vary over time and place, and it is arguable that the reaction of disgust is at least as malleable as the desire to which it is a reaction. On a criterion of exclusiveness and fixation, it is no more or less a perversion than heterosexuality of equivalent exclusivity. On a criterion of development and maturation, or arrest and regression, the answer is less clear. Some say that homosexuality is a developmentally immature stage or phase. I do not believe, however, that Freud's theory (despite incidental remarks) commits him to such a view. In the *Three Essays*, Freud notes that homosexuality "may either persist throughout life, or it may go into temporary abeyance, or again it may constitute an episode on the way to a normal development." He goes on, "It may even make its first appearance late in life after a long period of normal sexual activity" (1905d, VII, 137). In this case, it is heterosexuality that is the earlier phase. In passing, in the lecture on anxiety in the *New Introductory Lectures on Psycho-Analysis*, Freud indicates that "in the life of homosexuals, who have failed to accomplish some part of normal sexual development, the vagina is once more represented by [the anus]" (1933a, XXII, 101), thus presumably explaining why the vagina is avoided or (in the case of homosexuals who prefer sodomy) how the anus comes to take its place in sexual activity. But the main point (at 100–1) concerns the persistence of anal erotism in heterosexuals, and the point is that in the course of "normal sexual development" there is an equation of anus and vagina (that is, heterosexual intercourse involves displaced anal erotism), so homosexuals who prefer sodomy may in some sense be more direct. The point to notice here is that anal erotism (in its various forms) may be equally important for homosexuals and heterosexuals.[9] Freud does say that infantile sex is characteristically autoerotic (1905d, VII, 182), that is, involves no sexual object. In that respect, homosexuality is clearly not infantile. But then foot fetishism and bestiality also involve objects. Would one want to conclude that they are also not infantile, also not perverse? The presence of a whole person as object in the case of homosexuality doubtless makes a significant difference. (Inversion as such may, after all, be importantly different from perversion as such.)

Freud does occasionally seem to refer to homosexuality as an immature or arrested form of sexuality, for example in a letter in response to a mother who wrote him about her homosexual son (see also 1919e, XVII, 182 and 1940a [1938], XXIII, 155–6). Freud wrote:

Homosexuality is assuredly no advantage, but it is nothing to be ashamed of, no vice, no degradation; it cannot be classified as an illness; we consider it to be a variation of the sexual function, produced by a certain arrest of sexual development. Many highly respectable individuals of ancient and modern times have been homosexuals, several of the greatest men among them (Plato, Michelangelo, Leonardo da Vinci, etc.). It is a great injustice to persecute homosexuality as a crime – and a cruelty, too. . . . What analysis can do for your son runs in a different line. If he is unhappy, neurotic, torn by conflicts, inhibited in his social life, analysis may bring him harmony, peace of mind, full efficiency, whether he remains homosexual or gets changed. (1960a, 419–20, April 4, 1935)

Without support from his theoretical writings, the "arrest of sexual development" must be presumed to refer to (the social norm of) reproduction. At a theoretical level, it is only in the case of lesbianism that there looks like there is a stage-specific point to be made about object-choice. That is, given the basic premises of psychoanalytic theory, it is not entirely clear why all women are not lesbians. (Or, more tendentiously, how anyone can love a man.) Up to the genital phase, their development parallels that of little boys, and the beginnings of object relations should tie both little boys and girls to their mothers as the main supporting figure. Girls, unlike boys, are supposed to switch the gender of their love objects in the course of going through their oedipal phase. The incest taboo is supposed to lead boys to exclude their mothers, but not all women, as possible sexual objects. Under pressure of the castration complex, and through identification with their fathers, boys are supposed to search for "a girl just like the girl who married dear old dad." Girls, on the other hand, are supposed to switch from a female to a male love object. Why they do this is open to various accounts: Some accounts are in terms of penis envy (which needs more elaboration than can be provided here – in any case biological accounts in terms of a switch in interest from clitoris to vagina will not work). Some accounts are in terms of rivalry with the same-gender parent (something girls have in common with boys – it is just that their same-gender parent happened previously to have been the primary object of dependence and so love). Some accounts are in terms of a desire to please the mother (involving getting a penis for her). Whatever the account one gives of female psychosexual development, there is little reason to regard male homosexuality as involving arrest at or regression to an earlier phase of development, and so as infantile and (on that criterion) perverse.[10]

Still, perhaps something further can be extracted from Freud's general theory of development. It might be argued that there is a sense in which the basic mechanism of homosexual object-choice is more primitive than the mechanism involved in heterosexual choice. Freud distinguishes two basic types of object-choice: anaclitic and narcissistic (1914c, XIV, 87–8). On the anaclitic (or attachment) model, just as the sexual component instincts are at the outset attached to the satisfaction of the ego-instincts, the child's dependence on the parents provides the model for later relationships. On the narcissistic model, the individual chooses an object like himself. It might seem obvious that homosexual object-choice is narcissistic, and that narcissistic object-choice is more primitive than the other type. Neither point is correct. While the homosexual certainly has an object that is in at least one respect (gender or genitals) like himself, there are many other aspects of the individual, and in terms of those other aspects even heterosexual object-choice can be importantly narcissistic. Moreover, the mechanisms of homosexual object-choice are various (e.g., Freud sometimes gives emphasis to the avoidance of rivalry with the father or brothers), and the similarity of the object to oneself may not be crucial in all cases – indeed, an anaclitic-type dependence on the object may be much more prominent.[11] That narcissism as a stage, in the sense of taking oneself as a sexual object, may be more primitive than object-choice, in the sense of taking someone else as a sexual object, does not make the narcissistic type of object-choice more primitive than the anaclitic type. In both cases, unlike primitive narcissism, someone else is the object, it is just that on one model similarity matters most, on the other dependence matters most. Even if narcissism is considered the first form of object-choice (after autoerotism), dependence is present from the very beginning (and a whole school of psychoanalysis would argue object relations are present from the very beginning). Freud himself wrote:

At a time at which the first beginnings of sexual satisfaction are still linked with the taking of nourishment, the sexual instinct has a sexual object outside the infant's own body in the shape of his mother's breast. It is only later that the instinct loses that object, just at the time, perhaps, when the child is able to form a total idea of the person to whom the organ that is giving him satisfaction belongs. As a rule the sexual instinct then becomes auto-erotic, and not until the period of latency has been passed through is the original relation restored. There are thus good reasons why a child sucking at his mother's breast has become the prototype of every relation of love. The finding of an object is in fact the refinding of it. (1905d, VII, 222)

Homosexuality is no *more* a return to earlier modes of relationship than any other attempt at love.[12]

The American Psychiatric Association has struggled with the question of the classification of homosexuality. The classification is not without practical implications, and it is not surprising that the debate has taken political turns.[13] Nosology is not simply a matter of etiological theories in any case. At the minimum, classification sometimes takes account of symptomatic patterns and treatment possibilities as well as etiology. The argument against classifying homosexuality as a disease could well include the notion that it *should not* be treated (whatever its origin) as well as the political claim that the disease classification contributes to inappropriate discrimination (e.g., in jobs – should homosexuality be grounds for dismissal? should schizophrenia?). In 1973, the Board of Trustees of the American Psychiatric Association voted to remove homosexuality (as such) from the list of disorders in the *Diagnostic and Statistical Manual of Mental Disorders* (DSM-III, pp. 281–2). Nonetheless, something called "ego-dystonic homosexuality" was included. That is, if a homosexual does not desire his condition, or suffers distress at his condition, the condition is then regarded as a disorder. Clearly the criteria of mental disorder employed by the APA in this connection are not "neutral": Distress and undesirability can be traced to social attitudes (what produces distress and is therefore undesired in Iowa may be very different from what produces distress and is undesired in San Francisco – so homosexuality might be a "disorder" in Iowa but not San Francisco).[14] In any case, it does not follow from the etiological and developmental theories of psychoanalysis that homosexuality must produce distress and so be undesired.

It must be acknowledged, however, that even if homosexuality involves no developmental arrest or inhibition, even if homosexuality is as "genital" and mature as heterosexuality, it is, as things currently are, detached from the possibility of reproduction and in *that* sense perverse. Any sexual activity that must be detached in its effect from reproduction can be, and has been, regarded as perverse. (Note the relevant detachment is in effect, not in purpose. If the purpose of the persons engaged in the activity was what mattered, most heterosexual genital intercourse would have to be regarded as perverse.) Granting this sense to perversion, however, one should be careful what one concludes about people whose activities are in this sense perverse. For one thing, reproduction would in fact be excluded only if their activities were exclusively perverse. For another, whether it is socially beneficial to *bear* children (the care and upbringing of children is not excluded by perverse, i.e., nonreproductive, activity) depends on circumstances (other features of the parents, and social circumstances such as overpopulation). Moreover, new reproductive technologies may make the reproductive limitations of perverse activity of lesser concern, just as new contraceptive technologies have made the dangers of unwanted conception of lesser concern in "normal" sexual activity. Whatever the biological place of reproduction in human sexual life, it cannot settle the appropriate attitude to nonreproductive human sexual activity. Granting that it is the case that reproduction is one of the purposes of sex, it is equally certain that that purpose can be successfully achieved (and the survival of the species ensured) without all engaging in only reproductive sex. And after all, normal sex, that is, heterosexual genital intercourse between adults, can be multiply defective. There can be failures of reciprocity and mutuality, or interactive completeness (private sexual fantasies may make intercourse closer to masturbation in its experience, even if not in its possible effects). And even sex normal in the present sense, that is, of the kind that could in appropriate circumstances lead to reproduction, may fail in its actual effects (most intercourse does not lead to pregnancy, and intercourse between sterile partners or involving the use of contraceptives is most unlikely to). Does detachment from reproductive concerns in one's sexual activity make an individual defective? There is no reason to believe so. Freud frequently points out the great social contributions of homosexuals in history, sometimes even tying the contributions to the sexual orientation, deriving social energies from homosexual inclinations.[15] Not that Freud is blind to defects; he does not assume all homosexuals are mainstays of civilization: "Of course they are not . . . an 'elite' of mankind; there are at least as many inferior and useless individuals among them as there are among those of a different sexual kind" (1916–17, XVI, 305). Whether homosexuals contribute to society may be relevant to the question of the appropriate attitude to take toward homosexuality, but the same can be said for heterosexuals and those of mixed inclinations; there is no reason to expect uniformity of contributions within such groupings. It remains unclear whether homosexuality should be regarded as a perversion: It depends on which criterion for perversion is adopted (e.g., content, with disgust the marker; exclusiveness and fixation; or development and maturation, with reproduction the marker), and given certain criteria, on which developmental and etiological theories are believed. But it does seem clear that even if homosexuality is regarded as a perversion, that in itself gives no ground for condemning it or thinking it worse than heterosexuality; no reason to disapprove it in others or avoid it in oneself.

FOOT FETISHISM

One could reasonably conclude that Freud offers no systematically sustainable concept of perversion as pathological, and nonetheless should still recognize that his consideration of the issues provides valuable insight into what we mean by perversion and, more important, what perversion means – its psychological significance. If anything is a perversion according to prevailing attitudes, foot fetishism is, and Freud's discussion of exclusiveness and fixation helps us understand why.[16] But other criteria of perversion (content, maturation, reproduction, completeness, and so on) would doubtless yield the same result – indeed, it might be a condition of adequacy on such criteria that they yield that result. Classification is not the problem. Understanding the source and point of this sort of unusual interest in feet is.

Usually, when confronted with a desire one does not share, one can sympathize with the unshared desire at least to the extent of having a sense of what is desirable about the object. Part of the mystery of fetishism is making sense of the extraordinary value and importance attached to the object. Bringing out the link of fetishism to more ordinary overvaluation of sexual objects (which can in turn be tied to narcissism – 1914c, XIV, 88–9, 91, 94, 100–1) goes some way toward making fetishism intelligible (1905d, VII, 153–4), but it still leaves us wanting to know why desires should take such peculiar directions. Partly this is a question about the mechanism of object-choice, but, more important, it is a question about the mean-

ing of object-choice. What is it about a foot that makes it so attractive? Why are some particular feet more attractive than others? How
can they come to satisfy (or be seen to satisfy) needs? Psychoanalysis
offers answers. In the central cases, "the replacement of the object
by a fetish is determined by a symbolic connection of thought, of
which the person concerned is usually not conscious" (1905d, VII,
155). In the case of foot fetishism, in condensed form, psychoanalysis argues (among other things) that "the foot represents a woman's
penis, the absence of which is deeply felt" (155 n.). Thus condensed
the answer may seem wildly implausible. But in his paper on fetishism (1927e, XXI) Freud traces a chain of experience, fantasy, and
association that suggests how a foot might come to provide reassur-
ance about castration fears and so become the focus for sexual interests. Thus filled in, the story may still seem implausible. But notice
that the question of plausibility enters at two levels: One is the
plausibility of the beliefs ascribed to the fetishist (how could anyone
believe anything as implausible as that a foot is the mother's missing penis?), and the second is the plausibility of the ascription of the
(implausible) beliefs. The genius of the psychoanalytic account is
not that it seeks to make bizarre or ad hoc beliefs plausible, but it
takes beliefs that it gives us other reasons for ascribing to people and
shows how in certain cases they persist and give direction to desire.

Some of the relevant beliefs (e.g., in the ubiquity of the male
genital) are to be found in infantile sexual theories. Much of the
evidence for such beliefs, as well as for symbolic equations, comes
from the study of neurotics; which is as it should be, for, as Freud
repeatedly points out, "neuroses are . . . the negative of perversions"
(1905d, VII, 165). We should perhaps pause for a moment on this
point. The sexual instinct, we have seen, is complex, has several
dimensions (ibid., 162). It is not the simple, "qualityless" energy of
much of Freud's earliest theorizing (168, 217). It is thus possible to
reidentify the "same" instinct in different contexts because variation in (for example) object may leave the source clearly the same.
Instincts, unlike qualityless energy, meet one of the conceptual restrictions on "displacement": a change in object can be seen as "displacement" (rather than mere change) only against a background of
continuity. One of the things that may have concealed the underlying continuity between infantile and adult sexuality is that the infant is "polymorphously perverse" (191) – and the tie to adult sexual-

ity is clearest in relation to perverse sexuality (not heterosexual genital intercourse). Similarly, the role of sexuality in the neuroses was concealed partly because the sexuality involved is typically perverse. As Freud puts it, "*neuroses are, so to say, the negative of perversions*" (165) – so the sexual nature of neuroses tends to be hidden. What Freud means by the famous formula is spelled out a bit more fully in a note: "The contents of the clearly conscious phantasies of perverts (which in favourable circumstances can be transformed into manifest behaviour), of the delusional fears of paranoics (which are projected in a hostile sense on to other people) and of the unconscious phantasies of hysterics (which psycho-analysis reveals behind their symptoms) – all of these coincide with one another even down to their details" (165 n. 2). To make this claim persuasive, one must bring out the content of the unconscious fantasies of hysterics, but this is made simpler by that fact that, in the case of neurotics, "the symptoms constitute the sexual activity of the patient" (163), and "at least *one* of the meanings of a symptom is the representation of a sexual phantasy" (1905e, VII, 47). Thus Dora's hysterical cough could be analyzed in terms of an unconscious fantasy of fellatio (ibid., 47–52). None of this is very surprising if one remembers that neurotic sexuality, like perverse sexuality, is infantile (1905d, VII, 172) – whatever shape the sexual instinct eventually takes, it inevitably has its roots in infantile sexuality.

Returning to foot fetishism, whatever one thinks of the psychoanalytic story, it is clear that some story is needed. The attachment is, without further explanation, too peculiar. It is hard for one who does not share the desire to see what is desirable. With suitable hidden significances, the desire at least becomes intelligible as desire. Such understanding is needed for true sympathy. By the standard of exclusiveness and fixation, fetishism is doubtless perverse. But that does not take one far, and we have argued that the criterion of exclusiveness and fixation is itself inadequate if applied quite generally. Certainly there is something peculiar about fetishism, and insofar as psychoanalysis can help us understand that peculiarity, it may help us achieve an appropriate attitude toward perversions in general. In the case of fetishism, while we might not share the beliefs, we can see how given certain beliefs, certain objects and activities might become desirable. Fetishism allows a kind of simultaneous denial and acceptance of uncomfortable facts. It does not follow that all desires become equally uncriticizable once understood. The beliefs may have wider implications and having the beliefs and desires may have wider effects. So some perversions may be objectionable. Our ordinary standards for judging human action and human interaction do not lapse in the face of perversions; but the mere fact of perversion is not an independent ground for moral criticism. Remember: All of our desires are equally in need of explanation, they all have a history (more or less hidden), we may just feel the need for an explanation less in the case of more familiar desires.

Again, foot fetishism demands some explanation. Those who wish to reject the psychoanalytic account of foot fetishism have the burden of supplying an alternative. I believe that a simple stimulus generalization account will not do. Psychoanalysis readily includes the standard associationist points, though sometimes adding less standard associative connections as well; for example, Freud notes:

In a number of cases of foot-fetishism it has been possible to show that the scopophilic instinct, seeking to reach its object (originally the genitals) from underneath, was brought to a halt in its pathway by prohibition and repression. For that reason it became attached to a fetish in the form of a foot or shoe, the female genitals (in accordance with the expectations of childhood) being imagined as male ones. (1905d, VII, 155 n. 2; cf. 1927e, XXI, 155)

But Freud is also properly wary of attributing too much to early sexual impressions, as though they were the total determinant of the direction of sexuality:

All the observations dealing with this point have recorded a first meeting with the fetish at which it already aroused sexual interest without there being anything in the accompanying circumstances to explain the fact. . . . The true explanation is that behind the first recollection of the fetish's appearance there lies a submerged and forgotten phase of sexual development. The fetish, like a "screen-memory," represents this phase and is thus a remnant and precipitate of it. (1905d, VII, 154 n. 2)[17]

The connections Freud emphasizes are typically meaningful, rather than mere casual associations. The more general problem with simple stimulus generalization is that it tends to explain both too little and too much. Why do other people exposed to the same stimuli not develop fetishistic attachments? (Psychoanalysis may also have trouble with this question. See 1927e, XXI, 154.) Why do fetishists often attach special conditions (such as smell) to their preferred objects? (Here psychoanalysis has some interesting suggestions. See 1909d, X, 247 and 1905d, VII, 155 n. 2.) If stimulus generalization stands alone as an explanatory mechanism, it can appear able to explain actual particular outcomes of an association only at the expense of appearing equally able to explain any other outcome of a given early impression. The factors pointed to by the conditioning theorists are simply too pervasive and nondiscriminating. Something that would explain everything explains nothing.[18]

The desires of the fetishist are typically highly thought-dependent. He sees the fetish object as of a certain kind, as having certain connections. (This "seeing as" is another aspect of the situation generally neglected by behaviorist approaches.[19]) Psychoanalysis seeks to trace out these connections (some of them hidden from the individual himself) and their history. It seeks to understand their compulsive force and to enable the individual to specify more fully what it is that he desires in relation to the object. The thought of the object (including the thought of the reason for the desire or of the feature that makes the object desired desirable) specifies the desire. A proper understanding of the relevant thoughts may be a necessary condition of freedom, of the possibility of altering desire via reflective self-understanding. A too exclusive attention to the behavior involved in perverse sexuality may neglect the thought and so the desire behind the behavior. Since people may do observably the same thing for very different reasons (sometimes one person wants to, while another person might be paid to; the different meanings of the same behavior may be revealed in associated fantasies, conscious and unconscious, and other thoughts), behaviorist specifications of perverse activity, like sociological accounts of perverse activity, may inevitably miss the point. If we are to understand perverse (and also "normal") sexual desires (and activities) we must look to the thoughts behind them.[20]

THE MENTAL AND THE PHYSICAL

Plato draws a line between physical love and spiritual love, thinking the latter higher than the former. The line between the physical and the mental does not correspond to the line between the sexual and the spiritual. For whatever one thinks of spirituality and mentality, sexuality is not purely physical. Indeed, if it were, one might expect the objects and aims of sexual desire to be fixed by biology. But while human biology is relatively uniform, the objects and aims of sexual desire are as various as the human imagination. There are psychological conditions of sexual satisfaction. Sex is as much a matter of thought as of action. While the machinery of reproduction, the sexual organs themselves, the genitals, have determinate structures and modes of functioning, sexual desire takes wildly multifarious forms. Sexuality is as much a matter of thought or the mind as of the body. To think one can get away from sexuality via the denial of the body is to mistake the half for the whole.

While it would be an exaggeration to say sex is all in the mind, it would be less of a mistake than the common notion that sex is purely physical. Freud came closest to the truth in locating sexuality at the borderland or bridge between the mental and the physical. Writing of instincts in general, Freud explained his meaning:

By an "instinct" is provisionally to be understood the psychical representative of an endosomatic, continuously flowing source of stimulation, as contrasted with a "stimulus," which is set up by *single* excitations coming from *without*. The concept of instinct is thus one of those lying on the frontier between the mental and the physical. (1905d, VII, 168)

Thus the sexual instinct is not to be equated with neutral energy (as in Freud's earlier theorizing, e.g., in his *Project for a Scientific Psychology* – 1950a [1895], I). It has direction (aim and object) as well as a somatic source and impetus (or strength). The instinct involves both biologically given needs and thought-dependent desires. It is our thoughts that specify the objects of our desire (however mistaken we may be about whether they will satisfy our real needs). Via transformations and displacements of various sorts, our sexual instinct takes various directions. As Freud at one place puts it, "In psycho-analysis the concept of what is sexual . . . goes lower and also higher than its popular sense. This extension is justified genetically. . . ." (1910k, XI, 222; cf. the discussion of "The Mental Factor" at 1905d, VII, 161–2). The analysis of sexual desires starts with an instinctual need derived from a somatic source. But the psychical representatives of this instinctual need develop in the history of the individual, attracting him to a variety of objects and aims (modes of satisfaction). Given different vicissitudes, our original instinctual endowment develops into neurosis, perversion, or the range of normal sexual life and character. Our character is among those (perhaps "higher") attributes that Freud traces back to sexuality. In his essay on "Character and Anal Erotism" Freud says we can "lay down a formula for the way in which character in its final shape is formed out of the constituent instincts: the permanent character-traits are either unchanged prolongations of the original instincts, or sublimations of those instincts, or reaction-formations against them" (1908b, IX, 175). I cannot pursue the puzzles raised by these alleged transformations, and by the psycho-analytic explanation of the normal, here,[21] but it should be clear that our sexual character in large measure determines our character, who we are: whether directly, as suggested in the formula, or indirectly, as the model for our behavior and attitudes in other spheres.[22]

There are lessons in multiplicity to be learned from Freud. At a minimum, I would have us take the following from this essay on Freud's *Three Essays:*

1. Sexuality, far from being unified, is complex. The sexual instinct is made up of components that can be specified along several dimensions (source, object, aim). It is a composite that develops and changes, and can readily decompose. In particular, the instinct is "merely soldered" to its object.

2. The criteria for perversion are multiple, and no one of them is truly satisfactory if one is searching for a cross-cultural standard founded in a common human nature. Not that there are not ideals of sexuality (with corresponding criteria for perversion), but they too are multiple, and must be understood in connection with more general ideals for human interaction.

3. The purposes, functions, and goals of sexuality are multiple. It is not a pure bodily or biological function. There is a significant mental element that emerges perhaps most clearly in relation to the perversions, where the psychological conditions for sexual satisfaction are dramatically emphasized. Here we might find the beginnings of a defensible (Spinozist–Freudian) ideal in the sphere of the sexual: Health and maturity involve coming to know what we really want and why we

want it. Further, since what we want depends on what we think, if we wish to change what we want, we may have to change how we think.

Who we are is revealed in who or what and how we love. The structure of our desires emerges in the course of the transformation of the sexual instinct as we learn to live in a world full of internal and external pressures and constraints, as we learn to live with others and ourselves.

NOTES

1 While I here emphasize that the existence of some causal story does not render all evaluation out of place, I should perhaps also emphasize that some evaluations are almost always out of place. Whether homosexuality is the result of nature or nurture, it makes little sense to condemn homosexuality as "unnatural." For one thing, nature, or at least human nature, includes conditions of nurture: All humans must be somehow nurtured in order to survive and develop. The "somehow" of course allows for variations. The real point of the contrast of nature and nurture, two types of causes, may ultimately simply be in terms of uniformity versus variability. In terms of individual responsibility, nature and nurture may both be viewed as "external" causes (the individual does not choose them, and so does not control the result). For another thing, nature in general includes more than many would like to admit (one of the constant lessons of the Marquis de Sade). Insofar as charges of perversion are based on notions of unnaturalness, they may always be inapplicable. (See Michael Slote, "Inapplicable Concepts," *Philosophical Studies* 28 [1975]: 265–71. The various contrasts between the natural and the unnatural, and the historical development of the charge of unnaturalness against homosexuality, are interestingly traced by John Boswell in his *Christianity, Social Tolerance, and Homosexuality* [Chicago: University of Chicago Press, 1980].) In the coroner's verdict, "death by natural causes," the contrast is with other types of causes, basically causes involving the intervention of human intentions. Whatever the causes of homosexuality and homosexual desires, they must be of the same *type* as the causes of heterosexuality and heterosexual desires. This point is reflected in Aristophanes' myth in Plato's *Symposium*. Incidentally, one might note that if Freud had this myth in mind in his discussion at the start of the *Three Essays* (1905d, VII, 136), as the normally highly reliable editors of the *Standard Edition* claim in a footnote, his account there is misleading. Freud speaks as if the "poetic fable" is supposed to explain only heterosexuality, and as if the

existence of homosexuality and lesbianism therefore comes as a surprise. In fact, Aristophanes' story of the division of the original human beings into two halves, and their subsequent quest to reunite in love, allows for all three alternatives. Aristophanes starts with three original sexes: double-male, double-female, and "androgynous." Thus the myth offers an explanation (the same explanation) of homosexuality and lesbianism as well as heterosexuality. (One should perhaps also note that there is an Indian version of the myth that may conform better to Freud's account, and Freud refers to it explicitly later in *Beyond the Pleasure Principle* [1920g, XVIII, 57–8].) From the point of view of psychoanalytic theory, heterosexual object-choice and homosexual object-choice are equally problematic, equally in need of explanation (1905d, VII, 146n.).

Freud himself, in his published writings, only used the term "unnatural" three times in connection with perverse desires or practices. In each of the three instances (1898a, III, 265; 1916–17, XVI, 302; and 1920a, XVIII, 149), in context, the term refers to the views of others.

2 See Bernard Williams, "Moral Luck," *Proceedings of the Aristotelian Society*, Supp. vol. 50 (1976): 115–35; included in his *Moral Luck* (Cambridge: Cambridge University Press, 1981). See also the reply by Thomas Nagel, "Moral Luck," *Proceedings of the Aristotelian Society*, Supp. vol. 50 (1976): 137–51; included in his *Mortal Questions* (Cambridge: Cambridge University Press, 1979).

3 Freud spells out the content criterion for deviations in respect of source and aim: "Perversions are sexual activities which either (a) extend, in an anatomical sense, beyond the regions of the body that are designed for sexual union, or (b) linger over the intermediate relations to the sexual object which should normally be traversed rapidly on the path towards the final sexual aim" (1905d, VII, 150). The question remains, what is so objectionable about "extending" and "lingering"?

4 Freud summarizes his views on the child and feces in Introductory Lecture XX:

> To begin with ... He feels no disgust at his faeces, values them as a portion of his own body with which he will not readily part, and makes use of them as his first "gift," to distinguish people whom he values especially highly. Even after education has succeeded in its aim of making these inclinations alien to him, he carries on his high valuation of faeces in his estimate of "gifts" and "money." On the other hand he seems to regard his achievements in urinating with peculiar pride. (1916–17, XVI, 315)

5 "Not only the deviation from normal sexual life but its normal form as well are determined by the infantile manifestations of sexuality" (1905d, VII, 212).

6 Hence, as Erikson suggests, the infant is expelled from the oral paradise of an earlier stage (Erik Erikson, *Childhood and Society*, 2d ed. [New York: W. W. Norton, 1963], p. 79). Erikson is in general very helpful on the social contribution to and meaning of the psychosexual stages.

7 There has been some speculation on the possible evolutionary advantages of homosexuality in terms of altruistic and social impulses. See, for example, E. O. Wilson, *On Human Nature* (Cambridge, Mass.: Harvard University Press, 1978), pp. 142f.

8 The multiplicity of ends and essences for sexuality, and the corresponding multiplicity of criteria for perversion, is amply evidenced in a growing philosophical literature on sexual perversion (much of it collected in two anthologies: R. Baker and F. Elliston, eds., *Philosophy and Sex* [Buffalo: Prometheus Books, 1975] and A. Soble, ed. *The Philosophy of Sex: Contemporary Readings* [Totowa, N.J.: Littlefield, Adams and Company, 1980]). The authors tend to vacillate between on the one hand explicating the concept of perversion in a way that captures our ordinary classifications of particular practices, and on the other providing a sustained rationale for a defensible ideal of sexuality (with its attendant, sometimes revisionary, implications for what counts as a perversion). Here, as elsewhere, a "reflective equilibrium" between our intuitions and principles may be desirable. Perhaps most interesting from the point of view of the issues considered in this essay are Thomas Nagel's "Sexual Perversion" (*Journal of Philosophy* 66 [1969]: 5–17; and in his *Mortal Questions* and both the anthologies cited above) and Sara Ruddick's "Better Sex" (in Baker and Elliston, eds., *Philosophy and Sex*). Nagel finds the essence of sexuality in multileveled personal interaction and awareness, a dialectic of desire and embodiment that makes desires in response to desires central to sexuality. Hence the criterion for perversion that emerges is in terms of interactive incompleteness – according to which homosexuality need not be perverse, foot fetishism must be, and heterosexual intercourse with distracting fantasies might be. While the form of incompleteness is different, the emphasis on incompleteness might be suggestively connected with the sort of unification or totalization of components in Freud's final genital organization of sexuality – in terms of which perversions might be understood as component (or "incomplete") instincts. (Cf. Freud's statement, echoed often elsewhere, that the perversions are "on the one hand inhibitions, and on the other hand dissociations, of normal development" – 1905d, VII, 231.) In any case, Nagel's emphasis on a full theory of the nature of sexual desire seems to me right-headed. Also of special interest is Ruddick's "Better Sex," which, among other things, sorts out clearly the relation of reproduction to perversion in ordinary language and understanding.

Freud's emphasis on the role of pleasure (or discharge) in sexuality should be complicated by his emphasis on the psychological conditions of pleasure (thought-dependent conditions of discharge). Pleasure, as Freud well understood, is not itself simply bodily or otherwise simple. When the question shifts from sexuality and pleasure to the larger questions of love and falling in love, a whole range of additional factors has to be taken into account. Love and the family bring the Oedipus complex back to the center of the picture, and love relationships (whether the object is of the same or opposite gender) have to be understood in terms of transference, ego-ideals, and the splitting of the ego (1921c). The coming together of the sexual and affectionate currents in a mature love relationship raises all sorts of difficulties, but failures in this coming together tend to result in what might more properly be called "neurotic" love than "perverse" love (e.g., oedipal dependence or triangles are recreated, or needs for degraded or forbidden objects with accompanying patterns of psychical impotence emerge – see 1905d, VII, 200 and 1912d, XI, 180–7).

9 It might for some purposes be helpful to maintain the distinction between inversion and perversion. For it then becomes easier to ask whether it is their inversion (in object) that makes some individuals perverse (in aim), or whether it is their perversion (in aim) that makes some individuals inverted (in their choice of object). Or, to put it slightly differently, the question of perversion may be relatively independent of the question of choice of object (of homosexuality or heterosexuality).

10 Indeed, some analysts, such as Michael Balint, insist that many forms of homosexuality "are definitely not survivals of infantile forms of sexuality but later developments" ("Perversions and Genitality," *Primary Love and Psycho-analytic Technique* [London: Tavistock Publications, 1965], p. 136). But it must be noted that many of Balint's views are insupportable, or at any rate not provided with support. In particular, of homosexuals he claims "they all know – that, without normal intercourse, there is no real contentment" (p. 142). The development of psychoanalytic views of homosexuality from Freud onward is usefully traced in Kenneth Lewes, *The Psychoanalytic Theory of Male Homosexuality* (New York: Simon and Schuster, 1988).

The deeper problem raised by lesbianism (presuming that everyone starts with a female primary love object) may be how anyone (female or male) can love a man. Is it the sameness or the maleness of the object that matters for a homosexual? Again, how does maleness matter for women? For anyone?

11 Among the mechanisms of homosexual object-choice considered by Freud, the main one involves identification with the mother (1905d,

VII, 145 n.; 1910c, XI, 98–101; 1921c, XVIII, 108; 1922b, XVIII, 230–1)
and a secondary one involves reaction-formation against sibling rivalry
(1922b, XVIII, 231–2). Freud speaks elsewhere, in connection with a
case of lesbianism, of "retiring in favour of someone else" (1920a,
XVIII, 159 n.). Lewes, *The Psychoanalytic Theory of Male Homosexuality*, distinguishes four main strands in Freud's theorizing about the
etiology of homosexuality.

12 There is a difficult early passage in which Freud connects homosexuality
with a transitional phase of narcissism (1911c, XII, 60–1). It is thought-
fully discussed by J. Laplanche and J.-B. Pontalis (*The Language of
Psycho-Analysis* [London: The Hogarth Press, 1973], p. 259).

13 The basic facts are recounted in J. Marmor, "Epilogue: Homosexuality
and the Issue of Mental Illness," in J. Marmor, ed., *Homosexual Behavior: A Modern Reappraisal* (New York: Basic Books, 1980). A more detailed journalistic account is available in R. Bayer, *Homosexuality and
American Psychiatry: The Politics of Diagnosis* (New York: Basic Books,
1981). See also Lewes, *The Psychoanalytic Theory of Male Homosexuality*, pp. 213–29.

14 This may conflict with the APA's own general characterization of a
mental disorder, which includes the following restriction:

When the disturbance is limited to a conflict between an individual and
society, this may represent social deviance, which may or may not be
commendable, but is not by itself a mental disorder. (DSM-III [Washing-
ton, D.C.: American Psychiatric Association, 1980], p. 363).

C. Culver and B. Gert (*Philosophy in Medicine: Conceptual and Ethical Issues in Medicine* [Oxford: Oxford University Press, 1982]) raise
difficulties of their own with the APA definitions and classifications of
mental disorders, but they are less troubled than they ought to be about
the category of "ego-dystonic homosexuality." They write:

the primary reason why certain recurring sexual behaviors are maladies
is that they are ego-dystonic. The person engaging in the behavior is
distressed by it. Of course, such behavior is probably also a manifestation of a volitional disability, but even if it is not, the distress, if significant, is sufficient to make it count as a malady. Note that neither in the
case of distress nor of a volitional disability is the sexual condition a
malady because it is sexual, but rather because of some other characteristic attached to the condition. Thus, we believe that when homosexuality qualifies as a malady it is because of the distress the person experiences, not because of the person's homosexual phantasies or desires.
(p. 104)

But I believe that by their own criteria for what counts as a "malady"
they should be more equivocal. They argue (pp. 95–8) that grief should
not be regarded as a disease because it has a "distinct sustaining cause"

(namely, an external loss – if the sufferer came to believe the loss was not real, grief and suffering would cease). And so it would seem that it is unclear whether "ego-dystonic homosexuality" is, in their terms, a "malady." Doesn't the suffering (and even the putative "volitional disability") have a "distinct sustaining cause"? After all, if society changed its attitude, the suffering might disappear and there might be no need to overcome desires. Culver and Gert at one point write: "If a person is suffering or at increased risk of suffering evils principally because of conflict with his social environment, then his social environment would be a distinct sustaining cause of his suffering and he would not have a malady" (p. 94). A theory of the source of suffering is needed if suffering is to be the sign of a malady. Even supposing a change in social attitudes would not in a given case remove suffering, when a desire is ego-dystonic, it may be because the individual has internalized mistaken standards. Is the problem then in the desire or in the standards (it is the two together that produce the distress)? Which should be changed? An individual can suffer from an unjustified (but perhaps socially encouraged) self-loathing.

15 For example:

> It is well known that a good number of homosexuals are characterized by a special development of their social instinctual impulses and by their devotion to the interests of the community . . . the fact that homosexual object-choice not infrequently proceeds from an early overcoming of rivalry with men cannot be without a bearing on the connection between homosexuality and social feeling. (1922b, XVIII, 232)

The more usual connection that Freud makes is, of course, between social feeling and sublimated homosexuality (rather than active homosexuality):

> After the stage of heterosexual object-choice has been reached, the homosexual tendencies are not, as might be supposed, done away with or brought to a stop; they are merely deflected from their sexual aim and applied to fresh uses. They now combine with portions of the ego-instincts and, as "attached" components, help to constitute the social instincts, thus contributing an erotic factor to friendship and comradeship, to *esprit de corps* and to the love of mankind in general. How large a contribution is in fact derived from erotic sources (with the sexual aim inhibited) could scarcely be guessed from the normal social relations of mankind. But it is not irrelevant to note that it is precisely manifest homosexuals, and among them again precisely those that set themselves against an indulgence in sensual acts, who are distinguished by taking a particularly active share in the general interests of humanity – interests which have themselves sprung from a sublimation of erotic instincts. (1911c, XII, 61)

16 In understanding why here, we also understand what it means to de-

scribe a desire or practice as "perverse." Foot fetishism is not generally regarded as disgusting. What is disturbing or troubling about it is the idea that someone might be (sexually) interested *only* in feet. However much such focus might simplify life, it does seem to leave out other valuable possibilities.

17 The problem here is rather like the problem with certain other behaviorist attempts to explain complex psychological phenomena. For example, Wolpe and Rachman suggest, in relation to Freud's case of Little Hans, "that the incident to which Freud refers as merely the exciting cause of Hans' phobia was in fact the cause of the entire disorder" (J. Wolpe and S. Rachman, "Psychoanalytic Evidence: A Critique Based on Freud's Case of Little Hans," in S. Rachman, ed., *Critical Essays on Psychoanalysis* [Oxford: Pergamon, 1963], p. 216). The incident involved was Hans's witnessing the fall of a horse that was drawing a bus. Aside from other problems with their account (see J. Neu, *Emotion, Thought, and Therapy* [London: Routledge and Kegan Paul, 1977], pp. 124–35), Freud had pointed out fifty years before: "Chronological considerations make it impossible for us to attach any great importance to the actual precipitating cause of the outbreak of Hans's illness, for he had shown signs of apprehensiveness long before he saw the bus-horse fall down in the street" (1909b, X, 136).

Later additions to the psychoanalytic theory of fetishism (including emphasis on phases of development earlier than the phallic stage) are traced in Phyllis Greenacre, "Fetishism" (in I. Rosen, ed., *Sexual Deviation*, 2d ed. [Oxford: Oxford University Press, 1979], pp. 79–108).

18 See Neu, *Emotion, Thought, and Therapy*, pp. 126–7.

19 See C. Taylor, *The Explanation of Behaviour* (London: Routledge and Kegan Paul, 1964).

20 I, like Nagel ("Sexual Perversion"), wish to give special emphasis to the role of desires in perversion. For whether a particular activity or practice as engaged in by a particular individual should be regarded as perverse typically depends on the desires that inform his practice (though the force of this point might vary with alternative criteria for perversion and for sexuality). Description, here as elsewhere, is theory laden. Whether a particular observable action counts as "neurotic" depends on why it was done, on its meaning. A person who washes his hands fifteen times a day need not be obsessive–compulsive, he may be a surgeon. Similarly, a "golden shower" performed out of sexual interest has a very different significance in respect to the question of "perversion" than one done as an emergency measure to treat a sea urchin wound. Of course, actions can be overdetermined, motives can be mixed, and motives can be hidden. In any case, the full description of what a person is doing typically

depends on what he thinks (whether consciously or unconsciously) he is doing and why. Underlying thoughts and desires are essential in characterizing the nature of activities and practices.

And again, in understanding the nature of desires themselves, the role of thoughts can scarcely be overemphasized. As Stuart Hampshire concludes in the course of a discussion of the role of thought in desire:

the traditional scheme, which distinguishes the lusts from thoughtful desires, may turn out to be much too simple, and to reflect too grossly simple moral ideas. Any study of sexuality shows that thought, usually in the form of fantasy, enters into a great variety of sexual desires, which are normally also associated with physical causes. The traditional equation of physical desire, or lust, with unthinking desire is not warranted by the evidence. Nor is it true that the more reflective and fully conscious desires, which are in this sense rational, are necessarily or always the most complex. On the contrary, there can be preconscious and unconscious desires which are shown to have developed from very complex processes of unreflective and imaginative thought.   (*Freedom of the Individual*, 2d ed. [London: Chatto and Windus, 1975], p. 137)

21 I make a start in "Getting Behind the Demons," *Humanities in Society* 4 (1981): 171–96 (esp. 191–2).

22 As Freud puts it in discussing the case of the Rat Man: "a man's attitude in sexual things has the force of a model to which the rest of his reactions tend to conform" (1909d, X, 241). The thought also forms the basis for Freud's main doubt about masturbation: "injury may occur through the laying down of a *psychical pattern* according to which there is no necessity for trying to alter the external world in order to satisfy a great need" (1912f, XII, 251–2; cf. 1908d, IX, 198–200). We should perhaps note that he continues: "Where, however, a far-reaching reaction against this pattern develops, the most valuable character-traits may be initiated."

8 Morality and the internalized other

Often, when Freud mentioned morality, he was referring to a culture's restrictions on sexual behavior – a code regularly endorsed yet routinely defied. He was deeply interested in exposing the reasons for such restrictive sexual codes, and the dynamics of our deviations from them. Still, for Freud, it is not the sexual content nor the societal enforcement of certain constraints that makes them moral; moral constraints are, rather, constraints that play a particular role within the psychology of individuals – namely, the role of "superego." While the emergence of a superego is, according to Freud, bound up with the dynamics of sexual desire in general and the oedipal complex in particular, in the end it is the relational properties and not the content of the superego – specifically, its historical relations to other people and its ongoing relations to the ego – that make it a *super*ego and make it the agency of morality. An account of the formation and the character of the superego is, then, simultaneously an account of the formation and the character of morality.

To understand Freud's account of the superego, and the closely related ego-ideal, we must understand how a self or an ego is constituted and how characteristics of other people may be internalized to become parts of oneself. This story forms the crucial metapsychological background for Freud's account of morality, and I offer a somewhat novel interpretation of this background in the first and second sections of this chapter. The third section discusses the seemingly paradoxical situation in which an internalized other retains its otherness, and the fourth explores the distinction between the super-

I am particularly grateful to Sebastian Gardner and Jerome Neu for their comments on an earlier draft of this essay.

209

ego and the ego-ideal. In the final section, I try to locate Freud's account of morality with respect to some available options, and I defend it against some likely objections.

I. CONSCIOUSNESS AND THE DEFLECTIONS OF DESIRE

According to Freud, our fundamental desires or drives are few, the many and various desires we regularly experience being the result of more or less elaborate deflections and transformations of these.[1] At its most basic, a desire is directed toward some object or end whose attainment causes the satisfaction of the desire and the release of the energy that sustains it. If the object or end is not attainable, however, the desire will seek release through substitute objects. Almost any object may substitute for another as long as the person in some way associates the two, but the closer and the richer the associations – similar appearances, physical proximity, similar sounding names, and so on – the more satisfying and stable the substitutions.[2] A single desire may be deflected onto several new objects, and several distinct desires may be deflected onto a single object; these are the so-called primary processes of displacement and condensation – processes that take place automatically, driven by the pressure of unreleased desire and rewarded by the pleasure of regained equilibrium. Because almost all substitute objects are imperfect substitutes, however, the aquisition of a substitute object seldom results in the complete satisfaction of one's original desire; hence, one's original desire will tend to remain active to some extent and the processes of deflection and condensation will continue indefinitely.

This unconscious "logic" of desire – of substitution through association – is often at odds with the logic of conscious thought. Whatever the qualitative similarities between a mark on the tablecloth today and the desired mark on the sheets of years ago, consciously we know that the former is no substitute for the latter.[3] This is because conscious thoughts (i.e., thoughts that are part of the system Cs, and governed by the so-called secondary processes) are sensitive to temporal ordering, to causal laws, and to *dis*analogies – they are answerable to the constraints of reality, as it were – whereas unconscious thoughts (i.e., thoughts that are part of the system Ucs) answer only to the demands of imagination and pleasure, for which temporal order, causal laws, and negative facts are irrelevant.[4] Because we can never be conscious of all of our thoughts, and because consciousness often denies a desire its object (or, indeed, denies the desire itself), some reliance on and reversion to the unconscious logic of desire is inevitable. And, at bottom, it is by appeal to the conflict and the fluctuation between these two modes of thought – between conscious and unconscious processing, or between thought in accordance with the reality principle and thought in accordance with the pleasure principle – that Freud attempts to explain many cases of (apparent) irrationality.[5]

Bound up with the capacity for conscious thought are two other, related capacities: (1) the capacity to acknowledge one's own subjectivity – to acknowledge one's thoughts *as* thoughts, or one's point of view *as* a point of view, and (2) the capacity to use language. Freud is quite explicit about each of these connections. Unconscious processes, he asserts, "equate reality of thought with external actuality, and wishes with their fulfillment" (1911b, XII, 225) such that "the antithesis between subjective and objective does not exist from the first" (1925h, XIX, 237). With regard to language, Freud writes, "the conscious presentation comprises the presentation of the thing plus the presentation of the word belonging to it, while the unconscious presentation is the presentation of the thing alone.... [A] presentation which is not put into words ... remains thereafter in the Unconscious" (1915e, XIV, 207; see also 1923b, XIX, 20, 25). The claim is not merely that consciousness *employs* a language, rather that it is the employment of a language which *makes* one conscious.

Freud does not, however, explain *why* the capacity to recognize subjectivity and the capacity for language should be both correlated with and, indeed, definitive of consciousness. We might venture the following on his behalf: A subjective point of view is a subjective point of view for the same reason that a language is a language – namely, it is capable of representing the world as being a certain way whether or not the world is in fact that way; both a subject and a language must be capable of representation at a distance and, more important, they must be capable of *mis*representation. Acknowledging subjectivity and using a language as a language both presuppose the recognition of this possibility – the possibility of misrepresentation and, hence, the possibility of representation itself. It is the recognition of this possibility that, for Freud, seems to constitute the essence of consciousness.[6]

This interpretation of what Freud means by consciousness helps to explain Freud's shift away from the conscious/unconscious contrast toward the ego/id contrast: If the emergence of consciousness is equivalent to the emergence of a recognition of one's own subjectivity, it is also equivalent to the identification and delineation of a self or an ego. The id, in contrast, is an assortment of desires, wholly directed toward their objects and wholly oblivious to their subjective character.

The foregoing interpretation of Freud's notion of consciousness may help to explain two otherwise puzzling claims made by Freud: (1) the claim that *emotions* must be conscious, and (2) the claim that thought is *experimental* action.[7] As long as an impulse remains unconscious, it will be freely deflected from one object to another without regard to their causal relevance to the original object of one's desire, and it will immediately issue in actions directed at these objects without regard to the likely success of those actions. The impulse or desire, as long as it remains unconscious, will not be withheld or suspended pending a future appearance of its original object or an opportunity for more effective action. Emotion, however, seems to require just such frustration and suspension of desire; in anger, for example, one's most immediate destructive impulses are outwardly restrained but inwardly sustained. Emotion establishes a subjective as opposed to an objective site of action. So, too, with thought. In thought, I create a desired state of affairs inwardly rather than outwardly (I *imagine* it, I *represent* it), and this enables me to experiment with various possibilities and outcomes prior to committing myself to any one of them. Thus in thought, as in emotion, I withdraw to a subjective realm. But since the contrast between the subjective and the objective, or between the imaginary and the real, can only be grasped through consciousness (as Freud understands it), both emotion and thought (versus desire and belief, or impulse and cognition) will indeed depend on consciousness.

II. THE INNER AND THE OUTER

In attaining a sense of self – that is, in attaining consciousness, or attaining an ego – boundaries between myself and other things must be drawn. Fixing the physical and the psychological boundaries of a self, however, is a complicated and ongoing process. Desire is possessive, seeking to incorporate things we like into ourselves, while disowning things we dislike, seeking to expel them from ourselves. At a very basic level, this is manifested in our attempts to draw desirable objects toward and into our bodies while pushing away or pulling back from objects we dislike. (Children's preoccupation with various bodily orifices is not due merely to the fact that they are the sites of vivid sensations; capable of ingesting, retaining, or expelling material, they are also the sites of engrossing ambiguities concerning what is and is not mine, what does and does not belong to me.) At a more abstract level, though, it is properties that are owned or disowned in accordance with desire: We tend to attribute desirable features to ourselves (we "introject" them) while attributing undesirable features to things outside ourselves (we "project" them). So, for example, a child will view his difficulty with a toy as a problem with the toy, not himself, yet will view an accomplishment brought about through a parent's intervention as his own accomplishment, not that of the parent – a tendency that is not, of course, confined to children, and one that may be reversed when self-confidence is undermined.

With the ability to recognize other people as psychological wholes – personalities that combine both good and bad properties in distinctive ways, comes the possibility of internalizing not just individual properties of another but whole personalities. When I take a whole person rather than a selected aspect of some person as the object of my desire, the possession or incorporation of that object requires the internalization of a whole personality; satisfaction of my desire thus requires that I fantasize the internal presence of the desired person rather than merely the desired properties of that person. The result is the internal presence of not only the loved but also the hated aspects of the internalized other; in imaginatively acquiring that which I desire, I may also consign myself to the continued presence of much that I despise.

Just which people I internalize will depend on which people are most regularly the objects of intense but unsatisfied desire – those whom I most regularly and intensely *desire* to possess or control yet am usually *unable* to possess or control. Typically, and initially, the internalized other will be one's mother or one's father, for they are typically the objects of one's strongest desires and they are the people whom one first comes to see as psychological wholes. Eventually and in principle, though, any influential other may be internalized. Note, though, that it is my inability to fully possess or control others that both demonstrates their independence from me and creates the need to resort to fantasy in order to satisfy my desires; so some experience of conflict between my desires or actions and those of another is a precondition for my internalization of that person. The internalization of another is a way to *imaginatively* possess and retain a desired person who, in *fact*, cannot be possessed or retained.

The internalization of a desired person is an alternative to and, in effect, a compromise between two other options in the face of frustration: deflection of one's desire to new (external) objects, and retreat to narcissism (whereby oneself becomes the new object of desire).[8] One is continually confronted with a choice between redirecting desires outward, never wholly successfully, and redirecting desires inward, effectively withdrawing from the world. Internalization offers a third alternative; for with internalization, one's desires remain directed toward their original object, but that object is withdrawn from the external world and "housed" within.

III. IDENTIFICATION AND OTHERNESS

The internalization of another does not necessarily give rise to a superego. To the extent that we are able to simply add another's desires and personality traits to our own or to replace our previous desires and traits with those of someone else, the internalization of an other will amount, rather, to a kind of merger with that person. Given the frequency of conflict between the desires and personalities of different people, and given the difficulty of relinquishing one's most basic desires and dispositions, however, the internalization of another will normally engender some internal conflict. This introduces a question, familiar from current discussions of personal identity and self-deception, about how two apparently distinct and conflicting personalities might nonetheless constitute a single person.

Freud did not consider this to be an idle question, answerable by mere stipulation. He explicitly rejected the idea that the contrast between conscious and unconscious mental states, for example, could be understood on the model of two interacting selves for, in his view, the unconscious, or the id, is not a self at all.

This process of inference . . . leads logically to the assumption of another, second consciousness which is united in one's self, with the consciousness one knows. But . . . a consciousness of which its own possessor knows nothing is something very different from a consciousness belonging to another person, and it is questionable whether such a consciousness, lacking, as it does, its most important characteristic, deserves any discussion at all. . . . [W]hat is proved is not the existence of a second consciousness in us, but the existence of psychical acts which lack consciousness. (1915e, XIV, 170)

On Freud's view, the unconscious or the id cannot be considered a separate self because, as we have already suggested, creating a self is of a piece with becoming conscious. Thus, although the drives of the id (of the system Ucs) certainly are in some important sense *mine*, they are not part of my ego or my *self* until as they are taken up by consciousness.

An internalized other, clearly, may be aligned with either the system Cs or the system Ucs, depending on whether its desires and beliefs are acknowledged or not. Its *otherness*, however, will depend on its opposition to one's conscious self. (Opposition wholly within the unconscious not only fails to be opposition to one's self but, what actually comes to the same thing, it fails to sustain itself as an opposition for, as we saw earlier, it immediately resolves itself through the workings of displacement and condensation.) To the extent that an internalized other is unconscious, its opposition to oneself will amount to a rebellion against the regimentation imposed by consciousness; for consciousness is simply the agency through which previously unconscious material confronts the reality principle, and through which prudence is enforced. To the extent that an internalized other is conscious, on the other hand, it will amount to a set of second-order desires regarding one's conscious, first-order desires. In either case, the internalized other retains its otherness only insofar as it directs its desires toward aspects of one's self rather than toward objects in the external world – hence, a *super*ego (an "Über-Ich"). The superego is precisely that part of a person that remains opposed to or critical of the ego.

Acknowledging the superego – that is, becoming conscious of it without actually identifying oneself with it – thus depends on acknowledging its role as an overseer of the ego. Initially, of course, it is other people – parents, in particular – who "oversee" our actions and decisions; and when they are internalized, it is precisely in their role as overseers that they retain the independence from the self that is necessary for a superego, or a moral "conscience."

We may reject the existence of an original, as it were natural, capacity to distinguish good from bad. What is bad is often not at all what is injurious or dangerous to the ego; on the contrary, it may be something which is desirable and enjoyable to the ego. Here, therefore, there is an extraneous influence at work, and it is this that decides what is to be called good or bad. . . . A great change takes place only when the authority is internalized through the establishment of a superego. The phenomena of conscience then reach a higher stage. Actually, it is not until now we should speak of conscience. . . . (1930a, XXI, 124, 125)

My earlier remarks about consciousness and language may now help to explain why the superego is typically experienced as an inner *voice*. Points of *view* must be spatially distinguished, so that *looking* at myself from another's point of view requires that I view myself in relation to a real or imaginary other that remains outside of my physical self. What that other "sees" in me, then, will depend on what is publicly displayed and what is visible from the particular vantage point occupied by the other. I will modify my *behavior* in response to another that continues to be conceived of as external to me. Another's voice, on the other hand, need not be experienced as spatially external to me; to be distinct from mine, it is enough that it address itself to me, or carry on a conversation with me. Thus, unlike the gaze of another, the *voice* of another may influence me as I merely deliberate about what to do; it will influence mere *intentions* to act. The superego, as inner voice, oversees my conscious (hence, articulated) desires, not just the results of those desires; it comments on what my ego *is*, not just what it *does*.

Originally, renunciation of instinct was the result of fear of an external authority: one renounced one's satisfactions in order not to lose its love. If one has carried out this renunciation, one is, as it were, quits with the authority and no sense of guilt should remain. But with fear of the super-ego the case is different. Here, instinctual renunciation is not enough, for the wish persists and cannot be concealed from the super-ego. Thus, in spite of the renunciation that has been made, a sense of guilt comes about. (ibid, 127–8)

IV. JUDGES AND IDEALS

Freud thought of the superego as a harsh judge – harsher, in fact, than the parents or other authorities from which it is derived. I have already suggested two reasons for this. First, it is only those parts of another that stand over and against the self that, when internalized, retain their otherness. Aspects of an internalized other that easily merge with one's preexisting self will not be experienced as other; they will be assimilated into the ego (or id) rather than contribute to the character of a superego. Second, unlike real judges of our actions, the internal critic that is the superego observes our every thought, and thus recognizes the pervasiveness of our sins.

There is, however, another important reason for the harshness of the superego according to Freud. One of the features of our parents (and of adults in general) that we covet most is their power. As children, we seek control of our environment but are constantly confronted by others who wield greater power and who seek to control us. Furthermore, great as an adult's power may be, a child is bound to perceive it as still greater since adults' power tends to be most marked in their dealings with children and since adults' intervention tends to focus on just those desires – sexual desires and aggressive desires, for example – that are most intense. Desire for the parent's power thus becomes a prime reason for internalization of a parent figure, and the internalized parent figure thus becomes particularly powerful. Note, however, that the parent's power, now (imaginatively) possessed through internalization, remains power exerted over the child's ego or self. This allows two things to occur, strengthening the harshness of the superego still further. First, the superego may align itself with the id in its attack on the ego:

The way in which the super-ego came into being explains how it is that the early conflicts of the ego with the object-cathexes of the id can be continued in conflicts with their heir, the super-ego. If the ego has not succeeded in properly mastering the Oedipus complex, the energic cathexis of the latter, springing from the id, will come into operation once more in the reaction-formation of the ego ideal. (1923b, XIX, 38–9)

And:

Thus the super-ego is always close to the id and can act as its representative vis-à-vis the ego. (ibid., 48–9)

Second, insofar as the child has projected its own aggressiveness and hostility toward a parent onto that parent, he must now contend with that hostility as it is directed back toward himself:

> His aggressiveness is introjected, internalized; it is, in point of fact, sent back to where it came from – that is, it is directed towards his own ego. There it is taken over by a portion of the ego, which sets itself over against the rest of the ego as super-ego, and which now, in the form of "conscience," is ready to put into action against the ego the same harsh aggressiveness that the ego would have liked to satisfy upon the other, extraneous individuals. (1930a, XXI, 123)

Much as Freud emphasizes the harsh and aggressive aspects of the superego, he also, at times, seems to grant it a more positive role. He recognizes that we admire as well as fear our parents, and he speaks of an "ego-ideal" as well as of a superego.⁹ The two are closely related aspects of a single phenomenon, it seems, insofar as they both come about through the internalization of the qualities of another which one desires but cannot have. And just as a child's conception of a parent's power is typically an exaggeration, so too is the child's conception of a parent's virtue; the ego-ideal stands apart from the self partly on account of its idealized character.¹⁰ In its role as judge, the superego stands over the self as an aggressive critic while, in its role as an ideal, it stands over one as a possibility to which one aspires. In its response to the superego as ideal, the ego experiences a longing to improve while, in its response to the superego as judge, the ego experiences the anxiety of anticipated failure.¹¹

On one view of the matter, these two sides of the superego may be seen to cooperate; one setting the standards and the other enforcing them. Unfortunately, however, the stronger each aspect is, the more likely they are to work against rather than with each other. In setting oneself an unreachable goal and then condemning oneself for not being all that one should be, the stage is set for a debilitating sense of failure and self-loathing.

> The more virtuous a man is, the more severe and distrustful is his behaviour, so that ultimately it is precisely those people who have carried saintliness furthest who reproach themselves for the worst sinfulness. This means that virtue forfeits some part of its promised reward; the docile and continent ego does not enjoy the trust of its mentor, and it strives in vain, it would seem, to acquire it. (1930a, XXI, 125–6)

Much as Freud viewed the creation of a superego and an ego-ideal as essential to morality and to civilization itself, he worried about the results of their increasing strength in European civilization and religion. The presence of excessive internal demands and internal ideals tend to debilitate us with frustration and desire that are, eventually, bound to erupt in rebellious delinquency – individually and as a society.[12] Thus, a weakening of the superego and the ego-ideal were seen by Freud as generally desirable. To accomplish this, he favored more lenient parenting and more lenient social codes. Also, and more important, though, he favored strengthening and expanding the ego – that is, consciously acknowledging and prudentially managing more aspects of oneself – so as to lessen the oppressive character of one's superego. Indeed, to the extent to which one is able to truly understand the character of one's superego – its sources and its tactics – one becomes able either to extricate oneself from its demands (by realizing how unrealistic these demands are, for example) or to make its demands one's own (thereby transforming superego into ego).

V. MORALITY

Freud considered the presence of a superego – an inner critic and ideal – and the presence of a moral sense to be one and the same. This is a tempting equation, if morality is taken to require actions that oppose one's self-interest. The existence of a superego explains how it is that we may act in the service of something over and above our self-interest – that is, the interests of the ego – despite the absence of any external enforcement or reward, and it explains how it is that we may feel *required* – that is, commanded – to act against our self-interest.

Not all conceptions of morality require moral acts to be acts that oppose or disregard self-interest, nor do all conceptions of morality insist that moral acts be experienced as obligatory. Aristotle's account of morality, for example, makes no such assumptions. Freud's identification of a moral sense with a superego, however, only makes sense if morality must be both selfless and dutiful. If this seems an overly narrow (and overly German) conception of morality, two things might be said on Freud's behalf. First, there are many different and contested ways of distinguishing moral matters from ethical matters more generally. Fixing the boundaries of the moral is at least partly a stipulative matter, and the stipulations implicit in Freud's account of morality are certainly not unusual in contemporary thought. Second, it must be remembered that Freud is not endorsing the morality he seeks to analyze. He did not hold that a stronger moral sense was always a better thing (either for ourselves or for others); indeed, as noted above, he usually recommended a weakening of the superego and, hence, a weakening of our moral sense.[13]

Freud's conception of morality – as involving acts opposed to or indifferent to self-interest, and as involving a sense of obligation or duty – may be accepted, of course, without yet accepting his identification of a moral sense with a superego. Kant, for example, sought to derive obligations opposed to self-interest from the obligations of reason alone. His position, though, invites questions concerning the *medium* through which obligations are felt – the *motivational* basis for morality. Kant's blanket dismissal of inclinations as a basis for morality (because that would make duties contingent rather than necessary) seems to leave us without any basis at all; his appeal to the will seems only to invoke a special sort of inclination – a sort that floats free of self-interest, operating *on* the (phenomenal) self rather than *from* it. This, though, is precisely what Freud sought to capture in his account of the superego: the possibility of an inner agent that transcends and acts on the experienced self. His account of the superego is a naturalistic counterpart to Kant's account of the noumenal self, with the commands of the superego replacing the commands of the will. In some important respects, then, Freud's position should be seen as accommodating rather than competing with that of Kant.

Worries may remain, of course, concerning the content and the legitimacy of the superego's demands. The superego, after all, promotes the (often arbitrary) commands of particularly influential people rather than the (supposedly) impartial commands of reason. Can our moral sense depend so completely on the personalities and pronouncements of those we have internalized? Freud's answer, I suspect, would be another question: What else could it depend on? Once one accepts naturalism, the appeal to processes of internalization seems inevitable. It must be remembered, though, that internalized parents tend to be idealizations of actual parents. A child's perception of her parent is exaggerated and oversimplified in various ways, and after the parent is internalized, its personality will continue to stray from that of the actual parent – both because it is no longer dependent on the external reality of that person and because it will gradually become an amalgamate of many different personalities that have been similarly internalized. Thus the superego, although based on very particular individuals, tends to become a more abstract representative of societal authorities and societal ideals in general.

For this reason, it is unlikely that one's superego could be formed in such a way as to regularly command wickedness. Whatever parents themselves do, the commands they give to children and the ideals they espouse to children tend to accord with those of the society at large; and even if parents fail to espouse and enforce the norms of the society, others will eventually contribute to the formation of a superego so as to bring it more in line with societal norms. This does not, of course, guarantee that every superego commands only good things. But this will be true on any account of a moral sense: What I feel or think I ought to do will not always be what I actually ought to do.

The power and the appeal of Freud's account of morality, at least as I have laid it out here, do not depend on its specifically sexual sources – the story of how the superego emerges from the Oedipus complex, or the equation of moral anxiety with castration anxiety, for example. Its power and its appeal lie, rather, with its ability to make sense of dutiful selflessness within a naturalistic psychology. Freud accomplishes this through an account of the internalization of others, an account that I have tried both to elaborate and to defend. Whether or not one accepts this as an account of morality, it ought to help clarify an important aspect of our psychology – namely, the means by which the imagined presence of another may (for better or for worse) continue to control one's actions and intentions.

NOTES

1 Freud's view of the nature and number of basic drives changes over time, and it is never very precise. In "Instincts and Their Vicissitudes" he suggests that there are two groups of primal instincts – the sexual in-

stincts and the self-preservative instincts, adding that "this supposition has not the status of a necessary postulate ... it is merely a working hypothesis" (1915c, XIV, 120–1). By *Civilization and Its Discontents* (1930a, XXI, 59), the crucial distinction has become that between Eros and Thanatos, life-preserving and life-destroying instincts. See Freud's note reviewing the evolution of his position at the end of "Beyond the Pleasure Principle" (1920g, XVIII, 60–1), and see his *Introductory Lectures* (1916–17, XV, 413), where he discounts the importance of determining sameness versus difference of basic instincts.

2 The reinforcing effect of multiple associations between an original object of desire and substitute objects is especially clear in Freud's analysis of some of his own dreams, e.g., in *The Interpretation of Dreams* (1900a, IV, 282–4), and in his analysis of the Rat Man's obsession, e.g., in "A Case of Obsessional Neurosis" (1909d, X, 213–17).

3 I refer to the case of a woman whose husband was impotent on their wedding night, discussed by Freud in his *Introductory Lectures*, (1916–17, XVI, 261–4).

4 These contrasts between conscious mental processes and unconscious mental processes are stated most explicitly in "The Two Principles of Mental Functioning" (1911b, XII, 215) and in "The Unconscious" (1915e, XIV, 186).

5 I discuss and defend what Freud calls the "special characteristics of the system Ucs," and I consider their bearing on his analysis of the Schreber case and the Wolf Man case in my contribution to *Freud: Problems of Explanation* (London: Routledge and Kegan Paul, forthcoming).

6 Freud actually wrote a paper on consciousness that has now been lost. Clearly, by the time he wrote "The Unconscious," the term "consciousness," aligned with the system Cs, had acquired a somewhat technical meaning for Freud. Just how similar his theoretical concept is to our ordinary concept(s) of consciousness (or the rather different German concept of *Bewusstsein*) is an open question.

7 Regarding (1), see Section III of "The Unconscious" (1915e, XVI, 177–9). Regarding (2), see "Two Principles of Mental Functioning" (1911b, XII, 219); *The Interpretation of Dreams* (1900a, IV, V); *Jokes* (1905c, VIII, 191–2); and "Negation" (1925h, XIX, 237).

8 See Freud's discussion of this possibility in "On Narcissism: An Introduction" (1914c, XIV, 69) and in "Mourning and Melancholia" (1917e, XIV, 239).

9 The editor's introduction to "The Ego and the Id" (1923b, XIX, 9–11), recounts various stages in Freud's development of the notion of an ego-ideal and a superego.

10 In his paper "On Narcissism: An Introduction" (1914c, XIV, 94), Freud

also describes the formation of an ego-ideal as a means of recovering the
lost narcissism of infancy: "He is not willing to forgo the narcissistic
perfection of his childhood; and when, as he grows up, he is disturbed by
the admonitions of others and by the awakening of his own critical
judgment, so that he can no longer retain that perfection, he seeks to
recover it in the new form of an ego-ideal. What he projects before him
as his ideal is the substitute for the lost narcissism of his childhood in
which he was his own ideal."

11 The word we translate as "conscience" is the German *Gewissenangst*.
Freud makes the anxiety component of this concept explicit and relates
it to the Oedipus complex:

> Just as the father has become depersonalized in the shape of the super-
> ego, so has the fear of castration at his hands become transformed into
> an undefined social or moral anxiety. But this anxiety is concealed. The
> ego escapes it by obediently carrying out the commands, precautions
> and penances that have been enjoined on it. If it is impeded in doing so,
> it is at once overtaken by an extremely distressing feeling of discomfort
> which may be regarded as an equivalent of anxiety and which the pa-
> tients themselves liken to anxiety.
>
> ("Inhibitions, Symptoms and Anxiety," 1926d, XX, 128)

12 This worry is developed most fully in the final chapters of *Civilization
and Its Discontents* (1930a, XXI, 59).

13 This reminder ought also to help counter some objections to Freud's
portrayal of women as having a weaker moral sense than men (due to
their less resolved Oedipus or Elektra complexes). Moral inferiority, in
this sense, seems a good thing according to Freud.

9   Freud on women

Historically, psychoanalytic writing and everyday language have referred to "woman" as a unitary entity; psychoanalysis has compared
"the man" to "the woman," "the boy" to "the girl." Recent feminist
and postmodernist writing has taught us to be wary of such singular
referents and of theories that employ them. In particular, psychoanalysis has often been criticized for the limited class and cultural
location of its clinical sample – of the empirical "women" upon
which its purportedly universal theory of femininity has been developed. When we interrogate Freud's writings, however, we find that
his and other psychoanalytic references to "woman" are in dialogue
with an emphatically plural account of a multitude of "women."
Freud's descriptions of women and of his interactions with them
comprise a large cast of characters, a pantheon of higher and lesser
ideal-typical goddesses and mortals to complement and accompany
Oedipus, Narcissus, Moses, and others in psychological glory or igno-
miny. We also find actual, historically specific, late nineteenth- and
early twentieth-century named and nameless women in clinical
cases and vignettes.

This essay enumerates these women. I describe a number of implicit axes that differentiate them. Freud describes woman as subject
of her own psyche, that is, as living experiencer of self and conscious
and unconscious mental processes, as subject to herself. Woman as
subject expands into woman as subject-object, that is, object to her
own subjectivity as she internally relates to and identifies with or
against another internally experienced woman.

I thank Elizabeth Abel and Joseph Lifschutz for very helpful suggestions.

224

Woman as subject and subject-object contrasts with woman as object in the masculine psyche. Freud depicts for us clinically and theoretically how men experience women, and we can also, by examining his writings on women, find clues ourselves as to how they are characterized or imagined to be by men. Freud also expands his investigation of woman as psychological subject or object by considering woman's location in social-historical time and woman as object of cultural attribution or categorization.

Finally, Freud demonstrates for us a range of possible locations with the psychology and social organization of gender and sexuality. In his writings on sexuality and development, his cases, and his social theories, women are young girls, mothers (of daughters and of sons), daughters of mothers, daughters of fathers; they are heterosexual, lesbian, sexually inhibited or frigid altogether; they are substitute mothers, as nursemaids, servants, or governesses; they are wives, mother-symbols, or whorelike sexual objects of desirous or fearful men. This diversity stands as some response to the critique of singularity. It suggests that, although claims about limited class and cultural basis may be accurate, we miss, by looking only to cultural and social categories outside the relations of gender, the very great complexity and multiplicity of identities and social locations within it. Freud on women is a good place to begin to delineate this complexity and multiplicity.

At the same time, I will not be the first person to suggest some glaring limitations – to use Freud's word, scotomas – in Freud's account. The maternal, as a strong, intense feeling, preoccupation, and identity in women as subjects is almost entirely absent, along with adequate recognition or treatment of infantile attachment to the mother. Of prime importance is an account of mature female desire and heterosexuality that renders it at best as inhibited; at worst, this desire and sexuality is seen entirely through male eyes.

This essay is about Freud's writings on women. As I indicate, these writings have been contested from the beginning. There has also been both within the field of psychoanalysis and outside of it much revision, new formulation, challenge, and change, even as many psychoanalysts would still accept many parts or the whole of Freud's writings on this subject. These new formulations are beyond the scope of my concerns here.[1]

I take woman as subject here to refer to what we normally mean by a self, actor, agent, experiencer. I am not concerned with contemporary accounts that problematize such a self or agent but simply to distinguish in a general way this psychological, social, or cultural subject from an object seen or experienced by an other who is him or herself the experiencing knower in an investigation or account. I distinguish five approaches to women as subjects in Freud's writings: first, theoretical woman in the developmental theory; second, clinical woman; third, woman as subject-object – theoretical and clinical woman as she herself internally represents and experiences woman as object; fourth, women as they are socially and historically located; and fifth, women as creators of psychoanalytic technique and understanding.

Theoretical woman in the developmental theory

Conventionally, when we investigate Freud's writings on women, we are most concerned with his developmental account of woman and femininity – female psychology or sexuality. Woman's development here is reconstructed from adult clinical cases, her subjectivity observed and interpreted as generic femininity. In Daniel Stern's terms, Freud's account here, along with most early psychoanalytic accounts, is about "clinical" girl and woman as Freud reconstructs her development from a life narrative constructed through the transference and interpretations. It is not an account of "observed" girl, observed from infancy by analysts or developmental psychologists.[2] As Stern points out, this kind of psychoanalytic theorizing is "pathomorphic and retrospective":[3] it retrospectively singles out adult clinical issues as overall definers of normative phases and stages of development as well as of central personality and identity issues throughout the life span. In my definition here, this girl or woman whose development is being retrospectively described, is not empirically clinical – an actual patient or patients; rather, she is Freud's theoretical feminine subject, or theoretical subject of theoretical femininity.

Freud describes his theory of woman's development, or the development of femininity, in a series of articles written and published during an approximate ten-year span from the early 1920s to the early 1930s: "The Dissolution of the Oedipus Complex" (1924d, XIX), "Some Psychical Consequences of the Anatomical Distinction between the Sexes" (1925j, XIX), "Female Sexuality" (1931b, XXI), and Lecture 33 of the *New Introductory Lectures* (1933a, XXII), "Femininity." In addition, Ruth Mack-Brunswick claims in "The Preoedipal Phase of the Libido Development" that her account is based on typed notes taken after discussions with Freud in the early 1930s.[4]

In these writings Freud subsumes what we would later come to call gender, or gender identity, under sexuality, or sexual identity. "Femininity" and "female sexuality" are thus equivalent, and what psychoanalysis can presumably concern itself with, as he puts it: "I have only been describing women in so far as their nature is determined by their sexual function. It is true that that influence extends very far; but we do not overlook the fact that an individual woman may be a human being in other respects as well" (1933a, XXII, 135). There are several possible outcomes to woman's sexual development, but the "normal femininity" (ibid., 126) that is the preferred outcome is a heterosexuality entailing passivity and centering on the vagina as organ of sexual response and excitement. A girl to achieve this normal femininity makes three shifts in her development: from active to passive mode, from "phallic," or clitoridal, to vaginal aim, and from mother (lesbian/homosexual) to father (heterosexual) as object.

Freud developed his later theory in two stages. In the 1924 and 1925 articles, Freud begins quite explicitly from a male norm and compares female development to it. The foci of his discussions of female sexuality are the girl's originary phallic sexuality, her castration complex, and the simplicity of her oedipal configuration: "The girl's Oedipus complex is much simpler than that of the small bearer of the penis; in my experience, it seldom goes beyond the taking of her mother's place and adopting of a feminine attitude towards her father" (1924d, XIX, 178). Her castration complex – envy for the penis – leads up to her Oedipus complex; the Oedipus complex is never given up in as absolute a way as the boy, because she has no castration to fear. Upbringing, intimidation, and the threat of loss of love motivate some renunciation of oedipal wishes, but she does not develop the same strong superego nor really give up her infantile genital organization; her wishes simply modulate over time. Freud does not say so, but one could infer that this gradual giving up in disappointment of oedipal wishes could account for the lesser insistence of female libidinal drives in comparison to male: This notable lack of active female sexual desire in normal femininity results from a sort of postoedipal atrophy of desire. Indeed, female desire in this model remains only for the missing organ (the penis) rather than for the sexual object (the father or men more generally). Desire is thus quickly transferred to the desire for a baby, symbolizing the penis, from her father, preferably a boy baby who brings the missing penis with him. Freud thus explains most of what we conventionally mean, and what he explicitly means, by femininity, both the girl's heterosexuality – she turns to her father to get a penis (= child) – and her maternal desires – her desire for a child (= penis) – as a secondary by-product of penis envy. He also introduces the problematic masculine outcome, that of the girl who, when she must give up her father, identifies with him instead.⁵

The centrality of penis envy in this account cannot be overstressed. Freud contrasts the girl's reaction to the genital difference between the sexes to that of the boy. The boy's first reaction is denial or disavowal; he sees nothing (in other work, Freud describes how this reaction carries over into male fetishism, the grown man's attempt to fantasize a female phallus and deny the threat of his own castration). In the normal case, he gradually accepts the evidence of his senses, as the threat of castration terrorizes him into believing that he, too, could be penisless and that there really are penisless creatures in the human world. The boy's earliest sexual interests and curiosity may concern either the genital difference between the sexes or the riddle of where babies come from.

The girl, by contrast, "behaves differently. She makes her judgment and her decision in a flash. She has seen it and knows that she is without it and wants to have it" (1925j, XIX, 252); "she develops, like a scar, a sense of inferiority" (253). Both sexes develop contempt for women – the boy, "horror of the mutilated creature or triumphant contempt for her," the girl, "the contempt felt by men for a sex which is the lesser in so important a respect" (252 and 253). The girl gives up her clitoridal masturbation, a painful reminder of her castrated state, and eventually, during puberty, instigates in herself a "wave of repression" (255) that replaces her "masculine" sexuality with femininity. In the unsuccessful case, she continually struggles with compulsive renewed autoerotic demands through puberty and into her adult analysis. Unlike the boy, the girl's first sexual interests always concern the question of genital difference rather than the question of where babies come from.

Freud returns to these themes in "Analysis Terminable and Interminable" (1937c, XXIII, 250–3). Here, he suggests that the desperate female wish for a penis generates the "strongest motive in coming for [psychoanalytic] treatment" and constitutes biological "bedrock," a final, unanalyzable resistance to psychoanalysis. He claims that men's struggle against passive submission to men, signifying castration, has an equivalent bedrock position. Both stances center on the "repudiation of femininity" and the meaning of the penis.

In his 1925 article, Freud begins to query the "prehistory" of the Oedipus complex – the conditions in both sexes that lead to its emergence – but it is in his 1931 paper, "Female Sexuality," that this query is more fully developed. Freud indicates in all three papers, as well as in the lecture, "Femininity," that he is writing under pressure. He refers implicitly to his recent cancer operations and fear of death. He discusses explicitly the challenges of feminists, the number of other writers in the field eager to grab onto half-truths (presumably, to publish before him), the challenges to his position by Horney and Klein (and, presumably, by Jones), and the welcome contributions of women analysts who share his perspective. The contributions of this last group especially instigate the 1931 paper. Its main contribution is an extensive revaluation and discussion of the preoedipal mother–daughter relationship that precedes and leads up to the girl's turn to her father. Castration is still recognized, but it is not in this work the center of investigation. Freud acknowledges that the work of female analysts with patients – he refers especially to that of Jeanne Lampl-de Groot and Helene Deutsch – has led him to recognize an intense, long-lived, exclusive, passionate preoedipal attachment characterized by phallic (active, clitoridal) desires.[6] In this reformulation, the father suddenly declines in libidinal significance, as he is seen now as "not much else . . . than a troublesome rival" (1931b, XXI, 226), and the puzzling question of why the girl ever gives up this attachment to her mother emerges. Freud concludes, in fact, that the female Oedipus complex is never so absolute in the girl as in the boy: "It is only in the male child that we find the fateful combination of love for the one parent and simultaneous hatred for the other as a rival" (229). This attachment is in many cases never given up completely, and many women carry over the character of their attachment to their mother to their attachments to their father and husband.

One reading of the female Oedipus complex here would privilege Persephone, torn from and always maintaining her attachment to her mother Demeter. Such a reading is certainly supported by the 1931 and 1933 accounts, as well as by the accounts Freud draws upon and by later psychoanalytic writings. Freud, however, also stresses the turning of love into hostility, and the number of grievances the girl comes to have toward her mother. The mother does not and cannot reciprocate the intensive exclusivity of childhood love with its totalistic but unspecified demands for satisfaction, does not seem to feed sufficiently, has other children, arouses and then forbids sexual activity, and finally, is responsible for not providing her daughter with a penis. Freud puzzles on the different fate of the daughter's and the son's attachment, sometimes according most weight to the fact that only the daughter has received the extra blow of no penis, sometimes allowing that all such intense love – presumably the boy's as well, insofar as he isn't terrorized out of it by the threat of castration – is doomed to perish simply because it was so intense.

The "normal" outcome here is the femininity I have described, but Freud stresses two nonfeminine outcomes, one, a general revulsion from sexuality as the girl gives up (or struggles with, in clitoridal masturbation) her phallic sexuality along with her masculine identities, another as she "cling[s] with defiant self-assertiveness to her threatened masculinity" (229). In both these cases, she gives up her mother as sexual object and object of attachment without turning to her father as a sexual object rather than as an object of identification. Freud's account, then, of an unresolved oedipal outcome is closer to the model of Athena than of Persephone. It is that of the daughter who identifies herself totally with her father, does not recognize her mother, and remains object-sexually, if not autoerotically, virginal.

Clinical woman

Freud not only uses clinical material explicitly and implicitly in his reconstructive account of female development and female sexuality. In his cases, clinical fragments, and vignettes, women are also empirical, actual, often named, specific subjects in the analytic situation. We have a vivid sense of them and probably our own fantasies of what they were like. We think of Dora, Freud's most famous female case, struggling to name her own history and her own psychological and family situation, unheard like Cassandra, sacrificed and bartered by her father like Iphigenia (1905e, VII). Dora is the father's and mother's daughter in the worst situation, as she wistfully hopes for love and affection from a mother and mother-substitute who is in reality the father's lover. Consciously, she denies sexual desire – or expresses it symptomatically; unconsciously, she is primarily homosexually attached, at the developmental level of an adolescent crush that conflates the desire for merger and caretaking with sexual desire. She is rejected by Freud, who treats her as an objectively bad, vengeful fully grown woman rather than as a confused adolescent and who names her at least partially after a family nursemaid.[7]

Anna O., in actuality Breuer's patient rather than Freud's, is also the father's daughter, but victim of circumstance and her own inner conflicts and desires rather than of conscious manipulation and sacrifice (1895d, II, 21–47). We suffer with her as she watches over her sick father, as she feels guilty about her fleeting wish to be dancing, as her stiff arm turns into snakes (penis symbols, Freud will later consider them), as she is unable to drink or eat, to speak German, or even to speak at all, as various psychically instigated paralyses overtake her, as she alternates her lives daily from one year to another. We are relieved at her cure and happy to learn how successfully she later manages her life as active feminist and social worker.

We learn more fleetingly of Fraulein Elizabeth von R., Frau Emmy von N., and Miss Lucy R., and even less of Katharina, Fraulein Rosalia H., and Frau Cacilie (all in 1895d, II, 48–181), of the case of homosexuality in a woman (1920a, XVIII), of the many women in the *Introductory Lectures on Psycho-analysis* (1916–17, XV and XVI). Emmy von N., plagued with hysterical conversion symptoms and full of self-recriminations, also manages her large estates and houses, oversees the care and well-being of her two daughters, is an intelligent woman with "an unblemished character and a well-governed mode of life" (1895d, II, 103). Frau Cacilie, whose case is abridged for reasons of confidentiality, suffers from a "violent facial neuralgia" (ibid., 176), hallucinations and other hysterical symptoms, yet is highly gifted artistically, erudite, and wide ranging intellectually. Elizabeth von R., like Anna O., is attached to a father whom she then has to nurse through an illness, feels conflict between sadness at her father's situation and her desire to spend time in the social pleasures of late adolescence, develops hysterical leg pains in relation to the nursing situation, and later becomes guiltily in love with her brother-in-law. Freud suggests to us that sick-nursing, a woman's responsibility, often plays a role in the genesis of hysteria, as the nurse's fatigue combines with the need to suppress all emotion and as enforced immobility can lead to flourishing fantasy development. Miss Lucy R., a governess, suffers like Elizabeth von R. from conflicts over erotic desires and feelings of rejection, in this case by her employer. Katharina's trauma is more direct, as she has almost been an incest victim and has witnessed her father's incestuous success with her cousin; Rosalia H. has also suffered from unwanted sexual advances, though not, it seems, rape or seduction.

In all these cases, we see Freud's beginning understanding of the implication of sexual desire (the cases of Anna O., Elizabeth von R., and Lucy R. most explicitly) and sexual trauma (an explicit event in the cases of Katharina and Rosalia H.; trauma as conflict in the other three) in the genesis of hysteria. With him, we first see these in the actual lives of individual women. Sexuality is also a factor in cases of unnamed women: the "case of homosexuality" who developed desire for a woman of uncertain character partly in reaction to feelings toward her father; sexual shame, as far as we can make this out, in the case vignette of the woman whose obsessive symptom consisted in running into a room and calling her maid to a position where the maid could see a stain on a tablecloth, symbolizing in reverse the stain that was not on the wedding sheets when her newly wedded husband was impotent (1916–17, XVI, 261–4); the girl whose obsessively arranged bedclothes and pillow symbolized her separation of mother and father and substitution of herself for either mother or father in the parental bed (ibid., 264–9).

In a research study, I have interviewed many women members of the second generation of analysts – those trained in the 1920s and 1930s – and several claimed that one attraction to the field was that Freud saw women as sexual subjects rather than objects.[8] In the *Studies on Hysteria* and other clinical vignettes, we catch some glimpse of this sexual subjectivity, a subjectivity that, as I have indicated, is not present in Freud's account of theoretical woman as subject. I do not suggest that women in these cases are sexual free spirits – they are for the most part afflicted with the physical and mental pain of hysterical symptoms or the overriding insistence of obsessional neurosis – but their sexuality is clearly neither feminine-passive, that is, without lust, nor, with the exception of the case of homosexuality (following Freud's definition of masculinity in women), masculine. Inhibition or frigidity by convention characterize neurotics, but the conflicted sexuality described in some of these cases does not fit the closer to asexual model that Freud later describes.

Woman as subject-object

In considering woman as subject-object, or object to a self that constructs and reconstructs her subjectivity, we are led to consider further the mother–daughter relationship and its meanings for the daughter. We cannot consider the relationship from the mother's point of view. Possibly because of the centrality of the genetic and reconstructive approaches in psychoanalysis, in which the focus is on the developing child as this development is occurring or as it is (re)constructed, possibly, it might be argued, because of Freud's real inability to identify with mothers, Freud's writings show a striking lack of interest in the parenting relationship from the point of view of the parent, and especially of the mother (the father does, after all, threaten to castrate his son; the mother simply sits passively as her imagined sexuality goes from phallic to castrated and as she is and is not an object of attachment or sexual desire of son or daughter). We do learn of Frau Emmy von N.'s concerns about her daughters, as well as the concerns of Anna O.'s mother and the parents of Fraulein Elizabeth von R. The mother–daughter relationship, however, is a relationship seen from the point of view of the daughter.

There is a unique complexity of identificatory and object-relational experiences and tasks for the daughter as she sorts out this relation to her mother. Clinically, Freud describes for us Dora's attachment to her mother and to Frau K., as well as that of the girl who is the subject of his paper on female homosexuality. He tells us that all children originally experience the importance of the breast as first object and of early maternal care. Freud's late theory, following especially Lampl-de Groot, argues that the girl remains in the negative oedipal position – attached to her mother – for a long time. She may never give up this attachment completely, and she certainly does not dissolve her Oedipus complex as absolutely as does the boy.

Even as he describes this long period of attachment, however, Freud also describes how the girl strongly and forcefully turns on her mother – this mother who denied her milk, love, and the phallus. The mother has, in her daughter's view during this period in her development, withheld what she could choose to give. The girl goes round and round. At first, all children think everyone is anatomically constructed like them. The girl then learns that some people have penises, whereas she doesn't. She assumes her mother does and that she will have one when she grows up. She then realizes that she will never have one, and – Freud is unclear here – believes either that her mother has chosen never to give one to her and hasn't got one herself, or that, although she doesn't have one, could have arranged things so that her daughter did. In any case, there is great disappointment and a radical distancing from her mother. The daughter, as does the son, introjects an image of mother and breast as object; for the daughter, mother is an ambivalently loved and hated object in the daughter's psyche.

But the oedipal resolution, as Freud describes this (it seems generically, though possibly he speaks only of the boy), involves identifying with the same sex parent so that the ego itself is transformed through this identification. The girl, then, must identify with this same mother who is an ambivalent, narcissistic (an object like the self) object of attachment in order to attain her "normal femininity." The mother must be taken in as subject as well as object. But what should be the ego-ideal, the maternal object-become-subject that is taken in as "normal femininity," is a castrated, denying subjectivity. This castrated, denying subjectivity becomes, as a result of identificatory processes, part of the self of the girl, even as the identificatory object remains, psychologically, as an object of ambivalent love and hate.

Women as they are socially and historically located

When we think of Freud's writings on women as subjects, we generally mean the developmental account of theoretical woman, or, occasionally, the richly textured descriptions of clinical women. In both kinds of accounts, but especially in the latter, we also can find two other approaches to women as subjects, women as social-historical subjects and women as contributors to psychoanalysis.

Freud, as psychoanalyst, is most interested in the inner psychic worlds, self-constructions, and conflicts of women. However, he is also a man of his time, and especially in those writings that precede his mid-1920s discussions on female sexuality, one who expresses firm opinions about the social situation of women and sexuality. I have mentioned Freud's linking of sickbed-nursing with hysteria. He is firm in his strong defense of the morality and upstanding qualities and capabilities of the women whom contemporary neurologists and psychiatrists considered degenerate, morally and mentally contaminated, and inferior as a result of their heredity. In his early discourse on " 'Civilized' Sexual Morality and Modern Nervousness," Freud mounts a powerful critique of the societally, culturally, and familially induced constraint on women's (and men's) sexuality and of the trap that marriage is for many women (1908d, IX). These women, raised in restrictive sexual environments and held close to their families, are suddenly thrust into marriages with men who have themselves been constrained and whose sexuality has been autoerotic or engaged in with debased objects (on this, more below), men who are, for their own reasons, unlikely to make sympathetic initial sexual and marriage partners for properly brought up women. Freud implies that female neurosis may result from or be facilitated by – because all neurotic symptoms and character in general result in his view from both inner, early developmental and constitutional factors and from external factors in the current situation of the person – this marital situation, as neurotic symptomatology enables withdrawal from a difficult situation and expresses anger at the same time. Freud points to the problematic situation of upper-middle-class women in another vignette, which he labels "In the Basement and on the First Floor" (what we might now call "Upstairs, Downstairs"). He describes two girls of different classes who engage in childhood sex play, the lower class girl as part of her path toward a normal and healthy heterosexuality, the upper class girl, racked by guilt and educated in ideals of feminine purity and abstinence, as prelude toward sexual inhibition and neurosis (1916–17, XVI, 352–4).

Freud's defense of homosexuality parallels his defense of hysteria. In the *Three Essays on the Theory of Sexuality* (1905d, VII), and later in "The Psychogenesis of a Case of Homosexuality in a Woman" (1920a; XVIII), he argues that homosexual object-choice is on a continuum with heterosexuality – "one must remember that normal sexuality too depends upon a restriction in the choice of object" (151); that everyone is bisexual – "in all of us, throughtout life, the libido normally oscillates between male and female objects" (158); that homosexuality does not necessarily have to do with physical abnormality, as people of all sexual orientations may show secondary sex characteristics of the other sex; and that many homosexuals are morally and intellectually outstanding.

His own lesbian patient is a "beautiful and clever girl of eighteen, belonging to a family of good standing" (147), and "not in any way ill" (150). The story of her development to homosexual object-choice, via jealousy of her mother's pregnancy, desire for a baby from her father, and anger at him for not providing one, is an unremarkable story of oedipal development. The girl's intense attachment to her mother presages Freud's 1931 change in theoretical emphasis. Freud distinguishes here, more clearly than in any other part of his writing, gender identity – as he puts it, "the sexual characteristics and sexual attitude of the subject" (170) – from object-choice, arguing that either a "masculine" or a "feminine" woman might love women. Freud here is somewhat taken aback and somewhat amused at the willfulness and independence of his patient, including, as in the case of Dora, her attempts to deceive him and thwart the analysis. She is described as "a spirited girl, always ready for romping and fighting" and a "feminist [who] felt it to be unjust that girls should not enjoy the same freedom as boys" (169), even as her penis envy is emphasized. Freud is sympathetic toward her parents but seems, really, to agree with their condemnation of their daughter's object-choice and their desire to change it only to the extent that he also thinks that she has (partly out of a motive of revenge) picked as her love object a person of dubious morals and behavior.

Women as creators of psychoanalytic technique and understanding

Women are not only subjects of their psychological development and clinical experience or social and cultural subjects. Freud's writings on women and femininity make clear the ways that women, as patients and analysts, have helped to create psychoanalytic theory and technique, and he is often generous with his acknowledgments of these contributions. Anna O.'s "chimney-sweeping" created the talking

cure; Emmy von N.'s complaints about Freud's interrupting her associations and Elizabeth von R.'s inability to respond to hypnosis led to
the method of free association. Hysterical women taught Freud the
varieties of symptom formation, Cacilie showing how symbolic word
associations could be transformed – a grandmother's "piercing" look
leading to pain in the forehead, feeling "stabbed in the heart" to chest
pain, an insult, or "slap in the face," to facial neuralgia (1895d, II, 178–
181). Tracking down the source of Miss Lucy R.'s aversion to cigar
smoke and burnt pudding and Anna O.'s inability to drink water
helped create the trauma theory of symptom formation and the technical practice (no longer rigidly employed) of working back step by
step to the origin of each symptom. Women helped create and make
visible transference and countertransference – Freud sees clearly
Anna O.'s eroticized transference to Breuer and even Breuer's countertransference, though he has a name for the latter only much later;
he takes the transference of woman patient to male doctor to be
"paradigmatic and emblematic of transference in general" (1912b,
XII). Women also created or inspired those transferences that were
invisible to Freud – he does not link Miss Lucy R.'s preoccupations
with cigar smoke to his own smoking; he, notoriously, does not see
his own virulent negative countertransference to Dora nor his wist-
ful, fatherly hovering transference to Elizabeth von R., in whose future he interested himself to the extent of procuring an invitation to a
ball to which she was invited and acknowledging, ruefully, that
"since then, by her own inclination, she has married someone unknown to me" (1895d, II, 160).[9]

  Women were also, as analysts, direct contributors to Freud's understandings of women as well as to other aspects of psychoanalytic
theory and technique. Discussion of this contribution is beyond the
scope of this chapter, except to note confusion (see later) concerning
the extent to which women analysts made these contributions as
colleagues or, in direct and indirect ways, as patients, of Freud's.

WOMAN AS OBJECT

When we think about Freud on women, in the typical case we mean
Freud's conceptualization of female development or female sexuality.
I have reviewed the writings in which he addresses these conceptual-
izations. I believe, however, that a stronger, more pervasive treatment

of women in Freud's writings concerns what we might consider to be woman in the male psyche – woman as object, not subject.

Such a claim is in some ways self-evident: Freud was, after all, a man. Any account of women that he produced is, finally, an account of women viewed through the mind of a man. I mean something different. I refer to the fact that Freud gave us, both explicitly and implicitly, psychodynamic accounts of how men view women, or certain women, as objects or others, and of what femininity and women mean in the masculine psyche. There is something intuitively more convincing in these accounts of woman as object in the male psyche than in those of woman as subject and, indeed, they do not seem to have been widely criticized in the psychoanalytic (or in the feminist) literature since Freud. Both male and female writers seem more or less to agree with and elaborate upon Freud's claims in this area, in striking contrast to the way that female writers especially, but also some male writers, have taken issue with almost everything Freud claims about women as subjects.[10] We will also return to the question of the extent to which Freud's view of woman as subject might be seen to be a picture of woman whose experience is viewed or imagined by man, but except when unavoidable, that is not our concern until the end of this section.

Manifest, explicit, treatments of women as objects

One must, here, acknowledge, Karen Horney, who covered in her discussions of "The Flight from Womanhood" and "The Dread of Woman" most of what needs to be said on this subject.[11] Insofar as Freud's discussions of male development and masculinity center on the male castration complex, it can be said that Freud is preoccupied, indeed obsessed, with the meaning of the female, of sexual difference, and of what marks this difference, in the male psyche. Presence of the penis distinguishes the male, and "Nature has, as a precaution attached . . . a portion of his narcissism to that particular organ" (1927e, XXI, 153; I have rearranged the structure of the sentence).

Freud discusses women as sex objects to men in "A Special Type of Choice of Object Made by Men (Contributions to the Psychology of Love, I)" (1910h, XI) and "On the Universal Tendency to Debasement in the Sphere of Love (Contributions to the Psychology of

Love, II)" (1912d, XI) (Freud's developmental account here implies that this "universal" tendency is found entirely in men). Men, he suggests, split women symbolically and erotically into mothers, or mothers and sisters, on the one hand and prostitutes on the other. The former cannot be sexually desired, though they are supposed to be the kind of woman a man should marry, and the latter, though they are maritally and socially forbidden, can be sexually desired. As long as a woman symbolizes the mother, she is a forbidden oedipal object-choice, an indication of an attachment carried on too long. Fleeing to a woman who is or is like a prostitute protects the defensively constructed idea of the mother's sexual purity and denies oedipal desire. Alternatively, it equates mother with a prostitute, thereby giving her son access to her along with his father. Psychically derived impotence follows the same line of reasoning, so that men become impotent with women who are like, or who represent psychically, their mothers. Freud here gives us the psychodynamics of a split long present in Western culture, literature, and social organization. Indeed, the wife must eventually reciprocate her husband's setting her up as an asexual mother, as "a marriage is not made secure until the wife has succeeded in making her husband her child as well and in acting as a mother to him" (1933a, XXII, 133–4).

Some men do not stop with the simple expedient of separating sexual from asexual women; they must deny the female sexual constitution altogether. "Fetishism," claims Freud, is "a substitute . . . for a particular and quite special penis" (1927e, XXI, 152), the penis that the mother was once thought to have. All boys struggle with acknowledging female – originally the mother's – castration. Fetishists resolve the struggle by disavowal, or denial, creating a fetish that externally represents the maternal phallus and thus supports such disavowal. Disavowal also enters the realm of mythology, as the snakes of "Medusa's Head" (1940c, XVIII) condense signification on the one hand of the mature female external genitals and on the other of many penises, which in turn stand both for castration (because the one has been lost) and denial of castration (there are many penises). Medusa's decapitated head, the castrated female genitals, evokes horror and even paralysis – a reminder of castration – in the man who looks at it, but this paralysis is also an erection, thereby asserting that the penis is still there. This short two-page vignette captures the extreme horror at castration and the potential destructiveness of women and the female genitals that Freud glosses with milder words like "contempt" in other writings.

The phallic mother is also important in female development – the girl, when she first learns about sexual difference, believes her mother has a penis and that she will too when she grows up; for both sexes, the preoedipal mother is seen in Freud's view as "phallic," that is, active. But the recognition of the mother's castration seems more permanently traumatic to the boy: "No male human being is spared the fright of castration at the sight of the female genital" (1927e, XXI, 154). The girl, as we have seen, is, finally, much more traumatized by a castration of her own. In Freud's view, a more drastic solution to conflict over the mother's castration than fetishism – which still enables a heterosexual object choice with fetish added on as phallus – is homosexuality, in which the partner himself possesses the phallus directly.[12]

Like theoretical women and femininity, clinical women present themselves as objects as well as subjects in Freud's writings. In the "Irma" dream (1900a, IV, 96–121), several doctors inject, palpate, minutely examine, and try to cure Irma, who recalcitrantly and vindictively tries to undermine their efforts to cure her. Servant women – Grusha, seen from behind as she bends over scrubbing the floor (1918b, XVII, 90–6), the governesses Fraulein Peter and Fraulein Lina allowing their small charge to play with their genitals, Lina squeezing abscesses from her buttocks at night (1909d; 1955a, X, 160–1) – play important roles in the formation of neurotic symptomatology in both the Wolf Man and the Rat Man and specify clinically the class splits described in the "Contributions to the Psychology of Love." Class here intertwines with gender and sexuality in the formation of male erotic desire.

Freud's stance from within the male psyche toward both abstract woman and concrete clinical women and his ease of identification with men in this stance produce what has seemed to many commentators a notable amorality in his views of male behavior. I refer here not so much to his giving up of the seduction hypothesis – it seems clear that his exoneration of Fliess's behavior to Emma Eckstein ("Irma") was unconscionable and that he made his about-face for theoretical and social as well as for evidential reasons, but that he was certainly well aware of sexual abuse of children and of the prevalence of incest. I refer more specifically to particular clinical cases. Freud barely notes that Dora's father gave her mother syphilis and that his illness may have affected his children's health as well, and he condemns neither this father who handed her over at the age of fourteen to a grown man nor Herr K., who was willing to accept the gift and who tried to seduce her. The case of Paul Lorenz, the Rat Man, is presented with objectivity muted by empathy, and it is a masterful rendition of the phenomenology of obsessive neurosis. But Freud only mentions in passing, as interesting fact, that Lorenz may have seduced his sister and certainly felt free to seduce and use a range of other women, sometimes with drastic consequences, driving them to suicide. In the case vignette of the "dear old uncle" who had the habit of taking the young daughters of friends for outings, arranging for their being stranded overnight, and masturbating them, Freud remarks only on the creation of symbolic equivalence between clean or dirty money and clean or dirty hands and the possible problem of hands being dirty, rather than commenting forcefully on the man's hands being where they were in the first place (1909d, X, 197–8).

Woman as implicit, latent object in the male psyche

The mother is not only explicitly represented in Freud's account of the male psyche. She is also represented implicitly, or latently. In *Civilization and Its Discontents*, Freud contrasts the "oceanic feeling" with longing for the father as the origin of religious feeling (1930a, XXI, 64–73). This oceanic feeling, resonant with "limitless narcissism" (72) and in contrast to which mature ego-feeling in later life seems a "shrunken residue" (68), is very clearly, though not stated as such, the original feeling of the infant with its mother (see "On Narcissism: An Introduction," 1914c, XIV). It is not longing for the mother, for lost narcissistic oneness, then, that generates religious need, but longing for the father. This longing results from "infantile helplessness" (72) in the face of fear, and, as the account in *Civilization and Its Discontents* develops, it becomes clear that the fear Freud refers to is oedipal fear and fear of castration, precisely, the boy's fear of his father, merged with his love for him. What begins here as an impersonal oceanic feeling, held by generic human beings of both sexes, turns out to be contrasted with a specifically masculine relation to the father, which Freud thus sees emphatically as more important than the relation to the mother for the boy.

Even less explicitly acknowledged than the mother who signifies the limitless narcissism of childhood is the idealized mother, symbolized by her breast and her sometimes perfect love. In striking contrast to the denigration and contempt for the mother that he portrays elsewhere, in contrast to his minimizing of the importance of this early relation in *Civilization and Its Discontents*, Freud also claims that "sucking at the mother's breast is the starting-point of the whole of sexual life, the unmatched prototype of every later sexual satisfaction. . . . I can give you no idea of the important bearing of this first object upon the choice of every later object, of the profound effects it has in its transformations and substitutions in even the remotest regions of our sexual life" (1916–17, XVI, 314). Such sucking is gender-free, but Freud later implies that the satisfaction at that time and its later sequelae may be gender differentiated. It is hard to separate male wish-fulfillment from objective description of the female psyche when Freud tells us that "a mother is only brought unlimited satisfaction by her relation to a son; this is altogether the most perfect, the most free from ambivalence of all human relationships" (1933a, XXII, 133).

In Freud's Pantheon, then, masculine images of the mother seem to oscillate between Aphrodite, all mature heterosexual love and global eroticized giving, perhaps with a touch of narcissism, in love with her son and his penis, and, someone like Hera, more vengeful, strong, and insistent, resentful of men and their betrayals. This mother is not only herself castrated, she castrates, or threatens to castrate, both her son and her daughter. In contrast to Jungian writing, Demeter, the mother who loves the daughter and mourns her loss, is nowhere to be found.[13]

Woman as her subjectivity and character are imagined in the masculine psyche

In "The Taboo of Virginity (Contributions to the Psychology of Love, III" (1918a, XI), Freud suggests that women other than mothers, vengeful recently deflorated ex-virgins, might castrate a man or take his penis. In the ex-virgins' case, this would be in revenge for their painful defloration. Therefore, in many cultures, the custom is *jus primae noctis:* the right of strong, powerful, older men to perform a bride's defloration. Freud suggests in passing that a virgin might indeed be hurt or resent her first experience of intercourse; he has discussed elsewhere at length the girl's penis envy as well as her very problematic sexual socialization. To build our sense of horror, he invokes the decapitating (castrating) Judith and Holofernes: A husband, who must live with his wife for some time, should be spared her revenge and anger. But Freud is much more certain of the part of male fantasy in the custom: "Whenever primitive man has set up a taboo he fears some danger and it cannot be disputed that a generalized dread of women is expressed in all these rules of avoidance. The man is afraid of being weakened by the woman, infected with her femininity. . . . The effect which coitus has of discharging tensions and causing flaccidity may be the prototype of what the man fears" (198–9). Even worse, it seems, than the impotence and lack of sexual desire that Freud suggests in the first two "Contributions to the Psychology of Love," is the possibility of total weakening and "infection" with femininity. The young, innocent husband must be protected against such a psychic threat. We must ask, in this context, if the imagined reaction of the girl is not almost entirely that of a man imagining how he would feel being reminded by intercourse of his lack of a penis.

A final imagined version by the male psyche of woman as subject is, like the resentment of defloration, presented by Freud as objective truth about women. Freud describes for us a variety of traits that characterize women and that he attributes entirely to penis envy and women's lack of a penis: shame at her body; jealousy, which results directly from envy itself; a lesser sense of justice resulting from the weak female superego that never forms because the girl does not fear castration and does not therefore give up oedipal longings or internalize sexual prohibitions; narcissism and vanity, as the self-love that men center on their penis becomes defensively diffused throughout the female body (1925j, XIX, 257). As Freud points out, feminists in his time and since have accused him of male bias in his views here. He also acknowledges, in possible contradiction to his resting his case on clinical findings, that these are "character-traits which critics of every epoch have brought up against women" (ibid.). Freud as cultural man, then, seems to have borrowed a variety of (masculine) cultural attitudes about women whose origins he then coincidentally demonstrates to arise in female development.

We are led, finally, to our place of beginning, the theory of femininity. At various points in his writings, Freud claims that activity–passivity are our best approximations of masculinity–femininity, but he in fact is much more focused on the distinction phallically endowed or castrated: Women are castrated men. I am not the first person to ask where Freud's overwhelming preoccupation with castration and the penis – male organs and a threat to masculine body integrity, as Freud, along with later psychoanalytic commentators, verifies – comes from. We have good reason, from Freud's own account, to think that such a preoccupation comes from the boy, that as Freud wonders about femininity, he is asking, as one commentator puts it, "what is femininity – *for men?*"[14] I have tried to sort out women as subjects, women as objects to their own subjectivity, and women as explicit objects in the male psyche, but we are left with the problem of what part of the Freudian construction of woman as subject is really constructed after the fact from the centerpiece of Freud's theory of sexuality, based on an explicit and implicit male norm. Is Freud, as Horney suggests, asking how a man, or boy, would feel if he were someone without a penis? Here, woman as manifest subject becomes, possibly, latent projection of man.

Freud claims, quite rightly of course, that his theory comes from clinical experience, and he supports it further by drawing upon the writings of several women analysts. But the issue of clinical experience in early psychoanalysis is complicated. To begin, these several women analysts – Deutsch, Lampl-de Groot, and Mack Brunswick – were themselves analyzed by Freud (as was Marie Bonaparte, who later developed what was considered as Freudian orthodoxy on femininity). As with all analysands, these women analysts seem to have remained transferentially and in actuality attached. Lampl-de Groot, even as she provides the basis for a radically new theory, does not take issue with Freud's claim for the centrality of the female castration complex. Indeed, she reviews almost everything he has written before suggesting modestly, on the basis of two cases, that there might possibly be something that Freud left out, at least in these two cases. Deutsch and Anna Freud in their own writings give evidence that they wanted to please Freud by the kind of theories they created, and they have been taken to task on this account by others as well.

Moreover, as the biographical literature on psychoanalysts expands, we are becoming more aware of just how autobiographical the early writings often were. These first analysts, after all, did not have a lot of cases, and one knows – even as one doesn't know – oneself best. Freud is quite explicit that his theory of the Oedipus complex evolved from his own self-analysis; his *Interpretation of Dreams* stands as a classic account of psychoanalytic theory creation through self-analysis. We do not know about times when he might have used himself as a case without acknowledgment. Other writings are not so candid. Deutsch's autobiography and a biography of her make clear the autobiographical basis, translated into fictive case accounts, of much of her theory of femininity, and Deutsch is among early women writers on women a leading defender and supporter of the theories of primary penis envy, narcissism, masochism, and passivity. A recent biography of Anna Freud suggests that Freud's 1924 and 1925 papers on female psychology, as well as an earlier paper, "A Child Is Being Beaten: A Contribution to the Study of Sexual Perversions" (1919e, XVII), come at least partially in the former case and probably entirely in the latter from his analysis of his daughter, whose own writings on beating fantasies and on altruism are themselves autobiographical though presented fictively as cases. Both Deutsch and Anna Freud, in writings we now have available, affirm at some length their hatred and jealousy of mothers who are all bad, their idealization of fathers who are virtually all good.[15]

Freud's "clinical experience" with women patients then, from the end of World War I through the mid 1920s, just prior to his writings on femininity, was partly with those same women who wrote autobiographically and of their own patients as they supported and helped to create his position. Did, and how did, his analysis of these young women followers, including that young woman nearest and dearest to him – Anna – affect his theory? How much were their autobiographical and theoretical understandings, reflected in their writings on femininity, affected by their analysis with Freud – a Freud who, as we know him from his classic case reports, was not loathe to make interpretations to patients based on previously conceived theories? These understandings, translated at least in the cases of Deutsch and Anna Freud into fictive patient accounts, as well as into theory, must have emerged at least partially from interpretations and reconstructions made by that very powerful and charismatic person who later used their writings as independent corroboration of his own position. They may well have been reflecting their own experience in writings – there are certainly women with the particular configuration of love and hate for father and mother they describe, and women who, for a variety of reasons, express envy or desire for a penis or passive or masochistic sexual desires. However, they cast their writings in universal terms, as characterizing femininity per se, and Freud, for theoretical reasons, used them that way as well.

The problem here is not the partially autobiographical basis of these early psychoanalytic writings. It is only recently that, under the name of countertransference, analysts are willing publicly to open themselves as extensively to scrutiny. As I indicate, much early psychoanalytic theory (I do not speculate about psychoanalytic theory today) was autobiographically based, and in the case of the theory of femininity, as elsewhere, the opposition (Horney, for instance) almost certainly drew upon implicit autobiographical understandings as well.[16] I mean to draw attention to the especial complexities in the case of Freud's views on the psychology of women and the somewhat less than independently developed clinical and theoretical support he draws for these views. We can only begin to untangle the convoluted interactions in theory creation here.

Freud claimed that his understanding of women was "shadowy and incomplete," but he nevertheless developed a broad-sweeping theory about femininity and treated and discussed many women clinically. For the most part, we admire his clinical accounts, his forthright defense of hysterical women, and his condemnation of the conditions leading to repression and hysteria in women. We admire also his toleration and understanding of variations in sexual object-choice and sexual subjectivity. We are still not able completely to evaluate his theory of femininity; indeed, many evaluations find it to be extremely problematic.

By contrast, Freud's understandings about male attitudes toward women and femininity do not seem to be shadowy and incomplete at all. They are specific, informative, persuasive, precise, and clear, covering ingeniously a variety of sexual, representational, and neurotic formations. They illuminate for us with passion and empathy, and in full daylight, the mysteries of the male psyche.

NOTES

1 For an overview of modern psychoanalytic writings on women, see "Psychoanalytic Feminism and the Psychoanalytic Psychology of Women," ch. 9 in my *Feminism and Psychoanalytic Theory* (Cambridge: Polity Press, and New Haven, Conn.: Yale University Press, 1989).

2 Daniel N. Stern, *The Interpersonal World of the Infant* (New York: Basic Books, 1985), pp. 13–23.

3 Ibid., p. 19

4 Brunswick, "The Preoedipal Phase," in Robert Fliess, ed., *The Psychoanalytic Reader* (New York: International Universities Press, 1948), pp. 231–53.

5 According to Elizabeth Young-Bruehl, there is good reason to believe that the clinical model of the girl who compulsively maturbates, as she struggles with penis-envy and, presumably penis-preoccupation, as well as of the girl who leads Freud to "credit a single instance" (1925j, XIX, 256) of the masculinity complex, is Anna Freud, whose second analysis just preceded Freud's writing of his 1925 paper (Young-Bruehl, *Anna Freud* [New York, Summit Books, 1988], ch. 2). I discuss the complexities of the clinical bases of Freud's theories later in this essay.

6 See Jeanne Lampl-de Groot, "The Evolution of the Oedipus Complex in Women," 1927, in *The Development of the Mind: Psychoanalytic Papers on Clinical and Theoretical Problems* (New York: International Universities Press, 1965) and Helene Deutsch, *The Psychology of Women*, vol. 1, *Girlhood* (New York: Grune and Stratton, 1944), which summarizes Deutsch's earlier work.

7 See on Dora, Charles Bernheimer and Claire Kahane, eds., *In Dora's Case: Freud – Hysteria – Feminism* (New York: Columbia University Press, 1985). On Dora as an adolescent, see esp. ch. 2, taken from Erik H. Erikson, "Reality and Actuality: An Address." On Dora's name, see esp. ch. 9, Jane Gallop, "Keys to Dora," and Hannah S. Decker, "The Choice of a Name: 'Dora' and Freud's Relationship with Breuer," *Journal of the American Psychoanalytic Association* 30 (1982): 113–36.

8 See "Seventies Questions for Thirties Women," ch. 10 in my *Feminism and Psychoanalytic Theory.*

9 I am indebted for this point to Joseph Lifschutz (class lecture).

10 The areas of acceptance I have in mind include, for instance, discussions of male fetishism, analysis of masculine fear and/or contempt of women, and accounts of problems in heterosexual object-choice and experience.

11 See "The Flight from Womanhood: The Masculinity Complex in Women

as Viewed by Men and by Women," 1926, and "The Dread of Woman," 1932, both in *Feminine Psychology* (New York: W. W. Norton, 1967).

12 In *The Psychoanalytic Theory of Male Homosexuality* (New York: Simon and Schuster, 1988), p. 78, Kenneth Lewes points out that all preoedipal children are psychically male homosexual, since they are imaged by Freud to be sexually phallic and sexually desirous of a phallic mother.

13 See C. J. Jung and C. Kerenyi, *Essays on a Science of Mythology: The Myth of the Divine Child and the Mysteries of Eleusis* (Princeton, N.J.: Princeton University Press, 1963), and Erich Neumann, *The Great Mother* (Princeton, N.J.: Princeton University Press, 1963) (2d ed.). On Hera in the masculine psyche, see Philip Slater, *The Glory of Hera* (Boston: Beacon Press, 1968).

14 Shoshana Felman, "Rereading Femininity," *Yale French Studies* 62 (1981): 21. Felman also points out that accounts by women, like the present account, are really asking "What does the question 'What is femininity – *for men?* – mean *for women?*' " (ibid.).

15 On the autobiographical bases of Deutsch's and Anna Freud's writings, see Helene Deutsch, *Confrontations with Myself* (New York: Norton, 1973), Paul Roazen, *Helen Deutsch* (New York: Anchor, 1985), Nellie Thompson, "Helene Deutsch: A Life in Theory," *Psychoanalytic Quarterly* 56 (1987): 37–53, and Young-Breuhl, *Anna Freud*.

16 See Susan Quinn, *A Mind of Her Own: The Life of Karen Horney* (New York: Summit Books, 1987).

10   Freud and the understanding of art

Freud opens his ingenious and revealing essay on the *Moses* of Michelangelo with a disclaimer. He had, he said, no more than a layman's or amateur's knowledge of art: neither in his attitude to art nor in the way in which he experienced its attractions was he a connoisseur. He goes on:

Nevertheless, works of art do exercise a powerful effect on me, especially those of literature and sculpture, less often of painting. This has occasioned me, when I have been contemplating such things, to spend a long time before them trying to apprehend them in my own way, i.e., to explain to myself what their effect is due to. Wherever I cannot do this, as for instance with music, I am almost incapable of obtaining any pleasure. Some rationalistic, or perhaps analytic, turn of mind in me rebels against being moved by a thing without knowing why I am thus affected and what it is that affects me. (1914b, XIII, 211)

And then, as if for a moment conscious that he might appear to be imposing his own personal peculiarities, a quirk of his own temperament, upon a subject with its own code, with its own imperatives, he hastens to concede what he calls "the apparently paradoxical fact" that "precisely some of the grandest and most overwhelming creations of art are still unsolved riddles to our understanding." Before these works we feel admiration, awe – and bewilderment. "Possibly," Freud goes on with that irony which he permitted himself in talking of established ways of thinking

Some writer on aesthetics has discovered that this state of intellectual bewilderment is a necessary condition when a work of art is to achieve its greatest effects. It would be only with the greatest reluctance that I could bring myself to believe in any such necessity. (1914b, XIII, 211–12)

249

Anyone acquainted with Freud's style will at once recognize something typical in this whole passage, in the easy and informal way with which from the beginning he takes the reader into his confidence: typical, too, that Freud should be unable to renounce this natural way of writing even when, as here, the work on which he was engaged was ultimately to appear anonymously.

Nevertheless, for all its ease of manner, the passage that I have quoted is problematic. There are two questions to which it immediately gives rise, and to which some kind of answer is required, if we are to use it as providing us with an entry into Freud's views about art. The first is this: When Freud says that for him there is a peculiar difficulty in obtaining pleasure from a work of art if he cannot explain to himself the source of this pleasure, are we to take his words – as he says he wants us to – as a purely personal avowal? Or is it that what constituted for Freud the peculiarity of his situation is simply the deeper understanding he feels himself to have of human nature and human achievement: that the attitude to art from which he cannot free himself is one that must come naturally to anyone affected by psychoanalysis, and that it is only in ignorance of psychoanalysis that any other attitude – for instance, that of delight in bewilderment – could be conceived? And the second question is, What form of understanding or explanation did Freud have in mind? More specifically, we know that by 1913, the date of the Michelangelo essay, Freud had already subjected a large number of psychic phenomena, normal as well as pathological, to psychoanalytic scrutiny: dreams, errors, jokes, symptoms, the psychoneuroses themselves, fantasies, magic. And so it is only natural to ask which of these phenomena, if any, was to serve as the model, so far as the pattern of explanation it received, for the understanding of art?

The first question is one that I shall return to later. Meanwhile I should like to draw your attention to a passage from another and certainly no less famous essay that Freud wrote on a great artist, "A Childhood Memory of Leonardo da Vinci," which dates from the spring of 1910. Writing of Leonardo's insatiable curiosity, Freud quotes two sayings of Leonardo's, both to the effect that one cannot love or hate in any but a faint or feeble way unless one has a thorough knowledge of the object of one's love or hate. Freud then goes on:

The value of these remarks of Leonardo's is not to be looked for in their conveying an important psychological fact; for what they assert is obviously false, and Leonardo must have known this as well as we do. It is not true that human beings delay loving or hating until they have studied and become familiar with the nature of the object to which these affects apply. On the contrary they love impulsively, from emotional motives which have nothing to do with knowledge, and whose operation is at most weakened by reflection and consideration. Leonardo, then, could only have meant that the love practised by human beings was not of the proper and unobjectionable kind: one *should* love in such a way as to hold back the affect, subject it to the process of reflection and only let it take its course when it has stood up to the test of thought. And at the same time we understand that he wishes to tell us that it happens so in his case and that it would be worth while for everyone else to treat love and hatred as he does. (1910c, XI, 74)

Now, it must be emphasized that the two sayings of Leonardo with which Freud takes issue do not refer simply to personal loves and hates: they are addressed to what we feel about anything in nature. Indeed, in the longer of the two passages that Freud cites Leonardo is – or at any rate Freud takes him to be – expressly defending himself against the charge that a scientific attitude toward the works of creation evinces coldness or irreligion. If, then, Leonardo's attitude, so understood, is thought by Freud to deserve these strictures, it is worth setting them by the side of Freud's own attitude to art, as we so far have it, and wondering why they do not apply to it.

Turning now to the second of the two questions, I shall anticipate slightly by saying that Freud seems to find in a variety of mental phenomena suitable models for the interpretation of art: that in attempting to explain art he assimilates it now to this, now to that, psychic phenomenon, for the understanding of which he had already devised its own explanatory schema. The richness of Freud's aesthetic lies in the overlapping of these various suggestions; though, as we shall see, how the suggestions are actually to be fitted together is an issue to which Freud barely applied himself.

However, before either of the two questions that arise out of the Michelangelo essay can be answered, there is a third which requires our attention. And that is the question of what texts we are to consult, and what relative assessment we are to make of them, in arriving at a considered estimate of Freud's views. In addition to its obvious priority, this question has the additional advantage that, if taken early on, it might save us time later. For a mere review of Freud's writings on art and of their relative weight could show us where his central interests lay: it could show us the kind or kinds of understanding he sought and the significance that he attached to this. It could save us from certain mistakes.

For the first thing to be observed about Freud's writings on art is that some of them are only peripherally about art. A fact that emerges from Ernest Jones's biography is that Freud, for all his lack of arrogance, felt himself, in a way that is perhaps vanishing from the world, to be one of the great, to belong in a pantheon of the human race; and for this reason it was only natural that his thoughts should often turn to the great figures of the past, and that to understand the inner workings of their genius should be one of his recurrent ambitions. Freud, we may think, wrote *about* Leonardo in much the same spirit as later, at one of the dark moments of European civilization, he was to write *to* Einstein: it was the conscious communion of one great man with another.

My claim is, then, that the essay on Leonardo – and much the same sort of claim could be mounted for the essay on Dostoevsky – is primarily a study in psychoanalytic biography: and the connection with art is *almost* exhausted by the fact that the subject of the biography happens to be one of the greatest, as well as one of the strangest, artists in history. For if we turn to the text of the essay, and ignore the straightforward contributions to psychoanalytic theory, which are inserted, as it were, parenthetically, we shall see that the study falls into two parts.

There is, first of all, the reconstruction of Leonardo's childhood, the evidence for which is recognized to be scanty: and then there is the history of Leonardo's adult life, which is, of course, adequately documented, but which is deliberately presented by Freud in such a way that it can be connected up with earlier events. In other words, seen as a whole, the essay is an attempt to exhibit – not, of course, to prove but, like the clinical case-histories, to exhibit – the dependence of adult capacities and proclivities on the infantile, and in particular on infantile sexuality.

More specifically, the dependence of later on earlier experience is worked out in terms of fixation points and successive regressions. To Leonardo are attributed two fixation points. The first or earlier one was established in the years spent in his mother's house when, experiencing as an illegitimate child her undivided love, he was seduced into a sexual precocity in which intensive sexual curiosity and an element of sadism must have been manifestations. In time, however, a conjunction of internal and external factors – the very excess of the boy's love for his mother, and his reception into the nobler household of his father and his stepmother by his fifth year – brought on a wave of repression in which the blissful eroticism of his infancy was stamped out. He overcame and yet preserved his feelings for his mother by first identifying himself with her and then seeking as sexual objects not other women but boys in his own likeness. Here we have Leonardo's second point of fixation, in an idealized homosexuality: idealized, for he loves boys only as his mother loved him: that is, in a sublimated fashion.

It is against this childhood background that Freud then reviews and interprets the successive phases of Leonardo's adult life. First, there was a phase in which he worked without inhibition. Then, gradually his powers of decision began to fail, and his creativity became enfeebled under the inroads of an excessive and brooding curiosity. Finally, there was a phase in which his gifts reasserted themselves in a series of works that have become justly famous for their enigmatic quality. These last two phases Freud then proceeds to connect with successive regressions, in the manner that had become familiar since the *Three Essays on the Theory of Sexuality*. First, there is a regression to a strong but totally repressed homosexuality, in which the greater part of the libido, profiting from pathways laid down in a yet earlier phase, seeks and finds an outlet in the pursuit of knowledge – though, as we have seen, at a heavy cost to the general conduct of life. This, however, is then overtaken by a regression to the earliest attachment. Either through some internal transformations of energy or by a happy accident – Freud suggests a connection with the sitter for the *Mona Lisa* – Leonardo, now at the age of fifty, returns to enjoy his mother's love in a way that allows a new release of creativity.

Now it is in connection with this attempt to interpret Leonardo's adult life in the light of certain childhood patterns that Freud appeals to particular works of Leonardo all drawn from the later phase: the *Mona Lisa*, the Paris and London versions of the *Madonna and Child with St Anne*, and the late androgynous figure paintings. If we read the relevant section of Freud's essay (section IV) carefully, we see what his procedure is. He uses the evidence provided by the pictures to confirm the link he has postulated between this last phase of Leonardo's activity and a certain infantile "complex," as Freud would have put it at that date. Note that Freud does not use the evidence of the pictures to establish the infantile complex – that depends upon secondary sources and the so-called "infantile memory" from which the essay derives its title: he uses it to establish a link between the complex and something else. But, we might ask: In what way do the pictures that Freud cites provide evidence? And the answer is that the evidence that they provide comes from certain internal features plus certain obvious or seemingly obvious trains of association to these features. So in the Louvre picture Freud associates to St Anne's smile the caressing figure of Leonardo's mother; to the similarity of age between St Anne and the Virgin he associates the rivalry between Leonardo's mother and his stepmother; and to the pyramidal form in which the two figures are enclosed he associates an attempt on Leonardo's part to reconcile "the two mothers of his childhood."

I have said enough, I hope, to show how misleading it is to say, as is sometimes said, that in the Leonardo essay Freud lays down a pattern for the explanation of art based on the model of dream-interpretation. It is true that with certain very definite qualifications Freud does in the course of this essay treat a number of works of art in just the way he would if they were dreams; the qualifications being that the associations he invokes are not free and that the trains terminate on an already established complex. But there is nothing to suggest that Freud thought that this is the proper way to treat works of art if one wants to explain them as works of art: All we can safely conclude is that he thought this a proper way to treat them if one wanted to use them as biographical evidence. There are, indeed, ancillary pieces of evidence to suggest that Freud's interest in the Leonardo essay was primarily biographical. This certainly is in accord with the reception that the original draft of the essay received – and presumably invited – when it was read to the Vienna Psychoanalytic Society a few months before its publication.[1] The minutes reveal that in the discussion it was only Victor Tausk who referred to the paper as "a great critique of art" as well as a piece of psychoanalysis, and his remark went unheeded. Again, both in the original draft and in the final essay the feature most emphasized by Freud in

Leonardo's works is certainly not an aesthetic feature: that they are very largely left unfinished. And, finally, it must be significant that Freud made virtually no attempt to identify in the work of the last phase any correlate to the fact that, though this phase too marks a regression, nevertheless it was a regression that enabled a new release of creativity.

If we now turn back from the Leonardo essay to the essay on the *Moses* of Michelangelo, with which I began, we find ourselves involved with a totally different enterprise.[2] Indeed, if we consider both essays to be (roughly) studies in *expression*, then it looks as though they mark out the two ends of the spectrum of meaning that this term has occupied in European aesthetics. For, if the Leonardo essay concerns itself with expression in the modern sense – that is, with what the artist expresses in his works, or with Leonardo's expressiveness – then the Michelangelo essay is concerned with expression in the classical sense – that is, with what is expressed by the subject of the work, or the expressiveness of Moses. (The distinction is, of course, oversimple, and it is significant that there has been a continuous theory of expression in European aesthetics.)

Let us look for a moment at the problem that Michelangelo's great statue sets the physiognomically minded spectator. We may express it in a distinction used by Freud – and, of course, our aim anyhow is to get as close as possible to the problem as he conceived it – and ask initially whether *Moses* is a study of character or a study of action. Those critics who have favored the latter interpretation have stressed the wrath of Moses and contended that the seated figure is about to spring into action and let loose his rage on the faithless Israelites. The wrath is evident, Freud argues, but the projected movement is not indicated in the statue and would moreover contradict the compositional plan of the tomb for which it was intended. Those critics who have favored the former interpretation of the statue – that is, as a study in character – have stressed the passion, the strength, the force implicit in Michelangelo's representation. Such an interpretation can remain free of implausibility, but it seemed to Freud to leave too much of the detail of the statue uncovered and it insufficiently relates the inner to the outer. Freud's interpretation is that we should see the figure of Moses, not as being about to break out in rage, but as having checked a movement of anger. By seeing it as a study in suppressed action, that is self-mastery, we can also see it as a study in character and at the same time avoid any inconsistency with the compositional indications.

"Here we are fully back," Ernst Gombrich has written of this essay, "in the tradition of nineteenth-century art-appreciation,"[3] and this tradition he partially characterized by referring to its preoccupation with the "spiritual content" of the work of art. The evident conservatism of Freud's method in the Michelangelo essay does in large measure warrant Gombrich's judgment, and yet I think that if we look carefully at Freud's text there are some scattered counterindications that should warn us against taking it – what should I say? – too definitively.

It is a matter of more than local interest that in the Michelangelo essay Freud expresses his deep admiration for the critical writings of an art historian whom he had first encountered under the name of Ivan Lermolieff. This pseudonym, he later discovered, masked the identity of the great Giovanni Morelli, the founder of scientific connoisseurship. Now it was Morelli more than anyone else who brought the notion of "spiritual content" in art into disrepute. Admittedly what Morelli primarily objected to was not spiritual content as a criterion of value or of interpretation but its employment in determining the authorship of a particular painting; and it was to set this right that he devised his own alternative method, which consisted first in drawing up for each painter a schedule of forms, showing how he depicted the thumb, the lobe of the ear, the foot, the fingernail and other such trifles, and then in matching any putative work by a given painter against his particular schedule item by item. Nevertheless, once Morelli's method had been applied to determine authorship, the old idea of spiritual content had received a mauling from which it could not hope to recover.

It is, then, worth observing that it was precisely for his method, with all that it involved in the reversal of traditional aesthetic values, that Freud admired Morelli so much.[4] Nor was Freud's admiration mere generality. Quite apart from the intriguing but quite unanswerable question whether the anonymity of the Michelangelo essay might not have had as one of its determinants an unconscious rivalry with Morelli, Freud would seem to have used in pursuit of physiognomy a method markedly like that which Morelli evolved to settle issues of connoisseurship. The somewhat self-conscious attention to minutiae, to measurement, to anatomical detail suggests that, even if

Freud's critical aims were conservative, the methods he was prepared to envisage for achieving them were not so constricted. This point is one to which we may have to return. And, finally, it must be observed that Freud, both at the beginning and at the end of his essay, endeavors to link, though without indicating precisely how, the physiognomy of Moses with an intention of Michelangelo.

And now I want to turn to the third and only other extended essay that Freud wrote on art or an artist. (I exclude the Dostoevsky essay because, though almost the length of the *Moses* essay, it contains so little on its nominal subject.) In the summer of 1906 Freud had his attention drawn by Jung, whom he had not yet met, to a story by the north German playwright and novelist Wilhelm Jensen (1837–1911) entitled *Gradiva*. Though Freud referred to the work as "having no particular merit in itself," which seems a fair judgment, it evidently intrigued him at the time and by May of the following year it had become the subject of an essay, "Delusions and Dreams in Jensen's *Gradiva*." Unfortunately in the Standard Edition of Freud's works the practice of the original English translation, of printing Jensen's story as well as Freud's text, has not been followed. The reader who relies upon Freud's résumé is unlikely to appreciate fully the deftness and subtlety with which he interprets the text. In the résumé text and interpretation are in such close proximity that we may take the interpretation for granted.

Jensen's *Gradiva* is subtitled "A Pompeian Fancy," and it tells the story of a young German archaeologist, Norbert Hanold, who has so withdrawn himself from the world that his only attachment is to a small Roman plaque of a girl walking with an elegant and distinctive step, which he had first seen in the museum of antiquities at Rome and of which he has bought a cast. He calls the girl Gradiva, he spins around her the fantasy that she came from Pompeii, and, after several weeks of quite vain research into her gait and its distinctiveness or otherwise, he sets off to Italy, heavily under the influence of a dream in which he watched Gradiva perish in the Pompeian earthquake. On his journey south life is made intolerable for him by the endless German honeymoon couples and by the flies. He hates, we may discern, the untidiness both of love and of life. Inevitably he drifts to Pompeii and the next day at noon, entering the house to which he has in fantasy assigned Gradiva, he sees the double of the girl who is represented in his beloved plaque. Are we to believe that this is a hallucination or a ghost? In fact it is neither; it is, as Norbert Hanold has to realize, a live person, though she continues to humor him in the belief that they knew each other in another life and that she has long been dead. There is another meeting, there are two further dreams, and all the while there is the pressure on Hanold of having to accept how much of his fantasy is proving to be real. Ultimately there is a revelation, by which time Hanold is prepared for the truth. The girl is a childhood friend of his who has always been in love with him. He, on the contrary, had repressed his love for her and had only allowed it to manifest itself in his attachment to the plaque, which, it now turned out, in so many of its treasured aspects, some of which had been projected by him on to it while others must have been the causes of his initial attraction to it, precisely reflected her. Even the name that he bestowed on the plaque, "Gradiva," was a translation of her name, "Bertgang." By the end of the story his delusion has been cast off, his repressed sexuality breaks through, and the girl has restored to her "her childhood friend who had been dug out of the ruins" – an image obviously of inexhaustible appeal to Freud, who was to draw upon it over and over again each time he elaborated his favored comparison between the methods of psychoanalysis and the methods of archaeology.

It is natural to think of "Delusion and Dreams" as lying on the same line of inquiry as the later Michelangelo essay but at a point projected well beyond it. Both essays are studies in the character or mood or mind of the subject in a work of art, but in the Jensen essay the inquiry is pursued with what seems a startling degree of literalness. "A group of men," is how it begins, "who regarded it as a settled fact that the essential riddles of dreaming have been solved by the efforts of the author of the present work found their curiosity aroused one day by the question of the class of dreams that have never been dreamed at all – dreams created by imaginative writers and ascribed to invented characters in the course of a story" (1907a, IX, 7). And Freud then proceeds to grapple with this question in such detail, giving a lengthy analysis of Hanold's two dreams, that the reader might feel, on reaching the last sentence of the essay, that it could profitably have come somewhat earlier. "But we must stop here" Freud writes, "or we may really forget that Hanold and Gradiva are only creatures of the author's mind" (1907a, IX, 93).

But such a reaction on the part of the reader – or the feeling that

Freud here is guilty of misapplying his technique of dream-interpretation because he has falsely assimilated characters of fiction to characters of real life – would be inappropriate. For it overlooks one important, and indeed surprising, fact: that Hanold's dreams *can* be interpreted, that there is sufficient evidence for doing so. Of course this fact is purely contingent, in that we could have no general reason to anticipate it. Nevertheless, it is so. The overall point might be brought out by comparing the dream-interpretations in the Jensen essay with that part of the Leonardo essay where, as we have seen, Freud sets out to interpret some of the late works of the painter somewhat on the analogy of dreams. Now, the former, it might be argued, compares unfavorably with the latter. For anyone who accepts the leading ideas of Freudian theory will agree that there must in principle be a way of eliciting the latent content of the Leonardo works, the two open questions being whether the evidence permits this to be done in practice and, if so, whether Freud succeeded in doing it.[5] However, there can be no corresponding assurance that it is possible to elicit the content of Hanold's dreams, for Hanold's dreams are not actual dreams. Now, this argument is perfectly acceptable if what it points out is that there need not have been evidence adequate for the decipherment of Hanold's dreams. But Freud's discovery is that in point of fact there is, and this discovery is not only the presupposition on which the various dream-interpretations in the Jensen essay are based but also the most interesting feature about that essay.

Once this point is accepted, then Freud's effort to decipher the delusions and dreams of Norbert Hanold, so far from being merely the product of confusion between fiction and reality, can be seen as a genuine contribution to criticism. For it indicates the steps by which, explicitly to a certain kind of reader, implicitly to others, Hanold's beliefs and wishes are revealed – and in this respect it clearly refers to an aesthetic feature of *Gradiva*. And now an analogous point can be made for Freud's physiognomic researches into the Michelangelo *Moses*. For in this study Freud is to be seen, not simply as revealing to us the deepest mental layers of a particular representation, but as indicating how these layers, particularly the deepest of them, are revealed in the corresponding statue. And now perhaps we can see one way in which Freud diverges, if only in emphasis, from nineteenth-century appreciation. For Freud is at least as interested in the way in which the spiritual content of a work of art is made manifest as in the spiritual content itself: and when we take into account the "trivial" ways in which he thought deep content was most likely to manifest itself, the divergence visibly grows.

Let us stay for a moment with those arts in which revelation of character – of the character, that is, of the subject of the work, not as yet that of the artist – is a significant aesthetic feature. Now this feature cannot be unconstrained, otherwise it would cease to be of aesthetic interest. There must be some element in the work that at any rate slows down, or controls, the pace of revelation. Does Freud say anything about this other controlling factor – and the interrelation of the two? In *Gradiva* the controlling factor is not hard to identify: It is the growth of Norbert Hanold's self-consciousness or, as Freud calls it, his "recovery," which is in part an internal process and is in part effected through the agency of Gradiva. Now, Freud had an affection for this particular artistic compromise; it has a natural poignancy, and it also exhibits an obvious affinity with psychoanalytic treatment. As to the interrelation of the two factors, or how far the omniscient author is entitled to outrun his confused or unselfconscious characters, Freud has, implicitly at any rate, some interesting observations to make when he writes about the ambiguous remarks that abound in *Gradiva*. For instance, when Hanold first meets the seeming *revenant* from Pompeii, he says in reply to her first utterance: "I knew your voice sounded like that" (1907a, IX, 84). Freud's suggestion is that the use of ambiguity by an author to reveal the character of his subject ahead of the process of self-knowledge is justified insofar as the ambiguously couched revelation corresponds to a repressed piece of self-knowledge.

Freud, however, has no desire to impose the pattern of revelation controlled by the rate of self-knowledge upon all art for which it makes sense. In perhaps his most interesting piece on art, a few pages entitled "Psychopathic Characters on the Stage," written in 1905 or 1906 but only published posthumously, Freud writes of those literary compositions in which the alternate current is supplied by action or conflict.

A relevant question that Freud deals with in this brief essay is, How explicit is to be our understanding of what is revealed to us? Freud's view is that it need not be explicit. Indeed, even in the most deeply psychological dramas, generations of spectators have found it difficult to say what it was that they understood. "After all," Freud writes engagingly, "the conflict in *Hamlet* is so effectively concealed that it was left to me to unearth it" (1942a [1905–6], VII, 310).[6] Indeed Freud's point goes beyond this. It is not simply that our understanding need not be explicit but that in many cases there are dangers in explicitness, for explicitness could give rise to resistance if the character suffers from a neurosis that his audience shares with him. So here we have another virtue of what I have called the alternate current – namely that it serves what Freud calls "the diversion of attention." And one effective way in which it can do this is by plunging the spectator or the reader into a whirlpool of action from which he derives excitement while yet being secure from danger. And another contributory factor to this same end is the pleasure in play that is provided by the medium of the art: the element of "free play" that had been so heavily stressed in Idealist aesthetics.

And perhaps at this point we should just look back again for a moment at the Michelangelo essay. For we can now see a reason why in certain circumstances it might be, not merely just as acceptable, but actually better, that the revelation of expression should be achieved through small touches, through the trifles to which both Morelli and Freud, though for different reasons, attached such weight. For these trifles can more readily slip past the barriers of attention.

And now once again it is necessary to switch our point of view. For the diversion of attention as we have just been considering it would seem to belong to what might be called the "public relations" of the work of art. That is, its aim seems to be to secure popularity for the work or, more negatively, to avoid disapproval or even to evade censorship. However, if we now look at this process from the artist's point of view, we may be able to see how it can be regarded as contributing to the aesthetic character of the work. But first we must broaden our analysis somewhat. In the *History of the Psycho-Analytic Movement* Freud wrote: "The first example of an application of the analytic mode of thought to the problems of aesthetics was contained in my book on jokes"(1914d, XIV, 37; cf. 1913j, XIII, 187). We have now grown familiar with the idea that *Jokes and Their Relation to the Unconscious* could be made use of in explicating some of the problems of art, but it is perhaps insufficiently appreciated that the credit for this initiative must go to Freud himself.

Freud distinguished three levels to the joke, each marking a successive stage in its development. All three levels rest upon a primitive substrate of play, which initially comes into operation with the infantile acquisition of skills – specifically, so that we may single it out for attention, the skill of speech. Play generates what Freud calls functional pleasure, the pleasure derived from using idly, and thus exhibiting mastery over, a human capacity. Rising on this substrate, the lowest level is the *jest*, a piece of play with words or concepts with one and only one concession to the critical judgment: it makes sense. A jest is a playful way of saying something, but the something need be of no intrinsic interest. Where what is said claims interest in its own right, we move on to the second level and we have the *joke*. For the joke is constructed round a thought, though the thought, Freud insists, makes no contribution whatsoever to the pleasure that is specific to the joke. The pleasure – at any rate on the level with which we are concerned – derives entirely from the element of play, and the thought is there to give respectability to the whole enterprise by falsely claiming credit for the pleasure. And now we move to the third level – the *tendentious joke*. With the tendentious joke the whole machinery that we have so far considered – namely, the jest with a thought to protect it – is now used itself to protect a repressed purpose, either sexual or aggressive, which seeks discharge. But if we are to come to grips with this complex phenomenon, we must discriminate roles. Both jests and untendentious jokes are social practices, but their social side raises no real problems, nor is it of great significance. But with the tendentious joke it is significant. Let us see how this comes about. The joker makes use of the joke in order to divert his attention from the impulse that seeks expression, and the joke is expected to achieve this for him by the discharge of energy it can secure. But, unfortunately, the one person for whom the joke cannot perform this service is the joker: it is something to do with the fact that the joker has made the joke that prevents him from indulging freely in the possibility of play that it offers. The joke is incomplete in itself or, more straightforwardly, the joker cannot laugh at his own joke. Accordingly, if the joke is to fulfill the purpose of the tendentious joker, he requires a hearer to laugh at the joke – though, of course, the hearer, for his part, could never have laughed at it if he had made it himself. However, with the hearer, too, there is a danger, though the other way round, for it is the very openness of the invitation to play that might meet with censure if it is too blatantly extended. Hence the presence of the thought which is required to divert his attention from the play so that he may laugh at the joke. And his laughter licenses the joker in his ulterior purpose. Insofar as the joke falls flat or is denied acclaim, the joker will feel unable to afford the repressed impulse the release he had surreptitiously promised it.

How far this analysis of the tendentious joke may be applied to art is uncertain, and perhaps it would be out of place to demand a general answer. There would seem, however, to be two respects in which a parallel holds. In the first place, what Freud calls the "radical incompleteness" of the joke parallels in psychological terms what is often called the institutional character of art – as well perhaps as suggesting the psychological machinery on which that institution rests. Art is (among other things) what is recognized as art, and Freud's account of the tendentious joke may allow us to see an extra reason why this should be so, as well as to make a new assessment of its importance. Second, there is a parallel between the uncertainty in the hearer of the joke about the source of his pleasure, and the diversion of attention that is predicated on the spectator of the work of art. And this should help to make it clear why "diversion of attention" should be an aesthetic aspect of the work of art, and not just a cheap bid for popularity.

At this point it is worth observing that we are now in a somewhat better position to consider the first of the two questions that arose out of my opening quotation – when I said, you will recall, that it was unclear how far Freud's emphasis on understanding as a prerequisite of appreciation was a purely personal avowal, or whether it indicated a theoretical position. We have now gone far enough to see that part of understanding how it is that a work of art affects us is recognizing the confusion or the ambiguity upon which this effect in part depends. One of the dangers in psychoanalysis, but also one of those against which it perennially warns us, is that in trying to be clear about our state of mind we may make the state of mind out to be clearer than it is.

Indeed, it looks as though the "diversion of attention" required of the spectator of the work of art is far more thoroughgoing than the corresponding demand made on the hearer of the joke. For the spectator not merely uses the overt content of the work of art to divert his attention from the element of play, he may also have to use the element of play to divert his attention from the more disturbing or latent content of the work of art. In this respect he combines in himself the roles of the maker and the hearer of the tendentious joke. Freud, in dissociating himself from the traditional theory that "intellectual bewilderment" is a necessary ingredient in the aesthetic attitude, may have prepared the way for an account of art and our attitude toward it more thoroughly and more deeply challenging to a naïvely rationalist view.

And this leads us to a large question, to which so much of this essay has pointed. We might put it by asking, Is there, according to Freud, anything in the work of art parallel to the purpose that finds, or seeks, expression in so many of the other mental phenomena that Freud studied, and which variously provided models for his examination of art: the tendentious joke, the dream, the neurotic symptom? To this Freud's answer is, No. The artist certainly expresses himself in his work – how could he not? But what he expresses has not the simplicity of a wish or impulse.

Freud was guided in this by two rather elementary considerations, nonetheless important for that. The first is that the work of art does not have the immediacy or the directness of a joke or an error or a dream. It does not avail itself of some drop in attention or consciousness to become the sudden vehicle of buried desires. For all his attachment to the central European tradition of romanticism, a work of art remained for Freud what historically it had always been: a piece of work. And, second, art, at any rate in its higher reaches, did not for Freud connect up with that other and far broader route by which wish and impulse assert themselves in our lives: neurosis. "We forget too easily," Freud is reported as saying, "that we have no right to place neurosis in the foreground, wherever a great accomplishment is involved."[7] The *Minutes of the Vienna Psychoanalytic Society* reveal him over and over again protesting against the facile equation of the artist and the neurotic.[8] But once we abandon this equation, we lose all justification for thinking of art as exhibiting a single or unitary motivation. For outside the comparative inflexibility of the neurosis, there is no single unchanging form that our characters or temperaments assume. There are constant vicissitudes of feeling and impulse, constant formings and reformings of fantasy, over which it is certain very general tendencies pattern themselves, but with a flexibility in which, Freud suggests, the artist is peculiarly adept.

And, finally, we must remember that for Freud art, if expressive, was not purely expressive. It was also constructive. But here we come to a shortcoming or a lacuna in Freud's account of art which reduplicates one in his more general account of the mind, which was only slowly filled in. To understand this we have to look cursorily at the development of Freud's notion of the unconscious and unconscious mechanisms. Initially the notion of the unconscious enters Freud's theory in connection with repression. Then the notion proliferates, and the unconscious becomes identical with a mode of mental functioning called the primary process. Finally, Freud recognized that certain unconscious operations had a role that was not exhausted either by the contribution they made to defense, or by the part they played in the ongoing processes of the mind. They also had a constructive role to play in the binding of energy or, what is theoretically a related process, the building up of the ego. It was the study of identification, in which Freud included projection, that first led him to revise his views in this direction. But no shadow of this new development was cast over Freud's views on art, for the simple reason that there are not extended studies of art from this period. The unconscious appears in Freud's account of art only as providing techniques of concealment or possibilities of play. In a number of celebrated passages Freud equated art with recovery or reparation or the path back to reality.[9] But nowhere did he indicate the mechanism by which this came about. By the time he found himself theoretically in a position to do so, the necessary resources of leisure and energy were, we must believe, no longer available to him.

NOTES

1 *Minutes of the Vienna Psycho-analytic Society,* ed. Hermann Nunberg and Ernst Federn (New York, 1962–), vol. II, pp. 338–52.
2 On Freud's essay, see Hubert Damisch, "Le Gardien de l'Interprétation," *Tel Quel* 44 (1971): 70–84, and 45 (1972): 82–96.
3 E. H. Gombrich, "Freud's Aesthetics," *Encounter* 26 no. 1 (January 1966): 33.
4 See Richard Wollheim, "Giovanni Morelli and the Origins of Scientific Connoisseurship," collected in *On Art and the Mind* (Cambridge, Mass.: Harvard University Press, 1973), pp. 177–201. See also Jack J. Spector,

"The Method of Morelli and its Relation to Freudian Psychoanalysis,"
Diogenes 66 (Summer 1969): 63–83.

5 For discussion of the detail of the Leonardo essay, see Meyer Schapiro,
"Leonardo and Freud, An Art Historical Study," *Journal of the History of
Ideas* 17, no. 2 (April 1956): 147–78, and K. R. Eissler, *Leonardo da Vinci,
Psychoanalytic Notes on the Enigma* (London, 1962).

6 See also Jean Starobinski, "Hamlet et Freud" in Ernest Jones, *Hamlet et
Oedipe*, trans. Anne-Marie Le Gall (Paris, 1967).

7 *Minutes*, vol. II, p. 391.

8 Ibid., pp. 9–10, 103, 189, 224–5.

9 See 1908e [1907], IX, 153; 1910a [1909], XI, 50; 1911b, XII, 224; 1913j, XIII,
187–8; 1916–17, XVI, 375–7; 1925d [1924], XX, 64.

11 Freud's anthropology: A reading of the "cultural books"

How can the insights into individual psychology gained through the techniques of psychoanalysis illuminate the cultural, collective life of people in society? Freud returned to this question throughout his career in a series of works sometimes referred to as the "cultural books"; these include *Totem and Taboo* (1912–13); *Group Psychology and the Analysis of the Ego* (1921c); *Civilization and Its Discontents* (1930a); and *Moses and Monotheism* (1939a). In this essay, I give an exposition of these works in which I stress their unity, their evolution as psychoanalytic theory itself developed, and what I take to be their central argument. I also intend to show how vital aspects to this central argument may, despite the many difficulties these books present to the contemporary student of society and culture, contribute in powerful ways to our understanding of human social existence.

Before turning to the cultural books themselves, however, I want to begin by drawing attention to the fact that Freud was, from the first, concerned with ordinary cultural life. Of the book-length projects to which he applied himself as soon as he had completed the self-analysis which played so crucial a role in his intellectual development, three were nonclinical accounts of normal phenomena in which are visible the workings of unconscious thought processes, namely, dreams (1900a), slips of the tongue (1901b), and jokes (1905c). The effect of these works is to undermine the very distinction between normal and neurotic and to show that something other than rational, secondary process thought is a normal and essential aspect of all human life.

These three books are certainly "cultural" insofar as they explore aspects of thought, speech, and symbolization shared in the public arena of Western society. They do not, however, explicitly address the question of how human culture and society are constituted in general (though the examination of jokes in particular does involve a fine understanding of the social context and interpersonal strategizing involved in joke telling).

It must also be stressed at the outset that Freud's individual psychology itself was never the isolated, hermetically sealed internal system sometimes caricatured by its detractors. As he writes in the Introduction to *Group Psychology:*

In the individual's mental life someone else is invariably involved, as a model, as an object, as a helper, as an opponent; and so from the very first individual psychology, in this extended but entirely justifiable sense of the words, is at the same time a social psychology as well. (1921c, XVIII, 69)

Further, one may well consider "cultural" Freud's essays on art, literature, and myth, all undeniably "cultural" phenomena. True, in many instances Freud treats the characters in the work as if they were individuals whose motivations and psychodynamics exemplified clinical insights; while in others, such as in the studies of Leonardo (1910c) and Dostoevsky (1928b), his attention is focused on the psychology of the artist behind the work. In other instances, however, for example the work on folklore coauthored with Oppenheim (1957a [1911]), Freud makes clear that he considers the symbolism of the unconscious encountered in dreams and neurotic symptoms to be embedded in the language permeating public cultural discourse, so that folklore is amenable to interpretation along psychoanalytic lines.

One particular case of such public symbolism in myth deserves special attention because of its centrality and because Freud's position is so often misunderstood. When, in *The Interpretation of Dreams*, he discusses the theme of death wishes unconsciously felt by children toward a parent, he alludes to Sophocles' *Oedipus Rex*, it is neither to see the play as a manifestation of Sophocles' psychology, nor yet to examine Oedipus' own supposed motives and psychodynamics. It is, rather, to show how the play serves as a collective, publicly constituted fantasy that corresponds to the unconscious incestuous and rivalrous fantasies harbored by each member of the audience as repressed residues of childhood. Those critics who have gloated over the fact that Oedipus himself could not have had an

Oedipus complex miss the point: *We*, being humans and not fictional characters like Oedipus whose exploits are highly unrealistic, *do* have Oedipus complexes; the play thus serves as what Clifford Geertz calls a story people tell about themselves.[1] In *Oedipus Rex* we schematize and epitomize an aspect of our existence, and from this public text we learn how to understand ourselves and how to make ourselves who we are.

It is my contention that if we read Freud's cultural books replacing his search for historical origins with a focus on such fantasy schemas – individually experienced, but also collectively shared, communicated, and transmitted as symbolic representations and as phylogenetic templates – the main arguments take on persuasive force.

The 1907 essay "Obsessive Actions and Religious Practices" can be seen as an overture to the cultural books, a first statement of Freud's idea that neurosis and cultural phenomena can usefully be compared (1907b, IX). In this paper, Freud points to parallels between the private ceremonials of obsessional neurotics and the ritual observances of religion (and one must assume that he has in mind mainly Catholicism and Judaism). They are similar in the sense of guilt both engender if their performance is neglected, but they differ in that the one is variable from person to person, and private, while the other is stereotyped and collective.

The apparent distinction that the neurotic ritual, unlike the religious one, is meaningless disappears when it is realized that the surface triviality and absurdity of obsessional rituals are the result of displacements and other symbolic distortions of an originally perfectly clear idea (while the majority of religious practitioners actually have no inkling of the deep symbolic meaning of the rituals they perform, either).

Dynamically, Freud argues, the two are similar in being based on the renunciation of instinctual impulses. But they differ as to which instinct it is which is being renounced: Whereas in the neurosis it is exclusively the sexual instinct that is suppressed, in religion it is self-seeking, socially harmful instincts. At this relatively early stage in his thinking, Freud maintains that there are two classes of instincts whose opposition is at the root of psychodynamic conflict. One is the sexual instinct, or libido; the other is the class of ego instincts, concerned with survival of the organism, of which the foremost exemplar is hunger. The ego instincts are selfish in the literal sense, looking out at all times for the welfare of *numero uno;* the libido, by contrast, serves the purposes of the genome and the species by ensuring procreative copulation (though this is far from its only actualization in real life).

In the essay Freud puts forward the pithy formulation that one may describe obsessional neurosis "as an individual religiosity and religion as a universal obsessional neurosis" (1907b, IX, 126–7). This, I think, is the essence of his thought about civilization: Religion is the neurosis of civilization, the price civilized people pay for the instinctual renunciations demanded of them. Nor is it just any neurosis; it is specifically a neurosis of the obsessive-compulsive type.

One is so used to hearing that Freud developed his ideas through the treatment of hysteria common among the women in his clientele that one may be inclined to forget that by the time he turned his attention to cultural issues he had become considerably more interested in obsessional neurosis. Perhaps some impetus came from his self-analysis, in which he encountered obsessional features in himself. In any event, the only two published complete cases he himself treated were ones he diagnosed as obsessional – the Rat Man (1909d) and the Wolf Man (1918b [1914]). In one of his great final theoretical works, *Inhibitions, Symptoms and Anxiety,* he says quite explicitly "obsessional neurosis is unquestionably the most interesting and repaying subject of analytic research" (1926d [1925], XX, 113).

Because what is now called obsessive-compulsive personality disorder (but not the more full-fledged obsessional-compulsive neurosis) is typically seen in men more than in women, one might understand Freud's apparent privileging of obsessional psychodynamics in understanding civilization as an expression of his own well-known biases on the matter of the sexes. There is no doubt truth in this view; at the same time one should bear in mind that the problem of which it is a symptom – male domination and its historical and cross-cultural ubiquity – is also one that Freud's theoretical ideas help to explain. If "civilization" is in some meaningful way to be understood on the model of obsessional dynamics; if, furthermore, these dynamics are typical of men; and if, finally, the qualities of this constellation of conflicts lead to a need for control and the isolation of thought from affect, then this would go a long way toward explaining the enigmatic fact of universal gender inequality. That Freud was not himself free of the neurotic and cultural conditions he was able to diagnose does not invalidate his contribution to the understanding of the conditions in which he, and we, find ourselves.

The link between obsessional neurosis and the intertwined origins of religion, society, and civilized morality is the central theme of Freud's next and most important work on the application of psychoanalysis to the study of culture, namely *Totem and Taboo* (1912–13, XIII). The subtitle of the work, "Some Points of Agreement between the Mental Lives of Savages and Neurotics," has been enough to poison the atmosphere between anthropologists and psychoanalysts for most of a century now; but once again, we lose more than we gain if we allow the dated and objectionable aspects of the work to blind us to its positive contribution.

Freud accepted the notion prevalent in the anthropological thinking of his day that cultural history was to be understood as a unilinear progression of higher stages of civilization, and that contemporary non-Western, nonliterate peoples stood "very near to primitive man, far nearer than we do" and that "their mental life must have a peculiar interest for us if we are right in seeing in it a well-preserved picture of an early stage of our own development" (1912–13, XIII, 1). In these assumptions he was no different from the authorities upon whom he relied, including Frazer, Tylor, McLennan, Lang, Marett, and for that matter Durkheim (whose *Elementary Forms of the Religious Life* [1912] he consulted without, it seems, having been particularly impressed).[2]

In Freud's own thinking, the parallels he drew between obsession and civilization rested on the assumption that the history of civilization could be compared to a human lifetime, and that the customs of people closer to the childhood of the race could be understood on the analogy of the fantasies, conflicts, and phase-appropriate neuroses of individual childhood. These views are no longer tenable; nonetheless we must take them as the basis for reading Freud's work, and for finding our way toward a more plausible and useful interpretation of what he saw.

The first of the four essays that comprise that work, "The Horror of Incest," shows that Australian aboriginal peoples – "the most backward and miserable of savages" – are not only not unconcerned about regulating sexual life, but go to great lengths to prevent incest. Their marriage rules, section systems, and avoidance customs are the cultural equivalents of the prohibitions on incest enforced in each individual's psyche through the agency of the superego established in the wake of the resolution of the Oedipus complex.

In the second essay, "Taboo and Emotional Ambivalence," the "taboos" of the Polynesians and others are compared with the prohibitions and ceremonials of obsessional neurosis. Ambivalence, the central dynamic feature of obsessional neurosis, is the situation in which every affectionate relationship is offset by an equal but generally unconscious undercurrent of hostility toward the same person. The prohibitions and rituals of the obsessional are necessary to protect love and the loved ones from a danger, which, since it emanates from oneself, is ever present. The primary prohibition is against touching, which originally is understood in the sexual sense as masturbation, but is extended to any sort of contact. The sexual fantasies aroused by masturbation lead to the dread of castration in retaliation for murderous wishes against the oedipal rival; the sexual and hostile impulses are repressed, but displacement leads to a constant "seepage." The result is the obsessional's fear of contagion, and the preventive measures of isolation, in which thoughts are kept apart from each other and from the feelings appropriate to them (to keep them from "touching").

Freud shows that taboo states in many societies correspond in that taboo people and things are likewise "contagious," through constant displacement. Further, people and situations surrounded by taboo are those likely to evoke selfish and hostile impulses, just the ones repressed in the emotional ambivalence of obsessional neurosis.

Having shown the "points of agreement," Freud turns to the differences between ritual taboos and obsessional prohibitions. First, there is still, as in 1907, the difference between the instincts prohibited. In the neurosis, Freud says, it is a sexual impulse that must be controlled (because it brings with it hostile thoughts that are a source of danger). In the case of cultural taboos, the prohibition is on touching not in the sexual sense but "in the more general sense of attacking, or getting control, and of asserting oneself" (1912–13, XII, 73). The impulses prohibited are, then, a "combination of egoistic and erotic components into wholes of a special kind" (ibid.). What this unique instinctual blend might be will become clearer presently.

A second difference, as in the 1907 paper, is that the neurosis is a "caricature" of a cultural form; neuroses "endeavor to achieve by private means what is effected in society by collective effort" (ibid.). Freud goes further this time, though, and asserts that sexual instincts are unsuited to uniting people in society; that job is better done by the demands of self-preservation.

It seems at first contradictory to claim that egoistic instincts should be more suitable for leading people to unite in social groups than libidinal ones. The confusion is, I think, due to the state of flux in which Freud's instinct theory found itself at the time: He was about to jettison the distinction between ego and libidinal instincts altogether and replace them with a single instinct, libido, which could be directed either toward the self or toward an object (1914c). The "self-preservative" instincts thus turn out to be *both* "egoistic" and "libidinal." The "whole of a special kind" he had referred to would thus be narcissim, libidinal investment of the self. Social instincts, then, at this point in Freud's thought, become derivatives of narcissistic ones.

The point is elaborated in the third essay, "Animism, Magic and the Omnipotence of Thoughts." Both the "savage" and the obsessional neurotic, Freud argues, act as if they believed that wishes equal deeds, that they can have real effects on the world without any action, and, when they are bad, that they can and should be punished like bad deeds. Ideas about things, in short, are granted equal value with things themselves. Magic and "animism" – the postulation of an ensouled external world – which are said to typify "primitive" society correspond to the conviction, so typical of obsessional neurotics, that they are as guilty as murderers because of hostile wishes they have harbored, usually unconsciously. The basis of this attitude is the narcissistic overvaluation of one's own psyche and one's power to determine events. In at least part of the mind, the reality principle is rejected as too great a narcissistic blow (since it does not support the illusion of omnipotence); illusory satisfactions and ersatz control are clung to in the neurosis. The constant need for control and defense is required precisely because the neurotic believes he is dangerous – a conviction resting on the belief that wishes are deeds.

So far the book has been about "Taboo." In the fourth essay, surely the best known and most notorious, we at last arrive at "Totem";

the essay is called "The Return of Totemism in Childhood." Here Freud proposes to solve what was then – but is certainly no longer – an important anthropological issue, namely, how totemism and exogamy are related, which came first, and under what circumstances. James Frazer's four-volume opus *Totemism and Exogamy* was considered a work of paramount significance (it is now hardly ever read), and scholars struggled to place the two phenomena somewhere in the then accepted universal progression of evolutionary stages thought to characterize the development of religion and society.[3] "Totemism" refers broadly to those ideas according to which certain groups of people are linked with animal species, toward which they must observe some sort of ritual relationship and/or prohibition; "exogamy" refers to the institution whereby one is required to marry a person from outside one's own group (at whatever level that might be defined), and prohibited from marrying within the group. Thus, for example, in contemporary American society the nuclear family is exogamous, in that one may not marry a sibling, parent, or child.

After a conscientious review of the literature (to which the contemporary reader need devote only cursory attention, the debates having long since been completely superseded), Freud proposes his own theory of the origin of both totemism and exogamy. Taking these two features and the prohibitions associated with them to be the main foundations of primordial social life, he wants to show that the injunction not to kill the totem animal, interpreted as a displacement for the father, and the rule not to marry within the group, are respectively, negations of the two great oedipal wishes; to kill one's father (assuming a male ego here) and "marry" one's mother. The institution of society thus rests on the measures taken to suppress the wishes of the Oedipus complex.

Freud presents his argument as if it emerged from a consideration of three different theories and observations: Darwin's conception of the original social units in which humans may have lived; Robertson Smith's theory of the totemic sacrificial feast; and Freud's (1909b) and Ferenczi's observations of animal phobias in little boys.[4] The last named serve to prove that the totem animal is really the father, since in children, as presumably in "the childhood of the race," animals frequently represent the castrating father around whom phobic ideas nucleate. Robertson Smith's analysis is brought in to show that totem feasts, in which a prohibited animal is killed amid both mourning and rejoicing, are features of the supposed original religion of humankind.

Darwin's contribution to the scenario is his (really quite plausible, if not necessarily correct) suggestion that early humans probably lived in bands composed of a single adult male and those females and their young he was able to control and defend from competitors. The young males would be driven off as soon as they were sexually mature and thus potential rivals; after living a solitary life, they too would, in their turn, establish a mating unit with one or more females. Such an arrangement would, according to Darwin, prevent the dangers of too close inbreeding. (This model is, in fact, a fairly accurate schematic description of gorilla social organization.)

Freud's own theory weaves these strands together to propose that in one fateful era, inaugurating human culture and society, the excluded junior males rebelled against their father, driven by desire for his females, resentment of his tyranny, and new confidence perhaps arising from the possession of some new weapon. (I have elsewhere proposed that this new weapon would have been the capacity for culture itself.[5]) They killed and ate the father, thus by identification gaining some of his authority. The totem meal reenacts this "memorable and criminal deed, which was the beginning of so many things – of social organization, of moral restrictions and of religion" (1912–13, XIII, 142).

Their goal achieved and their hostility spent, the brothers' love for the slain father came to the fore, and in remorse, and through a fear of the war of all against all to which the succession would otherwise lead, they set up the first prohibitions in the name of the now deified patriarch: One must not kill the totem animal (father) and one must not commit what for the first time becomes the crime of "incest" with those women whose desirability instigated the revolt in the first place, that is, the father's consorts. The simultaneous sorrow and joy of the totemic feast represent both sides of the ambivalence: The rite both reenacts the triumph and expiates the crime. The prohibition on incest ipso facto inaugurates exogamy and the necessary exchange of wives between groups, while the memory of the dead father becomes the basis for the new moral system, authorized by the guilt felt by the brothers for their act.

Freud suggests that the memory of the original deed has remained in the human unconscious and continues to undergird and enforce human society, which is based on the incest taboo and the collective worship of progressively "higher" deities: first animals, then the hero, the polytheistic gods, and finally the returned superpatriarch of Judeo-Christian (and Islamic) monotheism. (The matriarchy, then widely believed to have been an important stage in the evolution of society, is slipped rather awkwardly into the interregnum after the father is killed and before the brothers have come to their wits and established civilized social organization.)

Freud's myth of the primal horde has struck a host of observers and critics as farfetched and overwrought; and certainly, from our point of view, the various arguments based on the assumption of a parallel between the evolution of society and the maturation of an individual – as well as the hypotheses about the matriarchy, the totemic stage of religion, and so on – have lost all but historical interest. It is my contention, however, that behind the melodrama lies the persuasive observation that the oedipal fantasies of human childhood, based on sexual and aggressive impulses within the nuclear family, have both a cultural and a phylogenetic basis, as would be expected given that we evolved under conditions of natural selection for maximum inclusive reproductive fitness. The primal horde probably never existed; but it does ideally embody the *fantasy* of what any male in a sexually reproducing species like ours might *aspire* to in his narcissistic and reproductive self-interest: to father offspring by as many women as possible, and to eliminate all rival males from competition by depriving them – one way or another – of reproductive potential, that is, by "castrating" them.

So well suited for reproduction in social mammals is this arrangement that stockbreeders of ungulates and other herd animals around the world have adopted it as usual practice, as I have pointed out elsewhere.[6] Breeders recreate the primal horde in their flocks by impregnating all the females with one or a few stud males, and killing and eating, castrating, or subjugating for forced labor the remaining males.

Once he had arrived at the formulation of the primal horde, Freud continued to organize his further thinking about culture and society around it. In his next major cultural work, *Group Psychology and the Analysis of the Ego* (1921c), he combines his earlier work on

narcissism (1914c), his idea of the primal horde, and the new dual
instinct theory he had proposed the previous year in *Beyond the
Pleasure Principle* (1920g.) A new instinct theory had been necessary
ever since the collapse of the old duality into a unitary view with
libido as the only instinctual drive. This situation left libido without
an antagonist among the instincts, and thus left Freud at a loss to
find a biological underpinning for the endemic conflict he found in
human psychology. The new instincts of 1920 are Eros, subsuming
the old libido; and a new instinct, Thanatos, the drive toward destruction and death.

The latter plays no active role in the *Group Psychology*; the revised version of Eros, however, contributes some new twists to
Freud's theory of culture and society. As we saw, sexual love in its
pure state leads to transient gratification and cannot form the basis
for lasting social bonds. Only erotic impulses that are partly aim-
inhibited can transform sexual interest into long-term love and affil-
iation. The sexual couple, then, stands in an equivocal position between narcissism and group psychology: a pair united in genital love
is a self-contained minimal unit, antithetical to the growth of larger
units. The primal father himself had been a pure narcissist, in the
sense that he gratified every wish, including sexual ones, as soon as
it arose. He did not, strictly speaking, lead a social existence in the
human sense; even his pairings with his consorts had complete but
only momentary pleasure, not lasting object relations, as their basis.
It was, rather, the brothers who, because of the sexual privation
forced upon them by their jealous father, first experienced social life
as we know it.

Prevented by the repressive father from achieving genital satisfaction with women, the brothers formed ties among themselves based
on aim-inhibited libido, sometimes expressing itself in homosexual
erotic ties among them. This aim-inhibited love became a part of
what cemented them into an enduring group. But narcissism once
again augments object love, through the process of identification.
Forced to renounce his own narcissism, each young man clings to it
in fantasy by creating the image of his own forfeited perfection as an
"ego-ideal" (a forerunner of the superego, a concept that appeared
first in *The Ego and the Id* [1923b]). This in turn is based on the
image of the full-fledged primal father he himself would like to be,
preserved for him in cultural and phylogenetic memory. Unable to

realize this ideal, and seeing the futility of competing with his brothers for supremacy, he turns his sibling rivalry, by reaction-formation, into a sense of equality and group solidarity, by the reasoning that "if one cannot be the favorite oneself, at all events nobody else shall be the favorite" (1921c, 120).

He introjects as his ego-ideal a leader who is, or at least can be mistaken for, a realization of what he aspires to. His fellows do likewise, and they thus share a common ego-ideal, identifying with the leader by trying to mold their own egos to a likeness of the admired one. The result is that they are all similar in having the same ego-ideal and similar egos, and therefore they are able to identify with each other and thus love each other in a way closer to narcissism than to object love. Thus aim-inhibited love spilling over onto others seen as like oneself is the basis of long-lasting social ties. Since the primal horde no longer exists, the leaders who emerge are not true narcissistic primal fathers, but simulacra of them who can overawe, fascinate, terrorize, and inspire love in a group. (Freud's prescience regarding fascism, then about to emerge, was uncanny.)

An implication of this analysis, not spelled out by Freud but with far-reaching implications for anthropology, is that social life among humans is structured around two axes. There is the axis of heterosexual coupling leading to biological reproduction, and there is the axis of society formed by aim-inhibited relations of identification based on libido that is neither hetero- nor homosexual, but which "shows a complete disregard for the aims of the genital organization of the libido" (1921c, 141).

It follows of necessity then that the social ties of the "brother horde," those which in fact constitute the more enduring "glue" of society, must be derived from pregenital erotic strivings, inhibited in aim and sublimated or transformed through reaction-formation into cultural forms. These pregenital elements would include the oral and dependent, the anal and sadomasochistic, and the exhibitionistic and narcissistic components of human sexuality, which make their appearance earlier in childhood than genital ones.

Any society has to reconcile the claims and principles of both the genital and the pregenital axes of society. Thus, in some non-Western, nonliterate societies, the two strands are visibly separated; there is a men's society different from the realm of heterosexual reproduction. The two are linked by the fact that senior men are both married householders and fathers, and also high-ranking members of the male society. The ritual symbolism of such male societies is often replete with more or less thinly transformed and sublimated pregenital erotic imagery.

By the time Freud wrote *Civilization and Its Discontents* in 1930, his theory had undergone still further revisions. He had introduced the tripartite ego–id–superego structural model of the psyche in *The Ego and the Id* (1923b); and he had finally faced up to the implication of his late dual-instinct theory, that aggression, pure and simple, is an instinctual drive on an equal footing with the sexual instinct. In 1930, Freud still sees culture and society arising out of love and common work, to be sure; but this love is more and more understood as derived from a primary narcissism that regards every other person as a potential enemy, rival, or inhibitor of one's freedom; the aggression aroused in defense of this narcissism is only by reaction-formation turned into the ambivalent love that characterizes society.

The first to thwart our boundless narcissism were our parents. We internalize their prohibiting authority as the superego, and keep it energized by using our own aggression, now turned against ourselves, to frighten ourselves into being "good" and renouncing our oedipal wishes in the interests of security and avoiding the punishments of loss of love and castration.

Now finally Freud has a grounding in his instinct theory for the ambivalence of obsessional neurosis and of civilization: Aim-inhibited object love and narcissistic identification as group bonds lie uneasily atop a repressed current of hatred and destructiveness, the inhibition of which imposes the "obsessive" defenses upon society. The great interest in beauty, cleanliness, order, and love of one's enemies so central to (Judeo-Christian) civilization's view of itself betrays the fact that culture has to work overtime to inhibit and defend against, by reaction-formation, the violent and anal sadistic urges that arise when narcissism is infringed.

The source of the superego, for Freud, which acts as internal guardian serving the interests of civilization rather than of our own happiness, is, in the 1930 work, a blend of both our own inhibited and inturned aggression and the fact of a real external punishing authority. Again, our descent from the primal horde, and our shared memory of the primal father and his murder, prepare us (men) to respond to our own less than titanic fathers with the awe and terror the original father inspired by his mere look.

With *Moses and Monotheism* (1939a [1937–9]), Freud's final major book, the journey is complete and the theory of culture can be viewed in its fully evolved form. Readers have been distracted, in approaching this work, by numerous difficulties (not the least of which being the question of why he wrote it at all, in the period of Nazi ascendency). A close reading of the book will reveal, I believe, that neither the question of Moses' nationality, nor of whether there were two Moseses, nor whether Moses was a follower of Akhnaton, nor even whether Moses was killed in a revolt, is central to the argument. Rather, the book is a new exposition of the primal horde theory this time explicitly set in the context of the history of Judeo-Christian civilization. Here for the first time the analogy between obsessional neurosis and Western religious history is systematically laid out.

The analogous pattern, repeated on the individual and collective level, is this sequence: "early trauma – defense – latency – outbreak of the neurosis – partial return of the repressed material" (1939a, 80). The trauma is an overwhelming experience of a combined sexual, aggressive, and narcissistic nature; in the individual, it is the oedipal fantasies, in society, the primal crime itself. The trauma gives rise to an active compulsion to repeat itself, and at the same time to an effort at defending against the impulse to repeat it. After remaining relatively dormant for a while, the conflict between impulse and defense reemerges under certain circumstances (such as in sleep or illness, when an instinct receives added strength as the libido does at puberty or when recent events remind one of the repressed material).

In a typical obsessional-compulsive neurosis, the initial trauma leaves a conflict between hostile wishes felt as deeds, and fear of danger, in the form of retaliatory castration. To ward off the danger, defenses are instituted including reaction-formation, whereby the hostile wish is converted into an elevated sense of justice and morality; isolation, in which thoughts and affects are kept apart and ideas left unconnected to avoid reexperiencing the whole fantasy; and undoing, in which the constantly asserted impulse needs to be counteracted with expiatory ritual. Latency is achieved in middle childhood with the installation of the superego and advancing cognitive abilities; but adolescence brings on new instinctual stresses leading to the outbreak of the repressed conflict in neurotic symptoms representing a compromise-formation between the ambivalent wishes to express and to defend against the impulses.

If, for the sake of exposition, we accept the analogy between culture and the individual life, the comparable sequence would be this: First there is the primal murder, the trauma enacting aggression and motivated by sexual and narcissistic impulses. The compulsion to repeat the deed is warded off by the defenses established as the social prohibitions on incest and on killing the deified representative of the father; these renunciations are enforced by the shared memory of the slain patriarch, whose internalized authority empowers the cultural superego. After a period of development and latency, certain historical circumstances, the upheavals of the biblical era, bring about a remembrance of the primal crime. In response to the threatened return of the traumatic situation and the feared retaliation from the still-living memory of the jealous deity who visits the sins of the father upon the sons down through generations, actions and observances are undertaken which, as compromise-formations, both express and defend against the hostile side of the ambivalent relations within society and toward the authority which maintains it. These observances become, first, the elaborate list of rules, prohibitions, and ritual observances of Judaism; and then the dramatic but ultimately failed attempt at liberation from them represented by Christianity. The latter, though ostensibly aiming at undoing the primal guilt through sacrifice and thus making the code of laws unnecessary, instead deepens the guilt by recognizing that even rebellious wishes, as well as deeds, require punishment and hoped-for forgiveness.

I am quite convinced that Freud arrived at the construct of the primal crime not from reading Robertson Smith and Darwin, but by performing upon the central Christian ritual, the Eucharist or Mass, the same sort of analysis and reconstruction of early events he would have carried out had the same constellation of ideas and actions been presented to him as the fantasy or ceremony of an individual obsessional patient. The endlessly repeated sacrifice of an "innocent" son could only be a resolution of neurotic guilt concerning an original murder of (or death wish toward) a father by the guilty ring leader of a "band of brothers." In the ritual the innocence of the rebel is proclaimed at the same time as his guilt is confessed by his execution; the original wish for patricide is enacted insofar as the slain son is asserted to be identical with the deified father.

My assumption that the primal crime is a reconstruction from Christian ritual is supported by this quotation from Freud:

From the manner in which, in Christianity, this redemption is achieved – by the sacrificial death of a single person, who in this manner takes upon himself a guilt that is common to everyone – *we have been able to infer* what the first occasion may have been on which this primal guilt, which was also the beginning of civilization, was acquired. (1930a, 136; my emphasis)

Freud himself recognized, of course, that the greatest difficulty in treating civilization as if it were an individual capable of having a neurosis is the question of how we are to suppose that contemporary people can be motivated, indeed compelled, by memories of events that occurred not in their own lives, but in ancient history. Though human actors and not a hypostatized "Civilization" are still the subjects of Freud's drama, his scheme requires them to act on knowledge they cannot be supposed to have gained by direct experience. How can this be?

In *Totem and Taboo*, contrary to widely held opinion, Freud does *not* suggest or even imply that the memory of the primal crime continues across generations by means of the "inheritance of acquired characteristics." While he does think that there must be inheritance of some psychical dispositions, he argues that these must be given "some sort of impetus in the life of the individual before they can be roused into actual operation" (1912–13, XIII, 158). And though he does not think that "direct communication and tradition" account for the transmission of the memories, he does not turn to genetic inheritance, but rather to the encoding of unconscious ideas in *cultural symbolism*, a mode of information storage that, like genetic information but independent of it, is transmitted across generations. The relevant passage is worth quoting in full, because misunderstandings of this text are so commonplace:

psychoanalysis has shown us that everyone possesses in his unconscious mental activity an apparatus which enables him to interpret other people's reactions, that is to undo the distortions which other people have imposed on the expression of their feelings. An unconscious understanding such as this of all the *customs, ceremonies, and dogmas* left behind by the original relation to the father have made it possible for later generations to take over their heritage of emotion. (158; my emphasis)

In other words, everyone can perform unconsciously the analysis Freud performs on, let us say, the Mass, and divines its real emotional message, which he or she then uses to give specific form to his or her own highly charged repressed fantasies – as I argued also that the audience does while watching *Oedipus Rex*.

As his career developed, Freud grew more and more convinced that symbolically disguised cultural inheritance in rites, symbols, and myths alone could not account for the strength of the oedipal fantasies, and did insist that they were phylogenetically inherited. But to say that something is inherited phylogenetically is not – as all of biology attests – the same as saying that it requires the "inheritance of acquired characteristics." As Freud pointed out, a comparison with the case of animals shows that they too "have preserved memories of what was experienced by their ancestors" (1939a [1937–9], 100). That is to say, the beaver has a phylogenetic "memory" of how earlier beavers built dams; the migratory bird has a phylogenetic "memory" of the constellations of the night sky used as signals by its ancestors. The question of the mechanism by which this "memory" was acquired is the province of genetics and evolutionary theory, and by no means Freud's problem alone.

I thus conclude that it is quite possible to suppose that humans have a phylogenetic predisposition to construct fantasies and attach affects to them as if they were vitally real according to the scenario of the primal horde – whether or not such a state of affairs ever really existed or not, or whether the phylogenetically inherited constellation is any more strictly speaking a "memory," in the narrow sense, than is the bird's innate knowledge of the stars and how to respond to them literally a "memory" of something its first ancestor experienced. Whether the "events" symbolized in the Eucharist, for example, actually once occurred or not is a moot point; what is relevant is that each generation is capable of acting as if it understood the meaning of the ritual and was under the peremptory sway of the impulses and fears it enacts.

We can see, then, that Freud supposes that the "memories" and fantasies at the root of our civilization are carried along three channels, the personal, the cultural, and the phylogenetic. The individual has a memory in the literal sense of his or her own actual infantile oedipal experience. This personal memory is formed against the backdrop of, and given shape to, on the one hand, by the species-specific human phylogenetic promptings that date back to our days as a social but precultural primate; and on the other by the culturally inherited symbolic forms – the "customs, ceremonies, and dogmas" – in which the particular traditions of the culture are encoded.

Personal memory can last only a lifetime, inscribed as it is in the tissue of a mortal organism. But civilization has continuity because memories, fantasies, myths, and ideas can travel across generations along two parallel tracks. One is genetic, and depends for its continuity on sexual reproduction; the other is cultural and involves the encoding of information in external vehicles – symbols in the broadest sense – the most highly charged of which draw energy from the libidinal, aggressive, and narcissistic impulses of childhood.

This "dual-inheritance model" of cross-generational information transmission[7] accounts for the existence of the two axes of society to which I referred earlier: The heterosexual one is necessary to accomplish sexual (genetic) reproduction, whereas the "band of brothers" is bound by aim-inhibited pregenital libido turned to cultural sublimations. These two must cooperate minimally to reproduce the totality of human society, but there is an inherent tension between them. As Freud says, "civilization behaves toward sexuality as a people or stratum of its population does which has subjected another one to its exploitation. Fear of a revolt by the suppressed elements drives it to stricter precautionary measures" (1930a, 107).

If, as I think we must, we reject the literal historicity of the primal crime, as well as the idea of the history of civilization being like maturation from infancy on through stages comparable to those in an individual life, then we cannot accept at face value Freud's analogy between Judeo-Christian religion and obsessional neurosis. But I propose that our rejection of these aspects of Freud's cultural thought should not lead us to ignore the fact that the parallels he cites are highly persuasive, indicating that the fantasies, impulses, defenses, and symbolisms observed clinically in obsessional personalities, and culturally in the rites, symbols, and traditions of our civilization, are closely related if not identical. The difference between them would remain that in religious institutions the instinctual conflict and its outcome are turned to the constructive function of uniting a group of surly individuals into an enduring society knit together by the strongest of instinctual emotions, namely libido, aggression, and narcissism. In the neurosis the same work is done to nobody's benefit.

If we accept that the individual memory of the childhood nuclear fantasy and its outcome is prepared for and augmented by the influence of both phylogenetic predispositions – the nature and extent of which has yet to be determined by research – and cultural tradition embodied in inherited symbolic forms and practices; and if we accept, furthermore, the implication of Freud's cultural works that there are two different social axes repesenting the two different modes of transmission of information across generations – the genetic, sexual one, and the cultural one based on aim-inhibited nonreproductive libido; then we also arrive at sound theoretical support for the tripartite model of the psyche. The agency of the organism proper (the ego) negotiates its way through reality always prompted by the (often conflicting) imperatives of the sexual, directly instinctual, phylogenetic "program" (the id); and the asexual, nongenital, cultural "program" (the superego). Individuals, as well as societies and cultures they form, must take the needs of all of these into account in any effective compromise. Investigating the ways they do this (or fail to do so) is the project for a systematic comparative ethnography yet to be undertaken.

NOTES

1 Clifford Geertz, *The Interpretation of Cultures* (New York: Basic Books, 1973), p. 448.
2 Emile Durkheim, *Les Formes Elementaires de la Vie Religieuse: Le systeme totemique en Australie* (Paris: F. Alcan, 1912).
3 James G. Frazer, *Totemism and Exogamy* (London: Macmillan, 1903).
4 Charles Darwin, *The Descent of Man*, 2 vols. (London: J. Murray, 1871). William Robertson Smith, *Lectures on the Religion of the Semites* (London, 1894). Sandor Ferenczi, "Ein Kleiner Hahnemann," *Internationale Zeitschrift fur Psychoanalyse* 1 (1913): 240.
5 Robert A. Paul, "Did the Primal Crime Take Place?" *Ethos* 4 (1976): 311–52.

6 Robert A. Paul, *The Tibetan Symbolic World: Psychoanalytic Explorations* (Chicago: University of Chicago Press, 1982).

7 Robert Boyd and Peter Richerson, *Culture and the Evolutionary Process* (Chicago: University of Chicago Press, 1985) and Robert A. Paul, "The Individual and Society in Biological and Cultural Anthropology," *Cultural Anthropology* 2 (1987): 80–93.

12 Freud's later theory of civilization: Changes and implications

Freud in the last phase of his work gave increasing attention to questions about civilization, about its roots in and effects on human psychology. He was particularly interested in whether civilization on the whole helped or hindered human beings in their search for happiness, and he dealt with this question in two well-known books, *The Future of an Illusion* and *Civilization and Its Discontents*, the first of which he wrote in 1927 and the second in 1930. This essay is a study of differences between the views that he expressed in these two books. The differences indicate a shift in his outlook, and the essay represents an attempt to understand the reasons behind this shift.

I

The Future of an Illusion ends in optimism. Briefly, Freud's hopeful conclusion was this: Just as healthy individuals overcome their childish ways as they mature, as reason comes to play a greater role in the governance of their lives, so too healthy societies should overcome their primitive practices as they mature, as science comes to play a greater role in the governance of their lives. Three years later, when he wrote *Civilization and Its Discontents*, Freud's optimism had dimmed. He ended the work on a somber note. No one, Freud observed, in this age of great technological advances can be confident that the struggle between life-giving and life-destroying forces that shapes civilization will not have a ruinous outcome. No doubt the rise of the Nazis and the Fascists during the intervening years partly explains this shift in his outlook. But his further reflections on the nature of civilization help to explain it as well. By the

287

time he concluded *Civilization and Its Discontents*, Freud had come to see problems in the development of civilization for which the ascendancy of science was not an obvious remedy.

The primitive practice on which *The Future of an Illusion* concentrates is that of religion. Freud saw religion as demanding and extracting from mankind unnecessary sacrifices of happiness and doing so in the service of irrational beliefs. Thus his optimism in foreseeing its decline and eventual replacement by less cruel and more rational practices. Freud based this optimism on an analogy he discerned between religion and obsessional neurosis (1927c, XXI, 42–4). In his view the degree of detail to which the analogy held, both in regard to origins and in regard to symptoms, warranted ascribing to civilization the same process by which individuals overcame the common obsessional neuroses of childhood. Essentially this process is one of gradually abandoning wishful and fanciful beliefs that were formed at an early age under the pressures of powerful feelings and drives that had not yet been tamed and channeled, and it occurs through the development of reason. That development brings increasingly intelligent reflections on the nature of things and an increasing confidence in those reflections, and as a result the system of irrational beliefs that immature minds naturally create and cling to gives way to a sounder view of the world. Thus the obsessions that are its products also lose their sway. Correspondingly, then, when social practices depend for their vitality on a system of beliefs that is similarly irrational and that similarly originates in immature thought, the development of science, which is to say the development of institutionalized reason, should have an analogous effect. The practices should decline as the system of beliefs they depend on gives way to sounder theories about the world. Religion, for Freud, was such a practice, and the diminishment in its influence was therefore a welcome sign.

Freud of course recognized that religion extended into areas of thought that were beyond the scope of science, and he acknowledged the historical importance of its teachings and doctrines in these areas. But he was unimpressed with defenses of religion that invoked these facts. In particular, he was unimpressed with the defense that invoked the importance of religion's teachings and doctrines in ethics, its traditional role in providing foundations for morality. Religion's defenders readily interpret this fact as a necessary truth, whereas

Freud interpreted it as merely a historical one. Consequently, he rejected the underlying premise of their defense, that godlessness meant amorality, and he dismissed as unfounded the common fear on which they liked to seize, that if God passed from the lives of men, nothing would be forbidden; all hell would break loose. Morality, Freud believed, could have other foundations than God's will, and accordingly he thought there was a possibility that human beings could be taught to accept morality's prohibitions and requirements without first investing them with religious significance (1927c, XXI, 40–1).

To be sure, Freud did not think this possibility existed at every stage of civilization. He did, however, think it existed at an advanced stage. And again he saw in the analogy between religion and obsessional neurosis reason to be optimistic. The very process by which the growth of science leads to the decline of religion should also expand the role of reason in the regulation of human relations. Rational acceptance of the prohibitions and requirements necessary for civilization's existence, acceptance based on a realistic assessment of human beings and their place in nature, should then replace acceptance based on illusions about such matters, illusions that have long served to allay certain deep-seated fears that have persisted since early childhood. At its most optimistic *The Future of an Illusion* contemplates a time when morality's prohibitions and requirements are not only divested of their religious significance but also subject to pruning and revision in the service of human happiness. At that time, Freud wrote, human beings will to a large extent be reconciled to civilization (ibid., 44).

How different his attitude in *Civilization and Its Discontents!* Yet one cannot say that Freud had been blindly optimistic in the earlier work and only later opened his eyes. For in its last chapter he expressed an awareness that his hopes for greater human happiness might themselves be founded on illusions about reason. In particular, he conceded that he might be overestimating the power of reason to master the emotional forces that gave religion a character analogous to obsessional neurosis. Perhaps, then, the doubt implicit in this concession grew in his mind and eventually brought about this change in his attitude. While he did not in *Civilization and Its Discontents* return to the analogy and its implications, he did take up questions about morality and the emotional forces that make it such a powerful factor in the inner life of human beings. And as he pondered these questions, he came increasingly to see morality, regardless of its foundations, as an irremediable source of human unhappiness. His view, by the end, leaves little room for hope that human beings, guided by reason, could remake morality into an instrument of their happiness and thereby become largely reconciled to civilization.

The first clear indication in *Civilization and Its Discontents* of Freud's doubts about the possibility of such a reconciliation occurs near the beginning of Chapter 3. Having traced human unhappiness to three sources, the degenerative character of our bodies, the merciless forces of nature, and human relations, Freud remarked,

> As regards the third source, the social source of suffering, our attitude is a different one. We do not admit it at all; we cannot see why the regulations made by ourselves should not, on the contrary, be a protection and a benefit for every one of us. And yet, when we consider how unsuccessful we have been in precisely this field of prevention of suffering, a suspicion dawns on us that here, too, a piece of unconquerable nature may lie behind – this time a piece of our own psychical constitution. (1930a, XXI, 86)

This suspicion immediately gives birth to a new thought, which becomes the essay's major theme:

> When we start considering this possibility, we come upon a contention which is so astonishing that we must dwell upon it. This contention holds that what we call our civilization is largely responsible for our misery, and that we should be much happier if we gave it up and returned to primitive conditions. (ibid.)

From here through Chapter 4 Freud proceeded systematically to develop this theme. Then, in Chapter 5, he began to close in on the suspicion from which it issued.

The argument of Chapter 5 signals a definite break from the view that informs his earlier optimism. The propensity of men to aggress against each other, man's appetite for brutality and cruelty, which did not figure in the argument of *The Future of an Illusion*, makes its appearance in this chapter and is reckoned by Freud to be a threat to civilization of such magnitude that, to subdue it, society has to place seemingly excessive and unreasonable demands on its members. In other words, for civilized society to control human aggression, some of the demands of its morality must seemingly exceed, in the restraint and sacrifice they require, demands that one could reasonably hope human beings would accept and meet out of mature reflection on what was in their self-interest or in the interests they had in common. Freud put the point this way:

In consequence of this primary mutual hostility of human beings, civilized society is perpetually threatened with disintegration. The interest of work in common would not hold it together; instinctual passions are stronger than reasonable interests. Civilization has to use its utmost efforts in order to set limits to man's aggressive instincts and to hold the manifestations of them in check by psychical reaction-formations. (112)

Freud arrived at this conclusion from reflection on the extent to which civilized society fosters attachments of affection – libidinal ties, in his words – among its members. For Freud, all affection is originally sexual, and hence affectionate attachments that are not overtly sexual indicate the influence of an additional factor. In the absence of such a factor, Freud thought, civilized society would consist of people paired off sexually, working together cooperatively out of common interests that the necessities of life create, but otherwise unconnected. That this is manifestly not the case, that within civilized society friendships and affections extend broadly to include outlanders and strangers even, meant that some additional, "disturbing" factor must be at work (108–9). And Freud concluded that this factor was human aggression: To preserve itself from this destructive force civilization had to foster and sustain widespread affection among human beings, and this task necessarily involved making excessive demands on human goodwill and self-control.

Freud offered as the one telling example the demand to love one's neighbor as oneself. Adopting the viewpoint of someone who had never before heard this demand, Freud argued that it was puzzling, indeed paradoxical. Love, after all, was something special, something to be given only to those worthy of it, something one could not give willy-nilly without greatly diluting its value for those who received it. Moreover, the demand was certainly nothing any sane person, knowing how unloving and selfish human beings could be, would agree to; for the advantages of treating complete strangers with the same love and concern one showed for oneself were small and improbable, while the dangers were just the opposite. In other words, to a rational individual concerned for his own well-being, even one mature enough to realize that to secure it he must work cooperatively with others, this demand would seem unreasonable and extreme. Yet its preeminence and authority in our civilization's morality, Freud maintained (having resumed his own voice and viewpoint), testifies to the importance to civilized society of binding its members together libidinally. Such ties among its members are necessary as a check on their own hostile impulses.

Once Freud concluded that civilization could not, without making demands of this sort, accomplish the vital task of fostering and sustaining affectionate attachments among human beings, his break from the hopeful views he expressed in *The Future of an Illusion* was complete. Those views included at their core the idea that human beings could learn to accept morality's prohibitions and requirements on rational grounds and independently of any religious belief. The grounds that Freud had in mind consisted of considerations of self-interest as they arose in circumstances in which one's survival and happiness depended on one's working cooperatively with others.[1] The circumstances of civilized society are circumstances of just this sort, and the central prohibitions and requirements of its morality, the prohibitions on killing and the use of violence, for instance, and the requirements of honesty and respect for property, constitute, from the perspective of self-interest, eminently reasonable terms of cooperation for someone placed in such circumstances. Thus Freud could contemplate men's eventually becoming largely reconciled to civilization: Once they came to a realistic understanding of themselves and their circumstances, they could so reform the morality that regulated their social relations as to exclude all prohibitions and requirements that, from the perspective of self-interest, constituted unreasonable terms of cooperation. The implicit assumption on which this hopeful view rested of course was that excluding such prohibitions and requirements would not gravely damage social cohesion, and this assumption serves to divide the views of *The Future of an Illusion* from those of *Civilization and Its Discontents*. The argument that we canvassed from Chapter 5 of the latter work rejects the assumption. To repeat the argument's conclusion, because of men's propensity to aggress against each other, "the interest of work in common would not hold [civilized society] together; instinctual passions are stronger than reasonable interests" (112).

It is not, we should note, incidental to this argument that it represents the propensity of men to aggress against each other as an instinctual disposition. Freud would not have regarded human aggression as *invariably* resistant to regulation by prohibitions and requirements that, from the perspective of self-interest, constituted reasonable terms of social cooperation if he had considered it as merely a form of conduct that humans engaged in or abstained from according as they thought it served their interests. For the argument to succeed then human aggression had to be both a central and an abiding part of human experience – and Freud challenged his readers to deny that it was. In particular, it had to be a phenomenon that would not largely disappear in a juster society or a more hospitable environment. Consequently, it was neither the bare fact of human aggression nor its amount that led Freud to his conclusion, but rather the instinctual character of the propensity behind it. Moreover, the more primitive and independent the aggressive instinct that gave the propensity this character, the stronger Freud's argument; and there is no doubt that when Freud advanced this argument, he conceived of the aggressive instinct as virtually primitive and independent of other instincts (122).² Ten years before, in *Beyond the Pleasure Principle*, Freud had revised his theory of the instincts in a way that made a place for an aggressive instinct of this sort, and in the argument we are now considering he filled it.³

Nothing of the revisions Freud made in *Beyond the Pleasure Principle* enters into the argument of *The Future of an Illusion*, however. In particular, Freud did not in the latter work specifically mention aggression as either a source of any of the unreasonable demands civilization placed on human beings or an obstacle to their becoming reconciled to it. This omission suggests that Freud's subsequent break from that work's hopeful views can be at least partially attributed to his coming firmly to accept the aggressive instinct as a virtually primitive and independent one. Indeed, if one were to read *The Future of an Illusion* as reverting to a much earlier stage in Freud's thinking about instincts, the stage at which he divided the primitive ones into two separate classes, those of sex and those of self-preservation, and conceived of aggression as deriving from and dependent on either, then one could cite the revisions he made in *Beyond the Pleasure Principle* to explain his subsequent loss of optimism.

A clear statement of this explanation must start with some general observations about Freud's theory of the instincts. That theory, no matter the stage of its development, presupposes as basic to an understanding of instinctual phenomena a distinction between reflex behavior, behavior that is an immediate response to some external stimulus, and motivated behavior, behavior that results from some inner spring. As Freud drew the distinction, the former is the product of the nervous system, the latter the product of instinct (1915c, XIV, 118–20). Accordingly, all human motivation, that is, all human desires and interests, can be traced to primitive instincts. Of course, one may have to pass in reverse through several transformations in tracing a desire or interest back to its original instinct, but that it must originate in some instinct directly follows from a principle that is implicit in the distinction the theory presupposes, the principle that all motivational energy is nothing but instinctual energy.

At the earliest stage of his theory, then, the stage to which I'm suggesting Freud may have reverted in writing *The Future of an Illusion*, all human desires and interests can be traced to the instincts of sex and self-preservation. A useful though admittedly oversimple way of putting this thesis is that human motivation in every instance is at bottom either sexual or self-interested. Now in view of this thesis, the possibility that human beings, once they achieved a mature and realistic understanding of themselves and their circumstances, could collectively reform the prohibitions and requirements regulating their social relations so that they constituted reasonable terms of social cooperation should not appear beyond hope. Indeed, this hope is substantially the same as that of classical utilitarians who, taking altruistic and egoistic motives to be the basic categories into which all human motives (or their elements) fell, saw the possibility of enlightened human beings reforming their political institutions in ways that, while preserving social cohesion, would enable society to promote rather than impede people's interests in happiness. For Freud, of course, at this early stage of his theory altruistic and egoistic motives, when taken as basic, represented the sexual and self-preservative instincts. But making this substitution, one can say that, like classical utilitarians, he saw the possibility of enlightened human beings, by revising morality's prohibitions and requirements, rearranging their social relations in ways that, while preserving social cohesion, served their interests in happiness, which is to say, afforded them a decent chance of acquiring and satisfying desires whose satisfaction effectively, even if at several removes, gratified their sexual and self-preservative instincts. Under such arrangements then human beings would be

largely reconciled to civilization: None of its prohibitions and requirements would compel renunciation of instinct beyond what,
from the perspective of enlightened self-interest, would appear reasonable. Thus the hope that Freud expressed in *The Future of an
Illusion* would seem to have a foothold in a version of his theory of
the instincts that he had by the time of this work jettisoned.

There is still of course the question of aggression. Freud, however,
as I mentioned above, conceived of aggression on this early version
of his theory as deriving from and dependent on either the instincts
of sex or those of self-preservation. Specifically, he conceived of the
aggressive instinct as an instinct of mastery that was an ingredient
in either of these primitive instincts. As an ingredient in the self-
preservative instincts, the aggressive instinct prompts a person to
exercise power over his environment when trying to satisfy his survival needs (1905d, VII, 193 n.1; 1915c, XIV, 137–9; 1930a, XXI, 117).
As an ingredient in the sexual instincts, it prompts a person to
conquer objects of his sexual desire when those objects resist his
charms (1905d, VII, 157–8).[4] On this version of his theory, therefore,
the aggressive instinct, whatever problem it creates for reconciling
human beings to civilization, creates no more of a problem than
either of the primitive instincts in which it is an ingredient. Consequently, if it is not utopian to think that enlightened human beings
can collectively settle on prohibitions and requirements to regulate
their social relations that, while preserving social cohesion, afford
them a decent chance of gratifying their basic desires for sexual
union and personal well-being, then it is not utopian to think that
such human beings can learn to moderate the aggressive tendencies
inherent in those desires so that those tendencies do not constitute a
grave threat to civilized society. And conversely, if one thinks that,
because of these aggressive tendencies, there exist grave problems in
reconciling human beings to civilization, problems that would not
arise in the absence of such tendencies, then one has good reason to
abstract the aggressive instinct from other instincts and to conceive
of it as primitive and independent of them. Thus the introduction of
an aggressive instinct of this sort into a theory that had previously
recognized as primitive, independent instincts only those of sex and
self-preservation could explain a retreat from hopeful views about
human beings' eventually becoming reconciled to civilization. In
other words, the revisions Freud made in *Beyond the Pleasure Princi-*

ple, inasmuch as they implicitly introduced into his theory an aggressive instinct conceived of as virtually primitive and independent, could explain his later retreat from such views. Put simply, the explanation would be that introducing this instinct removed the foothold the views had in the theory, though to apply it to Freud's retreat in *Civilization and Its Discontents* requires backdating, as it were, *The Future of an Illusion*.

II

So far we have followed the main argument of *Civilization and Its Discontents* to the point where Freud concluded that civilized society, in order to preserve itself from the destructiveness of human aggression, had to foster and sustain strong communal ties among its members, and this task necessarily involved making excessive demands on their goodwill and self-control. Freud's conclusion, then, was meant to establish that the set of prohibitions and requirements that regulate social relations in civilization, if social cohesion is to be preserved, had to include some that from the perspective of self-interest, even enlightened self-interest, appeared unreasonable. Morality, in other words, was revealed at this point to be an unavoidable obstacle to reconciling human beings to civilization.

Freud, however, did not stop here. His conclusion at this point was that morality represented an obstacle to reconciling men to civilization owing to its content; but he also saw that it represented such an obstacle, indeed a greater obstacle, owing to its mode of regulation. And he recognized too that the obstacle in this case, as in the other, resulted from the ways civilization contained and controlled human aggression. The final two chapters of *Civilization and Its Discontents* extend the argument to these conclusions and thereby bring to completion the development of the work's major theme.

By morality's mode of regulation I have in mind several features of the way morality governs our lives: the authority of its prohibitions and requirements, their stringency, their internalization, and the vigilance of their governance. These features come together in a conscience, which is morality's agent within our personality and the workings of which Freud assigned in his theory to the superego (1923b, XIX, 35–7; 1930a, XXI, 123; 1933a, XXII, 66). A short summary should suffice to make clear how these features are reflected in a conscience. Thus, first of all, the authority of conscience reflects the authority of morality, and it gives evidence of this authority in its judicial and punitive activity. To violate a dictate of conscience is to bring down on oneself its reproaches and irritations, which can be severe and unrelenting. Second, the importance of its authority corresponds to the stringency of the prohibitions and requirements it enforces, and traditionally conscience has enjoyed the reputation of having supreme authority over its possessor. Correspondingly, then, the stringency of the prohibitions and requirements it enforces has traditionally been regarded as maximal; all other social norms and personal concerns have to defer to moral prohibitions and requirements on questions of how a person should act. Third, conscience, in being morality's agent within our personality, is the product of the internalization of morality's prohibitions and requirements, and the degree of their internalization is indicated by the degree to which conscience, in exacting obedience and punishing disobedience, operates independently of external direction and pressure. Last, that one cannot hide from one's conscience, that in its surveillance of one's thoughts and feelings it is all-seeing, attests to its vigilance and so to the vigilance with which morality governs our lives. To use Freud's simile, conscience is "like a garrison in a captured city," which civilization has installed in our personality to watch over us and to keep us in line (1930a, XXI, 123–4).

A rhetorical flourish, of course, is no substitute for argument. The analogy depicts conscience as an antagonistic force in our lives, and our summary of these four characteristic features of conscience suggests much the same picture. But while conscience may have seemed and may still seem like a hostile opponent, a stifler of one's wishes and a producer of anxiety and trouble, escape from which would bring true relief and peace of mind, and while its character may therefore give one reason to think that civilization, by implanting a conscience in each of us, pits its morality against our own happiness, it remains to be shown that the opposition between the two would not dissolve once reason achieved ascendancy in civilized society. Hence, if the workings of conscience are to be proof that morality's mode of regulation is by itself (i.e., apart from morality's content) an unavoidable obstacle to reconciling human beings to civilization, some argument is needed to show that the antagonism dividing a person from his conscience will not yield to reason.

The final chapters of *Civilization and Its Discontents*, in which Freud gives an account of how the individual acquires a conscience, provide the argument.

Freud restricted his account to the development of this aspect of personality in early childhood.[5] The account, in its essentials, describes how young children come to have ambivalent attitudes and feelings toward their parents and how this ambivalence grows into an emotionally difficult situation. It then proposes that a conscience forms out of the way the child resolves this situation. Briefly, the condition of young children is that of helplessness and complete dependency of their parents for protection and nourishment. As a result they form strong, loving attachments to their parents. They love them as the very powerful protectors and providers in their young lives, and they see that protection and provision as sure signs of their parents' love for them. They also, of course, see their parents as the supreme authorities in their lives, and they then obey their parents out of fear, fear of the punishment with which parents threaten disobedience, but more important, fear of the loss of parental love that to them such punishment implies. Consequently, by learning to obey parental authority, children acquire a rudimentary ability to tell right from wrong. But they have not yet, at this stage, acquired a conscience; for as long as their motive of obedience is fear of loss of love, they have not yet internalized any of the prohibitions and requirements their parents have placed on them. Hence, unlike someone who possesses a conscience, a young child at this stage may sometimes feel safe misbehaving because he is confident that his misbehavior will go undiscovered. Children, in other words, in not yet possessing a conscience are not yet liable to be troubled by their bad behavior apart from whatever fear they may have of being found out. In not yet possessing a conscience, they are not yet liable to a sense of guilt. On these points Freud wrote directly: "A great change takes place only when the authority is internalized through the establishment of a super-ego. The phenomena of conscience then reach a higher stage. Actually, it is not until now that we should speak of conscience or a sense of guilt." (1930a, XXI, 125) Explaining how this great change takes place, how parental authority becomes internalized authority, becomes then the object of Freud's account.

The key to his explanation is ambivalence. On the one hand,

children love their parents as the most important benefactors in their lives. On the other, they develop a large amount of hostility toward them as the authorities who regularly prevent them from satisfying their urges and desires. These circumstances, moreover, are unstable. Obedience to parental authority provokes anger because it frustrates instinctual urges, and the child directs this anger at his parents whom he sees as responsible for the frustration. At the same time, the child cannot act on this anger for fear of losing parental love and so is forced to suppress it. Thus, once again instinctual urges, in this case the urges of an aggressive instinct, must be frustrated in the interest of preserving parental love, and this additional frustration breeds additional anger, and so on. The circumstances of the young child thus eventuate in unrelieved hostility toward parents as well as in manifest love for them. And because of the instability of these circumstances, the child's hostility grows in force, if not feeling, and so the ambivalence becomes increasingly difficult to live with. The child resolves this emotionally difficult situation, finally, by identifying with his parents. Unable to escape from or depose these authorities while preserving their love, the child incorporates them, as it were, into his personality and invests this part of his personality with all the hostility he had been unable to vent. Thus a severe conscience, a harsh superego, is formed as external authority becomes in the child internal. To quote Freud;

A considerable amount of aggressiveness must be developed in the child against the authority which prevents him from having his first, but none the less his most important, satisfactions, whatever the kind of instinctual deprivation that is demanded may be; but he is obliged to renounce the satisfaction of this revengeful aggressiveness. He finds his way out of this economically difficult situation with the help of familiar mechanisms. By means of identification he takes the unattackable authority into himself. The authority now turns into his super-ego and enters into possession of all the aggressiveness which a child would have liked to exercise against it. (1930a, XXI, 129)

The principal idea in this explanation is that conscience owes its initial severity to the large amount of hostility that, at the time of its inception, has developed within the child. This idea, therefore, identifies the aggressive instinct as the original source of the power one implicitly attributes to a conscience in characterizing it as severe.

By contrast, the idea's natural alternative, the rival hypothesis that the initial severity of a child's conscience is a continuation of severe treatment that the child has received from his parents, the external authorities on whose behavior his conscience is modeled, identifies no specific instinct as the original source of such power. Freud, however, rejected this rival hypothesis because it implies that the more severe a young child's conscience, the stricter his parents; and observation had shown that even children of very lenient parents developed severe consciences. What is more, though Freud did not express this point, the rival hypothesis does not fit the phenomena as Freud understood them: The idea that the severity of conscience is merely a continuation of the severe treatment one received from one's parents is incongruous with the view that a radical change in one's emotional and motivational capacities takes place with the acquisition of a conscience.

On the hypothesis Freud proposed, then, conscience draws its initial power from the store of hostility that has built up as a result of the young child's having repeatedly suppressed his aggressive impulses, and it thus works to redirect that hostility from its original, outward object, the child's parents, onto a new, inward object, the child himself. This redirection of the hostility establishes conscience as an antagonistic force in one's life, and the antagonism is typically exhibited in "bad" conscience or a sense of guilt. Freud then further proposed that the same process explained how conscience continued to be an antagonistic force in one's life after the initial store of hostility had been exhausted. After all, with the acquisition of a conscience, one is regularly forced to renounce the satisfaction of urges and desires in order to meet its demands, and many of these urges and desires derive wholly or in part from one's aggressive instinct. Thus conscience renews itself by tapping the power of the aggressive impulses one suppresses in placating it: It takes aggression that is directed outward onto objects in the world and, using its energy for its demands, reproaches, and irritations, turns that aggression back onto its possessor. As Freud summarily put it, "conscience arises through the suppression of an aggressive impulse, and . . . it is subsequently reinforced by fresh suppressions of the same kind" (1930a, XXI, 130).

The real work of conscience therefore, as Freud represented it in *Civilization and Its Discontents*, is to block and deflect its possessor's aggressive instinct so that it does not realize its destructive aim. Civilization, Freud maintained, implants a conscience in each of us to do this work. We are thus invited to see conscience as a device by which civilization ingeniously turns to its advantage anti-social drives that are part of every human being's native endowment and that, if allowed to realize their aims, would create an environ-ment too hostile for civilized life to go forward. Indeed, in Freud's view, implanting this device in each of us is the most important method that civilization uses to disarm the aggressive forces in all of us that threaten to destroy it (1930a, XXI: 123).

Freud's view, it should now be clear, constitutes an argument for the notion that the workings of a conscience cannot be brought fully within the control of its possessor's reason. And while the argument is only implicit in the text, one can easily reconstruct its last stages. Thus, to begin with, the thesis about the real work of conscience puts into question the ideal of a mature conscience working in the service of its possessor's happiness. A conscience that did not trou-ble one with reminders and urgings more often or insistently than was reasonably necessary, that did not make unwarranted accusa-tions, that did not censor mere thoughts and wishes, and that did not criticize or condemn more harshly than one's conduct deserved might not, if typical of most people, succeed in doing its real work. For it might not use up enough of the energy of our aggressive drives to preserve civilization from the hostility and brutality of which human beings are capable and which gravely threaten its cohesion. Furthermore, because conscience draws its power directly from the impulses of the aggressive instinct, the level of its activity is to a significant degree a function of the amount of aggression that it has suppressed, and so to a corresponding degree is independent of ra-tional regulation. Reason, in other words, because it cannot come between conscience and the source of its power, has only a limited influence on its severity.[6]

Nor is this last point a purely theoretical conclusion. Freud, as we saw, found evidence for his account in the observation that even children of very lenient parents develop severe consciences. In addi-tion, he was struck by the common observation that the more virtu-ous a person is, the harsher his conscience treats him (1930a, XXI: 125–6).[7] This paradox, as he called it, openly invites a psychoanalytic explanation, and he used it to stake his hypothesis that the instinctual impulses whose suppression conscience compels supply it with new power for compelling subsequent suppressions. Both observations, then, guided Freud's thinking as he worked out his account. The first implies that the severity of a conscience can exceed whatever model of reasonable and fair-minded authority a child's parents present, and the second implies that its severity, contrary to reason, is not proportional to one's actual guilt. Each therefore gives evidence of reason's limited influence on the severity of conscience, and it remained for Freud to determine, using the resources of his theory, the instinctual factor at work and its method of operation.

Near the close of his discussion of conscience in *Civilization and Its Discontents* Freud declared that his intention had been "to represent the sense of guilt as the most important problem in the development of civilization and to show that the price we pay for our advance in civilization is a loss of happiness through the heightening of our sense of guilt" (1930a, XXI, 134). Our sense of guilt, on Freud's conception of it, expresses the antagonism that divides us from our conscience; and because conscience uses the power of the aggressive instinct to do its work, this antagonism, he had argued, is inherent in its workings. Morality therefore, owing to its mode of regulation in advanced civilization, that is, once its authority becomes internalized, far from being something human beings could remake into an instrument of their happiness, becomes an intransigent source of human unhappiness. For Freud this argument, even more than the argument of Chapter 5, confirmed the suspicion he entertained early on in his inquiry. The aggressive instinct is that "piece of unconquerable nature" – that "piece of our own psychical constitution" – that defeats every effort we make to regulate our social relations in a way that furthers our happiness. At this point Freud's shift away from the optimistic conclusions he reached in *The Future of an Illusion* is most pronounced.

III

Freud's shift away from these conclusions raises questions that he did not himself address. Above all, it raises a question about how much of the optimism he expressed in *The Future of an Illusion* the argument of *Civilization and Its Discontents* implicitly retracts. It retracts, as we have seen, the optimistic conclusion about human beings' eventually becoming reconciled to civilization, but the question is whether it also retracts the optimistic conclusion about human beings' eventually overcoming their illusions about themselves and their place in the world. Specifically, does it retract the conclusion about human beings' eventually abandoning their religious beliefs? Freud based these conclusions, it is worth recalling, partly on the idea that morality could have other foundations than God's will and that human beings could learn to accept its prohibitions and requirements in light of them. And since he thought these alternative foundations created the possibility of revising morality in the service of human happiness and thereby reconciling human beings to civilization, the argument of *Civilization and Its Discontents* in casting doubt on this possibility indirectly challenges its underlying idea that these foundations are a real alternative to religious doctrines (i.e., that the notion of humans learning to accept moral prohibitions and requirements in light of them rather than religious doctrines is a real possibility). Hence, the other conclusions Freud based on this idea are also brought into question. Whether the argument implicitly retracts them, however, is something still to be settled.

That it retracts the general conclusion about human beings' eventually overcoming their illusions about themselves and their place in the world seems fairly clear. Unhappiness and the wish for escape that naturally accompanies it give rise to a need for illusion when the unhappiness is deep and the prospect of escape is nil; and *Civilization and Its Discontents* in its conclusion places human beings in just such a condition. Of course, it is possible, at least abstractly, that with the advance of science and reason in civilized society people could collectively learn to resist the pressures of this need, but optimism on this score could not be firmly based on such speculation. Bearing in mind, then, the corrosive effects of cynicism on the human spirit, we may conclude that the argument of *Civilization and Its Discontents* implies the continued importance of illusion to keeping up the authority of morality. That the argument has this implication, however, does not mean that it implies the continued importance of religious beliefs to keeping up morality's authority. There may be, after all, other beliefs that can serve this purpose. Consequently, whether the argument retracts the specific conclusion about human beings' eventually abandoning their religious beliefs remains an open question.

The argument, let us note, does not directly conflict with the main grounds on which Freud drew this conclusion, the analogy between religion and obsessional neurosis conjoined with his understanding of how individuals who suffered from such neurosis overcame it. Rather, it implies the continued existence of a motive for religious beliefs that, according to the optimistic views of *The Future of an Illusion*, was destined to disappear. And while the continued existence of this motive clearly makes Freud's inference from analogy more uncertain, it does not eliminate the basis for his conclusion. The conclusion, then, is not retracted by the argument.

At the same time, its basis would be rather shaky if religious beliefs were the only ones that could plausibly satisfy this motive. That is, if the need for illusion that the unhappiness arising from the possession of a conscience created could plausibly be satisfied only by religious beliefs – specifically, the belief in an almighty god in whose commands moral prohibitions and requirements originated and obedience to whom offered hope of protection and relief from suffering, then the staying power of religion might well prove great enough to withstand the skepticism of science even as science and reason expanded their influence. In other words, Freud's conclusion about the eventual decline of religion, a conclusion he reaffirmed in later works (e.g., 1933a, XXII, 168), would be much less threatened by the argument of *Civilization and Its Discontents* if secular beliefs that established the underpinnings of morality's authority and promised rewards for complying with its prohibitions and requirements could replace in the minds of human beings the religious beliefs that served these purposes.

Futhermore, one can find in the ethical and political writings of certain modern philosophers ideas that, if they could gain widespread acceptance, presumably in some popularized form, would be suitable secular replacements for these religious beliefs. I am thinking, in particular, of ideas that have emerged with the rise of democratic institutions in the West. These ideas, whose classical elaboration occurs in works by Rousseau and Kant, constitute an egalitarian creed.[8] On this creed, each fully rational human being, in virtue of his or her rational powers, is capable in principle of joining together with other similarly rational human beings to form a democratic republic in which all participate as equal, lawmaking citizens. What is more, the creed holds that each of us is in fact joined together with others under the common rule of morality, and the moral community we thus form is a realization of this notional democratic republic. Accordingly, morality's prohibitions and requirements are prohibitions and requirements we impose on ourselves: They originate in laws that we, as the legislators of this community, make and adopt. Correspondingly, then, morality's authority derives from our own legislative authority. That is, it derives from the community's sovereignty over its members, a sovereignty in which each of us, as an equal member of its legislature, partakes. Compliance with morality's prohibitions and requirements is therefore, in effect, obedience to laws that one gives to oneself. So in living a moral life – fully complying with morality's prohibitions and requirements out of recognition of their authority – one achieves a kind of freedom, which Rousseau called moral freedom and Kant called autonomy. It is freedom that comes from being subject to no alien authority, from being ruled by no other laws than laws of one's own making. And the inner satisfaction that such freedom brings more than compensates for the loss in gratification of instinctual urges and desires that obedience to moral law entails.[9] Or so the creed promises.

To be sure, these ideas do not correspond nearly as closely to the circumstances of the young child as the religious beliefs they would replace, and therefore they do not answer nearly as directly as those religious beliefs the fears that human beings carry foward from these circumstances into adulthood. God, after all, is a much closer analogue of the parents of our early childhood than the supreme legislature of a democratic republic, and the protection and relief from suffering that God bestows come much closer to the benefits of parental love than moral freedom and the inner satisfaction it brings. Nevertheless, these ideas, because they could establish the underpinnings of morality's authority and promise substantial reward for obeying its laws, could be true descendents of the young child's beliefs about parental authority and parental beneficence and so the analogues of those beliefs within the egalitarian creed. Consequently, despite their greater distance from the circumstances of early childhood, they could still come to replace religious beliefs as the latter, under the pressure of an expanding scientific culture, became increasingly difficult to accept.[10] This conclusion, it should be clear, is not meant to be a prediction. The point is merely to show that it represents, within the framework of Freud's theory, a real possibility and as such keeps Freud's optimism about the eventual decline of religion from being undermined by his argument in *Civilization and Its Discontents.* The irony of this, though, is that Kant's ethics, which Freud liked to cite for its seeming expression of traditional religious morality (1933a, XXII, 61 and 163),[11] is in fact no friend of such morality and actually rescues Freud's conclusion about religion's downfall from the implications of his own later argument.

IV

This essay has examined the shift in Freud's outlook that the difference between his reflections in *The Future of an Illusion* on the development of civilization and his reflections in *Civilization and Its Discontents* on the same subject reveals. Settled changes in Freud's theory help to explain this shift, but the shift was not itself a settled change. Indeed, in his next major work, his *New Introductory Lectures on Psychoanalysis,* Freud appears to have shifted back toward the outlook he expressed in *The Future of an Illusion.* Thus, in its last lecture, which summarizes the argument of *The Future of an Illusion,* he wrote:

Our best hope for the future is that intellect – the scientific spirit, reason – may in the process of time establish a dictatorship in the mental life of man. The nature of reason is a guarantee that afterwards it will not fail to give man's emotional impulses and what is determined by them the position they deserve. (1933a, XXII, 171)[12]

No new theoretical reflections, however, accompany this apparent restatement of his earlier hope. In particular, nothing is said to modify his account of the aggressive instinct's effects on morality's content and mode of regulation or to suggest how, despite these effects, morality could have foundations that enabled it to be an instrument of human happiness. Freud, it would appear, did not himself fully appreciate the implications of his argument in *Civilization and Its Discontents.*

NOTES

1 See 1927c, XXI, 40–1, where Freud described the practical reasons that lead men to accept a prohibition on murder and drew from this case the lesson that moral prohibitions and requirements generally could be grounded on such practical considerations, particularly, those of "social necessity."

2 The reason for the qualifier "virtually" is given in note 3.

3 The revision referred to here is Freud's introduction of the death instinct into his theory; 1920g, XVIII, 38–41. The death instinct, as the name implies, is destructive in character and originally directed onto oneself. On Freud's theory, however, instincts are readily modified and, in particular, readily take on new objects. Thus, though originally directed onto oneself, the death instinct can be easily turned around and directed outwardly onto others. When this happens, the instinct takes the form of an outwardly destructive or aggressive instinct. Freud initially took sadism to be the singular instance of the transformation of the death instinct into an aggressive instinct, an instance whose manifest erotic component is explained by the fusion of the sexual instinct with this aggressive instinct. See 1920g, XVIII, 53–4; 1923b, XIX, 40–1; and 1924c, XIX, 163–4. Finally, in *Civilization and Its Discontents* Freud attributed acts of hostility and destruction that were not distinctly sadistic (i.e., that did not manifest erotic interests) to this transformation of the death instinct into an aggressive instinct. See 1930a, XXI, 117–22, where Freud reviewed these and other developments in his theory of the instincts.

4 Note that Freud here explained sadism as occurring when "the aggressive component of the sexual instinct . . . has become independent and exaggerated." Thus, in a sense, his later explanation (see note 3), which introduces the idea of the fusion of distinct instincts, sexual and aggressive, reverses the explanation at this earliest stage, which uses the idea of one of the instinct's components' breaking away from the others.

5 I am drawing here on a fuller exposition of this account that I have given elsewhere; see my "Remarks on Some Difficulties in Freud's Theory of Moral Development," *International Review of Psycho-Analysis* 11 (1984): 207–25, esp. 208–15.

6 Freud made this point even more clearly in *The Ego and the Id*. Thus he wrote, "Although [the superego] is accessible to all later influences, it nevertheless preserves throughout life the character given to it by its derivation from the father-complex – namely the capacity to stand apart from the ego and to master it" (1923b, XIX, 48; see also 1923b, XIX, 55–9).

7 See also 1923b, XIX, 54.
8 Specifically, Rousseau's *The Social Contract* and Kant's *Groundwork of the Metaphysic of Morals* and *Critique of Practical Reason.*
9 See Rousseau, *The Social Contract and Discourses,* trans. G. D. H. Cole (New York: E. P. Dutton 1950), pp. 18–19; and Kant, *Critique of Practical Reason,* trans. L. W. Beck (Indianapolis: Bobbs-Merrill, 1956), pp. 121–3.
10 One might also see their replacing religious beliefs as a further development in the internalization by human beings of morality's prohibitions and requirements. Accordingly, the replacement of God's legislation with self-legislation, of the idea that moral laws originate in God's authority with the idea that they originate in one's own authority, would result from one's identifying with one's conscience. And while identification in this case would be with an internal figure rather than an external one, it would nonetheless seem, in view of the great tension that possession of a conscience creates, amenable to psychoanalytic explanation as (once again) identification with the aggressor. Moreover, it corresponds to Freud's belief that the growth of intellect and the increasing internalization of morality are characteristic of the advance of civilization. See 1933b, XXII, 214–15.
11 This view of Kant's ethics is also implicit in Freud's observation that the Categorical Imperative is the heir to the Oedipus Complex; 1923b, XIX, 35 and 1924c, XIX, 167.
12 Cf. 1933b, XXII, 213.

13 In fairness to Freud: A critical notice of *The Foundations of Psychoanalysis,* by Adolf Grünbaum

Adolf Grünbaum's provocative book, *The Foundations of Psycho-analysis*,[1] was quickly accorded an impressive reception. His earlier critical pieces on the subject caused a stir among their audiences, audiences that included philosophers, psychoanalysts, and other interested persons. As was expected, some of the pieces were incorporated in the book; indeed, because of them, its appearance had been anticipated with feelings that ranged from glee to dismay. Neither of those extreme feelings, however, has obtruded on the respectful tone of most of the book's wide notice. There are several reasons for that tone. Among them is Grünbaum's familiarity with important phases of Freud's work, especially those leading up to the public inception of psychoanalysis at the beginning of the century. Grünbaum's book also displays an acquaintance with a variety of Freud's later writings and with post-Freudian psychoanalytic developments. In addition it furnishes a compendium of the criticisms Freud's thought has evoked. Also, for interesting but disproportionate measure, a third of the book indicts hermeneutic construals of Freud, notably those of Habermas and Ricoeur. Finally, but surely not least, Grünbaum brings to those topics and related ones a rare discursive and polemical tirelessness.

The visible signs of the impact of Grünbaum's writings about psychoanalysis include the following. In 1984, when his book appeared, there also came out, as if to accompany it, a volume by a well-known psychiatrist (see note 12 of this essay) that answers some of the charges against analytic therapy that Grünbaum stated

Editors of *The Philosophical Review* and my colleague, Jerome Schneewind, made salutary suggestions. I am grateful to them and to William Taschek for his encouragement and guidance.

in his earlier pieces and again in his book. In 1985 Grünbaum gave the Gifford Lectures; they were advertised as an outgrowth of *The Foundations of Psychoanalysis*. The June 1986 issue of *The Behavioral and Brain Sciences* has a précis by Grünbaum of his book together with a large number of discussions of it and Grünbaum's rejoinders to them. In my judgment, the energy and broad scholarship of Grünbaum's work on psychoanalysis have understandably attracted favorable comment. Almost from the outset it had the makings of an "event" in philosophical criticism of psychoanalysis and it became one. It also warrants what I believe it has not yet occasioned: an examination of its claims as a ". . . critique of the foundations of Sigmund Freud's psychoanalysis" (p. 1).

I

A major concern of Grünbaum's book is – in his phrase – the clinical credentials of psychoanalysis. He regularly employs the epithet "clinical" to refer to what occurs in the psychoanalytic hour. Thus, plausibly enough, clinical data exclude both experimental and epidemiological findings; much less plausibly, they exclude all information provided by a patient's parents or other persons who may know him. By the credentials of clinical data Grünbaum means the evidence they furnish – or fail to furnish – for Freud's major doctrines. As Grünbaum sees it, no evidence whatever for those doctrines can be yielded by clinical data alone. That is perhaps the main claim of the book, a claim clearly implied by the last sentence of its author's abstract: "If there exists empirical evidence for the principal psychoanalytic doctrines, it cannot be obtained without well-designed extraclinical studies of a kind that have for the most part yet to be attempted."[2] To be sure, Grünbaum discerns a chink of light in the evidential darkness. He says that " . . . on the whole, data from the couch *acquire* probative significance when they are independently corroborated by extraclinical findings or when they are inductively consilient with such findings . . ." (p. 266). As Grünbaum views it, then, clinical data are not " . . . altogether irrelevant probatively. But this much only conditionally confers *potential* relevance on intraclinical results. . . ." (ibid.; all emphases in quotations from Grünbaum's text are his). Some pages later, however, he is pessimistic about the "potential" value of findings from the couch. (See p. 278.)

How does Grünbaum arrive at his estimate of Freud's clinical data?

II

Grünbaum's effort to deflate the value of Freud's clinical data is accompanied by a unique attempt to inflate their role in the Freudian enterprise. A successful deflationary effort would, of course, have been all the more telling if the inflationary attempt had succeeded. Two salient instances of the latter should be examined at the outset. Both are major misreadings of Freud.

(1) In a 1917 lecture Freud said: "After all, [a patient's] conflicts will only be successfully solved and his resistances overcome if the anticipatory ideas he is given [by his analyst] tally with what is real in him." (1916–17, XVI, 452).[3] Grünbaum calls that statement a " . . . bold assertion of the *causal indispensability* of psychoanalytic insight for the conquest . . ." of psychoneurosis; and claims it ". . . entails not only that there is no spontaneous remission of psychoneuroses but also that, if there are any cures at all, psychoanalysis is *uniquely* therapeutic for such disorders as compared to any *rival* therapies" (pp. 139, 140; cf. p. 159).

Freud's statement, however, was meant only to characterize psychoanalytic treatment and to fend off the charge that it works solely by suggestion. What it says is tantamount to the following: Unless the suggestions an analyst makes to his patient correspond to facts about him, an understanding of his conflicts will not be attained, and his resistances will not be defeated. Thus understood, Freud's statement has no implications as regards the failure or success of nonpsychoanalytic modes of therapy or the possibility of spontaneous remission. Indeed, three pages earlier in the same lecture, Freud, speaking of the results of the *hypnotic suggestion techniques* he had used from the mid-eighties into the nineties, remarks: "Admittedly sometimes things went entirely as one would wish: after a few efforts, success was complete and permanent. But the conditions determining such a favorable outcome remained unknown." That remark contradicts what Grünbaum says about Freud's "bold assertion." To his credit, Grünbaum quotes the remark (p. 156). How does he cope with it? Despite its straightforwardness he repeatedly says it is "cryptic" and irrelevantly cites an 1892 case where the effect of Freud's hypnotic treatment was not termed "permanent" by Freud.[4] Obviously none of that addresses what Freud's remark plainly asserts: that at times the therapeutic success of hypnotic treatment was complete and lastingly so.

Besides the 1917 passage, there is a 1909 passage that Grünbaum also says implies that psychoanalytic treatment is causally indispensable for the conquest of psychoneurosis. (See p. 139.) But the 1909 passage, like the 1917 one, is compatible with therapeutic success in other kinds of treatment.[5] As to spontaneous remissions: Grünbaum's main excuses for imputing the causal indispensability claim to Freud – the 1909 and 1917 passages – do not bear at all on spontaneous remissions, phenomena whose occurrence Freud never denied. In fact, in 1913, midway between 1909 and 1917, Freud explicitly affirmed the occurrence of spontaneous remission of the major types of disorder accessible to psychoanalytic treatment (1913j, XIII, 165). That affirmation is decisive against Grünbaum's attribution of the causal indispensability claim to Freud.

(2) In a 1916 lecture Freud, after stating that psychoanalytic therapy was powerless in regard to delusions, said: "Even if psychoanalysis showed itself as unsuccessful in every other form of nervous and psychical disease as it does in delusions, it would still remain completely justified as an irreplaceable instrument of scientific research." Grünbaum quotes the claim and says of it: "But in the face of the suggestibility challenge, this statement is a gratuitous piece of salesmanship . . ." (p. 141). Yet in the same set of lectures, Freud, again speaking of patients with delusions, says:

Nor must we fail to point out that a large number of the individual findings of analysis, *which might otherwise be suspected of being products of suggestion*, are confirmed from another and irreproachable source. Our guarantors in this case are the sufferers from dementia praecox and paranoia, *who are of course far above any suspicion of being influenced by suggestion*. The translations of symbols and the phantasies, which these patients produce for us and which in them have forced their way into consciousness, coincide faithfully with the results of our investigations into the unconscious of transference neurotics and thus confirm the objective correctness of our interpretations, on which doubt is so often thrown. (1916–17, XVI, 453; my emphases)[6]

That passage shows that the claim Grünbaum calls "gratuitous" was stated by Freud with all due seriousness. It gives Freud's reason for the claim, that is, even if psychoanalysis had proven helpless with transference neurotics, the discovery of the coincidence of many of their "free associations" with the avowals of nonsuggestible psychotics was a scientific advance. The passage also shows that Freud tried to meet the charge of suggestibility by relying on the avowals of nonsuggestible psychotics to confirm the suggestion-free character of identical associations made by suggestible neurotics. What is more, the passage is an important instance of Freud's dependence on data that played no therapeutic role: data provided by psychotics who were fundamentally unamenable to analytic therapy.

Freud's appeal to psychotics' avowals falsifies Grünbaum's claim that ". . . the attribution of *therapeutic* success to the undoing of repressions . . . was the foundation, both logically and historically, for the central dynamical significance that unconscious ideation acquired in psychoanalytic theory . . ." (p. 182). Ignoring that instance of a nontherapeutic foundation for Freud's tenets, Grünbaum mistakenly says that Freud ". . . gave the same epistemic sanction to the clinical etiologies of the two subclasses of psychoneuroses . . .," that is, the transference neuroses and the narcissistic, psychotic ones (p. 141). But the Freud passage makes it plain that the data supplied by untreatable psychotics were guarantees for Freud of the correctness of many of his interpretations, and so were not on a logical or epistemic par with the data concerning neurotics.

(1) and (2) are crucial instances of Grünbaum's inflationary endeavors. Both try to aggrandize the important role played for Freud by data of therapeutic upshot. Later it will become obvious that Grünbaum's inflation of their role is largely effected by slighting extraclinical sources of support for Freud's doctrines. First, however, I take up Grünbaum's main attempt to deflate the value of those data: the charge of suggestion.

III

The centerpiece of Grünbaum's book is its second chapter, "Did Freud Validate His Method of Clinical Investigation?" Viewed as criticism of Freud, the chapter has two main parts. In the first part Freud is saddled with an argument Grünbaum dubs the "Tally Argument" (p. 140). Though the argument is Grünbaum's chief claim to originality in Freudian exegesis, I shall not state it or discuss Grünbaum's assessment of it. It is enough to note that the argument cannot be mounted unless one attributes the causal indispensability claim to Freud, and, as I have already argued, any such attribution is unwarranted.[7] In the second part Grünbaum offers the familiar conjecture that Freud's clinical data may have been due to his patients' suggestibility and so may not have supported psychoanalytic doctrines.

The charge of suggestion, however time-worn, is vexing. Freud thought so and Grünbaum painstakingly reminds us that he did. (Cf. pp. 130–9). Grünbaum is discreet, however about one of Freud's caveats concerning suggestion. (See p. 145.) In 1909 Freud sarcastically complained of the "great . . . economy of thought effected by the use of the catchword 'suggestion'." "Nobody knows," he added, "and nobody cares what suggestion is, where it comes from, or when it arises" (1909b, X, 102). Seventy-five years later, Grünbaum's numerous appeals to suggestion are a case in point; they are unaccompanied by any discussion of the origin or character of suggestion. Since Grünbaum fails to specify the nature or limits of the relevant phenomena, his repetition of the charge proves as vague as earlier statements of it by other critics. Even so, the charge cannot be disregarded; Freud, despite its lack of articulation, tried to meet it several times; his fullest single attempt to meet it merits discussion.

In that attempt Freud, though he prefers his term "transference" to "suggestibility," speaks of psychoanalytic suggestion.[8] In his first defense against the charge, he contrasts analytic therapy with pure suggestion, saying that in ". . . every other kind of suggestive treatment the transference is carefully preserved" but that at ". . . the end of an analytic treatment the transference must itself be cleared away; and if success is thus obtained or continues, it rests, not on suggestion, but on the achievement by its means of an overcoming of internal resistances" (1916–17, XVI, 453). In his second defense, he argues that "The acceptance of suggestions on individual points is no doubt discouraged by the fact that during the treatment we are struggling unceasingly against resistances which are able to transform themselves into negative (hostile) transferences" (1916–17, XVI, 453). In his third defense, one that occurs in the same passage and at several other places (see note 6), Freud expresses his reliance on the coincidence of free associations of neurotics with the avowals of psychotics.

That passage is repeatedly cited by Grünbaum (p. 143) when he discusses Freud's efforts to distinguish analytic therapy from purely suggestive modes of treatment. As I have argued (Section II (2)), if Grünbaum had not ignored Freud's third defense he could have avoided some basic errors about Freud's views; also, since he nowhere answers that defense, his charge of suggestion seems much less than – to use his epithet – menacing. Against Freud's first defense, Grünbaum makes a criticism of some force. He observes that there Freud, while trying to respond to the charge of suggestion, appeals to the psychoanalytic conception of resolving the patient's transference; and says that Freud, by so doing, argues in a "viciously circular" way: "For clearly, the psychoanalytic dissection of the patient's deferential submission to his doctor already presupposes the empirical validity of the very hypotheses whose spurious confirmation by the analysand's clinical responses was at issue from the outset!" (p. 144).[9] For Freud it was essential to transference resolution that the patient be convinced that in his transference he has been ". . . *re-experiencing* emotional relations which had their origin in his earliest object-attachments during the repressed period of his childhood"(1925d [1924], XX, 43).[10] Since that conviction may be due to the analyst's suggestions, Freud's first point of defense fails; as Grünbaum says, it is "question-begging" (p. 144).

The objection is of course a formal one. It does not touch the substantive question, namely, when a patient becomes convinced that he is, in his transference, "reexperiencing," has his conviction been responsibly reached and is it a reasonable – even perhaps correct – conviction?[11] Various more or less unconscious patterns of relationship which disfigure many persons' lives suggest that an affirmative answer would often be plausible; but no philosopher of science or mind has, to my knowledge, advanced our understanding of the question or of kindred ones that psychoanalysis raises.

Except for his observation that one of Freud's three favorite defenses against the charge of suggestion is a *petitio,* Grünbaum's second chapter includes nothing original that is pertinent to the charge.[12] Signally, he fails to meet Freud's other two defenses.[13]

IV

Grünbaum's main attack on Freud is the claim that the clinical data cannot by themselves support psychoanalytic doctrines because *all* of them *may* owe their origin to suggestion. Understandably, he offers some other reasons for questioning those data and the doctrines Freud believed they helped confirm. Grünbaum's additional reasons are stated in Part II of his book, and are presented as a set of criticisms of Freudian views on repression. An adequate assessment of them requires a much larger perspective of Freud's thought than Grünbaum allows. The narrowness of Grünbaum's perspective is evident from the outset. He begins by speaking of "the credentials of psychoanalytic theory" (p. xi) but a few lines later and regularly thereafter he labels psychoanalysis a "clinical theory." (Cf. pp. xii, 3, 5, 6, 7, 8 and passim.) He takes the label, I assume, from his supposition that the theory is *"clinically* based" (p. 5) but the citations he gives in support of the supposition are transparently inadequate. (See pp. 5–6.) In this section I briefly try to indicate how confining the supposition is, and I suggest a comprehensive view of the materials on which Freud relied.

In 1915 Freud spoke of ". . . the broad basis of our observations, the repetition of similar impressions from the most varied spheres of mental life" (1916–17, XV, 67). If one were to look in Grünbaum's critique for some recognition of the broad basis of Freud's observations – for examples of Grünbaum taking into account the "similar impressions" Freud assembled from highly diverse spheres of mental life – one would turn to his chapters about Freud on parapraxes and dreams. But before reaching them one is forewarned. Grünbaum announces that he will ". . . argue for the following thesis: even if the original *therapeutic* defense of the repression etiology of neuroses had actually turned out to be empirically viable, Freud's compromise models of parapraxes and of manifest dream content would be *misextrapolations* of that etiology, precisely because they lacked any corresponding therapeutic base at the outset" (pp. 187–8). That thesis is surely original; a paraphrase may make it clearer: In the absence of a counterpart to therapy for the normal phenomena of parapraxes and dreams, Freud had no reason for thinking that repression plays a role in the occurrence of any of them.[14] In other words, since dreams and parapraxes are not thus comparable to clinically treatable disorders, there is no warrant for asserting about any of them that they occur in the form of unconscious conflict – and compromise – between a wish or motive and resistance to it. That thesis is the most extreme case of Grünbaum's insistence that the only data that Freud was both entitled and willing to draw upon were data of therapeutic upshot. Indeed, apart from the two chapters on parapraxes and dreams, and a solitary remark which refers to Freud on jokes – and embodies a fundamental mistake[15] – Grünbaum nowhere discusses Freud's conviction that he had found applications and confirmations of his doctrines outside the sphere of clinical practice. Thus a reader unaware of the range of Freud's work is not told by Grünbaum that Freud tried to show how his doctrines both threw light on and were supported by phenomena as diverse as psychotic manifestations, the vagaries of sexual orientation, jokes, taboos, religious practices and creeds, myths, folklore, so-called symptomatic actions, and sundry literary and biographical items. As one would expect, those sources of support for Freud's views differ in value – some are impressive, some negligible.[16]

Such a reader might be surprised to learn that in 1909, while reporting a case history, Freud said: "Therapeutic success, however, is not our primary aim . . .," and that as late as 1932 he remarked: "I have never been a therapeutic enthusiast" (1909b, X, 120; 1933a, XXII, 151). Of course Freud always held that therapeutic practice, and especially the experience of therapeutic failure, was invaluable for the development of psychoanalysis. But one cannot appreciate Freud's reservations about therapy if one mutes, as Grünbaum in effect does, Freud's proclamation that as early as ". . . the date of *The Interpretation of Dreams* psychoanalysis . . . was not only a new method of treating the neuroses . . . it was also a new psychology . . .," that psychoanalysis had "become the name of a science – the science of unconscious mental processes."[17]

In accord with the title of his book, Grünbaum claims that his critique will examine the "postulational" foundations of Freud's theory of unconscious motivation. (Cf. p. xii.) To see that the claim is exaggerated, one need only consider Freud's basic "assumption" of ". . . a strict and universal application of determinism to mental life . . .," a determinism that, in the absence of organic deficit, is itself psychical.[18] Freud programmatically tried to give the assumption some content and force by his various attempts to show that ". . . mental processes are in themselves unconscious and that of all mental life it is only certain individual acts and portions that are conscious"; and that, moreover, those unconscious processes determine what conscious mental life we possess (1916–17, XV, 21, 109; 1915e, XIV, 166, 167). Even so, was the assumption itself inchoate or idle and Freud's endeavor to substantiate it misguided or superfluous? Or did Freud's observations and doctrines support – and if so, how far – his postulate of psychical determinism? If any issues are foundational, those are; Grünbaum does not mention them.[19]

V

Grünbaum heralds his third chapter as an appraisal of Freud's arguments for the claim that repression is a causal factor in psychoneurosis. (See, for example, pp. 177, 194.) Most of the chapter, however, is a capsule history of Freud's disillusionment with the notion of repression and the related clinical techniques he and Josef Breuer shared before Freud founded psychoanalysis proper. The chapter also repeats matter Grünbaum has stated on ealier pages and contains, besides incidental detail, some promissory notes that may serve as an agenda for much of the book's later chapters. The main ones should be singled out: (a) "... the bare *existence* of the psychic mechanism of repression . . . is still a far cry from its Freudian role as a generic pathogen, as a dream-instigator, and as a begetter of parapraxes" (p. 188).[20] (b) Without "its *legitimation* by the presumed therapeutic dynamics of undoing repressions . . . or some other as yet unknown epistemic underpinning, not even the tortures of the thumbscrew or of the rack should persuade a rational being that free associations can *certify* pathogens or other causes! For, without the stated *therapeutic* foundation, this epistemic tribute to free associations so far rests on nothing but a glaring causal fallacy" (p. 186). As far as I can tell, (a) and (b) express Grünbaum's chief misgivings about Freud's claims that unconscious conflicts between wishes and resistances to them contribute to psychoneuroses and other psychological phenomena, and that the technique of free association, properly handled, can often uncover such conflicts.

In ensuing chapters, Grünbaum clarifies and deploys (a) and (b), but one will ransack his third chapter in vain for a reasoned appraisal of Freud's mature "repression etiology," the one he first expounded at the turn of the century and buttressed and altered thereafter.

VI

Among Freud's main works, no others, if they are to be evaluated fairly, demand as much care and tact as *The Interpretation of Dreams* and *The Psychopathology of Everyday Life*.[21] Nor can one appreciate them without an informed sense of Freud's two other major works that appeared in the same astonishing half-decade: *Jokes and their Relation to the Unconscious* and *Three Essays on the Theory of Sexuality*. The neglected book on jokes is singular for its clear and compelling statement of Freud's view of the *processes* of unconscious thought; and the essays on sexuality are indispensable for his view of the *materials* of unconscious thought, that is, erotic and hostile wishes and resistances to them. Grünbaum, however – and here he is far from alone – does not notice the interrelations of the four works. Instead, he focuses on objections to which he thinks *The Psychopathology of Everyday Life* is vulnerable, and then attacks *The Interpretation of Dreams*.

In taking up the *Psychopathology* before the *Interpretation*, Grünbaum follows Freud's expository practice.[22] Early in this century Freud became convinced that his most persuasive introduction to psychoanalysis was his account of *Fehlleistungen*, that is, the parapraxes of everyday life: anomalies of memory, slips of the tongue, eye, and pen, bungled actions, and – what to my mind prove most striking – combined parapraxes.

In the *Psychopathology*, Freud avoids examples that require "depth" psychology. Though he uses the term "repression," he often employs it interchangeably with "suppression." In his first two examples he utilizes the technique of free association extensively but in both cases the associations culminate in material that is suppressed rather than repressed.[23] As with those cases, so too with most of the other examples of parapraxes in the *Psychopathology*: They are not instances of the emergence of deeply "repressed" ideas or affects.[24] Nonetheless, much of the material Freud presents in the *Psychopathology* illustrates basic psychoanalytic tenets. As I have said, among the phenomena he discusses, combined parapraxes are particularly striking – at least by way of nudging me toward a psychoanalytic viewpoint. Freud's chapter on them is, however, meager.[25] To help supplement it, I shall briefly discuss certain phenomena closely akin to combined parapraxes, namely, accumulated ones.

Some readers of this piece may have had experiences of roughly the following kind: In the days just before an appointment that a person anticipates with barely felt anxiety, she quite atypically forgets some signal items, say, first, her money purse and, later, her keys. She then – and this too is unusual for her – makes an engagement that, unrealized by her at the time, conflicts with her appointment. She then recalls the latter and tries to postpone it; or recalls it only after the time for keeping it is past.

That sort of example of accumulated parapraxes is, as I have suggested, not unfamiliar. If one inquires among one's acquaintances, one may learn of a number of examples similar to it. The one I have sketched – drawn from an actual case – is of some evidential value in the following ways: First, in pointing to a disposition to more felt anxiety about the appointment than was actually experienced – a disposition that helps explain the resistance to keeping the appointment; second, the odd forgetting of the signal items, episodes emblematic of the resistance, trenches on the symbolism that Freud, though hardly the first to notice, was the first to employ systematically. In the *Psychopathology*, Freud often adverts to that symbolism. (His fullest account of it is in the *Introductory Lectures*, Chapter X.)

I do not know what Grünbaum would say about the evidential value for psychoanalysis of my mundane example and of numerous others like it. Since such phenomena are neither clinical nor, of course, epidemiological or experimental, I assume he would say they have no evidential value whatever. That, after all, is his staunch methodological commitment. In point of fact, Grünbaum nowhere mentions in his book either combined or accumulated parapraxes. The omission is regrettable; Freud himself thought they were his most convincing cases among parapractic phenomena of the need for psychoanalytic interpretation (1901b, VI, 238; 1916–17, XV, 56).

Likewise, in his chapter on parapraxes, Grünbaum does not mention Freudian symbols; and, in his discussion of *The Interpretation of Dreams*, he takes them up merely to set them aside (pp. 220–1). The way he sets them aside should be examined. After saying that Freud ". . . emphasizes that the interpersonally significant symbols play only an auxiliary, subordinate role in dream interpretation vis-

à-vis the 'decisive significance' of the dreamer's free associations . . . " (p. 220), Grünbaum adds: "Thus, when interpersonal
dream symbolism is present in the manifest content, its interpreta-
tive translation can yield only *bits* for the interpretation. Hence, for
the purpose of examining the credentials of his interpretation of
dreams, it will suffice to confine our comments to his reliance on
the method of free association as an epistemic avenue to the purported motivational cause of dreaming" (p. 221).

In fact Freud did say in the *Introductory Lectures* that "Interpretation based on a knowledge of symbols is not a technique which can
replace or compete with the associative one. It forms a supplement
to the latter and yields results which are only of use when introduced into it" (1916–17, XV, 151). Grünbaum (p. 220) refers to that
passage and also to the page before it; what he does not note is that
on the earlier page Freud says: "We are then forced to recognize that
whenever we venture on making a replacement of this sort [sc. a
symbolic one] we arrive at a satisfactory sense for the dream,
whereas it remains senseless and the chain of thought is interrupted
so long as we refrain from intervening in this way."[26] Nor does
Grünbaum intimate that in the first paragraphs of the same chapter,
as well as its penultimate one, Freud claims that ". . . even if there
were no dream-censorship, dreams would still not be easily intelligible to us, for we should still be faced with the task of translating the
symbolic language of dreams into that of our waking thought. Thus
symbolism is a *second and independent factor* in the distortion of
dreams, alongside of the dream-censorship" (XV, 168; my emphasis;
cf. 149–50, and IV, xxvii).

In my judgment, Grünbaum should not have demoted and then
ignored Freud's "second and independent factor" in dream interpretation, a factor that also often plays a crucial role in the interpretation
of neurotic symptoms, paraxises, literary works, and so on. To be
sure, as regards dream interpretation, if free association could be
shown wholly to lack epistemic value, that would call into question
the greater part of Freud's procedure concerning dreams; however, as
Freud implies, it would leave the interpretation of their symbolic
elements intact. In any case, Grünbaum nowhere else in his book
discusses Freud's views on the symbolism, views, incidentally, that
Freud did not develop until the second decade of this century.

If Grünbaum's slighting of the symbolism seems puzzling, it can, I suggest, be explained as follows. When Freud states how he came to know the meaning of the symbols, he does not depend on clinical findings. The position is rather the reverse:

[W]e learn it from very different sources – from fairy tales and myths, from buffoonery and jokes, from folklore (that is, from knowledge about popular manners and customs, sayings and songs) and from poetic and colloquial linguistic usage. In all these directions we come upon the same symbolism, and in some of them we can understand it without further instruction. If we go into these sources in detail, we should find so many parallels to dream-symbolism *we cannot fail to be convinced of our interpretations* (XV, 158–9; my emphasis; cf. for example, XII, 335–7; V, 351).

That, in outline, is the epistemic basis for Freud's notorious symbolism; and one of the evidential bases for his mature practice of interpretation in general. Again, the symbolism is not founded on clinical data or, a fortiori, on clinical data confined to instances of therapeutic success. Consequently, I take it, Grünbaum dismisses it. To do so is to give the go-by to one of the foundations of psychoanalysis.[27]

VII

On Freud's conception, combined parapraxes concur and in some cases cooperate in trying to fulfill the same wish. Accumulated parapraxes – as I am using the phrase – repeatedly express or allude to a wish and may also work toward fulfilling it. (In my example of accumulated parapraxes, the appointment the woman forgot was with a gynecologist and concerned a question charged with anxiety.) Single parapraxes either try to fulfill a wish or express or allude to it.

Both the single and combined parapraxes that Freud cites often involve unusual – unusual and perplexing – forgetting. His first example in the *Psychopathology*, the "Signorelli" one, is a single parapraxis of forgetting a proper name. It exemplifies a distinctive set of features: Before forgetting the name, one regularly had it – as one still has a plethora of other names, including less familiar ones – at one's command; one or more substitute names, names one knows are incorrect, obtrude themselves; some detail connected with the person whose name one is striving after is fixated on or is more or less isolated and vivid; when one recovers the name, one at once knows it is correct. That ensemble of phenomenological features is hardly unfamiliar.

In such cases, as well as similar ones, we say we "know" the name, and are confounded by its sudden inaccessibility to consciousness. At times we suspect a motive for our odd forgetfulness: one or another disagreeable item associated with the bearer of the name. Freud gave impetus to that suspicion by his novel elaboration of it, but it is absurd to suppose he was the first to entertain it. Neither, of course, was he the first to notice tendentious forgetting in general.

The innovations Freud introduces in his discussion of the "Signorelli" case can be briefly summarized: The context in which the name was forgotten was directly preceded by talk or thought on another topic, a topic the forgetter broke off or suppressed; the substitute names were displacements of the forgotten one, either allusive or phonemic or both; besides those external associations, an internal, disagreeable content associatively linked the later topic, especially the bearer of the forgotten name and the vivid detail, to the earlier, broken-off topic; the disagreeable content motivated forgetting the name. (See VI, 1–7, esp. 6; 12, n. 2; 13, n. 1; 20–21; 22; cf. V, 530.)

Freud says of his schema that it occurs with "uncommon frequency" in cases where one is trying to recover an anomalously forgotten name and other names come to mind which one knows are incorrect (VI, 7). In order to evaluate that claim one would need, at the start, an unbiased selection of relevant and careful introspective reports. No such compilation, so far as I know, has been made.

Grünbaum, in his short discussion of Freud's first example, follows Sebastiano Timpanaro.[28] Neither of them notices the example's distinctive ensemble of phenomenological features; consequently, neither of them sees that it may well require explanation as a whole. Nor does Grünbaum ever discuss tendentious forgetting, the overall psychological trend illustrated by Freud's initial examples and by a host of cases he goes on to cite. Grünbaum's failure to come to terms with Freud's first example could, however, be overlooked if his criticisms of Freud's second example, an example much like the first, did not prove baseless. Before substantiating that judgment, it will be useful to consider Freud's first two examples in some detail; and also to discuss tendentious forgetting in general.

Though Freud does not explicitly make the point, his second example, the "aliquis" case, has the same set of phenomenological features as his first one. (See VI, 12, n. 2 and 13, n. 1.)[29] Both examples are meant to illustrate conflict between an unconscious wish or motive and a conscious aim. The unconscious wish is to keep an anxious-making thought suppressed; the conscious aim, to formulate another thought and of course, in order to do so, to depend on one's memory for words and names. But the latter thought in fact – in unrecognized fact – flouts the unconscious wish. The wish then impedes the aim by prompting a curious memory lapse. It may more or less impede it: Since a constituent word or name is oddly and distractingly forgotten, the thought may be lost; at the other extreme, the thought, despite the memory gap, may be taken up and pursued. Because, ordinarily the unconscious wish is only to some extent successful and the conscious aim only somewhat hindered, Freud terms such lapses "compromises" or "compromise-formations." (See VI, 4, 234, 277–8.)

According to Freud, the "Signorelli" and "aliquis" cases illustrate both that conflict and compromise. In each case, a sequence of associations, external and internal, links the lapse to the unconscious wish. Each sequence converges on and is completed by the conscious retrieval of the wish together with the realization that, because the wish was at odds with the thought, it impeded it. Such realizations are not without affect, whether the affect is overtly limited or is markedly intense.

If one is willing to affirm the occurrence of tendentious forgetting then – perhaps surprisingly – some of the main points in Freud's discussion of his first two examples should seem reasonable. Notably, tendentious forgetting often presupposes a wish or motive and an aim in conflict with it. Above all, in tendentious forgetting the motive must, if only temporarily, *unconsciously* prevail. Also, Freud's claim that the conflict tends to result in a "compromise" is often supported by the cases of tendentious forgetting most likely to be generally acknowledged, that is, instances of forgetting intentions or experiences when there is a patently self-interested motive for forgetting them.[30] For example, unconscious reluctance to return a borrowed object may occasion a disconcerting but merely intermittent forgetfulness to return it. (Cf. VI, 230–1.)

In this section and the preceding one I have discussed several kinds of phenomena that Grünbaum either wholly or largely neglects. Instances of them often appear explicable by Freud's tenets concerning suppression and repression. None of them is based on clinical findings. They include combined and accumulated parapraxes, Freudian symbolism, the distinctive set of phenomenological features of certain sorts of forgetting, and normal tendentious forgetting in general. Grünbaum's disregard of them when he discusses the *Psychopathology*, together with his unfounded charges against that work, render his chapter on it a disservice. I now turn to those charges.

VIII

In Section IV, I mentioned a complaint Grünbaum has about both the *Psychopathology* and *The Interpretation of Dreams*. The reader may recall his epithet for it: "misextrapolation." A bald statement of it can be gotten by shaving one of his sentences: ". . . as I have . . . explained . . . in . . . my criticism of Freud's repression theory of parapraxes, his compromise model . . . rests on a *misextrapolation*; for he does not even try to adduce any counterpart to . . . *therapeutic* . . ." upshot (p. 231).[31] As I have said, Freud held that in a parapraxis there is an unconscious disturbing wish and a conscious purpose disturbed by it; and that a parapraxis is typically a "compromise" between them. He held, too, that dreams usually fit that pattern. (See, e.g., 1916–17, XV, 66, 130.) Moreover, he thought that psychoneurotic symptoms were modeled on it.[32] Grünbaum's complaint is that Freud does not try to find a further point of likeness: a counterpart to therapeutic upshot for parapraxes and also one for dreams. Since Grünbaum mistakenly claims that jokes too, according to Freud, are "compromises," he could also have complained that Freud did not try to find "cures" for them. (See note 15.)

Grünbaum's complaint is, of course, an artifact of his insistence that Freud was limited to therapeutic upshot in seeking support for his doctrines. Moreover, the complaint, on its own terms, is surrealistic. Consider parapraxes. Freud characterizes them as follows: they must be "momentary and temporary," and not exceed "the limits of the normal." They must, that is, be transient and infrequent intrusions on what we regularly, in thought and action, both believe ourselves to have at our command and in fact do. (See 1901b, VI, 239.) But what counterpart to therapeutic upshot could there be for a "momentary and temporary" untowardness that occurs within the limits of normalcy? Next, consider an ordinary dream. What would be a "cure" for that evanescent entity?[33] To be sure, if parapraxes or dreams were worrisomely repeated or were otherwise grave enough to be countered as neurotic symptoms, Freud would try to deal with them therapeutically. (See e.g., 1901b, VI, 39.) He also found it aided therapy to interpret his patients' dreams and parapraxes; by the turn of the century, interpreting them was part of his regular procedure.

While discussing the "aliquis" case, Grünbaum himself suggests a counterpart to therapeutic upshot for a parapraxis: Uncovering a repressed wish to which a parapraxis is attributed could, he says ". . . be 'therapeutic' in the sense of enabling the patient himself to correct the parapraxis *and* to avoid its repetition or other parapraxes in the future" (p. 193). He seems unaware of drawbacks to his suggestion. (i) Repetitions of a parapraxis or of related ones would soon extend beyond normalcy. (Combined and accumulated parapraxes evidently lie on the border between the parapractic and the neurotic.) (ii) Grünbaum applies his suggestion to a particular class of parapraxes: forgetting words or names. (Curiously, he overlooks Freud's examples of persons recovering, by way of sequences of association, names they had anomalously forgotten. See 1916–17, XV, 110–12.[34]) In fact Freud furnishes an analogue to therapeutic *treatment* that is both within the limits of normalcy and applicable to parapraxes in general: The affect-laden entry into consciousness of the wish that led to the parapraxis, an entry often achieved by free association. That analogue pertains to every type of parapraxis, including those for which – once they are perpetrated – there is no possibility of correction or repetition.

For several reasons I shall soon discuss, Grünbaum would reject the Freudian analogue to therapeutic treatment concerning parapraxes. The analogue applies to dreams too: the affect-laden entry into consciousness of the wish or wishes that led to the dream, an entry, again, that may be effected by using the technique of free association. Grünbaum, however, has his own "genial proposal" for a counterpart to therapeutic upshot for dreams.[35] Though tentative, it is startling:

Just as sexual repressions are deemed causally necessary for neurosogenesis, so also sundry sorts of repressed infantile wishes are avowedly the *sine qua non* of dream instigation. Thus, just as the therapeuticity of lifting pathogenic repressions is the corollary of the former, so also the latter may seem to entail the following: To the extent that the *analyzed* patient achieves conscious awareness of his previously repressed infantile wishes, that conscious mastery robs these very wishes of their power to engender dreams! Hence, in proportion as the analysand's buried infantile wishes are brought to light, he should experience, and exhibit neurophysiologically (e.g., via REM sleep), a striking reduction in dream formation. But what if this decrease fails to materialize? It would then seem to follow that, unless the typical analysand is chronically unsuccessful in retrieving his buried infantile wishes, Freud's account of dream instigation is false. (pp. 234–5)[36]

There is of course no textual support in Freud for the exclamatory salvo in the Grünbaum passage; nor does Grünbaum pretend there is. Grünbaum, I take it, knows Freud never held that, once some of one's parapraxes or dreams have been interpreted, one can look forward to a perceptible decline of those phenomena in one's life. I take it he also knows, though he does not cite, Freud's implicit warning against that folly. (See 1916–17, XVI, 456–7.) Why, then, take exception to Freud's common sense about the normalcy of parapraxes and dreams?

To put the answer somewhat tersely: Freud found a number of significant respects in which he could compare those normal phenomena to psychoneurotic symptoms. (See note 32, this essay.) Indeed, he said that dreams and parapraxes, and also innocuous fiddling and the like, are "the only symptoms" a "healthy" person can have. (See 1916–17, XVI, ibid.) Freud's laboriously won comparisons – not conflations – yielded him large classes of instances of his views concerning unconscious mental processes and contents in general. But Grünbaum throughout insists that the only data on which Freud was both able and willing to draw were data of therapeutic upshot. That insistence leads him to pose the question: Where is the therapeutic counterpart? He then presses the question because he knows that, notwithstanding interpretations of some of one's parapraxes and dreams, one will go on manufacturing both.[37] Grünbaum thinks he has embarrassed Freud thereby; that he may have caught him – not once but twice – in the act of *misextrapolating*.[38]

IX

In *The Interpretation of Dreams* Freud says he learned from Josef Breuer that *solving* hysterical phobias, obsessional ideas, and so on, could succeed in *dissolving* them (1900a, IV, 100). For a parapraxis or a dream, there was no question of its dissolution; but its formation and solution were alike for Freud analogous to those of neurotic symptoms. Free association, together with the symbolism, was the method he evolved to arrive at his solutions.

Free association from a dream's components or from a parapraxis is not invariably needed in order to grasp its motivation. Often young children and at times adults have dreams that are transparently wish-fulfilling (1900a, IV, Chapter III passim; 1916–17, XV, 126–35); and occasionally a parapraxis wears the wish that prompted it on its face. (Freud held that there were no comparably transparent neurotic symptoms. See for example, 1916–17, XVI, Lecture 23 passim.) If one looks to Grünbaum, one finds that he allows the "commonsense credibility" of the "preanalytic causal attribution of *some* dreams to wishes" (p. 219). What is more, he concedes that parapraxes whose motives seem to him transparent "share two significant features of the genuinely 'Freudian' ones: (1) they exhibit intrusions upon the agent's control of his own behavior, and (2) the intruding element is a wish or an affect" (p. 200).

That concession of Grünbaum's – henceforth, "his concession" – is explicitly applied by him to various allegedly transparent parapraxes. Among them are the following:

(a) "in the course of giving a lecture on human sexuality, a person misspeaks himself by saying 'orgasm' instead of 'organism' " (p. 199).

(b) "the man who turns from the exciting view of a lady's exposed bosom muttering [sic!], 'Excuse me, I have got to get a *breast* of *flesh* air!' " (p. 200; my brackets).[39]

It will, I believe, prove instructive to relate Grünbaum's concession to several charges he makes against the use of free association for the solution of opaque parapraxes.

(1) Post hoc ergo propter hoc

When he discusses the "aliquis" case, and also at other places, Grünbaum levels the charge of *post hoc ergo propter hoc* against

Freud's claim that free association from a parapraxis or a dream can uncover a wish that prompted it (pp. 192, 198; cf. 170, 207, 208, 214, 254, 256–7). According to Grünbaum, even if one thus located a wish which was prior to, and indeed was aptly expressed by, a parapraxis and its attendant associations, one could not be warranted in concluding that the wish prompted the parapraxis. If one so concluded, one would have argued *post hoc ergo* etc. yet Grünbaum takes it for granted that his concession as regards (a) and (b) is not vitiated by the post hoc fallacy. One may, however, wonder why not. After all, it is tantamount to the claim that each of those parapraxes *shows* that a wish or affect that was prior to it had occasioned it.

I am not just saying to Grünbaum: *tu quoque*. It may well be the case that his explanations of (a) and (b) are invulnerable to the post hoc charge. But why does he – however sensibly – suppose they are exempt from it?[40] Moreover, given that he does so suppose, he has no reason to claim that deliverances of free association could not be exempt from it. At any rate, he gives none.

(2) The "thematic affinity fallacy"

Consider a wish located by a sequence of associations to a parapraxis. Let the wish be as expressible by – or as "thematically affinite" to – both the parapraxis and the associations as you may possibly imagine. No matter; it will be fallacious for you to conclude that the wish gave rise to the parapraxis; so Grünbaum asserts. Any such inference, he says, runs afoul of his invention, "the thematic affinity fallacy" (pp. 55, 198, 199). Grünbaum, however, never states the mistake in reasoning or argument that would be made thereby. In fact, the only error in argumentation at all clearly in view is Grünbaum's begging the question against free association. His intimidating phrase, "thematic affinity fallacy," should not frighten anyone. Plainly it did not dissuade him when he made his concession as regards (a) and (b): in each of those cases, as well as others, he relies heavily on the thematic affinity of the parapraxis to a wish in order to infer that the wish prompted the parapraxis.[41] Once more, I suggest, it was not unreasonable for him to do so.

(3) The unconscious cunning of some parapraxes

Grünbaum says: "To endow the unconscious with cunning, un-canny powers of intrusion upon conscious actions is only to baptize the causal fallacy by giving it an honorific name" (p. 192). The causal fallacy, I take it, is post hoc, and so forth. I have noted that Grünbaum does not press that charge against his concession concern-ing (a) and (b) et al.[42] What, then, of the "cunning, uncanny powers" of the unconscious in its "intrusion upon conscious actions?" Some-thing less than cunning may be shown by (a), but (b) seems quite strategic and unsettling. Grünbaum, if he noticed that aspect of (b), was not deterred by it when he made his concession. Here, too, not being deterred seems reasonable.[43]

(4) The "causal reversal fallacy"

The parapraxes I have spoken of as "transparent" are called that by Grünbaum; he calls the unobvious ones "explanatorily opaque."[44] Grünbaum says that the use of free association to interpret opaque parapraxes – and many dreams and neurotic symptoms – is invali-dated by yet another fallacy. He labels it "the causal reversal fal-lacy." Both in his discussion of the "aliquis" example and elsewhere, Grünbaum invokes the charge (pp. 186–7, 192, 233–4). According to Grünbaum one makes that mistake in reasoning whenever one con-cludes that ". . . a repression which emerges at the end of a chain of free associations – as its *terminus ad quem* – was actually the origi-nal cause of the symptom [or parapraxis or dream] that initiated the chain as its *terminus a quo*" (pp. 186–7; my brackets).[45]

Several remarks about the complaint of fallacious causal reversal may be helpful. (i) Why does Grünbaum speak of a reversal of causal-ity? First, for the sake of argument he waives any likelihood of the "contamination" of sequences of free association by suggestion. Ac-cording to Grünbaum, if the steps in the sequence are free of that influence, they will exhibit a causal order. That is, the earlier steps will effect the later ones. (Oddly, Grünbaum does not think that claim open to post hoc, etc.) Next, Grünbaum makes the often false supposition that the putative wish or motive emerges only at the *end* of the sequence. He concludes that, if it is inferred that the wish prompted the parapraxis from which the sequence *began*, the causal order will have been reversed.[46] (ii) It is *logically* possible that Freud perpetrated both the alleged fallacy of causal reversal and the post hoc fallacy. Garnering the wish from the associations to the dream, say, Freud could have projected it backward in time, and then claimed that it occasioned the dream. But, of course, even if it had preceded the dream, it would not follow that it had helped form it. (iii) Still, Grünbaum's charge of causal reversal does not withstand examination. Once again, it is a matter of parallel reasoning but not merely a *tu quoque* point. Whether one's route, as with opaque parapraxes, is that of free association, or, as with transparent ones, the quick perception of a wish that intruded "upon the agent's control of his own behavior," one takes it that the wish anteceded the parapraxis. Thus in relation to (a) and (b) Grünbaum presupposes a backward reference, however short in time, for the wish. Moreover, he has no argument against a more extended backward temporal reference. But, again, I think he was sensible; that it was reasonable for him not to be moved by the threat of alleged causal reversal when he made his concession as regards (a) and (b) et al.

It is easy to see why it was sensible of Grünbaum to ignore his charges (1) to (4) when he made his concession concerning (a) and (b). It was so because each of those parapraxes, on its own, conveys an indication of having been motivated. Each of them, as it happens, also suggests a clue to its motivation. Moreover, the circumstances of their occurrence – their immediate backgrounds – tend to support those judgments. Accordingly, it was reasonable for Grünbaum to claim that those involuntary blunders of speech were motivated mental acts; to assert, in Freud's words, that "they have a sense" of their own; and to suppose that, in both cases, the wish that prompted the parapraxis was affinite to or associated with the sense of the parapraxis. (See pp. 199–200.)

Once it is seen that none of Grünbaum's charges, (1) to (4), damages what he says about seemingly transparent parapraxes, it becomes evident that those charges are without force in relation to Freud's procedure for interpreting opaque ones. For if those charges told against Freud's method for the interpretation of opaque parapraxes, they would also tell against Grünbaum's concession concerning apparently obvious ones. But since they are powerless against the latter, they are without strength against the former.

Grünbaum has one further criticism of the technique of free association. Luckily it can be dispatched in a footnote⁴⁷; I say "luckily" because it is time to conclude this assessment of Grünbaum's Freud.

X

Grünbaum's main attack on Freud's tenets concerning repression is indirect. He repeatedly tries to discredit Freud's invention, the method of free association. Had he succeeded, he could justifiably assert that Freud's chief procedure for ascertaining unconscious processes and contents, including of course repressed ones, was of no avail. But, as I have tried to show, none of Grünbaum's efforts to impugn the method of free association is successful. Grünbaum's subsidiary attack is a programmatic demand: Freudian claims about repressed motives must be tested in ways that conform to the canons of eliminative induction. Yet Grünbaum himself disregards that inappropriate demand when pronouncing on various sorts of dreams and parapraxes whose motivation is not conscious.

Besides the failure of those attacks, there is the sorry fate of Grünbaum's exaggerated charge of suggestion. (Cf. Section II (2), Section III, and notes 13 and 47, this essay.) Taken together, they signify the defeat of Grünbaum's anti-Freudian campaign. Freud's clinical data, so far as Grünbaum's criticisms of them go, continue to constitute evidence that can be marshaled on behalf of psychoanalysis. Quite apart, that is, from the other sources of support for Freud that I have emphasized and that Grünbaum neglects.

At the outset, I said that Grünbaum's book is provocative. Its value, by no means inconsiderable, lies mostly in its learned and energetic provocations. Above all it incites and repays study of both itself and Freud.

NOTES

1 The Foundations of Psychoanalysis: A Philosophical Critique (Berkeley: University of California Press, 1984), pp. xiv, 310.

2 Adolf Grünbaum, "Précis of The Foundations of Psychoanalysis: A Philosophical Critique," Behavioral and Brain Sciences 9 (1986): 217. For a statement to the same effect in the book, see p. 278.

3 My bracketed interpolations. Cp. Grünbaum, p. 139.

4 *Pace* Grünbaum; see pp. 156–7. Cf. 1892–3, I, 117–28.

5 It also should be noted that Freud occasionally remarked that psychoneurosis might in the future prove accessible to physical intervention, presumably one or another pharmacological regimen. See 1916–17, XVI, 436 and 1925e [1924], XIX, 214–15. On p. 156, Grünbaum discusses the passage at 1916–17, XVI, 436, but fails to see that it is incompatible with his causal indispensability attribution. In 1917 Freud spoke of therapeutic successes ". . . that could not have been achieved by any other procedure" than analytic therapy (1916–17, XVI, 458; cf. 1923a [1922], XVIII, 250). The boast is made in the same lecture in which he mentions his earlier successes with hypnotic suggestion; the other procedures to which he alludes were, it is only reasonable to suppose, ones practiced when he made the claim. (Cp. 1933a, XXII, 153.) Grünbaum cites the claim (p. 142) and groundlessly adds that Freud, in making it, rejects the possibility of spontaneous remissions.

6 Cf. 1901b, VI, 255; idem, note 2; 1905d, VII, 165–6, note 2; 1915e, XIV, 197; 1925d [1924], XX, 60ff.; 1933a, XXII, 22–23.

7 Since neither the claim nor the argument that depends on it can be found in Freud's texts or derived from them, it is not surprising that, as Grünbaum says, ". . . writers on Freud have simply failed to appreciate that he offered this argument . . ." (p. 171). (According to Grünbaum's story, Freud "gainsays" the claim in 1926. Cf. pp. 160, 172.)

8 Freud said that "suggestion can be traced back to transference" (1916–17, XVI, 451; cf 1925d [1924], XX, 42).

9 If, in Grünbaum's sentence, one substitutes, say, "so-called transference" for "deferential submission" – and deletes the idle use of "spurious" – the gist of the sentence may be less unclear.

10 Quoted more fully in Grünbaum, p. 143.

11 See 1912b, XII, 100f. For a number of cases Freud claimed "objective confirmation" of early object-attachments predicted in analyses (1926e, XX, 216). The objective confirmation was "information from parents or nurses" (ibid.), information of a kind that Grünbaum, by terminological fiat, rules out as extraclinical. (Cf. for example, pp. 39, 262–3, and cp. 1916d, XIV, 313.) That the early attachments played a part in the patients' neuroses and were reexperienced in their transferences are, of course, further issues. (See also 1920g, XVIII, 20–3.)

12 Marshall Edelson's *Hypothesis and Evidence in Psychoanalysis* (Chicago: University of Chicago Press, 1984) has a useful summary and criticism of claims that Grünbaum, both in his second chapter and elsewhere, derives from other writers. See, in Edelson, pp. 52–3 and ch. 9.

13 I have not taken up the difficult second defense in the Freud passage I excerpted above. Grünbaum, in a later chapter, discusses one of Freud's

formulations of it with unusual care (pp. 275–7; see esp. the top of p. 277); and then disappointingly begs the question by merely repeating the charge of suggestion. See p. 277; cf. pp. 32, 129, 240–2. He adds an appeal to the "defects of free association" (p. 277); I discuss those alleged defects in Section IX.

14 I discuss the thesis in Section VIII.

15 Grünbaum, p. 61. Cf. 1905c, VIII, pp. 172 et ca., 203–5, 234. The passage on page 172, where Freud expounds his view that jokes, unlike dreams, do not ". . . create compromises . . . ," disproves Grünbaum's assertion that Freud regarded jokes as "compromise-formations." The passage is conclusive and clarifies Freud's later remarks on pp. 203–5; the passage on p. 234 is, strictly taken, irrelevant to the issue. Also helpful are 1915d, XIV, 151, 1915e, XIV, 186, and 1925d, XX, 65–6.

16 Freud believed he could ". . . appeal to the fact that there is an intimate connection between all mental happenings – a fact which guarantees that a psychological discovery even in a remote field will be of unpredictable value in other fields" (1905c, VIII, 15).

17 See 1924f [1923], XIX, 200; 1925d, XX, 70; cf. 1915e, XIV, 173; 1940b [1938], XXIII, 282.

18 See, e.g., 1910a [1909], XI, 29, 38, 52 and 1901b, VI, 242, 253–4. It should be emphasized that Freud's determinism concerning mental life was purposive or teleological. See for example, 1901b, VI, 240.

19 Also foundational but barely touched on by Grünbaum is Freud's attempt to extend the notion of subintentional action to the formation of neurotic symptoms, dreams, parapraxes, et alia. See pp. 77ff.

20 As Grünbaum observes, other thinkers before Freud had asserted the existence of repression. Grünbaum does not tell us what sorts of mental items were subject to repression according to those earlier thinkers. As in (a) above, he speaks as if repression could be observed *in vacuo*.

21 The same degree of those qualities has to be exercised when reading Freud's truncated and revised versions of those works in his *Introductory Lectures on Psycho-Analysis*. At times, the lectures, both implicitly and explicitly, reflect on the works, and it can be helpful to read them side by side.

22 See, for example, 1915e, XIV, 166; 1916–17, XV, 25–79.

23 The gulf between the suppressed (or, more generally, the preconscious) and the repressed (or, more generally, the unconscious) was not, for Freud, unbridgeable. As he said, "whether spontaneously or with our assistance, the one can be changed into the other" (1940a [1938], XXIII, 164).

24 Accordingly, Grünbaum speaks of some of Freud's examples as "propaedeutic cases" and "didactic prolegomena." See pp. 199–201; cf. p. 205.

25 Earlier in the text Freud gives several other examples of combined parapraxes: see 1901b, VI, 34–5, 171, 221, 222. Both the chapter itself and the earlier examples were added after the first edition.

26 My brackets. Freud's rashness is qualified at 1900a, V, 353.

27 On pages 220–1, Grünbaum twice speaks of the "interpersonal dream symbolism" and once of the "interpersonally significant symbolism." It could have been instructive if he had indicated the epistemic basis for the claim that the symbols are interpersonally significant.

In 1933 Freud emphasized the independence of the symbolism: "Since *we* know how to translate these symbols and the dreamer does not, in spite of having used them himself, it may happen that the sense of a dream may at once become clear to us as soon as we have heard the text of the dream, even before we have made any efforts at interpreting it . . ." (1933a, XXII, 13).

28 See Grünbaum, pp. 195–6. Timpanaro's book, *The Freudian Slip* (Atlantic Highlands, N.J.: Humanities Press, 1976) is instructive in regard to Freud's optimistic generalizations about slips of the pen and eye. (See 1901b, VI, 271–3; 1940b [1938], XXIII, 284.) It is of little value on the main theme of the *Psychopathology*: disturbances and peculiarities of memory. (See for example, 1916–17, XV, 60.)

29 One difference between the two cases should be emphasized: The context in which "aliquis" was forgotten was not directly preceded by a topic the forgetter suppressed. As a result, Freud's second example can serve as a model for a wide range of cases, cases of material suppressed either recently or over an extended interval. (Cf 1916–17, XV, 65.)

There are a few minor differences due to the fact that the second example is one of forgetting a pronoun in a Latin quotation. Freud was fond of the quotation, a line from Virgil's *Aeneid* (IV, l. 625) and undoubtedly knew it in its correct form. Some years ago it was conjectured, and a recent article impressively argues, that the memory lapse reported in the example was actually Freud's; that he invented the interlocutor to whom he imputes it. Grünbaum refers to the article but chooses to "take Freud's text at face value" (p. 190). Of course had he not so chosen, he could not accuse Freud of "leading" the interlocutor. Still, Grünbaum makes that accusation a mere three times (pp. 30, 58, 192); and several of his other criticisms of the example are, as he says, independent of the charge of suggestion. (See p. 208 et supra.) One of them, however, also presupposes taking Freud's text at "face value": doubting that the interlocutor – unlike Freud – would ordinarily have had Virgil's line at his command (p. 195).

30 Charles Darwin gives a striking case of such forgetting in his *Autobiography:* "I had, during many years, followed a golden rule, namely, that

whenever a published fact, a new observation or thought came across me, which was opposed to my general results, to make a memorandum of it without fail and at once; for I had found by experience that such facts and thoughts were far more apt to escape from the memory than favourable ones." Quoted by Freud, 1901b, VI, 148, n. 3.

I should note that Freud is especially concerned with cases of tendentious forgetting that ". . . occur in people who are *not* fatigued or absentminded or excited, but who are in all respects in their normal state . . ." (1916–17, XV, 29; cf. 45).

31 I use "upshot" instead of Grünbaum's "support." By "therapeutic support" I take it he means therapeutic upshot, whether affected by psychoanalytic treatment or in fact by suggestion.

32 There are related attributes shared by neurotic symptoms, dreams, and parapraxes. Importantly, Freud says they are alike constructed by displacement or condensation or both – by, that is, the processes whose effects Freud most persuasively exhibits in his treatment of tendentious jokes. (See 1905c, VIII, 90–177.)

33 How, the reader may ask, did Grünbaum try to motivate his complaint? He may find the answer if he turns to a passage on pp. 192–3 in Grünbaum's book. There Grünbaum claims that Freud attempted to fill a certain ". . . prima facie glaring inferential gap" (p. 192); and that, in order to do so, he made two assumptions, assumptions that supposedly require the counterparts. But Grünbaum gives no textual evidence – there is none to be given – that Freud thought there was an inferential gap, or consequently, assumptions needed to fill it. To the contrary: Freud thought there was no gap; that a sequence of free associations to a parapraxis or dream could show that the disturbing wish or wishes revealed by the sequence had prompted the parapraxis or dream. (See for example, the "aliquis" 1901b, VI, 11; and cf. Section IX, this essay.)

34 Freud's interest in the recovery of an anomalously forgotten name was not aimed at correcting the parapraxis. His goal was not the schoolteacher's one of enabling a pupil ". . . himself to correct the parapraxis *and* to avoid its repetition or other parapraxes in the future." Freud was interested in the correct name, whether recovered by oneself or otherwise supplied, insofar as it helped to reconstruct the unconscious processes that produced the parapractic product.

35 Grünbaum does not offer it as a proposal but as an objection to Freud. It will be clear that it is a maneuver similar to the one employed when he offered his "therapeutic" counterpart for parapraxes.

I owe the characterization "genial proposal" to J. Allan Hobson's laudatory remarks on Grünbaum's "epochal work"; cf. *Behavioral and Brain Sciences*, pp. 241–2; see note 2 above for the issue and date.

36 Grünbaum's tentativeness is explained by the sentences that follow the lines quoted; see p. 235.

37 It may be asked, why shouldn't one parapract or dream the less? Freud thought it was because dreams and parapraxes and, though differently, jokes, enabled various healthy trends and purposes; importantly among them, that of allowing our invincibly enduring infantile wishes some expression. Had Freud been interested in *antitherapy*, he might have invented techniques to inhibit joking, dreaming, parapracting, et al. (For the claim about parapraxes see 1901b, VI, 276.)

38 Once again, Grünbaum overlooks an inconvenient passage. In 1913 Freud wrote, "Psychoanalysis cannot be accused of having applied to normal cases findings arrived at from pathological material. The evidence in the latter and in the former was reached independently and shows that normal processes and what are described as pathological ones follow the same rules."

Freud continues: "I shall now discuss in greater detail two of the normal phenomena with which we are here concerned (phenomena, that is, which can be observed in normal people) – namely, parapraxes and dreams" (1913j, XIII, 166; see 1940a [1938], XXIII, 165).

39 Grünbaum is mistaken about the transparency of the motives for (a) and (b). In both cases free association may be needed to ascertain "the intruding element" that disturbed "the agent's control of his own behavior." To give a few inklings: in (a) nothing is said about whose orgasm may be in question or why the speaker finds it problematic. In (b) the singular indefinite article is suspect, the more so because it takes advantage of the idiom "a breath of." It could be helpful to know something of the man's earlier relation to the "bosom."

In my discussion of (1) to (4) below, I shall, for the sake of argument, suppose that (a) and (b) are transparent; that they were respectively prompted by, say, the desire to experience and the wish to caress. (For an unquestionably transparent parapraxis, see the example Grünbaum takes from Freud, pp. 205–6. The other examples he quotes from Freud (pp. 201, 205) are less than obvious.)

40 Obviously in each case he relies on the proximity of the stimuli together with the expressive aptness of the parapraxis to infer that the wish occasioned it. Freud too relied on that aptness; but he did not regard human beings as ahistorical creatures of the moment, creatures capable of apt responses solely to proximate stimuli. In that connection, and also others, see the spare and trenchant criticism of Grünbaum's book by Arthur Fine and Mickey Forbes; in particular, their remarks on Grünbaum's "atomism." *Behavioral and Brain Sciences*, pp. 237–8. Cf. note 2.

41 I have dropped the disjunct "or an affect" from Grünbaum's formulation; I take it the affect would be desire-laden and therefore can be construed as wishful.

42 Grünbaum's concession, it ought to be remarked, flouts his insistence on epidemiological and experimental methods – on, in general, the methods of eliminative induction. In making the concession, he tacitly but reasonably opts for inference to the best explanation. (I am indebted here to an unpublished paper by Richard W. Miller.)

After the present article was completed, James Hopkins's valuable essay, "Epistemology and Depth Psychology: Critical Notes on *The Foundations of Psychoanalysis*" appeared. See *Mind, Psychoanalysis and Science,* ed. Peter Clark and Crispin Wright (Oxford: Basil Blackwell, 1988), pp. 33–60. There are several points on which Hopkins and I coincidentally agree; I do not, however, take up a number of issues he helpfully discusses.

43 Freud stressed the uncanniness of many a parapraxis. He chose as his epigraph for the *Psychopathology* Goethe's lines: "Nun ist die Luft von solchem Spuk so voll / Dass niemand weiss, wie er ihn meiden soll" (*Faust*, Part II, Act V, Scene 5). Fliess called Freud's attention to the couplet.

44 *Behavioral and Brain Sciences*, p. 277; see note 2.

45 A funny thing about the *terminus ad quem* of many a free association trip: when one arrives one sees that, at various stops on the way, one was already there. Cf. the "Signorelli" and "aliquis" examples (VI, ch. I and II).

46 A version of the "fallacy" was stated earlier by Clark Glymour. See his article, "The Theory of Your Dreams," in *Physics, Philosophy, and Psychoanalysis*, ed. R. Cohen and L. Laudan (Dordrecht, The Netherlands: D. Reidel, 1983), p. 61.

47 Due to the possible richness or paucity of a patient's free associations, the analyst may select among them or ask for more of them. In the one case, according to Grünbaum, the analyst will bias the material; in the other he will suggestively "lead" the patient (p. 209 et ca.). But why should all or most such interventions amount to *bias* or *suggestion*? (Obviously, some control of those concepts is badly needed.) The actual issue is one of analytic practice. Some insensitive analysts are open to the charges; other analysts are not.

BIBLIOGRAPHY

The indispensable resource for studying Freud is the twenty-four volume *Standard Edition of the Complete Psychological Works of Sigmund Freud*, translated from the German under the general editorship of James Strachey in collaboration with Anna Freud, assisted by Alix Strachey and Alan Tyson (London: The Hogarth Press, 1953–74). It contains invaluable introductions, notes, and cross-references. The citations of Freud's works in this volume are keyed to the chronological listing of Freud's writings in the *Standard Edition*, the essentials of which are provided following this bibliography.

The most useful biographies of Freud are Ernest Jones, *Sigmund Freud: Life and Work*, three volumes (London: The Hogarth Press, 1953–7) and Peter Gay, *Freud: A Life for Our Time* (New York: W. W. Norton, 1988). Gay's biography includes an extensive and argumentative "Bibliographical Essay" that helps guide one through the voluminous secondary literature. The most philosophically acute tracing of the development of Freud's theorizing is Richard Wollheim, *Sigmund Freud* (Cambridge: Cambridge University Press, 1971). Special mention should also be made of the very thoughtful conceptual guide through Freud's writings provided in dictionary form in J. Laplanche and J.-B. Pontalis, *The Language of Psycho-Analysis*, trans. D. Nicholson-Smith (London: The Hogarth Press, 1973).

BOOKS

Abel, Donald C. *Freud on Instinct and Morality* (Albany, N.Y.: State University of New York Press, 1989).

Abramson, Jeffrey A. *Liberation and Its Limits: The Moral and Political Thought of Freud* (New York: Free Press, 1984).

Anzieu, D. *Freud's Self-Analysis* (New York: International Universities Press, 1986).

Archard, David. *Consciousness and the Unconscious* (LaSalle, Ill.: Open Court, 1984).

339

Benjamin, Jessica. *The Bonds of Love: Psychoanalysis, Feminism, and the Problem of Domination* (New York: Pantheon Books, 1988).

Berger, Louis. *Freud's Unfinished Journey* (London: Routledge and Kegan Paul, 1981).

Bersani, Leo. *The Freudian Body: Psychoanalysis and Art* (New York: Columbia University Press, 1986).

Bettelheim, Bruno. *Freud and Man's Soul* (New York: Knopf, 1983).

Borch-Jacobsen, Mikkel. *The Freudian Subject* (Stanford, Calif.: Stanford University Press, 1987).

Brown, Norman O. *Life against Death: The Psychoanalytical Meaning of History* (Middletown, Conn.: Wesleyan University Press, 1959).

Chasseguet-Smirgel, Janine. *The Ego Ideal*, trans. P. Barrows (New York: W. W. Norton, 1985).

Dilman, Ilham. *Freud: Insight and Change* (Oxford: Basil Blackwell, 1988).

Draenos, Stan. *Freud's Odyssey: Psychoanalysis and the End of Metaphysics* (New Haven, Conn.: Yale University Press, 1982).

Edelson, Marshall. *Hypothesis and Evidence in Psychoanalysis* (Chicago: University of Chicago Press, 1984).

Ellenberger, Henri F. *The Discovery of the Unconscious: The History and Evolution of Dynamic Psychiatry* (New York: Basic Books, 1970).

Erdelyi, M. *Psychoanalysis: Freud's Cognitive Psychology* (New York: W. H. Freeman, 1985).

Fancher, Raymond E. *Psychoanalytic Psychology: The Development of Freud's Thought* (New York: W. W. Norton, 1973).

Farrell, B. A. *The Standing of Psychoanalysis* (Oxford: Oxford University Press, 1981).

Fenichel, Otto. *The Psychoanalytic Theory of Neurosis* (New York: W. W. Norton, 1945).

Fine, Reuben. *A History of Psychoanalysis* (New York: Columbia University Press, 1979).

Fisher, Seymour, and Roger P. Greenberg. *The Scientific Credibility of Freud's Theories and Therapy* (New York: Basic Books, 1977).

Forrester, John. *Language and the Origins of Psychoanalysis* (New York: Columbia University Press, 1980).

Grünbaum, Adolf. *The Foundations of Psychoanalysis: A Philosophical Critique* (Berkeley: University of California Press, 1984).

Holt, Robert B. *Freud Reappraised: A Fresh Look at Psychoanalytic Theory* (New York: Guilford Press, 1989).

Izenberg, Gerald N. *The Existentialist Critique of Freud: The Crisis of Autonomy* (Princeton, N.J.: Princeton University Press, 1976).

Kline, Paul. *Fact and Fantasy in Freudian Theory* (London: Methuen, 1972).

Kofman, Sarah. *The Enigma of Woman: Women in Freud's Writings* (Ithaca, N.Y.: Cornell University Press, 1985).

Küng, Hans. *Freud and the Problem of God,* trans. E. Quinn (New Haven, Conn.: Yale University Press, 1979).

Lacan, Jacques. *Ecrits: A Selection,* trans. A. Sheridan (New York: W. W. Norton, 1977).

Laplanche, Jean. *Life and Death in Psychoanalysis,* trans. J. Mehlman (Baltimore: The Johns Hopkins University Press, 1976).

Lear, Jonathan. *Love and Its Place in Nature: A Philosophical Interpretation of Freudian Psychoanalysis* (New York: Farrar, Straus and Giroux, 1990).

Levin, Kenneth. *Freud's Early Psychology of the Neuroses: A Historical Perspective* (Pittsburgh: University of Pittsburgh Press, 1978).

McGrath, William J. *Freud's Discovery of Psychoanalysis: The Politics of Hysteria* (Ithaca, N.Y.: Cornell University Press, 1986).

MacIntyre, A. C. *The Unconscious: A Conceptual Analysis* (London: Routledge and Kegan Paul, 1958).

Mackay, Nigel. *Motivation and Explanation: An Essay on Freud's Philosophy of Science* (New York: International Universities Press, 1989).

Madison, Peter. *Freud's Concept of Repression and Defense* (Minneapolis: University of Minnesota Press, 1961).

Mahony, Patrick J. *Freud as a Writer,* expanded ed. (New Haven, Conn.: Yale University Press, 1987).

Malcolm, Janet. *Psychoanalysis: The Impossible Profession* (New York: Knopf, 1981).

Marcus, Steven. *Freud and the Culture of Psychoanalysis* (New York: W. W. Norton, 1984).

Marcuse, Herbert. *Eros and Civilization* (Boston: Beacon Press, 1955).

Masson, Jeffrey Moussaieff. *The Assault on Truth: Freud's Suppression of the Seduction Theory* (New York: Farrar, Straus and Giroux, 1984).

Mitchell, Juliet. *Psychoanalysis and Feminism* (New York: Pantheon Books, 1974).

Olsen, Ole A., and Simo Koppe. *The Psychoanalysis of Freud* (New York: New York University Press, 1988).

Pribram, Karl, and Merton Gill. *Freud's 'Project' Reassessed* (London: Hutchinson, 1976).

Ricoeur, Paul. *Freud and Philosophy: An Essay on Interpretation* (New Haven, Conn.: Yale University Press, 1970).

Rieff, Phillip. *Freud: The Mind of the Moralist,* 3d ed. (Chicago: University of Chicago Press, 1979).

Roazen, Paul. *Freud: Political and Social Thought* (London: Hogarth Press, 1969).

Rudnyisky, Peter L. *Freud and Oedipus* (New York: Columbia University Press, 1987).

Rycroft, Charles. *Psychoanalysis and Beyond* (University of Chicago Press, 1985).

Sagan, Eli. *Freud, Women and Morality: The Psychology of Good and Evil* (New York: Basic Books, 1988).

Santas, Gerasimos. *Plato and Freud: Two Theories of Love* (Oxford: Blackwell, 1988).

Sherwood, Michael. *The Logic of Explanation in Psychoanalysis* (New York: Academic Press, 1969).

Spector, Jack J. *The Aesthetics of Freud: A Study of Psychoanalysis and Art* (New York: Praeger, 1972).

Stewart, Walter A. *Psychoanalysis, The First Ten Years, 1888–1898* (New York: Macmillan, 1967).

Sulloway, Frank J. *Freud: Biologist of the Mind* (New York: Basic Books, 1979).

Timpanaro, Sebastiano. *The Freudian Slip: Psychoanalysis and Textual Criticism* (London: NLB, 1976).

Wallace, Edwin R. IV. *Freud and Anthropology: A History and Reappraisal* (New York: International Universities Press, 1983).

Weber, Samuel. *The Legend of Freud* (Minneapolis: University of Minnesota Press, 1982).

ANTHOLOGIES

Bernheimer, Charles, and Claire Kahane, eds. *In Dora's Case: Freud–Hysteria–Feminism* (New York: Columbia University Press, 1985).

Clark, Peter, and Crispin Wright, eds. *Mind, Psychoanalysis and Science* (Oxford: Blackwell, 1988).

Hanly, Charles, and Morris Lazerowitz, eds. *Psychoanalysis and Philosophy* (New York: International Universities Press, 1970).

Hook, Sidney, ed. *Psychoanalysis, Scientific Method, and Philosophy* (New York: New York University Press, 1959).

Horden, Peregrine, ed. *Freud and the Humanities* (New York: St. Martin, 1985).

Meltzer, Françoise, ed. *The Trial(s) of Psychoanalysis* (Chicago: University of Chicago Press, 1988).

Post, Seymour C., ed. *Moral Values and the Superego Concept in Psychoanalysis* (New York: International Universities Press, 1972).

Wollheim, Richard, ed. *Freud: A Collection of Critical Essays* (Garden City, N.Y.: Doubleday, 1974).

Wollheim, Richard, and James Hopkins, eds. *Philosophical Essays on Freud* (Cambridge: Cambridge University Press, 1982).

CITED WORKS OF FREUD

(1888b) "Hysteria" and "Hysteria-Epilepsy," S. E. I, 41–59.

(1888–9) "Preface to the Translation of Bernheim's *Suggestion*," S. E. I, 75–87.

(1891b) *On Aphasia*, London and New York, 1953.

(1892–3) "A Case of Successful Treatment by Hypnotism," S. E. I, 117–28.

(1892–4) Preface and Footnotes to the Translation of Charcot's *Tuesday Lectures*, S. E. I, 133–43.

(1893a) With Breuer, J., "On the Psychical Mechanism of Hysterical Phenomena: Preliminary Communication," S. E. II, 3–17.

(1893f) "Charcot," S. E. III, 11–23.

(1894a) "The Neuro-Psychoses of Defence," S. E. III, 45–61.

(1895d) With J. Breuer, *Studies on Hysteria*, S. E. II.

(1896a) "Heredity and the Aetiology of the Neuroses," S. E. III, 143–56.

(1896b) "Further Remarks on the Neuro-Psychoses of Defence," S. E. III, 162–85.

(1896c) "The Aetiology of Hysteria," S. E. III, 191–221.

(1898a) "Sexuality in the Aetiology of the Neuroses," S. E. III, 263–85.

(1899a) "Screen Memories," S. E. III, 303–22.

(1900a) *The Interpretation of Dreams*, S. E. IV–V.

(1901a) *On Dreams*, S. E. V, 633–86.

(1901b) *The Psychopathology of Everyday Life*, S. E. VI.

(1905c) *Jokes and Their Relation to the Unconscious*, S. E. VIII.

(1905d) *Three Essays on the Theory of Sexuality*, S. E. VII, 130–243.

(1905e [1901]) "Fragment of an Analysis of a Case of Hysteria," S. E. VII, 7–122.

(1907a) *Delusions and Dreams in Jensen's "Gradiva*," S. E. IX, 7–95.

(1907b) "Obsessive Actions and Religious Practices," S. E. IX, 117–27.

(1907c) "The Sexual Enlightenment of Children," S. E. IX, 131–9.

(1908a) "Hysterical Phantasies and Their Relation to Bisexuality," S. E. IX, 159–66.

(1908b) "Character and Anal Erotism," S. E. IX, 169–75.

(1908c) "On the Sexual Theories of Children," S. E. IX, 209–26.

(1908d) " 'Civilized' Sexual Morality and Modern Nervous Illness," S. E. IX, 181–204.

(1908e [1907]) "Creative Writers and Day-Dreaming," S. E. IX, 143–53.

(1909b) "Analysis of a Phobia in a Five-Year-Old Boy," S. E. X, 5–149.

(1909c) "Family Romances," S. E. IX, 237–41.

(1909d) "Notes upon a Case of Obsessional Neurosis," S. E. X, 155–320.

(1910a [1909]) "Five Lectures on Psycho-Analysis," S. E. XI, 9–55.

(1910c) *Leonardo da Vinci and a Memory of His Childhood*, S E. XI, 63–137.

(1910d) "The Future Prospects of Psycho-Analytic Therapy," S. E. XI, 141–51.

(1910e) "The Antithetical Meaning of Primal Words," S. E. XI, 155–61.

(1910h) "A Special Type of Choice of Object Made by Men," S. E. XI, 165–75.

(1910i) "The Psycho-Analytic View of Psychogenic Disturbance of Vision," S. E. XI, 211–8.

(1910k) " 'Wild' Psycho-Analysis," S. E. XI, 221–7.

(1911b) "Formulations on the Two Principles of Mental Functioning," S. E. XII, 218–26.

(1911c [1910]) "Psycho-Analytic Notes on an Autobiographical Account of a Case of Paranoia (Dementia Paranoides)," S. E. XII, 9–82.

(1912b) "The Dynamics of Transference," S. E. XII, 99–108.

(1912c) "Types of Onset of Neurosis," S. E. XII, 231–8.

(1912d) "On the Universal Tendency to Debasement in the Sphere of Love," S. E. XI, 179–90.

(1912f) "Contributions to a Discussion on Masturbation," S. E. XII, 243–54.

(1912g) "A Note on the Unconscious in Psycho-Analysis," S. E. XII, 260–6.

(1912–13) *Totem and Taboo*, S. E. XIII, 1–162.

(1913c) "On Beginning the Treatment (Further Recommendations on the Technique of Psycho-Analysis, I)," S. E. XII, 123–44.

(1913d) "The Occurrence in Dreams of Material from Fairy Tales," S. E. XII, 281–7.

(1913f) "The Theme of the Three Caskets," S. E. XII, 291–301.

(1913i) "The Disposition to Obsessional Neurosis," S. E. XII, 317–26.

(1913j) "The Claims of Psycho-Analysis to Scientific Interest," S. E. XIII, 165–90.

(1914a) "Fausse Reconnaissance ('déjà raconté') in Psycho-Analytic Treatment," S. E. XIII, 201–7.

(1914b) "The *Moses* of Michelangelo," S. E. XIII, 211–38.

(1914c) "On Narcissism: An Introduction," S. E. XIV, 73–102.

(1914d) "On the History of the Psycho-Analytic Movement," S. E. XIV, 7–66.

(1914g) "Remembering, Repeating and Working-Through (Further Recommendations on the Technique of Psycho-Analysis, II)," S. E. XII, 147–56.

(1915a) "Observations on Transference-Love (Further Recommendations on the Technique of Psycho-Analysis, III)," S. E. XII, 159–71.

(1915b) "Thoughts for the Times on War and Death," S. E. XIV, 275–302.

(1915c) "Instincts and Their Vicissitudes," S. E. XIV, 117–40.

(1915d) "Repression," S. E. XIV, 146–58.

(1915e) "The Unconscious," S. E. XIV, 166–215.

(1915f) "A Case of Paranoia Running Counter to the Psycho-Analytic Theory of the Disease," S. E. XIV, 263–72.

(1916d) "Some Character-Types Met with in Psycho-Analytic Work," S. E. XIV, 311–33.

(1916–17) Introductory Lectures on Psycho-Analysis, S. E. XV–XVI.

(1917c) "On Transformations of Instinct as Exemplified in Anal Erotism," S. E. XVII, 127–33.

(1917e [1915]) "Mourning and Melancholia," S. E. XIV, 243–58.

(1918a) "The Taboo of Virginity," S. E. XI, 193–208.

(1918b [1914]) "From the History of an Infantile Neurosis," S. E. XVII, 7–122.

(1919e) "A Child Is Being Beaten," S. E. XVII, 179–204.

(1919j [1918]) "On the Teaching of Psycho-Analysis in Universities," S. E. XVII, 171–3.

(1920a) "The Psychogenesis of a Case of Female Homosexuality," S. E. XVIII, 147–72.

(1920g) Beyond the Pleasure Principle, S. E. XVIII, 7–64.

(1921c) Group Psychology and the Analysis of the Ego, S. E XVIII, 69–143.

(1922b) "Some Neurotic Mechanisms in Jealousy, Paranoia and Homosexuality," S. E. XVIII, 223–32.

(1923a [1922]) "Two Encyclopaedia Articles," S. E. XVIII, 235–59.

(1923b) The Ego and the Id, S. E. XIX, 12–66.

(1923d [1922]) "A Seventeenth-Century Demonological Neurosis," S. E. XIX, 72–105.

(1923e) "The Infantile Genital Organization," S. E. XIX, 141–5.

(1924c) "The Economic Problem of Masochism," S. E. XIX, 159–70.

(1924d) "The Dissolution of the Oedipus Complex," S. E. XIX, 173–9.

(1924f [1923]) "A Short Account of Psycho-Analysis," S. E. XIX, 191–209.

(1925a [1924]) "A Note upon the 'Mystic Writing-Pad,' " S. E. XIX, 227–232.

(1925d [1924]) An Autobiographical Study, S. E. XX, 7–74.

(1925e [1924]) "The Resistances to Psycho-Analysis," S. E. XIX, 213–32.

(1925h) "Negation," S. E. XIX, 235–9.

(1925i) "Some Additional Notes on Dream-Interpretation as a Whole," S. E. XIX, 127–38.

(1925j) "Some Psychical Consequences of the Anatomical Distinction between the Sexes," S. E. XIX, 248–58.

(1926d [1925]) Inhibitions, Symptoms and Anxiety, S. E. XX, 87–175.

(1926e) The Question of Lay Analysis, S. E. XX, 183–258.

(1927c) The Future of an Illusion, S. E. XXI, 5–56.

(1927e) "Fetishism," S. E. XXI, 152–7.

(1928a) "A Religious Experience," S. E. XXI, 169–72.

(1928b) "Dostoevsky and Parricide," S. E. XXI, 177–94.

(1930a) *Civilization and Its Discontents*, S. E. XXI, 64–145.

(1931b) "Female Sexuality," S. E. XXI, 225–43.

(1932a) "The Acquisition and Control of Fire," S. E. XXII, 185.

(1933a) *New Introductory Lectures on Psycho-Analysis*, S. E. XXII, 5–182.

(1933b [1932]) *Why War?* S. E. XXII, 199–215.

(1936a) "A Disturbance of Memory on the Acropolis," S. E. XXII, 239.

(1937c) "Analysis Terminable and Interminable," S. E. XXIII, 216–53.

(1937d) "Constructions in Analysis," S. E. XXIII, 257–69.

(1939a [1937–9]) *Moses and Monotheism*, S. E. XXIII, 7–137.

(1940a [1938]) *An Outline of Psycho-Analysis*, S. E. XXIII, 144–207.

(1940b [1938]) "Some Elementary Lessons in Psycho-Analysis," S. E. XXIII, 281–6.

(1940c [1922]) "Medusa's Head," S. E. XVIII, 273–4.

(1940d [1892]) "On the Theory of Hysterical Attacks," S. E. I, 151–4.

(1940e [1938]) "Splitting of the Ego in the Process of Defence," S. E. XXIII, 275–8.

(1942a [1905–6]) "Psychopathic Characters on the Stage," S. E. VII, 305–10.

(1950a [1887–1902]) *The Origins of Psycho-Analysis*, London and New York, 1954. Partly, including "A Project for a Scientific Psychology," S. E. I, 177–397.

(1955a [1907–8]) Original Record of the Case of Obsessional Neurosis (the "Rat Man") S. E. X, 259–318.

(1957a [1911]) With D. E. Oppenheim, *Dreams in Folklore*, Part I, S. E. XII, 180–203.

(1960a) *Letters 1873–1939* (ed. Ernst L. Freud; trans. Tania and James Stern), New York, 1960; London, 1961.

(1965a) *A Psycho-Analytic Dialogue. The Letters of Sigmund Freud and Karl Abraham*, London and New York, 1965.

(1966a [1912–36]) *Sigmund Freud and Lou Andreas-Salomé: Letters*, London and New York, 1972.

(1968a [1927–39]) *The Letters of Sigmund Freud and Arnold Zweig* (ed. E. L. Freud), London and New York, 1970.

(1974a) *The Freud/Jung Letters* (ed. W. McGuire; trans. R. Manheim and R. F. C. Hull). Princeton, N.J.: Princeton University Press, 1974.

(1985 [1887–1904]) *The Complete Letters of Sigmund Freud to Wilhelm Fliess* (trans. and ed. J. M. Masson), Cambridge, Mass.: Harvard University Press, 1985.

INDEX